The Galaxy Is Rated G

The Galaxy Is Rated G

*Essays on
Children's Science Fiction
Film and Television*

Edited by
R.C. NEIGHBORS *and*
SANDY RANKIN

McFarland & Company, Inc., Publishers
Jefferson, North Carolina, and London

LIBRARY OF CONGRESS CATALOGUING-IN-PUBLICATION DATA

The galaxy is rated G : essays on children's science fiction film
    and television / edited by R.C. Neighbors and Sandy Rankin.
        p.   cm.
    Includes bibliographical references and index.

    ISBN 978-0-7864-5875-2
    softcover : 50# alkaline paper ∞

    1. Science fiction films — History and criticism.   2. Children's
films — History and criticism.   3. Science fiction television
programs — History and criticism.   4. Children's television
programs — History and criticism.   I. Neighbors, R.C., 1982–   II.
Rankin, Sandy, 1962–
PN1995.9.S26G24   2011
791.43'615 — dc23   2011021777

BRITISH LIBRARY CATALOGUING DATA ARE AVAILABLE

© 2011 R.C. Neighbors and Sandy Rankin. All rights reserved

*No part of this book may be reproduced or transmitted in any form
or by any means, electronic or mechanical, including photocopying
or recording, or by any information storage and retrieval system,
without permission in writing from the publisher.*

Front cover design by David K. Landis (Shake It Loose Graphics)

Manufactured in the United States of America

McFarland & Company, Inc., Publishers
    Box 611, Jefferson, North Carolina 28640
        www.mcfarlandpub.com

To the teachers who helped us see the wonders
of the galaxy, and our families and friends
who help us reach for them.

Table of Contents

*Introduction. Horizons of Possibility: What We Point to When
We Say Science Fiction for Children* 1
    SANDY RANKIN AND R.C. NEIGHBORS

PART 1. D IS FOR DEVIANCE

ONE. Monsters Among Us: Construction of the Deviant
Body in *Monsters, Inc.* and *Lilo & Stitch* 15
    ELIZABETH LEIGH SCHERMAN

TWO. Susan Murphy, Ginormica, and Gloria Steinem:
Feminist Consciousness-Raising as Science Fiction
in *Monsters vs. Aliens* 31
    HOLLY HASSEL

THREE. Performing Gender, Performing Romance:
Pixar's *WALL-E* 53
    CAROL A. BERNARD

FOUR. Last in Space: The "Black" Hole in Children's
Science Fiction Film 64
    DEBBIE C. OLSON

FIVE. A Few Beasts Hissed: Buzz Lightyear and the Refusal
to Believe 83
    DANIEL KENNEFICK

Part 2. S Is for Structures of Power

Six. Forward to the Past: Anti-Fascist Allegory and "Blitz Spirit" Revisionism in *Daleks' Invasion Earth 2150 A.D.* 97
  Daniel O'Brien

Seven. The Search for a "More Civilized Age," or the Failure of Utopian Desire in the *Star Wars* Franchise 111
  R.C. Neighbors

Eight. Inexplicable Utterances: Social Power and Pluralistic Discourse in *Transformers* 123
  Jacqueline Wiegard

Nine. "Population: Us": Nostalgia for a Future that Never Was (Not Yet) in *The Iron Giant* 138
  Sandy Rankin

Ten. Doctor Who: A Very British Alien 161
  J.P.C. Brown

Part 3. F Is for Future Shock

Eleven. No Future Shock Here: *The Jetsons*, Happy Tech, and the Patriarchy 183
  Brian Cowlishaw

Twelve. "No One's Lazy in LazyTown": The Making of Active Citizens in Preschool Television 195
  Lynn Whitaker

Thirteen. Flash Gordon: Remembering a Childhood Hero (Past, Present, Future) 217
  Patrick D. Enright

Fourteen. Toys, a T-Rex, and Trouble: Cautionary Tales of Time Travel in Children's Film 228
  Kristine Larsen

Fifteen. "Manmade Mess": The Critical Dystopia of *WALL-E* ... 248
  Alexander Charles Oliver Hall

Sixteen. A Bumbling Bag of Ball Bearings: *Lost in Space* and the Space Race 262
  Jonathan Cohn

About the Contributors 279
Index 283

• *Introduction* •

Horizons of Possibility: What We Point to When We Say Science Fiction for Children

SANDY RANKIN *and* R.C. NEIGHBORS

Children's film and television, like any media or cultural artifacts, represent certain beliefs, ideas, and practices as natural, and conversely represent certain beliefs, ideas, and practices as unnatural, as questionable, impossible, or unthinkable, by their absence if not by their circumscribed or negated presence. Indeed, presence *and* absence, affirmation and negation, can delight, fascinate, instruct, interpellate (children or adults as subjects), irritate, alienate and shock. These are ideological and anti-ideological functions that science fiction (sf), perhaps better than any other genre, serves. Though the visual and aural spectacles of sf tropes — ray guns; spaceships; sentient robots; alien encounters; far-flung planets; laser weaponry; hybrids of animal, human, and machine; gender neutral or bi-gender/androgynous, or bi-curious, sentient-sapient beings; etc.— have become "part of the modern idiom, infusing our language, our media culture, and our children's world of play with its images and its concepts,"[1] sf emphatically maintains the ability to alienate and shock, even when it also disalienates, entertains, consoles, or conserves.

Thus, in the 21st century, it is unsettling that we find so little scholarly attention to the joining of children's visual media and sf: both with their hopes and anxieties, their possible united or conflicting ideological effects. Toward this end, which is a beginning, as we hope to spark more dialogue than currently exists, this book focuses on how children's film and television use sf to promote, evade, or discourage hopes, consolations, anxieties, in a word: ideologies. The 16 essays herein articulate the encoding of science-fiction tropes in children's media, conversations between children's film/TV and adult sf, science-fictional elements in other genres or between genres, and/or address the growing popularity of sf in children's media in postindustrial countries, such as the United States, Canada, the United Kingdom, Australia, Scotland, to name a few of the geographic spaces from which our contributors are researching, studying, writing, and, in some cases, teaching. One contributor Daniel Kennefick, for example, discusses *Toy Story* and Buzz Lightyear within the context of belief. Another, Debbie C. Olsen, considers the absence of black children in sf film for children, criticizing sf films for betraying white nostalgia for an idealized all white past. Sandy Rankin identifies in the film *The Iron Giant* a forward-looking utopian nostalgia for a future that never was not yet. R. C. Neighbors and Alexander Charles Oliver Hall look for a more civilized and thoughtful age than ours, via their respective considerations of the *Star Wars* films and Pixar's *Wall-E*. Patrick D. Enright pleasurably and usefully engages in nostalgia for the represented virtues of a sf hero from his childhood, *Flash Gordon*. Our contributors draw from and invoke theorists such as Ernst Bloch, Gloria Steinem, Jack Zipes, Fredric Jameson, Judith Butler, Istvan Csicsery-Ronay, Jr., and Adilifu Nama, and many others, as they critique sf film and television's ideologies for and about children.

As much as we, the editors of this collection, would find it convenient and efficient to avoid definitions (such as sf means the absence or presence of nostalgia, or sf means the absence or presence of the future), and to say along with Damon Knight that "it will do us no particular harm if we remember that, like 'The Saturday Evening Post,'" sf "means what we point to when we say it,"[2] and the same is true when we point to and say entertainment and instruction "for children," we recognize that an absence of definitions and descriptions would be, for us, ideologically disingenuous. Indeed, quoting Damon Knight (or, as he preferred, damon knight) out of context is disingenuous. Knight/knight's main argument is that sf "is a genre worth taking seriously and that ordinary critical standards can be applied to it: e.g., originality, sincerity, style, construction, logic, coherence, sanity, garden-variety grammar." Publishing the first edition of the book *In Search of Wonder* in 1957, Knight/knight says, "a bad book hurts science fiction more than ten bad notices," but also says that "if science-fantasy has to date failed to produce much great literature, don't blame the writers who work in the field, blame those who, out of snobbery, don't."[3]

To be sure, there has been, are, and will continue to be, bad sf film and television created for children, and bad sf films and television with fantasy tropes—wizards, elves, sword fights, supernatural deities and monsters, humans with supernatural abilities. For some people, the blurring of sf with fantasy robs sf of all that is good about sf (cognition, estrangement, scientific method, plus other beauties — many of them technological as well as psychological and social), and such blurring hurts sf worse than ten bad notices. Darko Suvin, for example, early in his career as a scholar of sf, said that because fantasy is "committed to the imposition of anti-cognitive laws,"[4] it is "a subliterature of mystification,"[5] is "proto-Fascist," anti-rationalist, anti-modern, and the blurring of sf and fantasy is not only "rampantly sociopathlogical"[6] but "a terrible contamination"[7] of sf.

We are compelled to think via contingent definitional boundaries, particularly between science fiction and fantasy, which is the between-space (pre- and post–Suvin, but particularly post–) in which most of the defining trouble occurs, rather than between science fiction and realism or naturalism. Damon Knight prefers the term "science fantasy" for that which we will otherwise call "science fiction," a term he uses as often as science fantasy, as if the two are interchangeable. There is also trouble with defining what we mean by or should mean or can mean by "for children." To say when adulthood begins, and childhood ends, requires a boundary line that historically has been ideologically fluid. Furthermore, when we are speaking of media for children we are speaking of media created by adults, who target not only children but also adults (such double-targeting, a contamination?), a phenomenon with particular consequences we will discuss later in this introductory essay.

What We Talk About When We Talk About Sf

In regards to sf, we are compelled to define, in part, because there is much scholarship available about that which scholars and non-scholars alike explicitly identify as fantasy in children's media. Furthermore, sf warrants a close consideration (and hence a temporarily bracketed separation from fantasy) because fantasy *appears* to have triumphed in popularity against sf. For example, Philip Marchand says, "Harry Potter Rules. The unflagging energy of his creator, J.K. Rowling, writing volume after volume, sustains this phenomenon. The success of the latest movie version, *Harry Potter and the Half Blood Prince*, confirms it." He adds, "One effect of this triumph seems to be the increasing presence of fantasy, or elements of fantasy, in works of science fiction, a genre traditionally opposed to magic and even to such folk-scientific phenomena as UFOs. In a way," he says, "the trend to fantasy is not due simply to its superior commercial appeal, as demonstrated by the *Potter* books ... but also to developments in science itself." He explains by quoting sf novelist Robert Sawyer, "We have reached the point where contemporary science is so far out, to most people it is indistinguishable from magic.... The notion, for example, that black holes might provide not only links between space but links to time is grounded in current theoretical thinking."[8]

Fans and scholars of Tolkien/Jackson or of Miyazaki/animé may contest Potter's rule, and among children younger than the Potter fan base, it may be that "Wall-E Rules" or "Transformers Rule" or "Buzz Lightyear Rules." In any case, the triumph of fantasy is a possibility or probability that some scholars and fans celebrate, while other scholars and scientists and fans, who view fantasy with its magic and supernatural beings as an irrational contamination of sf's rational cognition, bemoan and criticize that proclaimed triumph. Yet others, such as the editors of this collection, are skeptical that the tropes of sf have in fact lost their popular appeal and their real-world process-utopian significance. Borrowing from David Seed, editor of *A Companion to Science Fiction*,[9] we recognize that sf is, and has been, a "multigeneric field," inclusive of, or at least often containing moments of fairytales, horror, myth, bildungsroman, the Western, mystery/crime, realism, surrealism, poetry, etc., *and* fantasy. Indeed, it is difficult, perhaps not-yet possible, for example, to say precisely "where science fiction ends and fantasy begins," particularly since the narratives of science fiction "repeatedly challenge the stability of boundaries between categories and concepts."[10]

Vivian Sobchack, who, in *Screening Space: The American Science Fiction Film* (enlarged ed., 1991),[11] says one of the difficulties in discussing the sf film is that "the critic has to deal with the nagging conviction that he or she ought to define it before describing it, that the very act of definition is, indeed, an academic requirement as well as a personal cathartic."[12] However, Sobchack points out that definitions, striving for exclusivity, can become "too narrow, seem glaringly and disappointingly arbitrary." She reminds us that, as Lawrence Alloway (who reportedly coined in print, or popularized, the term "mass popular art" in the 1950s and the term "Pop Art" in the 1960s) suggests, when generic categories are taken "rigidly," the categories "lose their descriptive usefulness and assume a normative function."[13] On the other hand, Sobchack also says that there is "something suspect about a critic who plunges into his subject with the optimistic assumption that his readers know — a priori — precisely what he is talking about."[14] Sobchack, who ultimately does not define science fiction, but instead offers, and sometimes critiques, multiple definitions that scholars and science fiction writers had proposed pre-publication of her book, says that "above all, if it is to remain relevant, a definition must accommodate the flux and change which is present in any living and popular art form."[15]

Indeed, taking Sobchack's words to heart, we begin by characterizing sf as the living and popular art form of flux and change *par excellence*, a genre of difference and potentiality. The science-fictional world, which is a world alternative to our own, even when inscribed within our present or our past (alternate histories or time-travelers), is not only a world that is "different in time or place from our own, but one whose chief interest," as Carl Freedman says, "is precisely the difference that such difference makes."[16] However, sf is also a living and popular art form of identity, which is to say that the alternative worlds of science fiction are continuous with our world. Sf engages with contemporary language and culture, historical materiality, social and scientific processes, philosophy, religion, psychology, anthropology, but sf pushes the preceding to their limits, and possibly beyond.

On the other hand, Fredric Jameson, who argues that thinking or imagining "beyond" our own mode of production, i.e., postindustrial late-modern capitalism, is not possible for us, and who yet identifies sf as an heir of and sub-genre of utopian literature, writes in *Archaeologies of the Future: The Desire Called Utopia and Other Science Fictions* (2005):

> The fundamental dynamic of any Utopian politics (or of any political Utopianism) will therefore always lie in the dialectic of Identity and Difference, to the degree to which such a politics aims at imagining, and sometimes even at realizing, a system radically different from this one.... [But] even our wildest imaginings are all collages of experience, constructs made up of bits and pieces of the here and now.... On the social level, this means that our imaginations are hostages to our own mode of production (and perhaps to whatever remnants of past ones it has preserved). It suggests that at best Utopia [and therefore science fiction] can serve the negative purpose of making us more aware of our mental and ideological imprisonment ... and that therefore the best Utopias are those that fail the most comprehensively.[17]

While we might dismiss or accept Jameson's late-modern Marxist despair (and his yearning for socialism)—"our imaginations are hostages to our own mode of production," emphasizing comprehensive failure—we may also dismiss or accept the aesthetic-optimism and the material-optimism of Istvan Csicsery-Ronay, Jr., like, Jameson, a Marxist. Csicsery-Ronay implicitly accepts *and* dismisses Jameson's pessimism by arguing in *The Seven Beauties of Science Fiction* (2008) not for representations of failure but for representations that are, if not exactly of success, then intimations of success: "As the world undergoes daily transformations via the development of technoscience in every imaginable aspect of life (and, more important, as people become aware of these transformation)," sf, he says, "has come to be seen as an essential mode of imagining the horizons of possibility." Sf texts "share a mass social energy, a desire to imagine a collective future for the human species and the world."[18] Sf, Csicsery-Ronay says, "regularly employs radically new scientific concepts of material and social relations; these relations, in turn, influence our conceptions of what is imaginable or plausible. Indeed, sf is," he says, "ingrained within the quotidian consciousness of people living in the postindustrial world; each day they witness the transformations of their values and material conditions in the wake of technical acceleration beyond their conceptual threshold."[19]

For the aforementioned Suvin, who has been a major influence on Jameson and Csicsery-Ronay, science fiction is "a literary genre whose necessary and sufficient conditions are the presence and interaction of estrangement and cognition, and whose main formal device is an imaginative framework alternative to the author's empirical environment."[20] But when Suvin and Jameson speak of cognitive estrangement, of the imagination as a hostage, of an author's (or a reader's) alternative environment, and when Csicsery-Ronay speaks of the seven beauties of science fiction and of our quotidian consciousness, they are each speaking of the estrangement and consciousness of adults, and of science fiction and alternative-world beauty for adults, not of or for children. Suvin once addresses science fiction for children or youth thusly: sf has "historically had its roots in the compost heap of such juvenile or popular sub-literature" known as the "species of adventure-journey," such as that by Jules Verne. However, in order to "develop properly," sf has had to "subsume and outgrow" the juvenile adventure-journey "the quicker the better for its generic affirmation." Suvin says such voyaging "is an honorable" function for sf. However, in retrospect, "one can scarcely fail to note that" the adventure-journey [sf] tale is an "initial (and for the reader initiatory), function." Suvin adds, "When unduly prolonged, this adolescence of SF means arrested development." The sf adventure-journey "should be kept in its proper humbly useful place in the ontogenetic development of the reader as well as in the phylogenetic development of the genre." Such tales (which Suvin refers to as Gernsbackian) keep sf alive "at the cost of starving, stunting, and deforming it." He says, "Unfortunately, a majority of what is published as [sf] is still in that prenatal, or, better, regression-to-womb stage. It is simply the Western or some kindred sub-literary species masquerading" sf's structures, "generally for venal and ideological reasons — under the eternals of [sf]: rockets, rayguns, or monsters."[21]

Whether or not sf for children, particularly sf television and film, partakes of and causes "arrested development," we ask questions that Suvin, et al., who are not writing about sf for children, do not: how much "cognitive estrangement" and "negative purpose of making us more aware of our mental and ideological imprisonment" can the media market of film and television for children bear, tolerate, let alone appreciate, value, encourage? Against the possibility of arrested development? And to what degree do the target audience of this collection of essays want children to think about the transformation of their values and material conditions, about the flux of identities and real or imagined differences, and the real or imagined changes that the future may bring, for the sake of cognitive estrangement and awareness of ideological imprisonment? To what degree do children want to think about such pervasive contingency and flux, the horizons of possibility: utopian and dystopian? Do children need that confectionary journey-adventure, that Western masked as science fiction, as part of their ontogenetic development? Or, rather, whether they need it or not, will they have it because they want it, crave it, revel in it? Suvin says, "The ambitious reader and writer cannot for long be satisfied with such pap," though such pap—"shamefacedly passing off a juvenile idea of magic for cognition"—Suvin says, "breeds generations of readers with juvenile taste, unable to develop the standards by which to judge [sf] (not to mention empirical human relations)."[22] In other words, we find ourselves returning to Jameson's assertion that our imaginations are hostages, in this case, hostages to a juvenile idea of magic that pretends to be cognition, and we are then hostages, perhaps, not to our own mode of production, but to residual modes of production from our pre-modern and early-modern past, or to romanticized notions of our past.

We think the answer to the above questions is that whatever our various answers may be, and however we may wish that children experience the epistemological and ontological terrain as solid, unmoving, securely unmovable, and may wish to forget about flux, change, contingency—whether experienced as utopian or dystopian—flux, change, contingency, and ideological imprisonment will not (as Jameson says about history)[23] forget about us or our children. Thus, we risk assuming a normative function, but we hope without rigidity as we recognize that every word—and representational image or sound—is a bias, a metaphorical coin, part of a figurative mobile army, as Friedrich Nietzsche said, which means that normative functions cannot be avoided: even absence, as some of our contributors argue, is normative, as is the term "children" and the phrase "for children."

What We Talk About When We Talk About Sf for Children

Of course, delineating a definition of "cinema for children"[24] is as difficult and plagued with complications as is the task of defining science fiction. As Peter Brooks notes, in discussing the equally amorphous category of children's *literature*, "do we mean literature read by children, or literature written for children? The two are not coterminous."[25] Likewise, visual media intended for children and visual media children actually view do not describe the same groups of films and television programs. "There are films aimed at children,"

Ian Wojcik-Andrews states, "films about childhood, and films children see regardless of whether or not they are children's films."[26] Seeing the incongruity between these groups, he concludes that "defining a children's film ... is something of an impossibility."[27] That is not to say, however, that we cannot discuss the characteristics of media produced by adults with children as their planned primary consumers, no matter how blurry the boundaries of such a classification — i.e., media for children — may be.

At least three characteristics are central to a discussion of media intended for child consumption — form, content, and marketing. By content, we refer more to the absence of certain content deemed "mature" by, in film's case, the Motion Picture Association of America (MPAA), such as excessive violence, sex, nudity, profane language, etc., than to the presence of any specific material. The MPAA stance on such issues is based on cultural assumptions inherited from America's Puritan ancestors and from the late Victorian emphasis on the role of the family and the sanctity of the child, with adults thinking of the child as "innocent," an innocence to be protected rather than corrupted (at least not before adulthood). These prejudices against certain material are less than objective, however; for instance, cartoons, which are "notoriously violent [and] literally death-defying,"[28] are seen almost universally as children's fare in the West.

Nevertheless, films are given a seemingly objective rating based on the apparent presence or absence of such "mature" material. Films for a general audience are rated G and are largely considered for children. With films rated PG, the MPAA suggests parental guidance, and with films PG-13, the MPAA strongly suggests parental guidance, based on an increase in "objectionable" material, either in intensity or amount. Finally, the MPAA gives an R (restricted) rating to films which require an adult to accompany anyone under the age of 17 to the viewing.[29] The rating scale for television is similar, with its TV-Y, TV-Y7, TV-Y7-FV (fantasy violence), TV-G, TV-PG, TV-14, TV-MA, from least to most mature. However, American culture tends to place less emphasis on the ratings of television programs and any possible negative impact on children attached to said ratings, than on the ratings of film, likely because, unlike with theatrical releases, there is no mechanism other than parental intervention to restrict children from viewing material not intended for them. This lackadaisical attitude toward television also implies that films, as opposed to television, are the *real* threat to childhood innocence.

Because of the ratings system, films and television programs are marketed for children largely based on the content. Media that lack most "objectionable" material mentioned above, G and PG in film ratings, target children through advertising and merchandising (toys, books, video games, etc.). In fact, television advertisers for children's programs may withdraw advertising dollars if they think parents will disapprove of a show's content. Likewise, production studios continually pressure filmmakers to lower ratings (generally to at least PG-13), to remove a required amount of such material, in order to market films to the largest possible audience, inflating numbers at the box office and, of course, toy sales (where the real money is made anyway).[30] In many cases marketing for these media target adults as well — through humor, for instance — due to adults' ability to approve or disapprove of content and their inherent purchasing power, something children generally lack.

Indeed M. Keith Booker points out that children's films are "doubly coded, containing some elements that are designed to appeal to (and send messages to) young viewers and others that are designed for the adults who accompany [them]."[31] Perry Nodelman calls this appeal to adults the "shadow text"[32] of media for children. Examples of such shadow texts are myriad, but one humorous example that illustrates the point comes from the children's cartoon *SpongeBob Squarepants*. In one episode,[33] SpongeBob, who looks more like a yellow kitchen sponge than an actual sea sponge, sits watching television. As SpongeBob stares intently, a pink anemone gyrates suggestively on the screen. SpongeBob grows more interested, but when his pet snail Gary slithers in, the sponge yells, abruptly changes the channel, and pretends he was watching football. SpongeBob was watching sea porn (or at the very least some other sexually suggestive sea program). Now, at this point, the adults watching are either rolling in the floor or are quickly changing the channel in a sanctimonious huff, all while the children scratch their heads in utter confusion.

The ratings system and marketing strategies, taken together, would seem to indicate that media for children are those media specifically marketed toward children based on the lack of objectionable content. However, this is not always the case due to the *form* of the texts, in particular whether they are animated or live-action. The problem arises in that Hollywood has largely been unable to understand how to market animated films and programs for adults. In the East, animation finds a large adult audience due to the thriving genre of anime. However, in the West, as mentioned above, animation is still viewed almost universally as for children and, therefore, immature, childish, etc. The confusion surrounding animation for adults in the West has led to the difficulty of some films and programs in finding an audience and further confused what is meant by for children.[34]

This volume, however, contains essays written by and for adults, essays about sf in film and television created by adults for children (but of course with their parents in mind, who pay for their children's entertainment and ideological consumption and/or pay for their wresting with ideological consumption, for their cognitive estrangements, alienations and shocks). We have divided the essays into three thematic sections, suggested by the motions, gestures and critiques within the essays themselves: I. D Is for Deviance; II. S Is for Structures of Power; and III. F Is for Future Shock.

Boundaries and Beyond

Wishing to address a scholarly lacuna, we now offer a *contingent* distinction between fantasy and science fiction, though they may be conjoined twin-genres (perhaps conjoined triplets with horror). For a distinction, a difference between fantasy and sf, we look to their source of imaginative difference from our mundane world. In the case of fantasy texts (either written or visual/aural), the source, as we have suggested above, is usually magic or some other supernatural phenomenon. On the other hand, with sf, the source is usually technologically-based (no matter how impossible or not-yet possible) and grounded in the sciences (even if the technology is likely impossible, according to our contemporary understanding of science, such as time travel and faster-than-light travel).

There are instances of what can be called "scifi fantasy," such as the *Star Wars* franchise, discussed in this volume by R.C. Neighbors, a franchise which includes science-fictional tropes such as starships, aliens, and space, as well as fantasy elements such as wizards and magic, in the form of Jedi and the Force, respectively. In addition, this volume includes Elizabeth Leigh Scherman's discussion of *Monsters, Inc.* (2001), which also spans the boundary between sf and fantasy. It has ray guns, fantastic machines, and alternative energy sources, as well as seemingly magical portals to another world. It is unclear if the monsters of the title are like the creatures of fantasy or more akin to aliens from another dimension. Either way, we have included essays about texts that involve fantasy as long as the focus is on a sf element/trope or set of elements/tropes. However, to keep the essays as unified and connected as possible, as well as to begin a dialogue within the scholarly lacuna, we decided the book should be limited to few references to traditional fantasy — by that, we mean swords, elves, magic, etc., and the texts that incorporate them — though we kept in mind the possibility of a dialogue between science fiction and fantasy within a text or group of texts.

As for "for children," we take a similar stance: Our contributors keep the focus on films and television fairly indisputably for children, rather than for adults, even if some adults may find some of the content objectionable. For example, *Lilo & Stitch* (2002), like *Monsters, Inc.*, both of which Scherman discusses, and *Toy Story* (1995), discussed by Daniel Kennefick, are obviously children's films, primarily due, as mentioned above, to form, content, and marketing. However, films like *Transformers* (2007), which Jacqueline Wiegard discusses, may be crossing the boundaries, for while the film was heavily marketed toward children, many adults may object to a child's viewing the violence found on the screen. Furthermore, some of our writers mention texts that push the boundaries of what can be considered children's film or television if only because they are texts that seem at least *as much* for adults as for children, such as J.P.C. Brown, who discusses the British series *Doctor Who* and Sandy Rankin who discusses *The Iron Giant* (1999) — with its mild profanity, sexual allusions, and allusions to the American Beat era of the late 1950s. Daniel O'Brien, in discussing *Daleks' Invasion Earth 2150 A.D.*, argues that the filmmakers honed their "source material into a pointed, if unintended allegory of, and commentary on, British resistance to Nazi Germany and, by extension, Britain's position on the international stage at the time of the film's production," an argument that, while valid and immensely worthwhile, is an argument that an audience of "children only" cannot possibly see. Children have little to no knowledge of British resistance to Nazi Germany, and, hence cannot make that particular allegorical leap, unless by "children" we mean teens, 'tweens, or young adults.

But none of this is to say that what we point to when we say for children, any more than what we point to when we say for adults, when we say American, or British, or masculine or feminine, or absence or presence, or film or television, or what we point to when we say sf, signifies that we are in a world in which the terrain is that of objective empiricism, absolute and instrumental logic, and reified conceptual rigor. Instead, we are in a world (of worlds) in which "sf for children" points towards horizons of possibility that from our adult vantage-point or disadvantage-point may seem unmoving, when in actuality, the horizons *and* vantage-points are always moving. With Galileo — in an imaginary, sf or fantasy form, since he likely never said it when he was forced to recant his belief that the earth moves around the sun — we say, *Eppur si muove* (and yet it moves).

NOTES

1. Edward James, *Science Fiction in the 20th Century* (Oxford, U.K.: Oxford University Press, 1994), 208.
2. Damon Knight, *In Search of Wonder: Essays on Modern Science Fiction* (Chicago: Advent, 1996), 11.
3. Ibid. 12–13.
4. Darko Suvin, *Metamorphoses of Science Fiction: On the Poetics and History of a Literary Genre* (New Haven: Yale University Press, 1979), 8.
5. Ibid., *Metamorphoses*, 9.
6. Ibid., *Metamorphoses*, 69.
7. Ibid., *Metamorphoses*, 9.
8. Philip Marchand, "On How Fantasy Took Over Science Fiction," August 8, 2009, http://network.nationalpost.com/np/blogs/afterword.
9. David Seed, "Introduction: Approaching Science Fiction," in *A Companion to Science Fiction*, edited by David Seed (Malden, MA: Blackwell Publishing, 2008).

10. Seed, 6.
11. Vivian Sobchack, *Screening Space: The American Science Fiction Film* (New York: Ungar, 1991).
12. Ibid., 17.
13. Quoted in Sobchack, 17.
14. Sobchack, 17.
15. Ibid., 18.
16. Carl Freedman, *Critical Theory and Science Fiction* (Middletown, CT: Wesleyan University Press, 2000), 43.
17. Fredric Jameson, "Introduction: Utopia Now," in *Archaeologies of the Future: The Desire Called Utopia and Other Science Fictions* (London: Verso, 2005), xii–xiii.
18. Istvan Csicsery-Ronay, Jr., *The Seven Beauties of Science Fiction* (Middletown, CT: Wesleyan University Press, 2008), 1.
19. Ibid., 4–5.
20. Darko Suvin, "Estrangement and Cognition," 1972, in *Speculations on Speculation: Theories of Science Fiction,* eds. James Gunn, Matthew Candelaria (Lanham, MD: Scarecrow Press, 2005), 27.
21. Darko Suvin, "SF and the Genealogical Jungle," in *Speculations on Speculation: Theories of Science Fiction,"* eds. James Gunn, Matthew Candeleria (Lanham, MD: Scarecrow Press, 2005), 66–67.
22. Ibid., 67.
23. Fredric Jameson, *The Political Unconscious: Narrative as a Socially Symbolic Act* (Ithaca, NY: Cornell University Press, 1981).
24. Cary Bazalgette and Terry Staples in their study of children's cinema *In Front of the Children: Screen Entertainment and Your Audiences* describe children as "people under the age of about twelve," but due to its almost arbitrary nature, we hesitate to endorse such a number.
25. Peter Brooks, "Toward Supreme Fictions," in *The Child's Part* (Boston: Beacon Press, 1972), 5.
26. Ian Wojcik-Andrews, *Children's Films: History, Ideology, Pedagogy, Theory* (New York: Garland, 2000), 19.
27. Ibid., 7.
28. Ibid., 3.
29. The rating of NC-17 (formally X) also exists but is exceedingly rare, since it limits the audience to such an extent that such films have always failed commercially at the box office.
30. It has been argued elsewhere that all films below an R rating are "for children" in the sense that they are "for everyone," since, as its name suggests, the R rating is the only distinction that actually *restricts* viewing based on age. And restricting the audience leads to restricted profit margins.
31. M. Keith Booker, *Disney, Pixar, and the Hidden Messages of Children's Films* (Santa Barbara, CA: Praeger, 2010), xxi.
32. Perry Nodelman, *The Hidden Adult: Defining Children's Literature* (Baltimore, MD: Johns Hopkins University Press, 2008).
33. "Your Shoes Untied," *SpongeBob Squarepants*, Television Program, Walt Dohrn and Paul Tibbitt (November 2, 2000; Burbank, CA: Nickelodeon, 2004).
34. There are exceptions to this, such as *Beavis and Butthead, South Park*, and some of the programs shown on Cartoon Network's Adult Swim programming block, but these exceptions have failed to change the widespread Western perception of animation as a children's medium.

References

Bazalgette, Cary, and Terry Staples. "Unshrinking the Kids: Children's Cinema and the Family Film." In *In Front of the Children: Screen Entertainment and Young Audiences*, edited by Cary Bazalgette and David Buckingham, 92–108. Suffolk: BFI Publishing, 1995.

Booker, M. Keith. *Disney, Pixar, and the Hidden Messages of Children's Films*. Santa Barbara, CA: Praeger, 2010.

Brooks, Peter. "Toward Supreme Fictions." In *The Child's Part*, 5–14. Boston: Beacon Press, 1972.

Csicsery-Ronay, Istvan, Jr. *The Seven Beauties of Science Fiction*. Middletown, CT: Wesleyan University Press, 2008.
Freedman, Carl. *Critical Theory and Science Fiction*. Middletown, CT: Wesleyan University Press, 2000.
James, Edward. *Science Fiction in the 20th Century*. Oxford, U.K.: Oxford University Press, 1994.
Jameson, Fredric. "Introduction: Utopia Now." In *Archaeologies of the Future: The Desire Called Utopia and Other Science Fictions*, xi–xvi. London: Verso, 2005.
_____. *The Political Unconscious: Narrative as a Socially Symbolic Act*. Ithaca, NY: Cornell University Press, 1981.
Knight, Damon. *In Search of Wonder: Essays on Modern Science Fiction*. Chicago: Advent, 1996.
Marchand, Philip. "On How Fantasy Took Over Science Fiction." August 8, 2009. network.nationalpost.com/np/blogs/afterword.
Nodelman, Perry. *The Hidden Adult: Defining Children's Literature*. Baltimore: Johns Hopkins University Press, 2008.
Seed, David. "Introduction: Approaching Science Fiction." In *A Companion to Science Fiction*, edited by David Seed. Malden, MA: Blackwell Publishing, 2008.
Sobchack, Vivian. *Screening Space: The American Science Fiction Film*. New York: Ungar, 1991.
Suvin, Darko. "Estrangement and Cognition." In *Speculations on Speculation: Theories of Science Fiction,* edited by James Gunn and Matthew Candelaria, 23–35. Lanham, MD: Scarecrow Press, 2005.
_____. *Metamorphoses of Science Fiction: On the Poetics and History of a Literary Genre*. New Haven: Yale University Press, 1979.
_____. "SF and the Genealogical Jungle." In *Speculations on Speculation: Theories of Science Fiction*, edited by James Gunn and Matthew Candeleria, 59–79. Lanham, MD: Scarecrow Press, 2005.
Wojcik-Andrews, Ian. *Children's Films: History, Ideology, Pedagogy, Theory*. New York: Garland, 2000.
"Your Shoes Untied," from *SpongeBob Squarepants*. Television Program. Walt Dohrn and Paul Tibbitt. November 2, 2000. Burbank, CA: Nickelodeon, 2004.

PART 1. D IS FOR DEVIANCE

• One •

Monsters Among Us: Construction of the Deviant Body in *Monsters, Inc.* and *Lilo & Stitch*

ELIZABETH LEIGH SCHERMAN

"You're one of *them*! Get out of here, Stitch!"
— Lilo from *Lilo & Stitch*

The girl Lilo has just realized that her pet "dog," Stitch, is not what she supposed him to be. He has revealed himself to her: four arms and a row of spikes down the back. Although Lilo has fought to defend Stitch's difficult behavior and strange appearance to her family and friends, she cannot accept the fact that he is an alien. Betrayed, Lilo commands Stitch to leave.

The 2002 Disney film *Lilo & Stitch* is one of many that present their young audience with a storyline built around a "deviant" body — that is, a body that characters in the film as well as the audience may consider abnormal and undesirable. These bodies may belong to aliens, or monsters, or mutants, and their presence in science-fiction cinema targeting children is particularly intriguing as children's film can act as a bellwether for social attitudes. The construction of a profitable "family film" demands a fragile balance: the story may sanitize but should also innovate; it may moralize but should not offend.[1]

Fantastic stories have long been a mainstay of family film. These texts have drawn upon fairy tales and fables, but have also included themes that feature encounters and tensions between humans and an "alien or monstrous force."[2] The genres of fantasy and science fiction are ideal for pushing the envelope on social norms. Such films have been read as symbolizing or encoding issues of social class, gender, and sexuality; what Steven Neale describes as "the boundaries of the human and the issues of difference."[3] Foundational to our understanding of humanity is the manner in which we are embodied. The cinematic portrayal of the "monstrous" body actually addresses the question, what is the "human" or "normal" body? May it contain robotic parts? Extra limbs? Unusual faces? What are socially acceptable variations in the way we move about, perceive objects, communicate, think or behave? These elements are not merely the stuff of science-fiction stories. They speak to the real-life experience of millions who are identified by society as defective or impaired. "Images matter," writes disability studies scholar Paul Darke, "[F]or the disabled, images of themselves are especially important as they are presumed by virtually all critics and audiences to be essentially self-evident."[4] In exploring what may be considered the deviant or atypical body in film, then, we are exploring how cinema — and society — uses images to construct disability and impairment, constructions that become naturalized and are then taken as "self-evident." Two family films — *Monsters, Inc.* and *Lilo & Stitch* — feature characters that clearly break the rules of the "normal" body: in *Monsters, Inc.*, as an assorted array of monsters, and in *Lilo & Stitch* as aliens. Both animated films reflect production choices about presenting bodies that were clearly not human, yet which reflect enough humanity to be identifiable and accessible to children. As such, these embodied characterizations are fascinating opportunities to ask ourselves what we as a society consider to be humanizing or dehumanizing characteristics. The films each utilize the trope of the outsider coming in through a portal to another world, with connotative significations for those whom society considers "outsiders" because of appearance or function.

Moreover, both films challenge social norms with their portrayals of such beings as ultimately complete and whole, beings whose only disability is society's act of exclusion. In fact, the child "Boo" in *Monsters, Inc.* is constructed as a monster when not in her own society, illustrating this social constructionist model of disability. *Lilo & Stitch*'s alien creatures Stitch, Pleakley, and Dr. Jumba Jookiba become fully accepted as part of Lilo's family and are thus normalized in the plot. The films, then, create a tension between the tradition of casting deviant bodies as monstrosities and the possibility that the monster, like "Boo," is *us* — and that society can be constructed to recognize all bodies as valued and celebrated. In this exploration of two children's films, cinema studies joins with studies in disability, discourse and visual culture to explore cinematic constructions of "monstrous" embodiment. Such images reflect how we as a society construct impairment and how these constructions have real-life implications for those who identify or are identified as disabled.

Social Construction of Disability

In order to explore the possibilities that film invites us to consider, it is helpful to understand the basic models of disability that have been used in society through time. These models have been explained as falling within three overarching paradigms: the moral/religious model, the medical model, and the social model. These models are by no means set in stone nor are they the only possible options in explaining impairment, but they are useful in providing a framework in which to explore society's construction of "disability" or "impairment." These are constructions which are constantly undergoing change, and this change may be reflected in cinema and other media.

The religious or moral model of disability is consensually described by disability studies scholars as the oldest disability model traceable in history. It is the first recorded attempt by humans to explain why a baby is born impaired (or perceived to be impaired), or why people acquire impairments or disfigurements.[5] These explanations commonly associate disability with morality or fitness of character, ascribing meanings to the disabled body that go beyond simple biological incidence; these may suggest divine or supernatural favor, disfavor, or opportunity for "cure" as a miracle or sign.

The medical model, also called the scientific, biological, or individual model, considers disability to be located in the body of the individual, which may be considered diseased, abnormal, or deformed by cause of being atypical. Rather than considering disability as a supernatural or moral signifier, the post–Enlightenment scientific community saw disability as a device for scientific and medical discovery—a problem to be cured, rehabilitated, or prevented altogether. As Rosemary Garland-Thomson writes, this approach attempts "to standardize the body through medical technology."[6]

In the social sciences and humanities, modern discourse on disability commonly distances itself from the medical model and employs instead a social model. These social models—and there are several—identify disability not as a characteristic empirically existing in an individual,[7] but as in whole or in part a social construct which reflects the values of a particular society. Put another way, "disability is not a characteristic that exists in the person so defined, but a construct that finds its meaning in social and cultural context."[8] Many scholars differentiate between impairment and disability, with disability not seen as physiology, but rather as external barriers of policy, attitude, and architecture which exclude people with impairments from full participation in society.

Studies of individuals who are identified as "different" or disabled tell us more about the society that labels them than the impairment itself. By analyzing cinema for what is presented as "normal" or "different" (what in literature is called the Other), we are able to, as disability scholar Christopher Smit writes, "expose, critique, and reconsider social and political relations between normative and minority groups."[9] Tales of monsters and aliens invite us to play with the construction of the Other, but it is serious play: like any good children's story, the images and representations can influence us for a lifetime.

Monsters, Inc.: Right Body, Wrong World

Long before the time Alice fell through the rabbit hole, mythological, fantasy, and later science fiction, protagonists have been stumbling over, seeking out, or creating portals between worlds. In contrast to doors or devices which allow travel through time or between parallel versions of the same world, these gateways actually lead to another entirely separate world. This phenomenon is found in many such texts targeting children and family audiences, including Alexander Key's juvenile novel *The Forgotten Door* (Scholastic, 1970) and in such films as *The Chronicles of Narnia: The Lion, the Witch and the Wardrobe* (Walden Media/Walt Disney, 2005, based on the book by C.S. Lewis, 1950–1956) and *Stargate* (MGM, 1994). Recently, Phillip Pullman utilizes a version of this idea in *The Subtle Knife* (Del Ray, 1997). In *Monsters, Inc.*, the doors between worlds are literal — closet doors of all types and colors, dangling among thousands of other doors on a suspended assembly line. Monster employees enter these doors to temporarily step into the human world, frighten a scream out of the child who sleeps in the bedroom on the other side, and return to "Monstropolis," where the screams are used to generate the city's energy. A crisis arises when a toddler follows the monster "Sulley" back into his world. The duration of the story depicts Sulley and his friend Mike's efforts to return the girl to her own world, discovering in the process that a child's laughter generates more power than a child's screams.

No Abnormal Folks Here — Just Us Monsters

The word "monster" comes from the Latin word *monere,* which means "to warn." Monsters in myth could act as judgment upon a society or as agents of heroic test. They often met a messy end at the hands of the hero, the lesson being that monsters are evil and meant to be slain. In the everyday world, "monstrous" or malformed infants "might be read as embodiments of the divine, as good or bad omens of the future, or as indications of God's will or wrath."[10] In *Monsters, Inc.*, however, monsters are the norm. The inhabitants of Monstropolis refer to themselves as "monsters," but there is no negative implication to the term. The normalization of the monsters was key to the film. "People generally think of monsters as really scary, snarly, slobbery beasts," explains *Monsters, Inc.* director Pete Docter. "But in our film, they're just normal everyday Joes. They clock in; they clock out. They talk about doughnuts and union dues. They worry about things like having straight teeth. Scaring kids is just their job."[11]

The opening shots of the film establish this friendly, "everyman" normality, with every detail of the mis-en-scène carefully crafted to contribute to the mood. Gentle, happy music plays as we hear the ding-ding of an old-fashioned bicycle bell, and a monster child throws a paper onto the porch of a New York–style tenant building. In the distance, white, domed buildings rise: the backdrop of elegance and perhaps elitism in contrast to the working-class muted colors of James P. "Sulley" Sullivan and roommate Mike Wakowski's neighborhood. Monster children jump rope — using one of the kid's tongues as the rope — and exchange polite good mornings with their elders. And there are human — rather "monster" — foibles: the fire-breathing monster sneezes and incinerates his newspaper; the jelly monster dissolves down the sidewalk drain after being distracted by tipping his hat to others. Coworkers smile and greet one another by name; what are apparently teenage monsters are gawky and wear braces. Even the discourse normalizes what humans would see as monstrous: the monocular Celeste gushes to Mike about "the first time I laid eye on you"; the traffic signal tells pedestrians when to "Stalk" or "Don't Stalk," and the *Daily Glob*'s headlines carry the story of "Five-headed baby born: Parents thrilled."

Most notably, the environment reflects an attitude quite different than that of our world; it light-heartedly portrays what could be seen as the social model of disability. That is, differences which in the human world would be seen as impairments do not result in the disabling of the citizens of Monstropolis. The buildings are constructed to withstand huge bodies, but can also accommodate tiny ones; furniture comes in many forms; clothing can accommodate varied amounts of limbs, eyes, and antennae. Docter explains that the world was carefully created to accommodate different bodies: "Everything from doors to telephones to cars had to be multipurpose in order to handle everyone from eight-foot monsters to little guys who are only two inches tall."[12] Mike Wazowski is a spherical green fellow with one large eye; his boss, Mr. Waternoose, has five, and the monsters who make up the decontamination team at Monsters, Inc. represent a buffet of limbs, eyes, and body shapes. The narrative does not present a hierarchy related to the number of eyes or limbs or the size, color, or shape of a creature. Mr. Waternoose might have five eyes, but he doesn't patronize the two-eyed creatures for having relatively pathetic binocular vision, nor Mike Wazowski for his monocular vision.

Nor is there a pretense that everyone is the same or should be the same. When Sulley teases Mike for not wanting to walk to work, he points to a huge chicken-type monster and says, "Look, Ted's walking to work." Mike shrugs and replies, "Big deal. Guy takes five steps and he's there." Mike isn't mocking Ted for the fact that he clucks instead of vocalizes, nor for his immense height; Mike is merely whining because Sulley is making him walk instead of taking his shiny red car, and he's a bit jealous that he can't make it to work in five steps. Sulley calls Mike "butterball," which is an affectionate reference to Mike's shape, and Mike counters with a friendly, "Look at you! You have your own climate!" In addition, body differences are no excuse for antisocial behavior; for example, both Mike and Sulley dislike the chameleon-like character of Randall, who abuses his unique ability to vanish by listening into private conversations and sneaking around where he's not wanted.

Virtually every citizen of Monstropolis is unique, although groups may be seen to share commonalities: flying, sliding or creeping instead of walking on two legs; seeing out of a variety of eyes; or behaving in reptilian, arachnid, or mammalian fashions. In the human world, these would be seen as disfigurements or abnormalities; in Monstropolis, deviance and atypicality is the norm, and the environment is structured in expectation of this. Unlike the human world, Monstropolis does not appear to equate difference with "impairment," and therefore disability — what Jan Tøssebro calls "a mismatch between the individual and the environment"[13] — doesn't exist.

How to Pass for a Monster

What are the visual signifiers of monstrosity in film? They are remarkably conventional, not only in children's cinema but in all cinema. Of course, there are those who "pass" for human, but if a creature is designed to be visibly monstrous, the options fall into dependable categories: the body is of a different size than the average human body; it has fewer or greater than four limbs, it has fewer or greater than two eyes and one head; similar restrictions occur on facial characteristics, and these elements should be bilaterally symmetric. Eyes are particularly nonnegotiable; there should be two, and the slightest difference in their appearance or function can give the monster away. Characteristics are often taken from animals: the monster has horns, fur, talons, a beak, or is differently colored. Vocalizations or food preferences may be unusual, or the monster may possess superhuman or preternatural abilities. These animal-like attributes were used to sell tickets to "freak" shows in turn-of-the-century circuses and carnivals. A child with hypertrichnosis could be called a "dog-boy," or "lion-faced boy"; a teenager without arms or legs called a "lobster boy." In both medical and social realms, such terms are still used to describe the anomalous human body: a baby has a "cat's cry" (cri du chat syndrome) or a "hare lip" (cleft palate). These discursive indicators of "Otherness" translate into the visual representation of abnormality in film. Certain signifiers are so critical to being considered monstrous, in fact, that some of the monsters in the scream factory enhance their scare factor by adding false monster teeth or an extra eye or two. They sharpen their fangs and practice their roars — none of which they need for their everyday lives.

Monster Meets Monster

There are, however, the equivalent of "monsters" in Monstropolis: human children. The film quickly establishes that the employees of the company Monsters, Inc. are just as frightened by human children as children are of them, with the factory thrown into a panic of "decontamination" after a monster named George returns through a closet door with a "toxic" child's sock stuck on his back. The factory goes into red alert; a team of hazardous materials specialists in an outstanding array of body shapes converges upon George to remove and destroy the tiny sock. Each team member's yellow protective outfit is specially designed to fit his or her body shape and number of limbs, digits, and eyes. Later, the unthinkable occurs when Sulley enters a door left unattended by Randall and returns with a toddler clinging to his back. "Kitty!" shrieks the tot, identifying the tall blue monster as a pet. Sulley is beside himself with fright, and stuffs the child into a sports bag. She escapes in a sushi restaurant and yells "Boo!" in a playful manner to the patrons. Monstropolis erupts into a panic. News reports feature Child Detection Agency technicians who "can neither confirm nor deny" the presence of a human child. A monster is on the loose.

With no experience of humans, the monsters turn to exaggeration and outright invention. "Well, a kid flew right over me and blasted a car with its laser vision," claims one monster while being interviewed on television. Another monster claims, "I tried to run from it, but it picked me up with its mind power and shook me like a dog." Even Mike, despite Sulley's insistence otherwise, tells his friend, "That thing is a killing machine! I bet it's just waiting for us to fall asleep."

While the film pokes fun at humans who will do anything for the sake of being on television, there is also an element of truth in the portrayal. Historically, descriptions of atypical humans have included the dubious: the "monster of Ravenna ... [with] wings instead of arms, an extra eye on the knee, and legs covered in fish scales and ending in talons."[14] Epileptics were believed by some to be possessed by demons, and disabled children were suspected to be changelings, substituted by the fairies in place of real child, a "massa carnis," or soulless lump of flesh, as Martin Luther described.[15] We seem to need to distance ourselves from those whom we are certain must be different from us not only outside but inside, and this fear of the unknown has resulted in social policies of isolation and oppression for many who possess what we see as undesirable bodies or minds. In the end, Monstropolitans aren't monsters at all — they're us.

Sulley quickly learns this lesson as he watches Boo draw, sleep, and show fear and delight. She's not an "it" or a "thing" as Mike calls her, but a being more like than dislike himself. In a scene reminiscent of *E.T.* (Universal Pictures, 1982), where Elliott lays a trail of candy to entice the little alien, Sulley lays a trail of cereal for Boo to follow into the bedroom. Boo shows affection toward Sulley, whom she calls "Kitty," likening him to an animal, but a friendly, domesticated one. Later, Mike will come around to Sulley's way of thinking, and both monsters will help Boo return to her own world. To do so, they must smuggle her back into the factory, which means that they must disguise her abnormality. They put her into a baby monster suit: purple, with two eyes sticking up on antennae. With this perfectly normal appearance, Boo is free to move about the city. *Monsters, Inc.* complicates the very idea of abnormality in a manner that gently invites the audience to reconsider social assumptions about difference and barriers; it turns the idea of monstrosity upside down by positioning the audience member as the "monster." It challenges us but also assures us, as Sulley assures Boo when she shows fear over what's lurking in the closet. "There's no monster in here," he asserts, then realizes that he's standing in the closet. "Well," he grins, "now there is."

And that's okay.

Lilo & Stitch: Don't Look Now, But Your Extra Arms Are Showing

The character of Stitch in Disney's *Lilo & Stitch* (2002) is the ultimate deviant body: he has no prototype, no mother nor father, no peers. He is "experiment 626"— the invention of scientist Jumba Jookiba, who will, along with Stitch, be exiled from his own planet. Although the other inhabitants of the planet are a diverse group, with different body types, faces, colors, and eyes, Stitch is ultimately pronounced "an abomination" in part because he is unable to behave acceptably. It's not just that he curses at them (in his own language) but also that he's been designed as the first of a new species — a species programmed to destroy everything it comes into contact with. "It has no place among us," decrees the Grand Councilwoman, leader of the United Galactic Federation.

Stitch is banned to a prison asteroid, but manages to escape in a rocket, landing on the earth island of Kauai,[16] a location lacking the big cities he is programmed to destroy. There, he manages to escape being captured by getting adopted in the guise of a dog by the child Lilo and her big sister Nani, who were orphaned when their parents died in a car accident. Jumba and Agent Pleakley from Stitch's planet are sent to Kauai to retrieve him, while Nani tries to prove herself a worthy guardian to a dubious social worker, Cobra Bubbles.

"He Used to Be a Collie Before He Got Ran Over": The Cost of Passing as Normal

"The creature 626 is entirely Other," writes political scientist Utz McKnight. "Its existence does not reflect natural categories of difference ... 626 is the aberration, the perfect Frankenstein's monster."[17] Like Frankenstein's monster, Stitch ends up challenging the expectations that society would place upon him — both human society and his own, including the assumption that "scientific experiments" such as 626 have neither the inclination nor the right to expect to be treated with equality in society. Stitch is the "test tube baby" that didn't turn out to be at all what its creator had hoped, and as such is being discarded. He is "nature-gone-wrong," a concept which can relieve society of its accountability in creating an inclusive environment; unlike Monstropolis, the world that Stitch falls into hasn't learned to live peaceably with its differences, let alone a true outsider — an alien.

Stitch's position can be seen to parallel that of the disabled person in our society, who under the medical model of disability may also be seen to be the product of tragedy, of accident, of intentions (in this case, nature's) gone awry. "The interpretation of disability as 'misfortune' allows for the understanding that inaccessibility too is a misfortune and not necessarily an injustice," argue disability scholars Michalko and Titchkovsky. "Everyone belongs to (is) a race, and the same holds for gender. This cannot be said of disability. People belong to (are) disability only because of some misfortune. Disability is not framed within the idea of 'natural' in the same way that gender, race, and able-bodiedness are."[18] Stitch also experiences the isolation of knowing that he is one of a kind, and the frustration of what is portrayed as the necessity of changing in order to be accepted into the world of the "normals." Pioneer disability writer Irving Kenneth Zola explains that unlike many minority populations, disabled persons are not born and raised in a subculture nor expected to identify with a cohesive group; they are "born for the most part into normal families, [and] we are socialized into that world."[19]

Stitch must also assimilate into his new world; he patterns himself after the creatures he sees achieving success with the privileged class. That is, he becomes a dog. That he must subordinate and compromise himself to "pass" is distasteful to him, but the alternative is capture and exile. While in the dog pound kennel, Stitch sees a poster of adorable dogs and considers his own body. He retracts two of his four arms as well as the line of scales down his back. He can't change his blue color or torn ears, but his masquerade works: Lilo falls in love with him. She has prayed for "someone to be my friend. Someone who won't run away." She had specified an angel, "the nicest angel you have," but what she winds up with most certainly does not fit her order. However, there is a clear parallel between Stitch and Lilo: both are parentless, both are angry and destructive — they bite, spit, and growl — both are unusually intelligent, and both are misfits.

Lilo realizes that her "dog" is different; she explains Stitch's bizarre appearance to critical onlookers by saying that he "used to be a collie" but he got run over.[20] She knows she's lying, but she's choosing to associate her dubious pet with the all-American canine hero "Lassie," at once silencing Stitch's critics and reinstating the narrative theme of social acceptance. She beds Stitch down with a baby bottle filled with coffee and reads to him from a storybook about "The Ugly Duckling," Hans Christian Anderson's tale of an ugly, outcast water bird who grew up to be a swan. Stitch looks intently at the picture of the duckling and intones, "lost." He is not merely the soulless weapon Jumba claimed him to be; he is slowly revealing that despite his aberrant outward appearance, he has the same potential and the same needs as other creatures. When the social worker scolds Lilo for her "dog's" bad behavior, she accepts his challenge to make Stitch into a "model citizen." And what better role model for an ideal citizen than Elvis Presley?

Unwittingly, Lilo has selected yet another "first of his species" and social outcast — in certain circles of his time — Elvis.[21] She dresses Stitch as Elvis and has him perform on the beach, which ends badly. Stitch, however, keeps trying to fit in, even to the extent of entering the water to learn to surf with Nani, although he cannot swim nor float. Again, the outing ends badly, as the social worker watches Stitch nearly drown Lilo by clinging to her neck. Nani's boyfriend David turns to Stitch and says, "You know, I really believed they [Nani and Lilo] had a chance. Then you came along." Later, Stitch climbs the stairway to his house and meets a duck that resembles the one in the storybook. His eyes brighten — is this a creature alone, unique like himself?—until the duck quacks and is joined by a family of ducklings. They waddle off, and Stitch's expression saddens. He has no family, and he will never grow into a swan. He is who he is, and although he will change to fit into his chosen family, they will also have to change to adapt to him, four arms and all.

His "coming out," however, is traumatic to Lilo. As the aliens storm her house to retrieve their prey, Stitch is compelled to reveal his true form. With great angst, he pops out his extra arms and displays his scales. Lilo is horrified. Stitch, her "puppy," is "one of them," an alien. She tells him to get out. Her anger at him is short-lived, however, as he ends up orchestrating her rescue from the hands of the aliens, who mistakenly capture her along with Stitch. When an alien bounty-hunter catches up with him, Stitch asks, "Does Stitch have to go on the ship? Can Stitch say goodbye?" Although Jumba has told him he has no family, he begs to differ.

"This is my family," he explains to his captors, which include the kindly Grand Councilwoman. "I found it all on my own. It's little and it's broken but still good. Yeah, still good." The Councilwoman accepts Lilo's argument that the dog pound sales receipt serves as proof that Stitch belongs to her, and seems grateful for a peaceful resolution to the situation. Stitch has found acceptance: attitude, four arms, and all. He has resisted the efforts of his maker to remake him so as to better "fit" others' values or body ideals. When Jumba entreats Stitch with the promise that "I'll put you back together again ... I'll make you taller and not so fluffy!" Stitch retorts, "I *like* fluffy!" He is fine with his body the way it is, and even though he has modified his sassy attitude, it continues to define him.[22]

The story ends with snapshots of the newly formed family—including boyfriend David and extended family members Cobra Bubbles, Pleakley and Jumba—as they work to restore Lilo and Nani's burnt-out home, dress up for Halloween (Stitch is a superhero), visit Graceland, and pose around the Thanksgiving table in a tableau that directly alludes to Norman Rockwell's "Freedom from Want," the iconic painting of the wholesome American family ... with a four-armed troublemaker, a four-eyed, blue-tongued alien and a one-eyed, three-legged alien. The message is clear: society can choose to accommodate and value any type of body.[23]

In creating a situation in which two worlds meet and ultimately collaborate, *Lilo & Stitch* allows the spectator to consider cultural norms about bodies from different viewpoints. Both earthlings and aliens end up adopting or being adopted into a wider "family": Stitch into the family of Nani, Lilo, and David; that same family into the protection of the United Galactic Federation, and Pleakely and Jumba into the family of earthlings. McKnight writes that *Lilo & Stitch* "clearly brings into question the role humans have in creation and the foundation of communities of difference."[24] In order to create a community where difference could be given root to grow, writer-directors DuBlois and Sanders deliberated over the story location. They wanted a setting that was "remote, isolated ... that couldn't draw a crowd," first selecting the state of Kansas, then a forest, before settling on Kauai.[25] The concept of *ohana* came from the island culture. As Lilo puts it, *"Ohana* means family. Family means nobody gets left behind. Or forgotten." DuBlois explains, "It's not about blood relations, but rather about being part of a larger community family."[26] *Lilo & Stitch* brings this notion to its extreme: even aliens are part of our larger family. We do not have to "fit in" to fit in.

This concept, that aberration or strangeness does not or should not equate with revulsion, is woven into the film's narrative. We may be strange beings even to ourselves: early on, Lilo is shown snapping photographs of interestingly-shaped and colored tourists, such as the large, sun-burnt man whose portrait she places on her bedroom wall.[27] "Aren't they beautiful?" she sighs, as she refers to her photograph collection. For Lilo, bodies that are unlike her own are objects of delight and acceptance. Pleakley, too, embraces bodily difference, donning a page-boy style wig and makeup as he poses as Jumba's wife, and later revealing that he's quite attached to this adopted appearance; he considers himself "pretty" and doesn't want Jumba to try on his wig. Adult spectators of the film may recognize the ironic humor in Jumba and Pleakley's passing for tourists. After all, tourists are a strange lot to begin with; who would notice a green, one-eyed, three-legged "woman" among the horde? David's only concern with Pleakley's appearance is that her head looks a little "swollen." Humor is also used in the selection of props; for example, Pleakley is shown using a child's stereoscopic viewer, even though he only has one eye, and Jumba owns a pair of four-lensed binoculars — quadoculars? — one lens for each eye. In Jumba's experience, two eyes may be seen as an impairment, but Pleakley never indicates any diminishment of ability.

Producer Clark Spencer designed the film to complicate the traditional children's movie theme of good versus evil, of a villain that is punished in the end. In *Lilo & Stitch*, the "villains" become part of the extended family, and co-protagonists Lilo and alien Stitch are redeemed.[28] However, redemption — being brought back into the fold — is not to be mistaken with "cured." Stitch retains his difference both in phenotype and personality, as is evidenced right to the end of the story. For example, in his attempt to rescue Lilo from the spaceship meant to capture him, he angrily tries to bite through her transparent container. When even his maker, who has been sent to capture him, tells him, "You're vile! You're foul! You're flawed!" Stitch does not disagree, but simply adds, "Also cute and fluffy!" The "photo" images of the family that conclude the movie show that Stitch continues to use his four arms, act as he wishes, and proudly display his spikes.

Conclusion

On the surface, these films may be seen to promote the ubiquitous kids' film happy ending: we're all just one, big happy, family, and if we just try, we can get along. But beyond the common tropes and themes, there is an undercurrent of challenge to the very idea of normalization and the deviant body. The monsters in *Monsters, Inc.* as well as Stitch and his cohort of aliens are neither "cured" nor sent to isolated parts of their native or adoptive society to live out their pathetic, abnormal lives. Children's author Jane Yolen writes, "Good stories are dangerous. Dangerous, anarchic, seductive. They change you, often forever."[29] The wonderful danger in science-fiction films, and particular those targeting children, is that there are those in the audience who will start to get outlandish ideas; those who will ask, "Why not?" The implication to society of actually implementing "Ohana"— inclusion for all — is enormous in its economic, political, and social effects. A world that finds it "natural" to provide accessibility to every body type, such as in *Monsters, Inc.*, or interactive coexistence with those who look, act, or think differently, such as in *Lilo & Stitch*, is a world that may seem unattainable, but it is one that disability rights and other civil rights advocates ask us to consider. For all of its flaws and commodification, cinema is still uniquely situated to offer our youngest citizens a compelling window through which to contemplate such a world, and to consider the possibility of moving beyond contemplation.

NOTES

1. Disney's critics have long accused the studio of the "Disnification" of films — simplifying them to remove offensive elements, while promoting (if not proselytizing) what Annalee Ward describes as "American values." See, for instance, Elizabeth Bell, Lynda Haas, and Laura Sells, *From Mouse to Mermaid: The Politics of Film, Gender, and Culture* (Bloomington: Indiana University Press, 1995) and Annalee R. Ward, *Mouse Morality: The Rhetoric of Disney Animated Film* (Austin: University of Texas Press, 2002). However, when studios present themes that are considered to promote certain positions on social issues, they can also lose ticket buyers. For example, *The Golden Compass* (Twentieth Century–Fox), was the target of an ersatz "boycott" by conservative Christian organizations who saw the film as promoting atheism, and Warner Brothers *Happy Feet* drew the wrath of a number of conservative Christians, who posted on websites and blogs their interpretation of the film as encoding a "homosexual agenda."
2. Thomas Schatz, *Old Hollywood/New Hollywood: Ritual, Art, and Industry* (Ann Arbor, MI: UMI Research Press, 1983), 86.
3. Stephen Neale, *Genre and Hollywood* (London: Routledge, 2000), 103.
4. Paul Darke, "Understanding Cinematic Representations of Disability," in *The Disability Reader: Social Science Perspectives,* edited by T. Shakespeare (London: Cassell, 1998), 181.
5. Susan School Eberly writes that "congenital disorders" and "birth defects ... have produced feelings of fear and awe since earliest times ... [and] have evoked a religious response," and

describes Assyrian clay tablets from 2000 B.C. as one of the earliest written records where a society has recorded and categorized disability; the tablets detail the description by soothsayers of 62 babies who were considered deformed or abnormal . See Susan Schoon Eberly, "Fairies and the Folklore of Disability: Changelings, Hybrids, and Solitary Fairy," *Folklore* 99, no. 1 (1988): 58–77.

6. Rosemary Garland-Thompson, "Shape Structures Story: Fresh and Feisty Stories about Disability," *Narrative* 15, no. 1 (2007): 114.

7. "Impairment" may be identified this way (as originating in the individual body, not in social construction), but even this is debated among disability studies researchers.

8. Steven Taylor, Bonnie Schultz and Pamela Walker, introduction to *Disability Studies: Information and Resources*, The Center on Human Policy, Law and Disability Studies at Syracuse University, http://thechp.syr.edu/Disability_Studies_2003_current.html#Introduction.

9. Christopher R. Smit and Anthony Enns, *Screening Disability: Essays on Cinema and Disability* (Lanham, MD: University Press of America, 2001).

10. Lindal Buchanan, "A Study of Maternal Rhetoric: Anne Hutchinson, Monsters, and the Antinomian Controversy," *Rhetoric Review* 25, no. 3 (2006), 241.

11. "Monsters, Inc. Production Notes," *Pixar Talk*, http://www.pixartalk.com/featurefilms/monsters-inc/monsters-inc-production-notes/.

12. Ibid.

13. Jan Tøssebro, "Understanding Disability," *Scandinavian Journal of Disability Research* 6, no. 1 (2004): 3–7.

14. Buchanan, "A Study of Maternal Rhetoric," 243.

15. Martin Luther, *D. Martin Luthers Werke. Kritische Gesamtausgabe. Tischreden* (Weimar: H. Böhlau, 1912).

16. Director Chris Sanders had originally intended the film to be set in Kansas, "an isolated place where he could have an alien land and not be discovered right away." He later switched the location to Kauai for the same reason as well as the challenge of setting a full-length animated film is a place where none had been set before. "That choice went on to color the entire movie and rewrite the story for us," said Sanders. See Pat Davis, "Disney Goes Hawaiian," *Hana Hou! The Magazine of American Airlines* 5, no. 2 (April/May 2002), http://www.hanahou.com/pages/Magazine.asp?Action=DrawArticle&ArticleID=389&MagazineID=24.

17. Utz McKnight, "The African in America: Race and the Politics of the Diaspora," *African Identities* 6, no. 1 (2008): 66. McKnight explores the film from a perspective of race and politics.

18. Rod Michalko and Tanya Titchkovsky, "Putting Disability in Its Place: It's Not a Laughing Matter," in *Embodied Rhetorics: Disability in Language and Culture*, edited by J.C. Wilson and Cynthia Lewiecki-Wilson (Carbondale: Southern Illinois University Press, 2001), 208.

19. Irving Kenneth Zola, "Communication Barriers Between the 'Able-bodied' and the 'Handicapped,'" *Archives of Physical Medicine and Rehabilitation* 62, no. 8 (1981): 355–9.

20. Stitch's animator, Alex Kuperschmidt, explains that he wanted Stitch to move "in a fashion that would give people a start, very fast," so he modeled Stitch's movements after that of a lizard he watched run across a table. He designed Stitch as an image of "a Swiss army knife of destruction. He has all of these sharp things sticking out of him." See Frank Moore, "Lilo & Stitch, Disney Feature Animation Florida's Finest Hour, Remembered," *Orlando Sentinel*, April 1, 2009, http://blogs.orlandosentinel.com/entertainment_movies_blog/2009/04/lilostitch-disney-feature-animation-floridas-finest-hourremembered.html.

21. Unwittingly, perhaps, for director/screenwriters Chris Sanders and Dean DuBois as well. In interviews, neither has expressed intent for such a parallel, but rather wanted to make the character of Lilo "unique," with Sanders explaining that "Elvis to [Lilo] is a hero. She doesn't look at any of the bad sides of Elvis' life. It's all the good side!" Sanders is also a self-described Elvis fan whose family "idolized" Elvis. See Jérémie Noyer, "Lilo & Stitch: A Little More Conversation with Directors Chris Sanders & Dean de Blois!" *Animated Views* (2009), http://animatedviews.com/2009/lilo-stitch-a-little-more-conversation-with-directors-chris-sanders-dean-de-blois/. His heroic status with Lilo and Sanders aside, Elvis was ultimately seen as a groundbreaker and rule-breaker in the music industry, but like Stitch, a little on the naughty side, with then-contemporary Frank Sinatra, for instance, decrying the young Elvis' music as "deplorable,

a rancid smelling aphrodisiac. It fosters almost totally negative and destructive reactions in young people." See BBC News Online, "The Enduring Enigma of Elvis," *BBC News*, http://news.bbc.co.uk/2/hi/entertainment/6937441.stm.

22. In both trailers and sequels to *Lilo & Stitch*, it is clear that Stitch's unconventional and at times disconcerting behavior is being sold as part of his charm. The Disney trailers for the film actually read as a send-up *of* Disney *by* Disney, as Stitch pops up to disrupt key sappy, emotional moments in scenes from *Beauty and the Beast, The Little Mermaid, Aladdin,* and *The Lion King*. In the popular DVD sequels, Stitch continues to wreak happy havoc.

23. In her critique of *Lilo & Stitch*, McKnight considers Stitch's creation as challenging "natural species differences and categories of social order" and asks, "What if our genetic experiments in defining difference allow for the creation of new ways of living and acting?" See McKnight, "The African in America," 68. While McKnight frames the question as a unrealized phenomenon, the truth is that there have always been new or various ways of "living and acting," as well as various bodies with which to perform them; it is society which often refuses to accept these variations as valuable.

24. McKnight, "The African in America," 68.

25. See Noyer, "Lilo & Stitch: A Little More Conversation." Also, LeiLani Nishime has discussed science fiction films as offering liminal places where "boundary crossers" can exist; in such a place, visitors such as Stitch and his alien cohort may move about less noticed than elsewhere; as Hawaii is part of the United States but also an island unto itself with a distinctive, diverse culture, it could be seen as such a liminal place. See LeiLani Nishime, "The Mulatto Cyborg: Imagining a Multiracial Future," *Cinema Journal* 44, no. 2 (2005): 34.

26. Noyer, "Lilo & Stitch: A Little More Conversation."

27. Sanders and DuBlois refer to the Orlando animation studio tourists as "moving wallpaper." The gentleman who was the inspiration for this character was British, said studio artist Irma Cartaya-Torre. "They burn in a different way," she explained. See Roger Moore, "Lilo & Stitch, Disney Feature Animation Florida's Finest Hour, Remembered," *Orlando Sentinel*, April 1, 2009, http://blogs.orlandosentinel.com/entertainment_movies_blog/2009/04/lilo-stitch-disney-feature-animation-floridas-finest-hourremembered.html.

28. Jérémie Noyer, "Lilo & Stitch: Producer Clark Spencer on a Hawaiian Roller Coaster Ride!" *Animated Views*, http://animatedviews.com/2009/lilo-stitch-producer-clark-spencer-on-a-hawaiian-roller-coaster-ride/.

29. Jane Yolen, "The Alphabetics of Story," *Jane Yolen*, http://janeyolen.com.

References

Bell, Elizabeth, Lynda Haas, and Laura Sells, eds. *From Mouse to Mermaid: The Politics of Film, Gender, and Culture*. Bloomington: Indiana University Press, 1995.

Buchanan, Lindal. "A Study of Maternal Rhetoric: Anne Hutchinson, Monsters, and the Antinomian Controversy." *Rhetoric Review* 25, no. 4 (2006): 239–259.

Darke, Paul. "Understanding Cinematic Representations of Disability." In *The Disability Reader: Social Science Perspectives,* edited by Tom Shakespeare. London: Cassell, 1998.

Davis, Pat. "Disney Goes Hawaiian." *Hana Hou! The Magazine of American Airlines* 5, no. 2 (April/May 2002). http://www.hanahou.com/pages/Magazine.asp?Action=DrawArticle&ArticleID=389&MagazineID=24.

Eberly, Susan Schoon. "Fairies and the Folklore of Disability: Changelings, Hybrids and the Solitary Fairy." *Folklore* 99, no. 1 (1988): 58–77.

Garland-Thomson, Rosemary. "Shape Structures Story: Fresh and Feisty Stories about Disability." In *Narrative* 15, no. 1 (2007): 113–123.

Luther, Martin. *D. Martin Luthers Werke. Kritische Gesamtausgabe. Tischreden*. Weimar: H. Böhlau, 1912. http://www.pitt.edu/-dash/gerchange.html#LutherDessau.

McKnight, Utz. "The African in America: Race and the Politics of Diaspora." *African Identities* 6, no. 1 (2008): 63–81.

Michalko, Rod, and Tanya Titchkovsky. "Putting Disability in Its Place: It's Not a Laughing Matter." In *Embodied Rhetorics: Disability in Language and Culture,* edited by James C. Wilson and Cynthia Lewiecki-Wilson. Carbondale: Southern Illinois University Press, 2001.

Moore, Frank. "Lilo & Stitch, Disney Feature Animation Florida's Finest Hour, Remembered."

Orlando Sentinel, April 1, 2009. http://blogs.orlandosentinel.com/entertainment_movies_blog/2009/04/lilo-stitch-disney-feature-animation-floridas-finest-hourremembered.html.
Neale, Stephen. *Genre and Hollywood*. London: Routledge, 2000.
Nishime, LeiLani. "The Mulatto Cyborg: Imagining a Multiracial Future." *Cinema Journal* 44, no. 2 (2005): 34–49.
Noyer, Jérémie. "Lilo & Stitch: A Little More Conversation with Directors Chris Sanders & Dean de Blois!" *Animated Views* (2009). http://animatedviews.com/2009/lilo-stitch-a-little-more-conversation-with-directors-chris-sanders-dean-de-blois/.
_____. "Lilo & Stitch: Producer Clark Spencer on a Hawaiian Roller Coaster Ride!" *Animated Views* (2009). http://animatedviews.com/2009/lilo-stitch-producer-clark-spencer-on-a-hawaiian-roller-coaster-ride/.
Schatz, Thomas. *Old Hollywood/New Hollywood: Ritual, Art, and Industry*. Ann Arbor, MI: UMI Research Press, 1983.
Shakespeare, Tom. *The Disability Reader: Social Science Perspectives*. London: Cassell, 1998.
Smit, Christopher R. and Anthony Enns. *Screening Disability: Essays on Cinema and Disability*. Lanham, MD: University Press of America, 2001.
Taylor, Steven, Bonnie Schultz and Pamela Walker. Introduction to *Disability Studies: Information and Resources*. The Center on Human Policy, Law and Disability Studies at Syracuse University, http://thechp.syr.edu/Disability_Studies_2003_current.html#Introduction.
Tøssebro, Jan. "Understanding Disability." *Scandinavian Journal of Disability Research* 6, no. 1 (2004): 3–7.
Tremain, Shelley. "One of Us: Conjoined Twins and the Future of Normal (review)." In *International Journal of Feminist Approaches to Bioethics* 2, no. 1 (2009): 181–184.
Ward, Annalee R. *Mouse Morality: The Rhetoric of Disney Animated Film*. Austin: University of Texas Press, 2002.
Wilson, James C. and Cynthia Lewiecki-Wilson. *Embodied Rhetorics: Disability in Language and Culture*. Carbondale: Southern Illinois University Press, 2001.
Zola, Irving Kenneth. "Communication Barriers between the 'Able-bodied' and 'the Handicapped.'" *Archives of Physical Medicine and Rehabilitation* 62, no. 8 (1981): 355–9.

• *Two* •

Susan Murphy, Ginormica, and Gloria Steinem: Feminist Consciousness-Raising as Science Fiction in *Monsters vs. Aliens*

HOLLY HASSEL

> "If all the science fiction ever written filled a boxcar, the stories that deal maturely and seriously with women might fill a bushel basket."
> — Scott Sanders, "Women as Nature in Science Fiction"

Outlining the "woman problem" in science fiction in his essay, "Science Fiction Women before Liberation," Eric Rabkin observes that, as a genre, science fiction has evolved from its earliest incarnations: works that were male-centered or anti-feminist or stories that featured "unflattering roles" for women characters. At the time of the essay's 1981 publication, Rabkin argued that "even within these constraints, science fiction has been bolder in imagining alternative roles for women than has any other formula literature."[1] Likewise, narratives for children (both film and literature) have often presented a puzzling mixture of both liberal, progressive, conservative, and reactionary ideologies.

Other scholars have written extensively about such politics and economies of sex and gender in the Disney oeuvre (see Alexander, 2001; Bell, Haas, and Sells, 1995; Downey, 1996; Hoerner, 1996; Kutsuzawa 2004; O'Brien 1996; Do Rozario 2004; and Towbin et al 2003), but little critical attention has yet been paid to the emerging new powerhouse in animated children's film, PDI/DreamWorks, whose blockbuster animated films have been no exception to Rabkin's claims (as works aimed at a youth audience) in their mix of conservative and progressive ideological content, from their earliest films, *Antz* and *The Prince of Egypt*, both released in 1998, particularly in the construction of gender (see Parsons, 2004; Zipes, 2001 for discussions of the conservative nature of children's popular culture).

By contrast, however, the popular animation studio's 2009 entry into the animated children's film market, *Monsters vs. Aliens*, illustrates particularly vividly Rabkin's claim in its re-imagination of women's liberation through the use of generic conventions of science fiction. This chapter will argue that *Monsters vs. Aliens* radically departs from the earlier DreamWorks storylines (and from the industry standard) by drawing upon the feminist consciousness-raising narratives of second wave feminism in order to tell the story of its protagonist, Susan/Ginormica; essentially, this is a feminist (and subversive) text in line with a tradition of children's works that subvert dominant ideologies.[2] Interestingly, though, the extra-filmic merchandising and "branding" elide its feminist message and refocus consumer attention on subsidiary male characters; this either hints at the studio's reluctance to embrace its subversive ideology or the studio's acute awareness of the market's conservative and patriarchal tastes.

The Patriarchal DreamWorks Tradition

Early PDI/DreamWorks pictures have adhered very closely to the definition of patriarchy and patriarchal values offered by sociologist Allan Johnson in *The Gender Knot: Unraveling our Patriarchal Legacy*. Johnson's book-length study argues that "patriarchy" is "*not* simply another way of saying 'men.' Patriarchy is a kind of society, and a society is more than a collection of people. As such, 'patriarchy' doesn't refer to me or any other man or collection of men, but to a kind of society in which men *and* women participate."[3] He argues that ... a society is patriarchal to the degree that it promotes male privilege[4] by being *male dominated, male identified,* and *male-centered*. It is also organized around an obsession with control and involves as one of its key aspects the oppression of women"[5]; Johnson's definition is exceptionally useful for examining both the visual and textual rhetoric of popular culture artifacts, and the PDI/DreamWorks films are particularly ripe for analysis.

What makes *Monsters vs. Aliens* unique in the production company's work is its radical departure from the patriarchal storylines of previous films, ranging from the male-centered and male-dominated narratives of *Antz, The*

Prince of Egypt, Chicken Run, and *Shrek* to the comparatively more recent and androcentric *Flushed Away, Bee Movie, Madagascar,* and *Kung Fu Panda*.[6] As the film titles alone sometimes reveal, all of the previous films are male-centered in that the narrative focuses on a male protagonist who must overcome some obstacle. For example, *The Prince of Egypt* retells the story of Moses; *Madagascar* traces the evolution of the complicated friendship between Alex the Lion (predator) and Marty the Zebra (prey); *Antz* follows the character of "Z" (a worker drone voiced by Woody Allen) and his transformation from drone to war hero; *Chicken Run,* though ostensibly the story of a flock of British female chickens, is narratively dominated by the presence of a blowhard American rooster, Rocky, voiced by similarly larger-than-life star Mel Gibson.[7]

Though the 2001 film *Shrek* and its sequels depart marginally by embracing several ideologically progressive messages in the character of Fiona, they also retain their focus on the eponymous character and his male inner circle of friends and advisors. Princess Fiona as a character superficially reflects the film's satirizing of fairy tale conventions (she irrationally adheres to the narrative conventions of the princess/rescuer dynamic in which Shrek refuses to participate; it's clear she is not "in" on the film's joke), and in the end, the film's message rejects the princess film conventions of 1950s Disney when Fiona's "true form" is her "ugly" ogre-self instead of her "beautiful" human princess self. Simultaneously, though, the film reinforces cornerstones of conservative and patriarchal structures such as heteronormativity and male-centeredness (with its focus on the needs, desires, and emotional struggles of the titular character), or as Johnson explains male-centeredness as a pillar of patriarchy, "...women are portrayed as along for the ride, fussing over their support work of domestic labor and maintaining love relationships, providing something for men to fight over, or being foils that reflect or amplify men's heroic struggle with the human condition."[8] Princess Fiona's role within the narrative is primarily to reflect Shrek's transformation from misanthropic hermit to socially functional citizen of a larger, "fairy-tale creature" community, including his new friend Donkey.[9] All DreamWorks films replicate this dynamic, which is what makes *Monsters vs. Aliens* such a dramatic departure.

Monsters vs. Aliens as Subversive Text

Many contemporary children's films such as those Pixar and DreamWorks examples above present "realistic" stories, often using "fantasy" tropes (e.g., animal characters[10]), implicitly incorporating some features of the fantastic without fully drawing upon the subversive power of science fiction that *Monsters vs. Aliens (MvA)* strategically embraces. This latest entry into the DreamWorks canon is subversive because it maximizes the potential of science fiction to challenge prevailing ideologies by critiquing pervasive traditional ideologies in children's media: gender role conservatism and the centrality of heterosexual romance in women's lives. Thus, this section focuses on how the film uses the tropes of science fiction (the mad scientist, evil alien dictator, government conspiracy, radioactive growth, etc.) and Susan/Ginormica's physical gigantification to parallel the conventions of second wave feminist consciousness-raising narratives; the film uses these narrative conventions in order to radically challenge patriarchal hegemony, at least intra-filmically. Susan's transformation is both literal and metaphorical, with feminist empowerment at the heart of it.

As far as its genre goes, *MvA* belongs more to a subgenre of science fiction than to the broad category itself. Part parody/spoof, part homage, the film is on the one hand a send-up of the 1950s B movie craze[11] and simultaneously, I argue, an earnest documentation of its protagonist's inner transformation. In order to document that transformation, the film uses conventions of science fiction both to camouflage and frame Susan's consciousness-raising. Theorists of science-fiction narratives have traced such conventions, such as Annette Kuhn's classic in the field, *Alien Zone: Cultural Theory and Contemporary Science Fiction Cinema*. She admits that "any attempt to define science fiction as a genre calls for a piecing together of fragments from a critical literature on science-fiction films which has rarely addressed science-fiction cinema as a genre."[12] Simultaneously, however, Kuhn identifies some of the "codes" common to the science-fiction genre, including science-fiction cinema's "mobilization of the visible, the spectacle," and the classic visual tropes of "deep space, the inner geography of spacecraft, the contours of alien planets."[13] Other frequently called upon narrative conventions include the Frankenstein/mad scientist of classic science fiction, the opposing forces of human and nonhuman in more contemporary works like *Alien* (1979) and *Blade Runner* (1982), the human body as monstrous or Other as in *The Thing* (1982) and *The Fly* (1986), and alien creatures as both threats and redeemers (*Independence Day* versus *Close Encounters of the Third Kind*, for example).[14] And science-fiction criticism has long held that the imaginary worlds of science-fiction narratives can be read as reflective of or ideologically illustrative of modern cultural concerns, which is an approach to *Monsters vs. Aliens* that I turn to now.

Monsters vs. Aliens first introduces viewers to Susan as the camera "eye" follows a group of women into Susan's bedroom in the early morning hours of Susan's wedding day to local weatherman, Derek Dietl. The film does not reveal to viewers anything about Susan's own personal pursuits, occupationally or otherwise, inviting viewers to see her entirely in relation to Derek. For example, Susan's group of friends squeal with delight as they tune into the morning weather show with Derek, giddy about Susan's impending marriage and exclaim, "It's like a fairy tale: The weatherman and the weatherman's wife!" Susan's shared excitement over her engagement — and her self-identification with his professional ambitions — is further illustrated when she declares "Just think, this time tomorrow, I'm gonna be in Paris. And someday, we won't just be honeymooning there. Derek will become an anchor or a foreign correspondent and we'll travel all over the world."

The film initially does not hint at its ultimate critique of what Linda Parsons has identified as one of the key objectives of gender construction in our culture: "to prepare young girls for romantic love and heterosexual practices. Girls come to know that their value lies in men's desire for them and the characteristics and qualities that will assure their desirability are revealed in cultural storylines."[15] *MvA* appears at first to participate in this part of the patriarchal project, further constructing Susan as the traditional, passive heroine of fairy tales and Disney princess films when Derek announces immediately before their impending wedding ceremony, "There's been a slight change of plans. We're not going to Paris ... because we're going somewhere better.... Fresno!" When Susan manages to swallow her disappointment and muster enthusiasm, choking out "I'm so proud of you," Derek interrupts with "...Us — you're so proud of us. We're a team now!" This exchange invites Susan, and viewers, to understand women's identification with a male partner as "partnership" rather than the male domination it actually is, and it reinforces stereotypical gender dynamics that play out until this point in the film.

Alison Lurie, children's author and critic, observes in *Don't Tell the Grown Ups: The Subversive Power of Children's Literature*, "Most of the great works of juvenile literature are subversive in one way or another: they express ideas and emotions not generally approved of or even recognized at the time; they make fun of honored figures and piously held beliefs; and they view social pretenses with clear-eyed directness."[16] Children's film is no different, and *Monsters vs. Aliens* takes a surprising turn once the narrative begins to employ some of the standard tropes of science fiction. Viewers who are accustomed to the kind of female protagonist defined by the standard fairy tale ideology that "[w]hen the heroine is beautiful she need not do anything to merit being chosen by the prince; she is chosen simply because she is beautiful" are challenged by Susan. As a character, she initially reinforces Parsons' observation that fairy tales (the literary heritage of fantasy narratives) present "as natural the notion that passive, beautiful females are rewarded."[17] This film rejects both of these conventions.

Susan's storyline resists this assumption in two ways: first, she is "beautiful" (as culturally defined in Western society) and initially participates in the patriarchal project by defining her identity entirely in relation to her fiancé, and yet, she is struck by a meteorite and turned into a giantess shortly before her wedding ceremony; clearly, she is not "rewarded" for her beauty or passivity. Second, Susan's gigantification parallels her emotional and psychological "consciousness-raising," one she embraces not simply because she is now marginalized by society and rejected by Derek, but because she reflects the post second-wave feminist sensibility in which the female protagonist of children's literature, according to Roberta Trites:

> plays a variety of roles, takes an active part in shaping her destiny, and does not relinquish her personal power. If she does not already know how to speak for herself, she learns in the course of the novel. If she does not already know how strong she is, she learns. If she does not already know how to combine the strengths associated with femininity with the strengths that have not been, she learns.[18]

Though Susan's story documents her struggle to fully accept agency, personal development, and an autonomous identity, the film's narrative conclusion comes down firmly on the side of Susan's full independence and uses the conventions of science fiction to achieve it narratively.

Consciousness-Raising as Science Fiction

Once Susan is rendered enormous by the common science-fiction trope of a meteor strike, her emotional embracing of this newfound physical strength does not initially match with her physical power. After the meteor strikes Susan, she is imbued with what viewers will discover is the space element "Quantonium," sought by an alien ruler, Gallaxhar, and Susan's dream wedding ceremony is transformed into a nightmare. Ever the perfect and attentive hostess, she implores her wedding guests to "have some champagne while we work this out" even though the Quantonium has transformed her from blushing bride into a 50-foot giantess. She pleads for Derek to help her even as the US military is capturing, sedating, and transporting her by helicopter to a top-secret facility holding an array of "monstrous" creatures including Insectosaurus, a grub transformed into a 350-foot monster; Dr. Cockroach, a mad scientist turned by his own experiments into a hybrid cockroach/human, and the Missing Link, a prehistoric fish man, and B.O.B., an "indestructible gelatinous blob" (note each of these characters' hearkening back to the 1950s B-movie science-fiction classics the film parodies). This motley crew of monsters marvels at Susan's arrival, noting "we are in the presence of the rare female monster." Susan's repeated reaction is "I don't belong here," "I'm not a monster.... I'm just a regular person." Despite these frequent assertions, as General W.R. Monger notes, Susan's "enormous strength and size" is undeniable, and her plea that "I'm not a monster! I'm not a danger to anyone or anything!" is belied by her simultaneous, accidental crashing of a helicopter. When General Monger escorts her to her cell, he offhandedly informs her, "One other thing, the government has changed your name to Ginormica." The external imposition of this new identity — partly by meteor, partly by the military and government (especially significant because of their nature as highly patriarchal institutions) — explains her resistance to fully embracing this new identity. This is in part a narrative strategy that makes her eventual embracing of an independent identity all the more dramatic and is the set-up for the blending of feminist consciousness-raising and science-fiction motifs.

The "consciousness-raising," or "CR" group was central to the success of the second wave feminist movement in the United States, which itself was a reaction against the first-wave of feminist activism. With its focus on cultural change, the second wave of feminism stands in opposition even as it continues the first-wave of feminism's structural and legislative agenda for feminist change. Having accomplished major shifts in citizenship rights ranging from voting to property ownership to divorce and custody advances, the feminist movement shifted its attention to the more abstract forms of sexism and privilege that suffused social relations — sexual harassment, reproductive rights, patriarchal cultural attitudes. Since *Monsters vs. Aliens* is inspired by the filmic conventions of 1950s and 1960s B-Movies, it is sensible that Susan's awakening draws from the contemporaneous social movement of second-wave feminism.

Many women who eventually became part of the US "Women's Lib" movement of the 1960s published and self-published their stories as a way of circulating tales of their feminist awakening. In *Monsters vs. Aliens,* Susan's transformation to Ginormica parallels these primary texts, and illustrate how *MvA* and Susan's story can be considered part of the CR genre — and in particular, how the film simultaneously uses science-fiction tropes to achieve Susan's feminist awakening and to deny them. My discussion of Susan's gender epiphany is framed by CR and science fiction in several key ways: the CR process must be collaborative; it involves an epiphany; the new consciousness involves significant transformation; and the CR participant categorically rejects the old way of thinking. *MvA* adapts these principles to the tropes of science fiction in both provocative and problematic ways.

Primary texts that document the mass women's movement were published in the early 1970s, typically by independent or feminist presses. Central to their accounts of CR as a process is the notion of community. Gabrielle Burton's *I'm Running Away from Home But I'm Not Allowed to Cross the Street* is one such example. Burton traces her own feminist awakening and describes the structure of the CR group:

> In the group we use a specialized way to talk to one another, called raising consciousness. This technique increases our sensitivity to the various forms of

oppression in our lives. In order to adjust successfully to our conditions, most of us have had to develop elaborate blinders. Raising consciousness helps us recognize our blinders and let out our angers and frustrations to that we can take hold of our lives and rechannel ourselves. Ideally one raises consciousness to the point where one can and must change her life.[19]

Similarly, "Mrs. Albert Stern" reported in a 1970 *Wall Street Journal* piece that by joining a "feminist discussion group," in which she made "what she considers to be significant progress in changing some of the attitudes within her family,"[20] including patriarchal assumptions about the primary role of the male bread-winner and the gendered division of labor. For Susan Murphy in *MvA*, CR takes place in multiple scenes of intimate, supportive discussion with a group of like-minded individuals, who themselves benefit from the CR process. For example, in the CR group, Susan not only recognizes her own power, she also uses the techniques of the CR group to validate her fellow discussants during a key scene where the group rejects the social ostracism and oppression they have experienced as "monsters" and validates each member's strengths.

> SUSAN: You can crawl up walls! And build a supercomputer out of a pizza box, two cans of hairspray, and
> DR. COCKROACH: ...a paper clip.
> SUSAN: Yes! Amazing.... And you! You hardly need an introduction. You're the Missing Link! You personally carried 250 co-eds off of Cocoa Beach, and still had strength to fight off the National Guard!
> LINK: And the Coast Guard and, also, the lifeguard.
> SUSAN: Amazing! And BOB ... who else could fall from unimaginable heights and end up without a single scratch?
> BOB: Link?
> SUSAN: You!
> BOB: Amazing!
> Insectosaurus roars.
> LINK: Good point, Insecto! Susan, don't short-change yourself!
> SUSAN: Oh, I'm not going to short-change myself ever again!
> BOB: Testify!
> LINK: Yeah!
> COCKROACH: Oh yes!

Without this group helping Susan recognize her "blinders," the next stage of CR could not happen. Emerging from the "specialized way to talk to one another," then, is the second important ingredient of consciousness-raising, the epiphany.

Like Mrs. Stern, Susan relies upon her CR discussion group to achieve an epiphany about her identity and her life path. Following Susan's dumping by Derek, she commiserates with her monster companions outside "Lub's

Diesel," an abandoned gas station. Echoing the sentiments of the CR groups of the 1960s, Susan arrives at a new understanding (one that was apparent to viewers all along) of her relationship with Derek, explaining to her monster friends, "Derek is a selfish jerk." Though the film uses humor to show just how dramatic the experience of claiming agency and rejecting previous gendered scripts can be, the meteor metaphor matches Parsons' description of the impact of feminism on fantasy stories: "The issue of agency is often evident in the strong voice of the protagonist. The goal of agency is self-discovery and personal development rather than domination over others, and human interdependency, rather than competition, is stressed."[21]

The epiphany in the CR group is followed by transformation. Ginormica's initial refusal to recognize her own newfound physical power is illustrated by the battle with Gallaxhar's deployed robot probe. When military and presidential intervention fails, General Monger advises the US President: "We need ... monsters!" Cutting back to scenes of the imprisoned monsters, the film shows us how Susan is insistent upon returning to her previous, "normal" life, as she participates in Dr. Cockroach's attempts to return her to her previous size.... "I'm supposed to be in Fresno!" she frets, and "Soon I'll be back in Derek's arms."

For Susan, her awakening to her own literal power operates on more than one level, as her physical strength is actually synecdochal: it is her own independence, agency, and self-discovery that she has truly awakened to, as this dialogue of the monster CR group shows:

SUSAN: Derek is a selfish jerk.
BOB: No!
SUSAN: Yes! All that talk about "us." "I'm so proud of 'us.'" "Us" just got a job in Fresno. There is no "us." There was only Derek. Why did I have to get hit by a meteor to see that? I'm such an idiot! Why did I ever think life with Derek would be so great anyway? I mean, look at all the stuff I've done without him. Fighting an alien robot? That was me, not him. And that was amazing!

Viewers are reassured that Susan Murphy's transformation to the autonomous Ginormica is complete in her final confrontation with the alien invader, Gallaxhar. Confident in his defeat of the carbon-based life form also known as Susan, Gallaxhar contemptuously refers to her as "Susan Murphy"; in response, Susan asserts "...And the name is GINORMICA!" as she shoots Gallaxhar's escape capsule in order to regain the Quantonium and re-embrace her newfound physical strength and power. In the end, General Monger engages the monster cadre on a new mission in Paris to combat "a snail [that] fell into a French nuclear reactor.... Escargantua is slowly making its way to Paris," giving Susan the opportunity to visit Paris where she will arrive not as "the weatherman's wife" of the opening scene but as Ginormica, superhero and protector.

Finally, this makeshift CR group is a key part of the film's transgressive message and reinforces the final result of CR: rejection of the previous way of thinking. Early in the film, before her full transformation, Susan is still longing for the comfort and familiarity of her previous life vision. In a painful confrontation with Derek, Ginormica comes to realize her fiancé's shallow and conditional relationship. As she celebrates her newfound strength, he undermines it, declaring his mobility to put his life and career on hold to await Susan's return to normalcy. Derek's previous rhetoric about teamwork is quickly revealed to be part of a patriarchal assumption about exactly whose team it is, illustrating the definition Johnson provides of patriarchy as a value system that is male-dominated, male-centered, and male-identified. Derek breaks off their engagement, selfishly asserting, "I'm not looking to get married and spend the rest of my life in someone else's shadow. And you're casting a pretty big shadow," even as he expected Susan to take on the very same, secondary role in their marriage. What makes *Monsters vs. Aliens* ideologically progressive is that Ginormica not only willingly embraces her new identity once her old life is left behind, she rejects her old life even when it is made available to her. At the film's conclusion, Derek retracts his previous "break-up" speech with a typically self-serving proposal:

> DEREK: Baby, I thought long and hard about what happened between us and I want you to know.... I forgive you.
> SUSAN: You forgive me?
> DEREK: Of course. It wasn't your fault you got hit by a meteor and ruined everything. And you know what? I say maybe you didn't ruin everything. I just got a call from New York. They offered me network. All I have to do is get an exclusive interview from you.
> SUSAN: Really?
> DEREK: Yeah. I get my dream job and you get your dream guy. It's a win-win for Team Dietl.
> SUSAN: Derek. That's amazing. Is the camera rolling?
> DEREK: Absolutely.
> SUSAN: Good, because I wouldn't want your fans out there to miss this. This is Susan Murphy saying, "Goodbye, Derek." [Ginormica picks him up and flicks him into the sky; he lands in B.O.B. who spits him out.]

It isn't until after her break-up confrontation with Derek that Susan is able to reject her previous co-optation by patriarchy and embrace an independent identity. Though Susan is initially heartbroken over Derek's abandonment of their shared future, after what could be viewed as a "consciousness-raising" group scene with her fellow "monsters," Susan experiences an epiphany that is modeled on the second-wave grassroots feminist phenomenon, the consciousness-raising group. That is, the break-up with Derek is important in Susan's emotional transformation, but her monster CR group is the true mechanism through which Susan *becomes* Ginormica psychologically. It's clear at the film's denouement that Ginormica's transformation is complete, but what is less clear is the role of the gender-confused group of monsters who have been so central to that transformation.

Gender Confusion

As Fritz explains, "Since the main point of consciousness-raising is to acknowledge the deeply felt pain women have repressed — to regain, as Gloria Steinem's phrase, 'the dignity of our own suffering'— feminists deliberately resist the temptation to refer to the problems of men."[22] This is what makes the film's use of the CR group methodology so interesting; even though the "monsters" are coded male in the film (in the sense that they are voiced by male actors), they are also socially marginalized and disempowered, so the film is able to make use of their subject positions in multiple ways; they can commiserate with and function as companions oppressed by a male-dominated system when narratively convenient at the same time as, extra-filmically, they perpetuate patriarchal values in the marketing of the film.

This extra-filmic gender dissonance manifests itself early intra-filmically when the monsters first arrive in San Francisco to battle Gallaxhar's robot. As they first stumble upon the robot probe, Susan reacts, "I can't fight that thing! I never ... I can't even ... [*gasping*] ... I'm hyperventilating.... Does anybody have a giant paper bag?" and "No, wait! You didn't tell us it was huge!" Her monster comrades, all male or coded male, send her into the city to hide, adopting the typical masculine-associated impulse to protect women, as Dr. Cockroach instructs, "Hide in the city, Susan. You'll be safe there. But stay away from the Tenderloin. It's a little dicey!" They initially take on the active responsibility of eliminating the threat (one of the few examples in the film where her male-coded CR group demonstrates traditionally masculine characteristics, contributing to the film's sense of "transgendering"). Susan complies, running in fear of the robot, "skating" on convertibles down the winding hills of San Francisco, finally arriving back at the Golden Gate Bridge. When the robot probe threatens travelers, Ginormica's impulse to protect the innocent overcomes her fear, and she takes on the probe, reassuring herself, "Susan, you can do this!" Ultimately, it is Susan who issues orders to her male-coded monster companions about how to defeat the threat, how to protect the innocent citizens, and how to conduct themselves in "heroic ways," a gender reversal that later contributes to the gender confusion within and without the film.

As promised, General Monger frees the monsters from their imprisonment; though Susan is giddy with her own efficacy, she is still irrationally attached to the promise of marital bliss and her wifely identity — and her fellow CR participants, namely Missing Link, are going through their own gender awakening.

> SUSAN: Three weeks ago, if you had asked me to defeat a giant alien robot, I would have said, "no, can do." But I did it! Me! I'm still buzzing. Did you see how strong I was?! Probably isn't a jar in this world I can't open.
> COCKROACH: You were positively heroic, my dear. I especially loved how you saved those people on the bridge. It was a nice touch. Wasn't she amazing, Link?
> LINK: (dejected and sarcastic) Yeah, she was great. Really cool. Loved it.

Though all of Susan's CR group characters experience gender confusion to some degree, this scene captures not simply Susan's struggle but Link's struggle as well. Link is coded early on as a traditionally masculine character who embraces the traditionally patriarchal and heteronormative values of dominance, strength, physical power, and virility. For example, when Susan first arrives at the secret facility, Link poses and postures, lifting weights, and challenging her: "First day in prison, you want to take down the toughest guy in the yard. Well, I'd like to see you try!" and later, when bidding Susan escape to the city, "Relax. Old Link's got this under control" (though he clearly does not). As a result, Link is the most threatened by Susan's newfound strength and power. In another of the key CR scenes following the group's victory over the robot, Link's gender identity is profoundly threatened.

> COCKROACH: Oh poor Link. After all that tough talk, you were out-monstered by a girl. No wonder you're depressed.
> LINK: Hey, I'm not depressed. I'm tired.
> [...]
> SUSAN: So Link's a little rusty — I mean sleep-deprived. You'll be back to your old self in no time. And so will I.

In this way, Susan's feminist consciousness is not fully formed until she experiences multiple CR group conversations as Leah Fritz explains it in *Dreamers and Dealers: An Intimate Appraisal of the Women's Movement*: "the forms we normally use: consciousness-raising, the speak-out, the *circle* of discussion where decisions are made by consensus."[23] Neither Link nor Susan at this early point in the film has fully come to embrace the challenges they have experienced to their gendered identity and in fact, they are both profoundly troubled by the potentiality of having to reject their previous assumptions about gender, gender identity, and their inherent sense of selves.

This gender confusion is further embodied in the figure of B.O.B. Midway through the film, as Susan and the CR group become more and more intimate, B.O.B's gendering becomes part of the film's humorous storyline. When the group boards the plane that will take them to battle the robot probe, Bob imagines his life after freedom:

> B.O.B.: I'll be a really giant lady.
> MISSING LINK: That's Susan.
> B.O.B.: Then I'll go back to Modesto and be with Derek.
> MISSING LINK: That's still Susan.

Later, when meeting Susan's parents, B.O.B. clutches Susan's mother, exclaiming, "Oh, Derek! I missed you so much! Thinking that we'd be together again. It's the only thing that got me through prison! I love you! I love this man," and when confronting Derek at the end of the film, B.O.B. sassily states, "Derek, you are a selfish jerk, and guess what? I've met someone else. She's lime green. She has 14 little chunks of pineapple inside her, and she's everything I deserve in life! I'm happy now, Derek, without you. It's over!" What this "gender trouble"—the adoption of male voice actors and confusingly gender-coded social functions, B.O.B.'s gender confusion—reflects is the film's own sense of internal gender dissonance that unfolds both within the narrative and extra-narratively in the marketing.

Intra-Filmic and Extra-Filmic Anxiety

An especially provocative aspect of *Monsters vs. Aliens* is the tension between the film's subversive message about gender, at least for its female protagonist, and its extra-filmic construction of its viewership.[24] Sands and Frank, in their study of print juvenile science fiction, have noted that science fiction has often "been the realm of boy readers"[25] and that "women and girls typically fare better in children's science-fiction series than in those for young adults," a relevant observation here because of the construction of *Monsters vs. Aliens* as targeted at male youth. Cynthia Freeland's "gender ideology" method (described in the essay "Feminist Frameworks for Horror Films") can be productively applied not simply to horror but to other popular film genres. What Freeland's framework helps to illustrate is that *Monsters vs. Aliens* itself reflects cultural anxieties about feminism even as it simultaneously promotes a feminist message.

Freeland distinguishes between "intra-filmic" and "extra-filmic" questions as two ways of producing feminist readings of films, suggesting that "we should focus on their representational contents and on the nature of their representational practices, so as to scrutinize how the films represent gender, sexuality, and power relations between the sexes."[26] Notably, she invites viewers to consider not only "the representation of women and monsters within the films" but also what she calls "gender ideology," or "a film's presentation of certain naturalized messages about gender — messages that the film takes for granted and expects its audience to agree with and accept."[27] Intra-filmically, the narrative arc of the story and the "ensemble" cast of the film demonstrate a discomfort with identifying the acceptability of Susan's feminist transformation.

First, the representation of Susan's transformation as "monstrous" places her in the same ranks as true monsters: B.O.B., a sentient blob; Dr. Cockroach, the scientist who blended his DNA with a cockroach; The Missing Link, a fish-ape hybrid; and Insectosaurus, a grub transformed by nuclear radiation into a 350-foot giant, suggesting Susan's development of agency, autonomy, and an identity distinct from her unctuous fiancée is, at least intra-filmically, similarly "monstrous." For example, when Susan Murphy arrives at the secret government facility, the monster occupants try to frame her in ways she does not self-identify:

> COCKROACH: Might we ask for your name, madam?
> SUSAN: Susan.
> B.O.B.: No, we mean like your monster name. You know, what do people scream when they see you coming? Like "Look out! Here comes...?"
> SUSAN: Susan.
> COCKROACH: Really?
> B.O.B.: [*spookily*] SUUUUSSAAANN! Ooh, I just scared myself! That is scary!

Though this exchange is played for humor and was part of the film's trailer and marketing campaign, it positions Susan's transformation as externally imposed by a masculine system and male group rather than internally claimed as part of a feminist epiphany, part of setting up Susan's eventual self-determined shift in identity from Susan to Ginormica (even though the name itself was conferred by the patriarchal institution of the military).

The film uses many of the tropes of science-fiction movies of the 1950s to parody earlier films, which on the one hand makes the film's subversive message possible; simultaneously, the use of such tropes invites viewers to consider the impact of framing Susan's rejection of patriarchal values as synonymous with the defining conventions of the genre, ranging from extraterrestrial invasion to mutations resulting from nuclear waste to mad science. Here, Carl Freedman's theoretical examination of science fiction as a genre — which extends Darko Suvin's original work — is useful (though there is certainly critical debate about the utility of the categories).[28] Freedman argues that science fiction is defined as such because of a "*dialectic* between estrangement and cognition."[29] That is, when compared with realistic or fantasy fiction, science fiction creates an "alternative fictional world," one in which the reader and the text are cognitively able to "account rationally for its imagination world and the connections as well as the disconnections of the latter to our own empirical world."[30] There is some rational way to account for the narrative events. Realistic fiction does not estrange readers from the empirical world, while fantasy, in Freedman's theory, estranges its readers from the empirical world but does not attempt to account for this estrangement or appeal to a reader's cognition.[31] In the end, Susan's transformation becomes science fiction because of its critical role in the film's overall parodic function.

Monsters vs. Aliens accounts for the monstrous creatures who become Susan's confidantes in cognitively justifiable ways. As General Monger presents his solution to alien invasion to the policy wonks and presidential sycophants during a key transition scene, he describes the coevals who will become key to Susan's feminist awakening:

> Insectosaurus.... Nuclear radiation turned him from a small grub into a 350-foot-tall monster that attacked Tokyo. Here we have the Missing Link.... A 200,000 year old frozen fish man who was thawed out by scientists. He escaped and went on a rampage in his old watering hole. This handsome fellow is Dr. Cockroach, Ph.D. the most brilliant man in the world. He invented a scientific machine that would give humans the cockroach's ability to survive. Unfortunately there was a side effect [shows picture of cockroach-human hybrid].... Now we call this thing B.O.B.... A genetically altered tomato was combined with a chemically altered ranch-flavored desert topping at a snack food plant. The resulting goop gained consciousness and became an indestructible gelatinous mass.

And yet, if Susan's transformation is both literal and metaphorical, then viewers and critics mustn't overlook the significance of paralleling her physical gigantification and subsequent feminist awakening with the biological mutations of her fellow monsters. The General's description of B.O.B. as a food item that "gained consciousness" and the fact that B.O.B. frequently mistakes Susan's story with his own provides a subtext that can camouflage or even mock the emotional work Ginormica does in the story. This may suggest that claiming feminist consciousness, while cognitively explicable and a familiar part of the empirical world is at the same time "monstrous" or the result of a freakish accident.

Even though the film seems to endorse an ideology that values women's liberation from the shackles of dependence and subordination, it simultaneously displays a discomfort with *explicitly* endorsing that ideology; masking Susan Murphy's feminist awakening as nothing more than another technological and cosmological catastrophe is one example of this discomfort. The offhandedness with which General W.R. Monger informs Susan, "Oh, by the way, the government has changed your name to Ginormica" is another. It seems important to emphasize that even though the film itself is conflicted about feminist empowerment, it nonetheless overcomes what Eric Rabkin calls the "oldest, most consistent and most profound difficulty women had to overcome in their presentations in science fiction," which is "getting presented in science fiction at all."[32]

Extra-Filmic Anxiety

Extra-filmically, the marketing of both the film and video game camouflage the film's feminist message in movie posters, product tie-ins, and other merchandising that highlight the male or male-coded secondary characters (such as the monsters, above) rather than the protagonist of the narrative, thus reinforcing patriarchal values and presuming that male consumers simply will not purchase products that strongly feature either women or feminist rhetoric. Fairytale and children's literature critic Jack Zipes has argued that:

> For anything to become a phenomenon in Western society, it must become conventional; it must be recognized and categorized as unusual, extraordinary, and outstanding. In other words, it must be popularly accepted, praised, or condemned, worthy of everyone's attention; it must conform to the standards of exception set by the mass media and promoted by the culture industry in general. To be phenomenal means that a person or commodity must conform to the tastes of hegemonic groups that determine what makes up a phenomenon. It is impossible to be phenomenal without conforming to conventionality.[33]

The filmmakers behind the production company PDI/DreamWorks may recognize the truth of Zipes' claim; the company's body of work suggests that it is highly profitable to write, produce, and market narratives that reinforce patriarchal values. *Monsters vs. Aliens* has accumulated international box office receipts totaling almost 400 million dollars as of this printing; it's clear that the mismatch between the film's "message" and its marketing has not had an impact on its commercial success, nor does the film fit Zipes' claim that phenomenal success requires conventionality. At the same time, its progressive message is not part of the film's marketing and merchandising.

MvA, then, is especially interesting, because of its reluctance, extra-filmically, to embrace the feminist message as part of its marketing, perhaps because the primary target of advertising is young male consumers who are the primary audience for film-related merchandising like video and computer game versions of the story. Freeland takes extra-filmic analysis to include "feminist investigations, in a sociologically, anthropological, or historical vein, into actual concrete issues concerning the historical context, production, and reception"[34] of the film. Extra-filmically, then, the marketing and merchandising of *Monsters vs. Aliens* denies the centrality of Susan/Ginormica's feminist awakening to the film's narrative.

Advertising for the film sometimes, but not always, includes Ginormica, but she is more typically subordinated to the glamorous, science-fiction conventional monsters that appeal to a male viewing audience, especially in the early version of the film's "teaser posters." For example, Jason Lynch's review of the film in the popular *People Magazine* is not the only review to point out that the movie is an "enjoyable send-up of 50s B movies"[35] such as *Attack of the 50-Foot Woman* and *The Blob* (both released in 1958), and the film's marketing capitalizes on this subtext. In one of the teaser posters, for example, the marketing production co-opts the fonts and layout reminiscent of the 1950s and 1960s B monster films that the *MvA* parodies, which is a natural artistic decision; the bold, geometric fonts are paired with similarly bold visual imagery. However, what is interesting is the decision to feature the figure of Insectosaurus — the 350-foot tall grub who has no speaking role beyond grunts and roars — in a prominent role. Since the purpose of a teaser poster is to generate hype for the upcoming film, it's no surprise that the film's feminist message was not highlighted by the early promotion. Another film poster similarly obscures the role of Ginormica as the narrative's protagonist by featuring B.O.B. solely, even though the film and its characters are referred to variably in reviews as an "ensemble" (Thilk), a "gang" (Neman), a "genial bunch" (Soergel), a "squad of monsters" (Marr), and "misfit oddities" (Vincent).

Similarly, the visual rhetoric of the cross-promotional products and merchandising, particularly the video games, use imagery that privileges the brainless character, B.O.B., voiced by cult favorite actor Seth Rogan, most noted for playing "lovable stoner" characters; this privileging is usually at the expense of the central character, Ginormica. Keeping with the "B Movie" theme of the film posters, the video game art for the Playstation version of *Monsters v. Aliens* foregrounds B.O.B. and de-emphasizes the other four "monster" characters, including Ginormica, using perspective that suggests they are far behind the gelatinous (and less important) blob.

Of course, film promotion consists of multiple components including trailers on TV and in theaters, the internet, in print venues like magazines and newspapers, merchandising tie-ins, and promotional giveaways, so the film posters and video games are not the only way to measure the mismatch between the film's ideological content, its narrative focus, and its marketing. The film is referred to in reviews as an "ensemble" film and the voice talent includes multiple high-profile and commercially successful actors (in addition to Reese Witherspoon, comic actors like Stephen Colbert, Rainn Wilson, Will

Arnett, Seth Rogan, Hugh Laurie, and Kiefer Sutherland). Promotional materials include character posters and other readily available add-ons accessible from the film's website.

Other character posters that were part of the marketing of the film illustrate the extra-filmic and intra-filmic tension with the progressive message of the film's storyline and the adherence to traditional patriarchal values (including male-dominance, as Allan Johnson describes it) suffusing the marketing and merchandising. With just one woman character in a central role, the composite character card features 7 other film characters, all male or "coded" male (like B.O.B, who is clearly not biologically defined as male but other cues, like his name and the actor voicing him, communicate to viewers the character's gender). As a result, the visual rhetoric minimizes Susan's role in the film and suggests she is as narratively important as non-speaking characters like Insectosaurus or flat, stock characters like General W.R. Monger.

Notably, Ginormica's "character card" continues to promote the message of feminist empowerment, since in it, she is seated at the "site" of her feminist awakening (the gas station where her epiphany monologue takes place) and the image includes the tagline "Brains and Brawn." Thus, Johnson's' definition applies here as Ginormica (and Reese Witherspoon, unfortunately) become token women among a largely male cast in a genre that tends to appeal to and strategically target male viewers. In this way, the film's message of feminist empowerment may not have the kind of impact it might if marketed to a different demographic.

Conclusion

Monsters vs. Aliens occupies a liminal place in the tradition of science fiction and children's film. Though the film partly rectifies Rabkin's "profound difficulty" of getting women presented in science fiction, it simultaneously communicates a profound ambivalence about its central female character and her narrative fate. It remains to be seen whether the future of children's science fiction on film will embrace this explicit, ideologically progressive trajectory that promises to engage new viewerships or whether science fiction will cling stubbornly to its androcentric heritage in the service of predictable commercial success.

NOTES

1. Eric Rabkin, "Science Fiction Women Before Liberation," in *Future Females: A Critical Anthology*, edited by Marlene Barr (Bowling Green, OH: Bowling Green State University Popular Press, 1981), 25.
2. For example, Elizabeth Rose Gruner has observed that school is a "powerful institution of social control," and that many works of children's fantasy such as the Harry Potter series by J.K. Rowling and books by James Patterson and Philip Pullman endorse a subversive message

about school and schooling (218). Linda Hutcheon has similarly observed that children's literature is especially ripe for analysis within the context of postmodern theories because "these narratives are intrinsically subversive." See Linda Hutcheon, "Harry Potter and the Novice's Confession," *The Lion and the Unicorn* 32 (2008): 171.

3. Allen Johnson, *The Gender Knot: Unraveling Our Patriarchal Legacy* (Philadelphia: Temple University Press, 1997), 5.

4. Johnson (citing Peggy McIntosh's essay, "White Privilege and Male Privilege") defines privilege as "any unearned advantage that is available to members of a social category while being systematically denied to others." See Johnson, *The Gender Knot*, 5.

5. Ibid., 5.

6. It should be noted that PDI/DreamWorks' production of androcentric and patriarchal films is quite in line with the industry standard. Disney/Pixar's list of animated films for children similarly uses male-centered narratives and subordinate, stereotyped, or "stock" female characters (or does not include any). Examples include *Monsters, Inc.*, *Toy Story 1,2, and 3*, *Finding Nemo*, *Cars*, *Ratatouille*, *Wall-E*, and *Up*. For further discussion of the gender and racial politics of Disney's animated films, Elizabeth Bell, Lynda Haas, and Laura Sells, eds., *From Mouse to Mermaid: The Politics of Film, Gender, and Culture* (Bloomington: Indiana University Press), 1995.

7. Other DreamWorks films are similarly focused on central male characters with subsidiary female characters who, as Johnson says, serve to "amplify men's heroic struggle." For example, *Madagascar* features only one female character, the gender and racially stereotyped Gloria, a hippopotamus voiced by Jada Pinkett Smith, who seems to be only tangentially functional in the films. She takes on a somewhat more central role in *Madagascar: Escape 2 Africa* when the male giraffe Gelman takes a romantic interest her, though she seems primarily to serve in a token role and, as Johnson says, "provide something for men to fight over," as the neurotic (and culturally stereotyped) Gelman must win Gloria's heart from a competing suitor, a hefty African hippopotamus.

8. Johnson, *Gender Knot*, 10.

9. In the third entry in the series, *Shrek the Third*, the film self-consciously embraces images of female empowerment in the form of a group of Fiona's friends — storybook princesses Cinderella, Snow White, Sleeping Beauty, among others — who use martial arts style combat skills to break out of prison and rush to Shrek's rescue.

10. For example, Ann Swinfen has written extensively on subgenres of fantasy (sometimes considered an umbrella category under which science fiction can fall). See Ann Swinfen, *In Defense of Fantasy: A Study of the Genre in English and American Literature Since 1945* (London: Routledge, 1984). Swinfen has observed that writers' "profound sense of man's identity with the rest of the animal kingdom helps to account for the continued fascination with beast tales but the attempted re-establishment of the old relationship does not exhaust the resources of such tales," noting that animal fantasy tends to be set in the primary world (true of many DreamWorks and Pixar films such as *A Bug's Life, Toy Story 1, 2 and 3, Finding Nemo, Madagascar, Ratatouille*, and *Up*) and also borrows more heavily from its antecedent literature. Post-war animal fantasy has drawn from folklore, animal fable, animal satire, naturalists' tales, and earlier modern fantasies.

11. *MvA* satirizes and honors several specific films from the era of the 1950s B-movie science fiction era, including *Creature from the Black Lagoon* (1954), *It Came from Beneath the Sea* (1955), and *The Amazing Colossal Man* (1957).

12. Annette Kuhn, "Cultural Theory and Science Fiction Cinema," in *Alien Zone: Cultural Theory and Contemporary Science Fiction Cinema*, edited by Annette Kuhn (London: Verso, 1990), 5.

13. Ibid., 6.

14. Ibid., 8.

15. Linda Parsons, "Ella Evolving: Cinderella Stories and the Construction of Gender-Appropriate Behavior," *Children's Literature in Education* 35, no. 2 (2004): 135–154.

16. Alison Lurie, *Don't Tell the Grown-ups: The Subversive Power of Children's Literature* (Boston: Little, Brown, 1990), 4.

17. Parsons, "Ella," 137.

18. Roberta Trites, *Waking Sleeping Beauty: Feminist Voices in Children's Novels* (Iowa City: University of Iowa Press, 1996), 11.

19. Gabrielle Burton, *I'm Running Away from Home But I'm Not Allowed to Cross the Street.* (Pittsburgh: Know, Inc., 1972), 33–34.
20. Ellen Graham, ed., *What Do Women Really Want?* (Chicopee, MA: Dow Jones Books, 1971), 96.
21. Parsons, "Ella," 140.
22. Leah Fritz, *Dreamers and Dealers: An Intimate Appraisal of the Women's Movement* (Boston: Beacon Press, 1979), 11.
23. Ibid., 9.
24. Though at least one source calls the target audience for *Monsters v. Aliens* "kids and their moms" (see Chris Thilk, "Movie Marketing Madness: Monsters vs. Aliens," M3: Movie Marketing Madness), other marketing tools suggest otherwise, namely the 125 million pairs of 3D glasses that were distributed so Super Bowl viewers could watch the premier of the 3D trailer. It should be noted that even though demographic data shows that 40 percent of Super Bowl viewers are women, marketing researchers like Martha Barletta have observed that ads in the Super Bowl disproportionately skew toward a presumed male audience.
25. Karen Sands and Marietta Frank, *Back in the Spaceship Again: Juvenile Science Fiction Series Since 1945* (Westport, CT: Greenwood Press, 1999), 35.
26. Cynthia Freeland, "Feminist Frameworks for Horror Films," in *Post-Theory: Reconstructing Film Studies*, edited by David Bordwell and Noel Carroll (Madison: University of Wisconsin Press, 1996), 204.
27. Ibid., 205.
28. See China Miéville, "Cognition as Ideology: A Dialectic of SF Theory," in *Red Planets: Marxism and Science Fiction*, edited by Mark Bould and China Miéville (Middletown, CT: Wesleyan University Press, 2009), 234. Miéville has usefully complicated Suvin's and Freedman's theorizing about the theory of cognitive estrangement as a mode of understanding generic differences between sf and fantasy, praising Freedman's challenge to "...a certain generic commonsense that has allowed generations of readers and writers to treat, say, faster-than-light drives a science-fictional in a way that dragons are not, despite repeated assurances from the great majority of physicists that the former are no less impossible than the latter." Miéville's questioning of the value of an uncritically analyzed "cognition" and his interrogation of "scientific accuracy" as ways of framing discussions of sf may be of use to readers interested in a strictly Marxist approach to the genre, though questions about the nature and ideological bent of "cognition" are beyond the scope of this essay.
29. Carl Freedman, *Critical Theory and Science Fiction* (Middletown, CT: Wesleyan University Press, 2000), 16.
30. Ibid., 17.
31. Except, as Swinfen has argued (see Swinfen, *In Defense of Fantasy*, 3), in the sense that in a text that can be categorized as fantasy rather than science fiction, in the "...imaginary world it is necessary to observe faithfully the rules of logic and inner consistency which, although they may be different from those operating in our own world, must nevertheless be as true to themselves as their parallel operations are in the normal world." In this sense, Freedman's argument is not neatly categorizable because fantasy may not have to account for the estrangement it requires of readers from the empirical world, but it does not abandon the rules of logic or consistency, in many cases.
32. Eric Rabkin, "Science Fiction Women Before Liberation," in *Future Females: A Critical Anthology*, edited by Marlene Barr (Bowling Green, OH: Bowling Green State University Popular Press, 1981), 13.
33. Jack Zipes, "The Phenomenon of Harry Potter, or Why All the Talk?" in *Sticks and Stones: The Troublesome Success of Children's Literature from Slovenly Peter to Harry Potter* (New York: Routledge, 2001), 175.
34. Freeland, "Feminist," 204.
35. Jason Lynch, "Review of *Monsters vs. Aliens*," *People*, April 6, 2009, 35.

REFERENCES

Alexander, Jonathan. "Family Friendly?: Review of *Tinker Belles and Evil Queens: The Walt Disney Company from the Inside Out*." *The Lesbian Review of Books* 7, no. 3 (2004): 14.

Barletta, Martha, and G. Mark Alarik. "Why Do Super Bowl Advertisers Ignore Women?" *Advertising Age*. February 14, 2005. http://adage.com/article?article_id=45099.

Barr, Marlene, ed. *Future Females: A Critical Anthology*. Bowling Green, OH: Bowling Green State University Popular Press, 1981.

Bell, Elizabeth, Lynda Haas, and Laura Sells, eds. *From Mouse to Mermaid: The Politics of Film, Gender, and Culture*. Bloomington: Indiana University Press, 1995.

Burton, Gabrielle. *I'm Running Away from Home But I'm Not Allowed to Cross the Street*. Pittsburgh: Know, Inc., 1972.

Do Rozario, Rebecca-Anne. "The Princess and the Magic Kingdom: Beyond Nostalgia, the Function of the Disney Princess." *Women's Studies in Communication* 27, no. 1 (2004): 34–59.

Downey, Sharon. "Feminine Empowerment in Disney's Beauty and the Beast." *Women's Studies in Communication* 19, no. 2 (1996): 185–213.

Freedman, Carl. *Critical Theory and Science Fiction*. Middletown, CT: Wesleyan University Press, 2000.

Freeland, Cynthia. "Feminist Frameworks for Horror Films." In *Post-Theory: Reconstructing Film Studies*, edited by David Bordwell and Noel Carroll, 195–218. Madison: University of Wisconsin Press, 1996.

Fritz, Leah. *Dreamers and Dealers: An Intimate Appraisal of the Women's Movement*. Boston: Beacon Press, 1979.

Graham, Ellen, ed. *What Do Women Really Want?* Chicopee, MA: Dow Jones Books, 1970.

Gruner, Elizabeth Rose. "Teach the Children: Education and Knowledge in Recent Children's Fantasy." *Children's Literature* 37 (2009): 216–235.

Hoerner, Keisha. "Gender Roles in Disney Films: Analyzing Behaviors from Snow White to Simba." *Women's Studies in Communication* 19, no. 2 (1996): 213–228.

Hutcheon, Linda. "Harry Potter and the Novice's Confession." *The Lion and the Unicorn* 32 (2008): 169–179.

Jackson, Rosemary. *Fantasy: The Literature of Subversion*. London: Methuen, 1981.

Johnson, Allen. *The Gender Knot: Unraveling Our Patriarchal Legacy*. Philadelphia: Temple University Press, 1997.

Kuhn, Annette, ed. *Alien Zone: Cultural Theory and Contemporary Science Fiction Cinema*. London: Verso, 1990.

Kutsuzawa, Kiyomi. "Disney's Pocahontas: Reproduction of Gender, Orientalism, and the Strategic Construction of Racial Harmony in the Disney Empire." *Atlantis: A Women's Studies Journal/Revue d'Etudes sur les Femmes* 2 (2004): 43–53.

Lurie, Alison. *Don't Tell the Grown-Ups: The Subversive Power of Children's Literature*. Boston: Little, Brown, 1990.

Lynch, Jason. "Review of *Monsters vs. Aliens*." *People* (April 6, 2009), 35.

Marr, Merissa. "DreamWorks Reboots for Life Beyond *Shrek*." *Wall Street Journal*. January 23, 2007, Eastern Edition.

Miéville, China. "Cognition as Ideology: A Dialectic of SF Theory." In *Red Planets: Marxism and Science Fiction*, edited by Mark Bould and China Miéville, 231–248. Middletown, CT: Wesleyan University Press, 2009.

Monsters vs. Aliens. DVD. Directed by Rob Letterman and Conrad Vernon. 2009. Glendale, CA: DreamWorks Animation, 2009.

Neman, Daniel. "Film Review: *Monsters vs. Aliens* Is Merely Mortal." *McClatchy: Tribune Business News*. March 27, 2009.

O'Brien, Pamela Colby. "'The Happiest Films on Earth': A Textual and Contextual Analysis of Walt Disney's *Cinderella* and *The Little Mermaid*." *Women's Studies in Communication* 19, no. 2 (1996): 155–183.

Parsons, Linda. "Ella Evolving: Cinderella Stories and the Construction of Gender-Appropriate Behavior." *Children's Literature in Education* 35, no. 2 (2004): 135–154.

Rabkin, Eric. "Science Fiction Women Before Liberation." In Barr. 9–25.

Sanders, Scott. "Woman as Nature in Science Fiction." In Barr. 42–59.

Sands, Karen, and Marietta Frank. *Back in the Spaceship Again: Juvenile Science Fiction Series Since 1945*. Contributions to the Study of Science Fiction and Fantasy, Number 84. Westport, CT: Greenwood Press, 1999.

Soergel, Matt. "*Monsters vs. Aliens* a 'Wacky Good Time': Heroes in Computer-Animated Sci

Fi Spoof Have Big Hearts and Decent Sense of Humor." *McClatchy: Tribune Business News.* March 27, 2009.

Swinfen, Ann. *In Defense of Fantasy: A Study of the Genre in English and American Literature Since 1945.* London: Routledge, 1984.

Thilk, Chris. "Movie Marketing Madness: *Monsters vs. Aliens.*" M3: Movie Marketing Madness. http://www.moviemarketingmadness.com/blog/2009/03/25/movie-marketing-madness-monsters-vs-aliens/.

Trites, Roberta. *Waking Sleeping Beauty: Feminist Voices in Children's Novels.* Iowa City: University of Iowa Press, 1997.

Vincent, Mal. "*Monsters vs. Aliens*: Animated Spoof Is a Lively Romp." *McClatchy: Tribune Business News.* March 27, 2009.

Zipes, Jack. *Sticks and Stones: The Troublesome Success of Children's Literature from Slovenly Peter to Harry Potter.* New York: Routledge, 2001.

• *Three* •

Performing Gender, Performing Romance: Pixar's *WALL-E*

Carol A. Bernard

    WALL-E was released on June 27, 2008. As an eagerly anticipated Pixar film, it garnered many reviews from all kinds of sources. Just a brief examination of some of the reviews from that release date illustrates the range of news media that reviewed *WALL-E*. Salon.com's tag line for its review is, "This new Pixar movie is an environmental cautionary tale and a story of robot love."[1] The title of NPR's *Morning Edition's* review is "'WALL-E': A Robot Love Story with Heart to Spare."[2] In *Entertainment Weekly's* review, Owen Gleiberman comments on the two primary characters, WALL-E and EVE. He remarks that "These two don't talk, exactly, but they hold hands and burble each other's names. It's love at first mechanized heartbeep."[3] *Newsweek's* David Ansen argues that "'Wall*E' is part sci-fi adventure, part cautionary fable, part satire and part love story, which may be the best and most improbable part of all."[4] From *MTV Movie News*, Kurt Loder in "-'WALL-E': Heavenly Creatures," also comments on the emotional desire of WALL-E, noting that the robot is "happily bleeping at his only companion, a cockroach; rerunning an old VHS tape of 'Hello, Dolly!' and pining for ... something. Romance?"[5] Finally, in the review from *The New York Times*, A. O. Scott states the film is "a disarmingly sweet and simple love story."[6] In each of these reviews, which are representative of how the film was generally received, the commentators and reviewers focus again and again on the "romance" between EVE and WALL-E.
    Certainly, the film sets up a classic theme of "boy meets girl." The problem with this is that neither robot actually has a sex. However, the filmmakers

definitely have gender in mind as they construct the characters, particularly the two protagonists. WALL-E is clearly read throughout the film as male. Partly, this is due to his name sounding like the male name, "Wally." Partly, this reading is due to the introduction of EVE, who is obviously constructed in the film as female. (For ease in this paper, I will be following these constructions and referring to WALL-E as "he" and EVE as "she.") Certainly, attributing female and male characteristics to objects that are technically neither is nothing new in animation. However, in this film, those attributes are taken to a new level when romance is introduced, especially as that constructed romance provides insight into queer desire.

Using Judith Butler's ideas of performativity allows for greater investigation of not only how gender is performed but also at how romance is performed. In looking at the performance of both gender and romance, we are also allowed glimpses of how queer romance can be remodeled as straight. The two robots switch stereotyped notions of romance, with the "male" robot being the one interested in such indicators as hand-holding and the "female" robot being much more aggressive and violent. Further, WALL-E, the "male" robot, learns his ideas of romance from a film, the musical, *Hello, Dolly!*, potentially calling up stereotypes of gay men who enjoy Hollywood musicals. All of his ideas of romance stem primarily from one scene in *Hello, Dolly!*, not even the entire movie. Thus, what Pixar does is demonstrate boldly the unnaturalness of romance: romance is not inherent; it is learned. In fact, the learning of romance is part of the overall arc of the storyline, for both WALL-E and EVE need to practice romance before they get it "right." The multiple reviewers of the film, by focusing on the romance, generally miss the central premise that robot romance must be learned; it is not innate. Further, most of the reviewers read the film as a priori heterosexual. However, it is this romance that allows for greater investigation of the performative nature of gender. Further, in highlighting the performative nature of gender, Pixar gives us glimpses of queer desire between the two robots. Again and again, throughout the film, the moviemakers consistently emphasize the fact that these are two robots falling in love. While the movie clearly genders the robots with masculine and feminine characteristics, nonetheless, the robots remain the "same" sex, as they are both literally asexual.

Judith Butler in her chapter, "Subversive Bodily Acts," from her classic work, *Gender Trouble*, focuses primarily on the ways in which gender is not part of an essential self. Rather, she elaborates on how gender is, in fact, a performance. In the lengthy passage that follows, Butler outlines her argument for problematizing gender:

> Gender is an identity tenuously constituted in time, instituted in an exterior space through a *stylized repetition of acts*. The effect of gender is produced

through the stylization of the body, and, hence, must be understood as the mundane way in which bodily gestures, movements, and styles of various kinds constitute the illusion of an abiding gendered self. This formulation moves the conception of gender off the ground of a substantial model of identity to one that requires a conception of gender as a constituted *social temporality*. Significantly, if gender is instituted through acts which are internally discontinuous, then the *appearance of substance* is precisely that, a constructed identity, a performative accomplishment which the mundane social audience, including the actors themselves, come to believe and perform in the mode of belief. (original emphasis)[7]

Perhaps the most relevant part of Butler's ideas for this paper is the argument that gender comes as a result of a "*stylized repetition of acts.*" That and the argument that "the *appearance of substance* is precisely that, a constructed identity, a performative accomplishment" both help to illuminate how Pixar is able to create gender for asexual creatures so easily. At least some of the ways that Pixar is able to create gender for the robots have to do with appearances, actions, and names. The title character's name, WALL-E, is, of course, a play on the name Wally, and the second robot's name is EVE, bringing to mind the biblical first female. As if these signifiers weren't enough, the film also highlights appearance.

The "male" robot is dirty, square, squat, and compact. The "male's" face is simply two very expressive eyes. Andrew Stanton, the writer and director of *WALL-E,* when interviewed by MoviesOnline.com, explains how he came to create WALL-E's "face." He reports that while at a baseball game, he was loaned a pair of binoculars, and simply looking at the binoculars began the process of designing WALL-E's expressiveness. He says:

> I knew he [WALL-E] was going to be a box at the most basic thing. I knew he was going to collapse to possibly show that he's shy and that's all I had. [...] then when I got handed these binoculars at a baseball game, I missed the entire inning. I just turned the thing around and I started staring at it and making it go sad and then happy and then mad and then sad [...]. There's no nose, there's no mouth, there's nothing and it's not trying to be a face.[8]

In Stanton's description of the creation of WALL-E, what is interesting to this argument is the complete and total lack of gender emphasis. In fact, the emphasis is on emotive possibility, i.e., happiness, anger, sadness, etc., not on the gender of the being that is doing the emoting. While Stanton clearly refers to WALL-E as "he," nonetheless the description is of a gender-less being. In fact, the being is not even supposed to be human-like. Stanton first states that he knew WALL-E was going to be a box, which is not humanoid at all. He then emphasizes clearly that "there's nothing" to WALL-E's face, except the very expressive eyes. This is not a description of a "male" character, but simply of a character. With EVE, though, there does appear to be more emphasis on gendering her appearance. EVE, the "female" robot, is a sparkling, dazzling white and is vaguely ovoid in shape, and the "female's" face is more rounded, more closely mimicking the human female face. At work here is a convoluted presentation of the characters. On the one hand, Stanton clearly indicates that his interest in WALL-E is of a character that is not necessarily gendered. However, once romance is introduced into the story line, the characters had to assume genders, and those had to be the complementary masculine and feminine, suggesting that EVE was created after WALL-E. Pixar could not allow a film to present too obviously same-sex love on screen, which again shows the performative nature of gender in the film. While these signifiers — names and shapes — are embedded in the characters, Pixar focuses on the last aspect of gender, actions, to hammer home the gender identity of both robots. It is through actions that the robots come to be seen as "gendered" throughout the film, thus further distancing the audience from the fact that the two robots are the "same" sex.

These actions are rooted in a very particular scene from a very specific source, the musical, *Hello, Dolly!* The scene is very brief. It primarily focuses on dancing and then hand-holding. The section that we are shown first begins with a large dance number, including a significant number of people dancing in unison. The scene then cuts to a scene where the male and female love leads are singing to one another and holding hands. Unlike almost everything else in the movie, the scenes from *Hello, Dolly!* feature real people, not animation. We are introduced to the background influence of *Hello, Dolly!* from the very beginning of *WALL-E*. The music that starts the movie, "Put On Your Sunday Clothes," is from the musical, and it is the beginning of our understanding that the musical helps to define and create both gender and romance for WALL-E.[9] The scene from *Hello, Dolly!* is replayed multiple times throughout *WALL-E*, emphasizing Butler's argument that gender comes from a "*stylized repetition of acts.*"[10] It is the repetition of the scene from the musical that indicates most prominently gender assignment as well as romance. By showing the scene multiple times, Pixar focuses on the need for repetition to instill in the movie audience an awareness of a clear gender for both main characters. Moreover, by highlighting a scene from another movie, Pixar indicates the performance, or the act, of gender. For neither robot is gender inherent. It is always and only can be performance.

If gender, which can seem like an essential quality, is a performance, then certainly romance is performance. Throughout the film, romance is indicated through the brief scene presented from *Hello, Dolly!*, particularly the action of holding hands. The character of WALL-E seems to long for a romantic connection through hand-holding. After he sees EVE, he wants to hold hands with her, particularly. She, on the other hand, is, initially, only interested in the fulfillment of her directive, to find living plant material and bring it back to the spaceship so that the humans can return to Earth. Just as WALL-E learns romance from the musical, so EVE also learns romance through the musical, via WALL-E. However, before she views the musical, EVE is focused on doing her job and blasting anything that comes in her way, including shooting at WALL-E before she acknowledges that he is not a threat either to her or her mission. She is, in fact, acting as what she is — a robot. It is only when danger is approaching, in the form of a sandstorm, that she assents to enter WALL-E's "home" and engage more directly with him. However, by entering WALL-E's "home," EVE is, in effect, agreeing to learn how to perform "romance." WALL-E uses the sandstorm as an opportunity to teach EVE about himself as well as to school her in the most obvious forms of "romance," both by showing her some of his many treasures he has found in the junk of Earth as well as, and perhaps more importantly, by screening the clip from *Hello, Dolly!* WALL-E uses the film to define the heteronormative stance that the musical indicates as necessary to create romance. However, WALL-E is attracted to EVE when he first sees her, and that attraction is of same for same, robot for robot, not masculine for feminine because at that moment, EVE has not learned femininity.

There are several elements in this scene that highlight the performative nature of both gender and romance. The elements focus, though, on the musical. When she first enters WALL-E's home, EVE is introduced to items that WALL-E has found. He shows the VHS tape to EVE, and she immediately begins to unravel the tape. This worries WALL-E, and he immediately takes back the tape, finds a tool to rewind the loose tape, and then he puts it into his scrapped together VCR — all the while tapping his fingers in anxiety, lest his beloved tape be ruined. As soon as the tape starts, EVE scans the screen, taking in the colors, movements, and actions of the characters on screen. WALL-E then tries to teach her to dance, and she imitates some of his moves, but does so badly, almost disengaging his stuff from its shelves and throwing him into the wall of the container. In all of this, EVE is learning from WALL-E and the film how to act feminine. WALL-E constantly has to hold EVE back — to prevent her from shooting an animatronic fish on the wall, to keep her from destroying his possessions.[11] He has to restrain the robotic EVE in order to train the feminine EVE, putting into practice Butler's concept that the acts of gender are "internally discontinuous" for EVE.[12] For EVE, there is no internalization of gender in the film at this point. She acts as what she is, a robot on a mission. Thus, gendered behavior is "discontinuous" in EVE at this moment.

The next element that highlights the teaching of romance is when EVE discovers the Zippo lighters. She picks one up, flicks it open, lights the flame, and becomes fascinated by the fire. In having her perform this action, Pixar is reminding the audience of the connections between fire and romance and love. It is at this precise moment that WALL-E attempts to hold EVE's "hand." She immediately dismisses him, but she becomes fascinated by the video again, and its focus on hand-holding, which is the final element of learning romance. She maintains the flame from the lighter as she scans the screen again.[13] It is at this moment that she is more firmly schooled in what it means to be feminine and what it means to be romantic. As Butler argues, it is the "*stylized repetition of acts*"[14] that helps to create gender; EVE is clearly beginning the process of repeating certain acts — leading her to encompass more fully a gendered identity, particularly a feminine gendered identity. Furthermore, as EVE becomes more and more feminine, she also learns how to "do" romance. While we don't see her put into practice this education in this scene, over the course of the film, EVE becomes more and more clearly gendered as feminine and exhibits certain romantic characteristics, up to and including hand-holding. While EVE learns to behave in a manner seen as more stereotypically feminine, she remains a robot who, eventually, falls in love with another robot.

This scene also indicates a new kind of masculinity, one already seen in other Pixar movies. In this scene, it is WALL-E who is instigating romance, who is taking on attributes more commonly associated with femininity, or a new kind of masculinity. Ken Gillam in his article, "Post-Princess Models of Gender: The New Man in Disney/Pixar," outlines how some earlier Pixar films represent masculinity. He looks at *Toy Story, The Incredibles,* and *Cars.* He says of the main male characters that "as these characters begin the film in (or seeking) the tenuous alpha position among fellow characters, each of them is also stripped of this identity — dramatically emasculated — so that he may learn, reform, and emerge again with a different, and arguably more feminine, self-concept."[15] For WALL-E, he is already in the "more feminine" self-concept. WALL-E's identity in this film is not that of an individual in an alpha position; his very nature, his program, is to clean up after others, a role stereotypically given to females, e.g., Cinderella or Snow White. The film begins, and spends quite a bit of screen time on, WALL-E's central order to clean and organize, to be what he is, a waste allocator. He is, in this sense, already "emasculated." As such, WALL-E's gender assignment is fairly ambiguous. While the filmmakers clearly want the viewers to see WALL-E as masculine and EVE as feminine, they have created two characters who do not fully embody either gender's characteristics. When WALL-E begins to interact with other robots, particularly EVE, but also the other robots aboard the spaceship, the Axiom, he is viewed as an oddity, at best. He already has a self-concept that is different from other robots, and is not constructed as being particularly masculine. Rather, his identity throughout the film, not just at the end, more fully encompasses Gillam's idea of the "new man." The character in the film that seems to go through the most change, in terms of identity, is EVE. She learns, from WALL-E and from *Hello, Dolly!*, how to be both feminine and romantic, to a limited degree. That education is seen most clearly when she watches a video recording of how WALL-E cared for her when she was incapacitated. Her programming shuts her down immediately after he shows her the plant life he has found.

When EVE shows the captain of the Axiom the plant life, he demands to see what Earth actually looks like in the present. He has been reviewing earlier tapes and videos of Earth, and he wants to see what it looks like now. He is disappointed because the blue sky and green grass have disappeared. However, as he is looking at the film of EVE's adventures on Earth, she is focusing on all of the activities that show how WALL-E cared for her. She looks first at the scene where WALL-E is showing her his clip from *Hello, Dolly!* She fixates on the hand-holding, and opens her own "hands" and interlocks her own "fingers." Then, the focus is on WALL-E protecting her, holding an umbrella over her during a storm and being electrocuted. Throughout this montage, the emphasis is on EVE witnessing WALL-E's acts of affection and learning from those acts both the idea and practice of romance. As has already been noted, *Hello, Dolly!* is instrumental in educating EVE in romance.[16] It is by re-seeing the film clip that she begins to understand more fully WALL-E's actions and behavior. She replicates some of the actions for herself, such as the interlocking of her fingers. She is no longer focusing solely on her directive, in part because she has completed it by bringing the plant life to the captain. However, she is also not focusing solely on her directive because her attention is given to WALL-E. By watching the security video that went into place as soon as she shut down on Earth, and by watching it outside of the presence of WALL-E, she learns very clearly what romance means, at least in the context of *Hello, Dolly!* and WALL-E's world. In this moment, we see again the emphasis on romance. Here, though, the filmmakers continue to play with traditional gender assignments. In problematizing both gender and romance, the film allows space for the presentation, albeit obliquely, of queer romance. In this moment in the film, EVE is copying WALL-E, again showing same for same, not difference. In this scene particularly, we understand that both EVE and WALL-E combine traditional ideas of masculinity and femininity, highlighting their sameness as robots more than any differences.

We see the culmination of the blending of gender and romance towards the end of the film. WALL-E has successfully aided the humans aboard their spaceship in returning to Earth. However, in the process, he is squashed by a retractable column where the plant is to be placed, to prove that life can exist on Earth. Upon reaching Earth, EVE rushes WALL-E back to his container where he has amassed spare parts so that she can literally re-make WALL-E. In this scene, EVE uses her robotic skills to find what WALL-E needs. She scans the container to find the parts needed to help reconstruct WALL-E. She uses a car jack to restore WALL-E to his proper shape; she changes his tires, replaces an arm, and replaces his eyes. She then shoots a hole through the top of the container so that he can recharge using sunlight. She waits anxiously for him to revive; when he does, he does so as a robot, as a Waste Allocation Load Lifter-Earth class, not as the character she has to come to know. She tries to show him the things he had been interested in previously, like a Rubik's cube and a standard incandescent light bulb. When he evinces no interest in these items, she turns to the VCR, puts in *Hello, Dolly!* and plays it. When she turns around, he has taken materials from the container and crushed them into a cube. He leaves, running over the cockroach — which has been his companion, and goes out to do his job. She follows and grabs his hand, precisely the action that he had attempted with her previously in the film.[17]

It is at this moment that the culmination of performing gender and performing romance happens. EVE is no longer just a robot, doing her job; she has internalized many of the characteristics of the feminine, nurturing the injured WALL-E. Further, she has internalized the signifiers for romance, like hand-holding. It is the action of holding WALL-E's hands that begins the resuscitation of the character of WALL-E; she leans forward and gives him what can only be called a robotic "kiss," including a spark of energy between them. In this moment she is humming music from *Hello, Dolly!*, right before she leans in to "kiss" WALL-E. She then moves away, but he continues to hold her hand. He then, slowly, comes back to "life," acknowledging EVE and excitedly recognizing that she is holding his hand. In this moment, a brief scene from *Hello, Dolly!* is interposed into the scene between WALL-E and EVE. The movie cuts to the male lead of *Hello, Dolly!* singing to the female lead and walking to her, and then the movie continues, focusing back on WALL-E and EVE, with the music of *Hello, Dolly!* rising behind them.[18]

This is the only moment in the film where the filmmakers present *Hello, Dolly!* out of the context of actually watching it on the makeshift TV with WALL-E. By cutting to this scene, the filmmakers help to remind the viewers of the film that the romance that EVE and WALL-E are engaging in is a performance, mimicking the earlier performance of a Hollywood musical. EVE hums music from the film clip; a scene from the film is inserted into the joyful connection between EVE and WALL-E. We are reminded again and again that the moment is a performance, highlighting Butler's claim that, "Significantly, if gender is instituted through acts which are internally discontinuous, then the *appearance of substance* is precisely that, a constructed identity, a performative accomplishment which the mundane social audience, including the actors themselves, come to believe and perform in the mode of belief."[19] For EVE earlier in the film, the acts of gender were "internally discontinuous" as they become for WALL-E at the end, after he has been physically crushed. However, she has changed over the course of the movie; she now performs more fully the constructions of gender and romance. EVE now behaves as a gendered being, and as a romantic being. Her anxiety about WALL-E and her actions to resurrect the character he had been indicate her immersion into a self that is both feminine and romantic—a self that is different from the self we are introduced to at the beginning of the film. By the filmmakers highlighting the importance of *Hello, Dolly!* at this crucial moment in the storyline, they emphasize that romance is not an essential element of identity but one that must be created and performed. In this context, the question naturally arises—which came first for EVE: the romance or the gender? Both are learned to a great degree by watching a film clip, and each informs the other. By creating both gender and romance using such an obvious artifice as a Hollywood musical, the filmmakers clearly highlight that both are only and always performances. This emphasis on performance also demonstrates the problematic nature of the emphasis on an apparently heterosexual romantic storyline.

By looking at gender and romance and their construction over the course of the movie *WALL-E*, I have focused on how the identities of both WALL-E and EVE are performances. By constructing *WALL-E* as a romance, and by showcasing the performative nature of both gender and romance, Pixar effectively circumvents the radical, queer desire between the two robots. Returning to the title of one of the reviews of *WALL-E*, Kurt Loder's "'WALL-E': Heavenly Creatures," we can see a hint of homoeroticism even in a review of the film. Whether intentionally or not, Loder's title immediately references Peter Jackson's 1994 film, *Heavenly Creatures*. In this complicated and dark film, two teenage girls are charged with the brutal murder of one of their mothers. Over the course of the film, though, the two girls become obsessed with one another and form a clearly romantic and sexual bond with one another.[20] By including the title of Jackson's film in the title of his review of *WALL-E*, Loder, inadvertently or not, suggests that the relationship between WALL-E and EVE is homoerotic. WALL-E and EVE are both robots; their gender is performance. Their desire for one another is same for same, not same for different.

In creating a film whereby two creatures that have no sex become not only sex-identified but also of different genders, Pixar negates and/or sublimates any hint of same "sex" desire—making the film more palatable both for Hollywood and for families. However, just by scratching the surface of how gender and romance are performed over the course of the movie, we are able to see how tenuous those identities are. At the end of the film, WALL-E's mechanical brain has been wiped clean, and he becomes what he is initially, a robot, just like EVE at the beginning of the film. EVE, by holding WALL-E's hand, re-ignites the romance in WALL-E, but in the moment before that, we, the viewers, recognize that WALL-E and EVE are the same — both robots. It is in that moment of sameness that we can see the flowering of "same" sex love and romance. While the film clearly wants to create an image of a heterosexual relationship, what is presented is not heterosexual at all. It is, instead, the union of two beings who are quintessentially the same, not different. At the end of the film, we are presented with two characters who consistently struggle with a stable gender identity and who long for romance — on their own terms, with neither having to assimilate completely any one gender. There is no tension between opposite sexes because there is no sex. When EVE holds WALL-E's hand, it is the joining of one robot with another, not a woman holding a man's hand, not even the feminine holding the masculine, giving us a glimpse, however fleetingly, of what queer romance can be.

NOTES

1. Stephanie Zacharek, "WALL-E," *Salon.com*, June 27, 2008, http://www.salon.com/ent/movies/review/2008/06/27/wall_e/print.html.
2. Kenneth Turan, "Wall-E: A Robot Love Story with Heart to Spare," NPR, June 27, 2008, http://www.npr.org/templates/story/story.php?storyId=91896053.
3. Owen Gleiberman, "WALL-E," *Entertainment Weekly*, June 26, 2008, http://www.ew/com/ew/article/0,,20209111,00.html?print.
4. David Ansen, "What a Dump!" *Newsweek*, June 27, 2008, http://www.newsweek.com/id/143466/output/print.
5. Kurt Loder, "WALL-E: Heavenly Creatures," *MTV Movie News*, June 27, 2009, http://www.mtv.com/movies/news/articles/1590067/20080627/story.jhtml.
6. A. O. Scott, "In a World Left Silent, One Heart Beeps," *The New York Times*, June 27, 2009, http://movies.nytimes.com/2008/06/27/movies/27wall.html.
7. Judith Butler, *Gender Trouble: Feminism and the Subversion of Identity* (New York: Routledge, 1990), 140–141.
8. Andrew Stanton, interview by Movies Online, *MoviesOnline*, June 27, 2008, http://www.moviesonline.ca/movienews_14899.html.
9. *WALL-E*, DVD, directed by Andrew Stanton (2008, Emeryville, CA: Disney*Pixar, 2008).
10. Butler, *Gender Trouble*, 140.
11. *WALL-E*, 2008.
12. Butler, *Gender Trouble*, 141.
13. *WALL-E*, 2008.
14. Butler, *Gender Trouble*, 140.
15. Ken Gillam, "Post-Princess Models of Gender: The New Man in Disney/Pixar," *The Journal of Popular Film and Television* (2008): 5.
16. *WALL-E*, 2008.
17. Ibid.
18. Ibid.
19. Butler, *Gender Trouble*, 141.
20. *Heavenly Creatures*, DVD, directed by Peter Jackson (1994, New Zealand: Miramax, 2002).

REFERENCES

Ansen, David. "What a Dump!" *Newsweek*, June 27, 2008, http://www.newsweek.com/id/143466/output/print.
Butler, Judith. *Gender Trouble: Feminism and the Subversion of Identity*. New York: Routledge, 1990.
Gillam, Ken. "Post-Princess Models of Gender: The New Man in Disney/Pixar." *The Journal of Popular Film and Television* (2008): 5.
Gleiberman, Owen. "WALL-E." *Entertainment Weekly*, June 26, 2008, http://www.ew/com/ew/article/0,,20209111,00.html?print.
Heavenly Creatures. DVD. Directed by Peter Jackson. 1994. New Zealand: Miramax, 2002.
Scott, A. O. "In a World Left Silent, One Heart Beeps." *The New York Times*, June 27, 2009. http://movies.nytimes.com/2008/06/27/movies/27wall.html.
Stanton, Andrew. Interview by Movies Online. In *MoviesOnline*, June 27, 2008. http://www.moviesonline.ca/movienews_14899.html.
Turan, Kenneth. "Wall-E: A Robot Love Story with Heart to Spare." NPR, June 27, 2008. http://www.npr.org/templates/story/story.php?storyId=91896053.
WALL-E. DVD. Directed by Andrew Stanton. 2008. Emeryville, CA: Disney*Pixar, 2008.
Zacharek, Stephanie. "WALL-E." *Salon.com*, June 27, 2008. http://www.salon.com/ent/movies/review/2008/06/27/wall_e/print.html.

• *Four* •

Last in Space:
The "Black" Hole in Children's
Science Fiction Film

DEBBIE C. OLSON

In the discourse of children's film there is an astonishing and disquieting lack of African American voices, and in the lucrative business of producing science-fiction films for young audiences, where is the African American child? Within the vast collection of Hollywood produced science-fiction (sf) family films, the majority star white children, usually male, who embark on an adventure to outer space, face an alien (either on another planet or here on Earth), or are displaced and need to find their way home. With the advent of technologically advanced CGI and special effects, these space adventures effectively capture the imaginations of a young viewing audience, and, more importantly, suggest a particular vision for the future of humanity. Unfortunately, that future vision in sf films tends to function as a type of nostalgia for an idealized, all-white past that hints at "white racists who view the elimination of blackness as 'biological destiny,' and who see 'no place' in their [future] design for the black American."[1] For many of these youth-centered sf films, the project is not the acceptance of the difference in alien life, but instead, a reaffirmation of white, patriarchal power structures. The alien creatures in these films often visually reinforce a metaphorically "coded connection between blackness and alienness, [which] is a recurring feature in SF cinema in general."[2] The aliens in children's sf are most often dark and mysterious (*E.T., Flight of the Navigator*), or silly and cartoonish (*Explorers*), but all are constructed as an Other to the human child in such a way as to reinforce social, cultural, and ideological norms of whiteness.

The science-fiction film (and fantastic films in general) is one vehicle that, as Jack Zipes argues, "sets the terms for socialization and education in the Western world. Cultural institutions ... are centered around profit, power, and pleasure through power," and the sf film's epic narrative, white protagonist, and the "civilizing" or "saving" of an alien or an alien world, or the fear of an alien invasion of Earth, allows the young audience to experience an imagined power over the construction of and participation in an advanced future, all while being swept away by the dazzling array of strange creatures and high-tech geography.[3] Most sf films present the *white* child as the only voyager to outer space, the only savior of aliens or alien worlds, and the only holder of technological know-how. But those films that center around a extraordinary voyage to other worlds — such as *Lost in Space* (1996), *Explorers* (1985), *Star Kid* (1998) — present a romanticized version of a historically white-male privilege achieved through a colonial-style power (*Avatar*), which is deceptively packaged in childhood imagination, magic, and wonder at the "discovery" of new creatures or worlds who "need their help." Western-based transnational corporations have helped promote this cinematic hijacking of the future by reconfigured childhood as a commodity through mass production of products based on popular sf films. Those sf films function as an integral part of that commodification, which creates a nostalgia for the idealized stability of the past — a nostalgia that is a privileged part of these films' narratives.

What are the implications for the black child viewer's conception of the future when they do not see themselves (in cinema) as a part of the future? Does their absence within mainstream children's film inform the black child's notion of his or her role in science or technology? Why isn't there a black Luke Skywalker (*Star Wars*) or a black Elliot (*E.T*)? From the Disney classic *The Black Hole* (1979) to the *Star Wars* films (1977–2005), (of which the original is the third highest grossing film of all time[4]), the child of color is barred from the science-fiction adventure, a hegemonic exclusion that reinforces the sf films' white-only futuristic narrative. While there are several superb instances in very recent years of adult African American actors starring as the protagonists in sf films — primarily Will Smith in *Independence Day* (1996), *Men in Black* and its sequel (1997, 2002), *I, Robot* (2004), and *I Am Legend* (2007) — there are no black *child* protagonists, or even major supporting characters, in children's sf films. Beneath the visual magic of science-fiction films lies a vision of the future that is bleached, "white"-washed by young protagonists who reaffirm whiteness as the only source of technological savvy or interaction with, and domination of, creatures from outer space. In this paper, I will examine some of Hollywood's most popular children's sf films and their underlying racial discourse of exclusion — a discourse that I argue is rooted in a nostalgia for an idealized homogenous white past, presented within an imperial rhetoric that masquerades as acceptance of Other (alien) cultures and peoples. For within the sf film's surface discourse of wonder and acceptance of "alien" life-forms, lies the very real subtext of marginalization and exclusion of the child of color.

A Scientific Exclusion

Historically, African Americans have had a wary relationship with science. It was Francis Galton, Charles Darwin's cousin, who coined the term "eugenics" in 1883 as a moral philosophy to improve human worth by promoting the selective breeding of the smartest and healthiest people. (Galton's ideas influenced Adolf Hitler's "final solution" during World War II.) From its very beginnings, science was manipulated to frame dominant white culture as biologically superior and deserving of the power to discriminate against "inferior" races. Race became a focus of a group of nineteenth century scientists who used "the technique of categorizing people according to their apparent biologically determined intelligence ... as a method of justifying both the class structure and the racial discrimination of imperialist societies."[5] In the early twentieth century, eugenicists argued that those persons deemed "defective" should not be allowed to breed. This type of "sophisticated" scientific thinking unfortunately infected early twentieth century scientific rhetoric and resulted in a number of horrific sterilization laws throughout the United States. But the eugenics movement had a much more sinister purpose: it was a pseudo-science justification for racial cleansing and was used to reinforce beliefs in the biological superiority of the white race, and, by those same scientific means, demonstrate the "natural" inferiority of blacks and other peoples of color. Such scientific rhetoric pushed blacks away from participation in scientific creation or discovery, and instead, continually positioned blacks as the subject of scientific study in order to support notions of white superiority.[6]

What is startling is that such unfounded beliefs in white genetic superiority are still alive today. Such science-based racism informs R. Herrnstien and C. Murray's infamous 1994 study on race and intelligence, *The Bell Curve,* in which they argue that whites and Asians are "naturally" more intelligent than blacks or Hispanics. In Vincent Sarich and Frank Miele's 2004 study, *Race: The Reality of Human Difference,* they argue that the non-white races, and particularly blacks, are an evolutionary-based, less developed form of homo sapiens, who are *naturally* less advanced than whites and therefore face their own extinction. The pervasiveness of these racist notions in some segments of the science community attests to the sad and desperate struggle of some whites to reinforce their belief in their own superiority. As Adilifu Nama argues, scientific ideas about African Americans such as these are "of particular value for unveiling how past racist constructions of the black body as primitive, a repository of unbridled sexuality, and a phallic danger — constructions that have been deemed overtly stereotypical, racist caricatures and too politically taboo and incorrect to discuss openly — [are today] returned camouflaged in science-fiction film."[7] While historically African Americans have been excluded from being creators of or practitioners in science, they are regularly included in sf — as the alien Other, the "lesser" being to the white protagonist. With a tradition of such exclusionary and racist rhetoric in the realm of science, it is no surprise that Hollywood, a most conservative entity, has not considered African Americans as relevant characters within children's sf films.

Throughout its history, however, the sf genre as a whole has been exclusively white. Sf films from the early years of cinema were typically constructed with "a host of white protagonists who confronted the science-fiction metaphors of American cultural crisis."[8] According to Christine Cornea, "science fiction has traditionally remained a remarkably white genre and it was rare to see a black character at all in films before the 1960s," especially in children or family sf films.[9]

The majority of sf films from the 1950s ultimately "depict[ed] exclusively white worlds" where white men confronted the alien threat (*Destination Moon* [1950], *The Thing* [1951], *The Day the Earth Stood Still* [1951], and *War of the Worlds* [1953] to name just a few).[10] Within those worlds, alien beings took on the outward, however exaggerated, characteristics of African Americans, Asian Americans and any ethnic groups that were viewed as socially Other. Many of the aliens from the 1950s were constructed to visually caricature ethnic minorities; for example, the black bug-like aliens from *Them* (1954); the large, bulging eyes and heavy brow of the alien invaders in *It Came from Outer Space* (1953); the bulbous head, large eyes and lips of the alien in *This Island Earth* (1955); and the lizard-ape-like alien from *It! The Terror from Beyond Space* (1958), with its giant flared nostrils, large lips, and gorilla-shaped head. Many of the sf films of the '50s created aliens creatures that visually reflected social fears of the Other, and, during the era of Jim Crow, that Other was the African American. As Nama argues, science-fiction film is "too often [a] representational site where the black body is used as a cipher to symbolize fear and contamination,"[11] which is evidenced by the many similarities in sf film aliens to Jim Crow era caricatures of African Americans (see Elizabeth Abel, 2010 and William Henry Chafe, 2001).

Future Space

In the arena of children's science-fiction film, the viewer is "held in thrall by a future continually deferred by time itself, constrained to pursue the dream of a day"[12] when tomorrow and yesterday are united in a white-only cinematic future with its "new constructions of ethnicity [that] betray an inability to imagine a future that is post-ethnic" or post-racism.[13] Such worlds as portrayed in children's sf films, do not create a vision of new politics or new humanity, but rather, these films inscribe a white science and technology as the only way to a future that is a disciplined and idealized image of our once exclusionary racist past. Through cinema, this repackaged past-as-the-future is sold to our children as a desirable future, what Jean Baudillard calls a "desperate rehallucination of the past"; a re-idealizing of a eugenics-based hallucination of an all-white society.[14] In such films, the alien character (or population) is either troubled or in need of assistance, which the white child rescuer then resolves; an age-old narrative that positions the white protagonist as a paternal power to the alien Other. Such "rehallucinations," of colonial power structures function in these children's films to normalize and naturalize the dominant white power structure. In many sf scenarios, aliens bring new technology and knowledge that are only passed on to the deserving white children. In other narratives, aliens may seek admittance to the child's human world and are inducted into "a new 'white future-time' open to all ... aliens [i.e. minorities] who are willing to be assimilated to this ostensibly progressive society ... based on a white American norm."[15] The 1986 film *Howard the Duck* is one example of such assimilation attempts. In this film, Howard is a child-like adult alien duck who is accidentally sucked into a worm hole that delivers him to planet Earth. The film's comedy arises from his attempts to assimilate into white society while trying to find a way home. The moment Howard arrives on Earth, he becomes victim to discrimination. He is thrown out of a club, chased out of an alley, told he doesn't belong and "needs to return to his own kind." Howard's misadventures and child-like persona provide a humor that is reminiscent of Jim Crow–era stereotypes of African Americans in children's books and cartoons. The human reaction to Howard's alienness is similar to white reactions to African Americans during that era. Throughout the film, Howard is maligned at every turn, made fun of because of his difference, is talked to as if he were a child, elicits fear from some, and is rarely taken seriously. *Howard the Duck*'s subtext is summed up by his friend Beverly's crooked manager: "Different lifestyles is one thing, different life forms is another." The film's blatant antimiscegenation message ("My God! This relationship defies nature!") is informed by similar themes found in the 1968 *Planet of the Apes* with the hints of romance between Zira the ape and Taylor the human (Green and Slotkin 60–61). The diner scene near the end of *Howard* functions as a metaphorical "lynching," complete with stereotypical "rednecks." The final scenes show Howard, who cannot go back to his own planet, as an entertainer — the only acceptable role open to the Other.

On the screen, the world the alien is introduced to is often significantly *not* multicultural or multiethnic, but is a homogenous, bourgeois whiteness that is then validated by the alien's desire to assimilate into it: "the result is a fiercely Manichean visual field of human whites and nonwhite aliens that invites the audience to experience the coded racial 'other' as unequivocally abnormal and threatening" under the guise of acceptance and assimilation."[16] The aliens onscreen, as well as the spectator, learn to "associate whiteness with order and regulation ... [and] blackness ... [as] an intrusion of chaos into order."[17] In *Howard the Duck*, Howard must learn to assimilate and accept his Other status, even in a world that to him is cannibalistic (humans eat ducks).

A number of new social attitudes and circumstances came together in the 1980s which allowed sf films to blossom once again. Stung by Civil Rights victories, white society focused on nurturing the new computer and information industries, inventing and redefining new media outlets (the Internet), and creating a social conservatism that fused with the upwardly-mobile mystique of the new "yuppies." Hollywood, free of the restrictions of the production code, experimented with new film technologies and special effects, allowing sf to burst onto the scene in what is considered the second "Golden Age" of sf films.[18] But many Hollywood films from the 1980s reflect a resistance to the civil rights gains of the 1960s and 1970s, featuring racially coded aliens that threaten bourgeois white society. Children's films of the 1980s were no exception. What is surprising, however, is that those same stereotyped ethnic images are found in more recent children's SF films, as well.

E.T.: The Extra-Terrestrial (1982)

In 1982, Steven Spielberg's *E.T.: The Extra-Terrestrial* earned a prominent place on the Hollywood map as one of the topmost grossing films of all time. The film also inspired numerous other alien-meets-child films, though none enjoyed the wide success that *E.T.* did. But behind Drew Barrymore's cutsie smile and Henry Thomas's continual wide-eyed fascination with E.T., lies a distinctly racist tone. The alien visitor is treated as dumb by the children. Even when E.T. begins to show that he can understand and speak some English words, he is treated much like a parrot or a monkey that can mimic human language, but with no real understanding. He is not a child, yet is treated as if he were. The children view E.T. as a pet, an attitude that most of the others in the film express to a certain extent — even the government scientists, who are so enamored of the idea of meeting an extra-terrestrial, that "the object is no longer there, only the *idea of the object*," and E.T. becomes an abstract symbol for the white colonial fantasy of what a alien creature *should* be: a childlike being in need of paternal protection and guidance."[19]

The film begins with a lynching-style posse chase by white men of E.T. E.T. himself is drawn very ape-like, which is confirmed in one particularly conspicuous scene: E.T. is hiding in the closet with stuffed animals, the camera halts momentarily to frame both E.T.'s head and a stuffed monkey's head, both clearly positioned and framed as to reinforce the allusion of E.T. to the monkey (a common trope for African Americans). E.T. is constructed not only to look ape-like, but to act ape or animal-like. For instance, E.T. is lured by Elliot's candy through the woods, much like an animal is lured with food (of course the "lure" resulted in some very lucrative advertising for Reese's Pieces). E.T. makes small mewling noises and waddles when he walks. He is dark brown, wrinkly, with large eyes and wide nostrils. According to Cornea, "racialized oppositions were obviously indicated in the costuming and casting" in the alien vs. human sf films such as *E.T.*[20] E.T. is shorter than the children, but can also stretch his neck up so that his head then towers over the children. This duality functions here to reinforce by height the superiority of the white children over the alien being. When E.T. stretches his neck, he merely affirms his alienness, rather than his equality to the white children.

In the film, each character's encounter with E.T. is not about the meeting of different cultures or worlds, but rather, works to reaffirm the sententious nature of white society. The camera in *E.T.* continually revisits the visual disruption of the "normal," the psychic jarring that takes place during the moment of alien encounter. The camera's lingering caress on the shocked faces of the characters when they first see E.T. functions as a visual loop which reinforces the Otherness of the alien. Each character's encounter with E.T. is accompanied by a captivating and lingering close-up of that person's reaction to seeing an alien being. This looping of the moment-of-encounter throughout the film, rather than normalizing the alien being, visually contradicts the narrative message of human acceptance of the alien and reinforces the not-human/not-us condition of E.T. The fact that the majority of the cast in E.T. is white presents to the spectator the "naturalness" of white superiority on a galactic level.

D.A.R.Y.L. (1985)

In the 1985 film *D.A.R.Y.L.*, whiteness is not only reinforced as the most naturally American, but even *alien* whiteness is accepted, and indeed welcomed, into the classic Western bourgeois family. There are no African American characters in this film at all; the featured world is completely inhabited by white people and filled with romantic Americana scenes — white children skipping stones in a lake, picture perfect main streets, perfect family groups, and touching postcard type scenes like the child D.A.R.Y.L. holding the dying old man's hand framed by bare, stark trees whose limbs seem to lovingly embrace the pair. Nature is equated with whiteness in this film, particularly the power of creation.

D.A.R.Y.L. opens with a bird's-eye view of a claustrophobic canyon, a car speeding through it, and a helicopter giving chase: scenes that are metaphorical for the dark, tight, womb-like space that precedes a child's birth. The speeding car stops, D.A.R.Y.L. hops out and climbs up the bank into the forest, and the car continues speeding down the winding mountain road until it purposely speeds itself off a cliff. The camera cuts to the helicopter's view of the amniotic river at the canyon bottom, searching for the car remains. The next cut is to young D.A.R.Y.L., wide-eyed, slightly disheveled, being discovered—"birthed"—in the woods by an elderly white couple. The opening birth scene emphasizes the unnaturalness of D.A.R.Y.L.'s beginnings and helps construct him as "alien."

D.A.R.Y.L. is a Pinocchio story about a child created in a test tube by a heartless military defense lab, who strives to become a "real boy." The film's project is to reinforce conservative, white, small-town patriarchy through a process of de-alienizing the alien; an alien that the film infers should never have been created at all. (The term "alien" in this film symbolizes not a being from outer space, but a being created within military space, and alien to nature.) This film presents a positive alien Other, a white child who was created through a scientific experiment to construct artificial life for the battlefield. But in order to maintain Western patriarchal family values, the film portrays the alien child as "just like us" in order to "assert and dramatize a resemblance" with which to establish white, capitalist, Americans as the "norm." Rather than the alien falling short of an idealized human model, as in other sf narratives, D.A.R.Y.L. is framed as the "ideal child," which disconcerts his human foster parents, particularly his mother, who is robbed of her desire to mother by a child who does not need a mother. D.A.R.Y.L.'s perfection functions to "maintain [his] alien-ness as the difference that makes a difference" in restoring the bourgeois family unit. D.A.R.Y.L.'s passivity and innocent flawlessness merely highlights the undesirability of a perfect human; thereby, in a clever hegemonic twist, the film establishes the flawed white human as the real perfection.[21]

The film's finale is D.A.R.Y.L.'s visual "rebirth": to escape the military officers who have orders to destroy him, he steals a plane and ejects into the lake. The camera focuses on his rise to the surface as a symbolic new and "natural" birth through the amniotic fluid he was denied. But he is later pronounced dead and a female scientist, in the Blue Fairy role, resuscitates the micro-chip in his brain and the final scene of the film shows *Daryl,* now a "real boy," free of the scientists (and by association science) and able to live the American dream. In classic Hollywood style, Daryl runs down the road into the waiting arms of his picture-perfect family.

In contrast to the other sf films I've mentioned here, in *D.A.R.Y.L.* "the 'difference' of the alien Other becomes absorbed in homogeneity ... [suggesting] that the 'difference' of the alien Other," if that alien is white, "is not so much absorbed as diffused and even erased," even if that alien is an "unnatural" one.[22] Whiteness is made particularly normative and natural by the films' two "birth" scenes: *white* scientists create life and *white* children "drop" from heaven. Such diffusion or erasure of difference is never an option if the alien in any way resembles a person of color. There is no "natural" presence for the black child; in fact, in a perfect world, no presence at all.[23]

Explorers (1985)

Explorers follows the adventures of three boys: Ben (a young Ethan Hawke), Wolfgang (the late River Phoenix), and Darrin (Jason Presson). Ben and Wolfgang are both dark blonde white boys who are a bit nerdy and obsessed with science. Ben "dreams" his scientific experiments, which suggests divine inspiration for his desire to explore outer space, similar to the divine inspiration claimed by the colonial European explorers who wanted to create a new Eden and bring civilization to primitive peoples. Significantly, the film opens in one of Ben's dreams where he is flying through the heavenly clouds, arms outstretched as he flies back down to earth. Darrin, on the other hand, is an outcast, a rebel, from a dysfunctional and violent home, who has dark hair and wears mostly dark clothing — the visual symbol for "does not fit in." It is also significant that the character of Darrin is a visual reaffirmation of stereotypes about "dark" people being more prone to dysfunctional behavior. The only black character in the entire film is one helicopter pilot, who is only shown for a very brief time.

Ben and Wolfgang build a space craft, designed from information Ben, and then Wolfgang dreamed, which they use to blast off into outer space. Though Darrin does go into space with them at the last, he has no participation in the "dreaming" of advanced scientific information that the other two boys enjoy.

The aliens, who were actually "feeding" the boys' with the dreams, are children themselves and direct Ben and Wolfgang's spaceship to their own. The aliens are bug-like (à la Sid and Marty Krofft), shiny dark green and pink, with bulbous bodies shaped like pears. Again the alien creature is dark with specific stereotypical ethnic characteristics. The female alien is pink with large eyes, flared nostrils, cantaloupe-sized cheeks, and large lips. The male alien is constructed to resemble Asian stereotypes: small nose, buck teeth, and slightly slanted eyes.

The aliens have learned all about earth by watching television, but the film emphasizes that the aliens have seen a majority of white media. The only image of any person of color in the montage of television series the aliens show the boys is a brief clip of Otis Redding and his band. As the sole image of black Americans, the film merely reaffirms age-old stereotypes about the roles African Americans are assumed to play in white society: entertainment. The film ends with the boys crashing their ship into the lake, and after escaping, standing together to watch it sink out of sight. They all later meet in an alien-induced dream where the three boys, and Ben's love interest, are all flying together through the heaven-inspired clouds. They then break out from under the clouds to fly over an alien city. The viewer is left assuming that the aliens will continue to guide the boys,' and now girl's, lives by controlling their acquisition of higher knowledge through telepathic alien interference. The lack of characters of color in this film, particularly given its name, is a compelling comment on the media exclusion of the black child from the adventure of discovery, as well as the acquisition of knowledge.

Flight of the Navigator (1986)

The world in the 1986 film *Flight of the Navigator* is also completely white. It is the story of a young boy who, in 1979, disappears only to reappear eight years later. He has no memory of where he was and to him he has only been gone one night. It is eventually revealed, after NASA captures a disabled space ship, that the child had been abducted by a kindly alien ship. In this film, there are no black characters at all, and most significantly none during the NASA scenes, which gives the appearance of an all-white, government organization. In reality, NASA in the 1980s had numerous African American employees, as well as black scientists and astronauts (for instance, Charles F. Bolden, Jr., recently chosen by President Obama to head NASA, joined NASA in 1980 and became an astronaut in 1981). Though the "the structured absence of blackness has historically been a signature feature of the [sf] genre,"[24] all-white images in sf films like *Flight of the Navigator* function to reinforce a long history of the exclusion of black characters from such futuristic narratives, and particularly from their participation in the science that brings about such a future.

The complete erasure of black characters from the creation of future technologies suggests an unconscious desire to erase people of color from the future as a whole. In children's sf, the future is always envisioned as predominantly white. The white protagonist David's (12 years old) desire to just "go back to the way things were" is also the film's message about the future. Lee Edelman explains that "the pleasurable fantasy of survival ... requires ... more than anything else the survival of a fantasy."[25] This fantasy "survival mode" is played out in *Flight of the Navigator,* as David is confronted by a future that he *consciously chooses* to disavow. His fear of future technological advances outweighs any desire to question or explore the new knowledge that the alien ship, Max, can offer him. David's singular goal is to return to his own time, to take his rightful place within the established patriarchal family structure, and to forget all notions of technological advancements and proof of alien life. Rather than show interest in the new technology of 1986, David is resistant and uninterested. Whereas in *Explorers* the children's goal was to seek, and then own, the higher knowledge that is assumed to come from alien life, David is particularly averse to confronting his own body's ownership of such advanced knowledge. In David, the aversion to the Other and the Other's culture is complete. The fact that David's brain is functioning at levels he neither understands, nor *wants* to understand, positions the film as presenting a future that is really only a desire to *return to* the past, rather than to explore the possibilities of the future. The past for the characters in *Flight of the Navigator* is a homogenous, patriarchal, youthful past. I say youthful because one of the "shocks" David experiences in the future is when he first sees his parents again and they have *aged.* David's reaction is tantamount to horror as he stares, particularly at his mother, whom he asks, "Mom! What happened to you?" The camera lingers on David's shocked expression, then cuts to frame his mother's aged and lined face (the father's face is not so framed), reinforcing not only a fear of the future, but of the female aging process as well.

Both of these films, *The Explorers* and *Flight of the Navigator,* have child characters who "stumble" onto an advanced science. Though one attempts to "capture" and "own" it, the other protagonist rejects and disowns the future, and both films simultaneously visually preserve and advocate for historically white predominance reinforced by a colonial rhetoric towards the Other.

Space Camp (1986)

The 1986 film *Space Camp* is a film about a group of nerdy students who get a chance to attend the NASA space camp. There is one African American character, Rudy, who is a supporting character, and one Asian character, who plays no part in the adventure. The film opens with one of the quintessential icons of American childhood: a white girl, Andie, standing in a field of gently waving golden wheat, a large farmhouse her backdrop, watching the night sky and declaring she will "go up" there someday. The allusion to traditional middle–America and "pure" rural sensibilities is clear here, particularly when the film next cuts to two fighter jets screaming across the sky overhead and the camera pans down to the adult air force member the girl child has become.

Rudy's role throughout this film is, stereotypically, the comic relief. Rudy's excitement at being chosen to attend Space Camp is sarcastically shot down by Andie, who, reluctantly, has been assigned to work at Space Camp. Throughout the film, Andie continually criticizes Rudy's enthusiasm for Space Camp and for science in general. Like an excited child in a toy store, Rudy grabs things, knocks things off shelves, and generally acts as the comic sidekick to the two main protagonists, Kathryn and Kevin. When Kevin asks Rudy why he's at space camp, Rudy's first response is that he wants to be the first "to have a fast food franchise in space ... Astronauts got to eat too!" Rudy reinforces stereotypes of African American men having low ambition and childlike unintelligence. But then, sheepishly and embarrassed, Rudy admits that he likes to learn and loves science, though he's "not very good at it." It is disheartening that the character is almost ashamed for others to know that he loves to learn and loves science. The film's rhetoric, however, nips Rudy's desire to learn in the bud by his admission he's "not very good at it." The entire scene, though poignant, merely reinforces the paternal attitudes of the white characters toward Rudy, who is "trying to measure up" to the white standard but is "not very good at it."

In a pleasantly surprising twist at the film's climax, it is Rudy who saves the day. As the oxygen runs low, Rudy reads a chart to tell Andie how to hook up the oxygen tanks: the wrong wire/valve combination and they all blow up. Rudy at first tells Andie the wrong valve color, then corrects himself. Kathryn pulls the chart from him in disgust, her impatience a visual reaffirmation of stereotypes that a person of color could never be intelligent enough to be a "hero," but Rudy insists he knows the right valve. Rudy has to work hard to convince Andie to trust him and his knowledge. She finally follows Rudy's directions, and all ends well. It is also Rudy who thinks to land at White Sands, NM, when they miss their first landing opportunity. But after those two critical saves, Rudy slips back into the shadows and into his "comic relief" character. For the rest of the film, he is rarely seen. A brief, bright spot at the climax where it is the black child who saves the day, and he is then returned to the background, to his proper "place."

Though Rudy's role is stereotypical in many ways, in other ways, *Space Camp* broke with convention by allowing Rudy, however momentarily, to heroically save the shuttle from disaster. For the decade of the '80s, that one save demonstrated progress.

Lost in Space (1996)

The 1996 film remake of the 1965 TV series *Lost in Space* removed the positive ideal family-on-an-adventure theme of the original series and replaced it with an extremely dysfunctional family whose members are significantly isolated from each other. In fact, the film's central focus is the palpable lack of relationship between Will Robinson and his father, Professor John Robinson (William Hurt), who rarely speaks to or acknowledges his son. That the family is lost in space only serves as the vehicle around which the family must mend itself and return to a cohesive, traditional unit. The film continually posits the past as a position to which all should aspire to return, similar to the *Flight of the Navigator* narrative. From Penny's constant reminders of missing her "old life" to Dr. Smith constant lamenting his return to his past life, the theme of "past life" is a persistent rhetorical device within the film's narrative. Significantly, the final "alien evil" of the film, is not the mutated Dr. Smith (Gary Oldman), but the "alien-ation" between father and son. The film's climax is the work-obsessed, absent father facing his own creation — a wild and slightly insane, "Robinson" Crusoe-like, adult son Will, who has been marooned on the planet with Dr. Smith. The planet is collapsing into itself — a metaphor for the collapsing father-son relationship. Because of adult Will's lack of fatherly guidance his unrestrained, scientific experiment threatens to destroy them all.

The film does not allow any other alien races or civilizations to intrude on the all-white world of the vast space station. As Vivian Sobchack explains,

> in a culture ... in which subjectivity and affect are regularly decentered, dispersed, spatialized, and objectified, and in which even alienation is alienated and literalized, it is hardly surprising that the figure of the 'alien' no longer poses the political and social threat it did in the SF of the 1950s.... Today's SF films either posit that 'aliens are like us' or that 'aliens R US.' Alien others have become less other ... they have become our familiars, our simulacra, embodied as literally alienated images of our alienated selves.[26]

And though the true alien in *Lost in Space* is the lost father-son relationship — the alienated image of ourselves Sobchack refers too — the film still presents a distinct lack of any substantive black characters in its diegetic future world other than the menacing evil transformed Dr. Smith.

The only black character in the film, Jeb, appears during the film's opening scenes of a spaceship dogfight. Jeb's ship is hit and disabled by laser fire, and his friend, the white Major West, defies orders to save him. It is a common trope among sf films that the person of color, if there are any at all, is the first to be eliminated (for example, the original *Planet of the Apes*). Though we do not see Jeb killed in this opening scene (the only scene in which Jeb actually appears), his rescue by Major West merely foreshadows Jeb's death later on in the film when the family discovers an abandoned ship from the future — a ship sent to rescue the family piloted by the now long-deceased Jeb.

During the film's final scenes, the white Dr. Smith has been transformed by a [black] space-spider bite into a tall, black, cloven-footed "alien" whose facial features contain an elongated head, flared nostrils, large lips and wide eyes. Given the very obvious absence of black characters in the film, the Dr. Smith transformation into a *black* alien sporting exaggerated African American facial features alludes to the white fear of "an irreversible crossing toward the loss of the terrestrial reverential" of whiteness.[27] The alien encounter with a now black Dr. Smith in this film functions as a subjectivity marker where "the alien, monster or robot ... provide an example of Otherness, against which a representation of 'proper' [white] human subjectivity is established, interrogated and, on occasion, problematized,"[28] and in this particular film, it is an alienated white male fatherhood that is problematized and interrogated by the now black Dr. Smith. The child Will must now choose to continue under the influence of the "black" Dr. Smith, or accept his white father's apology, a choice that is forced via an attack by the *black* alien Dr. Smith. In this film, blackness is equated with evil science, isolation, and insanity.

Conclusion

Do sf films for children romanticize and glorify a white-only future? Do they visually design nostalgia for a bold imperial future-as-the-past? And how much of these films' rhetoric reflect the recent predominantly white, conservative culture which celebrates a cowboy ex–President who flexed his imperial muscle in the invasion and occupation of Iraq? Does such colonialist nostalgia in children's sf reinforce for the child viewer and his or her parents a longing and expectation for a future filled with the "natural" racial hierarchies of a bygone era? It would appear so. How then does the African American child negotiate both viewing (and enjoying) the sf adventure and the inevitable sea of products that are an integral part of the sf-film package? How does the black child perceive an advanced future world when they see that future world in popular culture imagined only as white? Even when there are people of color in a children's sf film they are usually the first to die, or they are alien creatures (caricatures) who are the "natural" recipients of paternalistic conquest through the white protagonist's "fixing" or "saving" of the alien creature — who, more often than not, is constructed through CGI and special effects as a symbol for the Other-as-black. Through the visual absence of African Americans from sf films, their *exclusion* from active participation in, and creation of, the future is normalized. The effect of this "rehallucination" of the past-as-future in sf cinema within the discourse of childhood occurs "when narrative text and images become a pervasive part of the cultural environment [and] also become part of the identity of people who read and consume the images and narratives."[29] Childhood in sf films "seems to shimmer with the iridescent promise of Noah's rainbow, serving like the rainbow as the pledge of a covenant that shields us against the persistent threat of apocalypse now — or later" — an apocalyptic threat to white identity brought about by the uncontrolled encroachment of people of color into a collective future so vividly laid out for the child viewer on the sf screen.[30]

Through these white sf film adventures, black children are perhaps enticed to desire a hegemonic fantasy-future that presents to them their own absence and marginalization, a condition in which they are "constantly heading for deception ... but spurred on by [that] very deception."[31] For African American children, the space adventure is "space"-less. Hollywood has created a position of "spaceless-ness" for the black child character, a "black" hole into which their representation is exiled. A black hole is defined as a "theoretical entity" that "is formed when a star of sufficient mass undergoes gravitational collapse, with most or all of its mass compressed into a sufficiently small area of space, causing infinite spacetime curvature at that point (a 'singularity'). Such a massive spacetime curvature allows nothing, not even light, to escape": a fitting description of the "theoretical nature" behind the comparable "black" hole where the silenced black children excluded from Hollywood films reside.[32]

Another significant factor in black children's exclusion from the sf film is the market saturation of film-related products, which satisfy the child consumer's desire to re-experience the futuristic adventure of the film. Even though a black child may not have seen the actual film, the multitude of visual consumer products so saturate their real lived space, that the products thus function in lieu of actually viewing the film — the numerous product's images, textures, sounds, colors, and tastes entice the child to view the film in order to become a part of the cultural adventure, even though the black child is visually excluded in the film from that same adventure.

The visual reinforcement of white children as the only space adventurer or savior of worlds in sf films also suggest a normalized belief in both an ideal white childhood of which the black child can never be a part, and a constant Othering of the black child's image of herself by her absence in the film's narrative. The sf film is an imaginary window to a better, brighter future that "in a sense close[s] up again [by] universalizing itself"[33] and its message for all child spectators is this: the best future, the one we all should desire, is the return to a fabled white purist past.

Lee Edelman argues that the image of the Child functions "as the preeminent emblem of the motivating end, though one endlessly postponed, of every political vision *as a vision of futurity*."[34] Edelman's discussion of the

Child as a symbol of futurity provides a framework for my examination here of the visual *exclusion* of black children in sf family films. Edelman uses "Child" in a "universalizing" sense, but that is not the case in actuality: white child and black child signify very different historical, social, economic, and cultural meanings. It is symptomic in American culture that "Child" assumes a universal meaning that is rooted in the belief that "childhood" is always symbolically aligned with whiteness.

Although imaginative stories "teach people how to 'subjunctivize'— how to go beyond their personal selves and the actualities of their everyday reality, and explore all kinds of human possibilities,"[35] such racially limited sf portrayals beg the question: what is the effect on the black child's imagination for the future when the majority of *sf* films are exclusively *white* adventures? For African American children who view these films, their negotiation with the images would seem to require a "dual suspension of disbelief: that the [futuristic] world exists, and that black children *can also* be a part" of that imagined future, including access to, and knowledge of, new and fascinating technologies.[36]

Because culturally "ideas, values, and visions exist in a constant and complex dialectical relationship to the 'material,'"[37] the absence of children of color from the discourse of the future, as framed in sf films, replays again within children's material, lived culture. The unfortunate stereotype of black children as non-technologically savvy is supported through their exclusion in future-themed films. As Adam Banks argues, "Racism is enforced and maintained through our technologies and the assumptions we design and program into them — and into our uses of them," and those assumptions have become a subtle part of sf film and the underlying racist notions of who can create and use science and technology.[38]

The quotidian visibility of an idealized white child protagonist, visually prominent in almost every product within children's culture, serves as the subtle roar of adult desires for the return of past racial hierarchies. The exclusion of the African American child from a techno-based future, as portrayed in cinema, creates an *expectation* of their exclusion in a high-tech or space-based future, or even worse, no *surprise* at their absence. Geoff King and Tanya Krzywinska argue that, "much of the dramatic and structural tension of science fiction derives from the construction of a primary difference between the 'human' and the 'other.'"[39] And though the black child may identify with the *role* of the adventurer protagonist, the films typically codify blackness as the alien Other to the white human. The absence of actual black faces in a sf film with which the child can relate to his or her actual lived experience functions to reinforce "the message of the relative unimportance of these children"[40] and their place in a universalized human future. The sf film text then continues, through its absence of identifiable faces of color, "the problem of pervasive, internalized privileging of Whiteness ... which consistently reinforces an ideology of White supremacy"[41] and continues the perception of inherently race-based differences in the condition of childhood today, and most significantly, in the future.

Ultimately, science-fiction film's discourse of the future as the exclusive province of whiteness consistently suggests a broad cultural denial of diversity. As Kim argues, children's sf films "like postmodernism itself, both invoke and deny the discourses and politics of race, while sweeping other salient and concrete issues under the rug."[42] The "black hole" of exclusion may be a popular cinematic sf discourse, but the reality here on earth is that black children have witnessed the first African American President of the United States, Barack Obama, and their parents can tell them that "the sky's the limit" in pursuit of their dreams. Perhaps if there were a greater African American presence *behind* the camera, there would be more diversity in front of it. There is a prodigious need for a firm African American presence in the production realm of children's science-fiction films, particularly writers and directors who could present a future where a black child protagonist embodies the norm, rather than difference. But unfortunately, in today's Hollywood cinema, futuristic sf worlds are firmly entrenched in the racism of the past. In the space adventure, the African American child is, indeed, the last in space.

NOTES

1. Laura Dawkins, "Black Babies, White Hysteria: The Dark Child in the African American Literature of the Harlem Renaissance," in *The American Child,* edited by Caroline E. Levander and Carol J. Singley (New Brunswick, NJ: Rutgers University Press, 2003), 173.
2. Adilifu Nama, *Black Space: Imagining Race in the Science Fiction Film* (Austin: University of Texas Press, 2008), 83.
3. Jack Zipes. *Happily Ever After: Fairy Tales, Children, and the Culture Industry* (New York: Routledge, 1997), 7.
4. "Box Office Charts," *Yahoo! Movies*, http://movies.yahoo.com/mv/boxoffice/alltime/.
5. Stephen Rose, John Hambley, and Jeff Haywood, "Science, Racism, and Ideology," *The Socialist Register* (1973): 238.
6. Debbie C. Olson, "Techno-Utopia and the Search for Saraba," in *The Black Imagination: Science Fiction and Futurism,* edited by Sandra Jackson and Julie Moody-Freeman (publication forthcoming), 4.
7. Nama, *Black Space, 71.*
8. Ibid., 39.
9. Ibid., 180.
10. Ibid., 41.
11. Ibid., 95.
12. Lee Edelman, *No Future* (Durham, NC: Duke University Press, 2004), 30.
13. Isiah Lavender III, "Technicity: AI and Cyborg Ethnicity in *The Matrix,*" *Extrapolation* 45, no. 4 (2004): 439.
14. Jean Baudrillard, *Simulacra and Simulation* (Ann Arbor: University of Michigan Press, 1994), 123.
15. David A. Kirby, "Extrapolating Race in GATTACA: Genetic Passing, Identity, and the Science of Race," *Literature and Medicine* 23, no. 1 (2004): 186.

16. Nama, *Black Space*, 30.
17. Dawkins, "Black Babies, White Hysteria," 173.
18. Vivian Sobchack, *Screening Space: The American Science Fiction Film* (New York: Ungar, 1988), 300.
19. Jean Baudrillard, *The Conspiracy of Art* (New York: Semiotext, 2005), 92.
20. Christine Cornea, *Science Fiction Cinema: Between Fantasy and Reality* (New Brunswick, NJ: Rutgers University Press, 2007), 182.
21. Sobchack, *Screening Space*, 294.
22. Ibid., 293.
23. Ibid., 293.
24. Nama, *Black Space*, 10.
25. Edelman, *No Future*, 45.
26. Sobchack, *Screening Space*, 293.
27. Baudrillard, *Simulacra*, 123–124.
28. Cornea, *Science Fiction Cinema*, 176.
29. Elizabeth Heilman, *Critical Perspectives on Harry Potter* (New York: Taylor and Francis, 2003), 1–2.
30. Edelman, *No Future*, 18.
31. Baudrillard, *Conspiracy*, 194.
32. Andrew Zimmerman Jones, "What Is a Black Hole?" *About.com*, http://physics.about.com/od/astronomy/f/BlackHole.htm.
33. Baudrillard, *Simulacra*, 123.
34. Edelman, *No Future*, 13.
35. Debra O'Keefe, *Readers in Wonderland* (New York: Continuum, 2003), 20.
36. Debbie C. Olson, "Faces of Fantasy," *Red Feather Journal* 2, no. 1 (publication forthcoming), 19.
37. Sue Kim, "Beyond Black and White: Race and Postmodernism in the *Lord of the Rings* Films," *Modern Fiction Studies* 50, no. 4 (2004): 887.
38. Adam J. Banks, *Race, Rhetoric, and Technology: Searching for Higher Ground* (Urbana, IL: National Council of Teachers of English, 2006), 10.
39. Geoff King and Tanya Krzywinska, *Science Fiction Film: From Outer Space to Cyberspace* (London: Wallflower Press, 2000), 30.
40. Dorothy Hurley, "Seeing White: Children of Color and the Disney Fairy Tale Princess," *The Journal of Negro Education* 74, no. 3 (2005): 228.
41. Ibid., 223.
42. Kim, "Beyond Black and White," 875.

References

Abel, Elizabeth. *Signs of the Times: the Visual Politics of Jim Crow*. Berkeley: University of California Press, 2010. http://www.afrofuturism.net/.
Banks, Adam J. *Race, Rhetoric, and Technology: Searching for Higher Ground*. Urbana, IL: National Council of Teachers of English, 2006.
Baudrillard, Jean. *The Conspiracy of Art*. New York: Semiotext, 2005.
_____. *Simulacra and Simulation*. Ann Arbor: University of Michigan Press, 1994.
Chafe, William H., Raymond Gavins, and Robert Korstad, eds. *Remembering Jim Crow: Americans Tell about Life in the Segregated South*. New York: New Press, 2008.
Cornea, Christine. *Science Fiction Cinema: Between Fantasy and Reality*. New Brunswick, NJ: Rutgers University Press, 2007.
Dawkins, Laura. "Black Babies, White Hysteria: The Dark Child in the African American Literature of the Harlem Renaissance." In *The American Child*, edited by Caroline E. Levander and Carol J. Singley, 167–183. New Brunswick, NJ: Rutgers University Press, 2003.
Donalson, Melvin Burke. *Black Directors in Hollywood*. Austin: University of Texas Press, 2003.
Edelman, Lee. *No Future*. Durham, NC: Duke University Press, 2004.
Green, Eric, and Richard Slotkin. *Planet of the Apes as American Myth: Race, Politics, and Popular Culture*. Middletown, CT: Wesleyan University Press, 1998.
Green, Nicola. "Beyond Being Digital: Representation and Virtual Corporeality." In *Virtual

Politics: Identity and Community in Cyberspace, edited by David Holmes, 59–78. London: Sage, 1997.

Heilman, Elizabeth, ed. *Critical Perspectives on Harry Potter.* New York: Taylor and Francis, 2003.

Hurley, Dorothy. "Seeing White: Children of Color and the Disney Fairy Tale Princess." *The Journal of Negro Education* 74, no. 3 (2005): 221–232.

Kim, Sue. "Beyond Black and White: Race and Postmodernism in the *Lord of the Rings* Films." *Modern Fiction Studies* 50, no. 4 (2004): 875–907.

King, Geoff, and Tanya Krzywinska. *Science Fiction Cinema: From Outer Space to Cyberspace.* London: Wallflower Press, 2000.

Kirby, David A. "Extrapolating Race in GATTACA: Genetic Passing, Identity, and the Science of Race." *Literature and Medicine* 23, no. 1 (2004): 184–200.

Lavender, Isiah, III. "Technicity: AI and Cyborg Ethnicity in *The Matrix.*" *Extrapolation* 45, no. 4 (2004): 437–458.

Levander, Caroline E., and Carol J. Singley, eds. *The American Child.* New Brunswick, NJ: Rutgers University Press, 2003.

Massè, Michelle A. "Constructing the Psychoanalytic Child: Freud's *From the History of an Infantile Neurosis.*" In *The American Child,* edited by Caroline E. Levander and Carol J. Singley, 149–166. New Brunswick, NJ: Rutgers University Press, 2003.

Nama, Adilifu. *Black Space: Imagining Race in the Science Fiction Film.* Austin: University of Texas Press, 2008.

O'Keefe, Debra. *Readers in Wonderland.* New York: Continuum, 2003.

Olson, Debbie C. "Faces of Fantasy: The Discourse of Exclusion in Hollywood's Magical Realms." *Red Feather Journal* 1, no. 4 (2010). www.redfeatherjournal.org.

_____. "Techno-Utopia and the Search for Saraba." In *The Black Imagination: Science Fiction and Futurism,* edited by Sandra Jackson and Julie Moody-Freeman. Publication forthcoming.

Rose, Stephen, John Hambley, and Jeff Haywood. "Science, Racism, and Ideology." *The Socialist Register* (1973). http://socialistregister.com/index.php/srv/article/view/5356/2257.

Telotte, J.P. "Disney in Science Fiction Land." *Journal of Popular Film and Television* 33, no. 1 (2005): 12–20.

Sobchack, Vivian. *Screening Space: The American Science Fiction Film.* 2d ed. New York: Ungar, 1988.

Weinstock, Jeffrey A. "Freaks in Space: 'Extraterrestrialism' and 'Deep-Space Multiculturalism.'" In *Freakery: Cultural Spectacles of the Extraordinary Body,* edited by Rosemarie Garland Thompson, 327–337. New York: New York University Press, 1996.

Zimmerman Jones, Andrew. "What Is a Black Hole?" About.com. http://physics.about.com/od/astronomy/f/BlackHole.htm.

Zipes, Jack. *Happily Ever After: Fairy Tales, Children, and the Culture Industry.* New York: Routledge, 1997.

• *Five* •

A Few Beasts Hissed: Buzz Lightyear and the Refusal to Believe

DANIEL KENNEFICK

"Do you believe?" he cried.
Tink sat up in bed almost briskly to listen to her fate.
She fancied she heard answers in the affirmative, and then again she wasn't sure.
"What do you think?" she asked Peter.
"If you believe," he shouted to them, "clap your hands; don't let Tink die."
Many clapped.
Some didn't.
A few beasts hissed.
—from *The Adventures of Peter Pan*, by J. M. Barrie, 1904[1]

Why did those beasts hiss? Perhaps they didn't like fairies and hoped Tink would die. Perhaps they didn't like the tone of Peter's appeal, with its presumption that fairies cannot continue to live unless we believe in them. Nothing admits disbelief more than the demand that we must all believe or what we each believe will no longer be true. That is the language of make-believe. To those who believe in fairies, Peter's appeal can only be insulting. Even Tinker Bell's puny size in the story is probably illustrative of the decline in fairy belief. Traditional fairy belief centers around tall, warlike, euphemerized Gods (the Danaans in Ireland, for instance) or murderous creatures of the night. The dwindling of these awesome creatures to a tiny non-threatening size is often interpreted as a symptom of the decline in fairy faith, a decline which was accelerated by migration from the country to the cities in the era after the industrial revolution. Barrie's twee Victorian fairies appealed to his audience undoubtedly because they nurtured a deep nostalgia for their own rural childhoods, a nostalgia entwined with anxiety about continued societal transformation. Tinker Bell is a tinsmith by profession, as her name implies, thus embodying an archetypal vanishing class of rural artisans. In *Peter Pan* adult anxieties about social change are assuaged by forcing their children to express belief in a bowdlerized version of a faith their parents no longer hold. The children who believe in fairies were the ones who didn't clap. The more vocal of them might have hissed. Peter Pan would have hissed, had he been present in the audience during the play.

Why has it become, in recent times, such a trope of children's literature and entertainment that childhood is the age of belief and that children's belief can work wonders? After *Peter Pan* the best known example is the *Velveteen Rabbit*, with its premise that the Rabbit will become real only if loved by the boy, and its reference to the mechanical toys who "were full of modern ideas, and pretended they were real."[2] Perhaps this is more evidence of bourgeois anxiety at the threat posed to their own social standing by the mechanization of production which had previously brought about the collapse of traditional rural culture. Nothing seems to please parents better than when "traditional" toys or pastimes appeal to modern children. Just as biologists used to theorize that ontogeny replicates phylogeny, so we may speculate that childhood patterns of belief are expected to replicate historical beliefs no longer current in adult society. Hence it is as appropriate for children to believe in fairies, in an age when adults don't, as it is for children to favor old fashioned toys over modern mechanical ones, while their parents favor the automobile over the horse and car.

The movie *Toy Story*, with its protagonist, Buzz Lightyear, is this same story as told from the point of view of one of these mechanical interlopers into the traditional nursery.[3] At the same time Buzz is an interloper from another genre, a science-fiction character in a quintessentially fantasy story. Just as science fiction borrows from fantasy while introducing mechanistic explanations for the fantastic elements of the stories, so Buzz refuses to abide by the rule that inanimate objects become real only if they are toys loved by a child. He even dares to ask, to the confusion of the other toys, whether they are powered by crystalline fusion when we, and they, know they are powered by love and belief. Buzz's mechanistic belief in his own essential reality violates the rules of the nursery, and the bulk of the film deals with Buzz's disillusion, which is actually a re-illusion. He comes to believe he is real only in so far as Andy's imaginative belief makes him so. But is it imagination or belief that Andy possesses sufficiently strongly to make Buzz and Woody real?

Science Fiction and Fantasy: Belief Versus Imagination

Considering the differences between the genres of fantasy and science fiction may give us a clue as to the distinction to be drawn between belief and imagination. Are we to understand that children are more imaginative than adults, or simply more credulous, more easily prone to belief?

In science fiction we deal with tales of the imagination in which elements of the story are reworked so as to appeal to the beliefs of a modern audience, rather than to a pre-modern one. Fantasy, on the other hand, tries to maintain the actual "look and feel" of the older tales, even though we know that the modern audience will not really believe these stories. Thus fantasy is characteristically different from both folk tales, which were once told to audiences who may have believed them, and from science fiction, which is told to another audience which may believe that we are dealing with something that could be, or may yet be, true.

Let us consider another story which fits our general theme of belief and what it means to be real, the story of Pinnochio. Written in Italian as a serial for children by Carlo Lorenzini, under the pen name Carlo Collodi, with the title *The Adventures of Pinnochio* and completed in 1883, Pinnochio is one of the archetypal stories based around the notion of the relation of imagination and belief to childhood.[4] It indeed gives us a little clue to the reasons for the enduring popularity of this genre in the fact that it is actually about the belief and wish fulfillment of an adult, Geppetto the woodcarver, who wishes that he could have a real son. In addition the obvious religious overtones, in which a carpenter becomes the father to a child with obviously divine origins, betray that we are dealing with a children's story which appeals to adults who select reading material for their children.

Still, Pinocchio is considered (by adults) to be suitable for children. What are we to make of its recent science-fictional remake *AI: Artificial Intelligence?* Inspired by and partly based on a short story by Brian Aldiss, the plot was worked into a film treatment at the behest of Stanley Kubrick, who seems to have been the prime mover in introducing the parallels to Pinnochio, and directed by Steven Spielberg, though only completed after Kubrick's death.[5] In *AI* we have a small boy who is actually a robot, created to give comfort to a mother grieving for a dying child. When the robot child is displaced, following the recovery of the real son who was ill, he gradually becomes distanced from his "family," primarily as a consequence of sibling rivalry with his real "brother." The robot continues to love and pine for his human mother, and comes to wish he was real, believing that then he would find the love he seeks. Enamored of the story of Pinnochio, which seems to echo his own dilemma, he seeks for the Blue Fairy, who turns out to be nothing more than an inanimate fairground attraction, but who the robot boy believes will make him real. Eventually, as a result of this quest, he becomes trapped under the sea and, as time passes, is buried in a glacier, only to be uncovered and reactivated in the distant future by a race of robots who have succeeded humans on Earth. They cannot grant the little boy robot's wish to "make him real," but with the aid of arbitrarily advanced technology they do provide him with a version of his long lost mother who will "really" love him (in a bizarre but telling touch, they can only maintain this technological miracle for a few hours, which we are told is all the robot boy desires).

There are two points of interest in this science-fictional adaptation of a fantasy story. First, it is science-fictional because it adopts believable rationales for its main plot points. The good fairy is seen to be a fiction at first, and eventually replicated by "technology" in the far future. The little boy made of wood becomes an advanced robot. Even trendy science-fictional tropes are brought in to explain the need for robot children (climate change and population control). Thus a modern audience may more willingly suspend disbelief for this story than they will for the story of *Pinnochio*. Secondly, *Pinnochio*, with its conscious echoing of folk beliefs, especially in the person of the fairy, was and is a story intended for children, whereas *AI* was made for an adult audience. Thus fantasy stories, with their relatively frank admission that we no longer really believe in such things, are for children, while science-fiction stories, with their effort to boost the believability of the text, with increasingly strained exertions at plausibility, are more often for adults. When science fiction borrows motifs from fantasy or folklore it may be at its most strained. Indeed *AI* has displeased some science-fiction buffs, including the author of the original story, Brain Aldiss, who noted "It's crap. Science fiction has to be logical, and it's full of lapses in logic."[6] Aldiss, by his own testimony, spent years trying to persuade Kubrick against the idea of introducing the Pinnochio motif.

In fact, although science fiction has been highly popular as a film genre at least since the making of Star Wars in the mid-seventies, the genre's chief role has been to provide a more acceptable format in which fantasy films can be presented to the mass market. Star Wars itself is an important case in point, since despite its superficial science-fictional elements, its plot rather faithfully follows that of a well known international folktale best remembered in the form of the myth of Perseus (or in Ireland as the story of Balor and Lugh).[7] The tale is that of a king, often a sorcerer, who is warned by an oracle that his grandson will bring about his death. Accordingly he locks his only daughter in a tower, into which a hero or God penetrates, in a double sense, bringing about the birth of the hero who eventually slays the tyrant. Of course the influence of Joseph Campbell's monomyth on George Lucas has been widely remarked upon, but film critics are usually too busy noting stylistic resemblances to old westerns and Kurosawa movies to wonder where the plot itself came from.

Imagination and Belief

Margery Williams (she wrote under her maiden name; her married name was Bianco), the author of the *Velveteen Rabbit*, was influenced by the ideas of Walter de la Mare on the nature of the imagination, especially the childhood imagination. This influence seems particularly clear in the *Velveteen Rabbit*, told from the point of view of the toy, for whom the child's imagination congeals into a form of belief which accomplishes the miracle of transforming the rabbit into a real rabbit. At the end of the story, the former toy goes to live with its real cousins on the edge of the woods.

It is important to distinguish between two ideas which are conflated in much of the popular thinking on this subject. One idea is that childhood is associated with the imagination. This is the inspiration that lies at the heart of writing for children by those like Williams and de la Mare. The other idea is that childhood is a time of belief, what one might call the Disney hypothesis, but which is clearly present and implicit in the *Velveteen Rabbit*. The connection seems clear. Children have a vivid imagination, which causes them to be visionaries, seeing what is not there, and *then to believe in the reality of these visions*. I would call into question at once the necessity of this connection. If children are imaginative (and I am not certain they are more or less imaginative than adults), it is not clear that they are heavily invested in the imaginary visions which they do perceive. Indeed it could be argued that they are more imaginative than adults precisely to the extent that, not being invested in any of these imaginings, they are freer to run through them more quickly. Thus we could say they are *more* imaginative, to the extent that they have *less* belief, because by stopping more briefly at each imaginary place they can visit more widely amongst them than is true of those (for instance, adults) with stronger belief.

Let us examine de la Mare's views, as expressed in his essay *Rupert Brooke and the Intellectual Imagination*, since they are said to have informed Williams in writing the *Velveteen Rabbit*.[8] To de la Mare early childhood was a time in which the human imagination, being less experienced in the ways of the physical world, was freer and more indulged in each individual. As harsh reality more and more intrudes with disappointments on this imaginative vision world, the child begins to revert to a form of imagination based more upon reason and experience. This take on the interplay between experience and the imagination seems reminiscent of William Blake's thought. Blake had undergone a revival, spurred by W.B. Yeats, in the early years of de la Mare's life.

De la Mare's take on the childhood imagination seems a plausible one. His depiction of the imagination as an inborn human faculty is shared by many other thinkers, and not just in the arts. Albert Einstein, for instance, emphasized how dependent scientific work was on the freedom of the human imagination from external constraints. If we accept that such an inborn faculty exists within the human mind, it seems natural to suppose that it would enjoy freest reign during the early years of life, when experience of the external world must be limited.

However I am not willing to accept de la Mare's thesis unchallenged. To my mind it could also be argued, in direct reverse of his plausibility argument, that small children are forced by circumstance to be empiricists. This is the problem with plausibility arguments, that they are so easily inverted. Recall Oscar Wilde's dictum that nothing is really true unless its contradiction is also true. Precisely because children have little experience of the world, they must pay constant attention to it as they learn its rules. It is only later, when they have internalized these rules that their imagination will have freer play to impose itself on the external world, rather than being imposed on by it. The fact that they respond so readily to imaginative flights, frequently initiated by their parents, should tell us that here also they are being exposed to things they will need to learn. After all, where else do small children learn about Santa Claus, fairies and so on, except from adults? It is usually not until a little later in life that they begin to learn things from other children rather than from adults. Note that children learn belief in Santa Claus from adults, while skepticism about his existence is generally learned from other children, or evolved by the child independently.

In observing childhood we must be careful to distinguish it from that closely related entity, the parental re-experience of childhood. Parenthood is a time in life when humans are free to indulge their imaginative faculties, because parents feel enabled by their pedagogic role in pursuing a freer play of imagination than is normally considered socially acceptable. The adult inhibition of free play imagination seems to me directly linked to the issue of belief. It is considered bad form in the adult world to play with belief. It is a serious topic and must be treated seriously. With what relief do many adults turn to the world of the nursery when given the chance, where they may give freer rein to the playful aspects of the imaginative faculty.

In short we may say that imaginative play is closely associated with "make-believe." When we play imaginatively we say, "Let us believe in this for now." I would see this as preparatory play for adulthood, in the sense that one must eventually achieve sufficient practice to be able to hold one belief for long periods, in defiance of experiential evidence to the contrary. By practice one's imaginative faculty becomes able to maintain a single belief for long periods, essentially indefinitely. Then one has achieved adulthood, and one is expected not to "play around" with this belief any longer (though exceptions are made, for the purposes of humor, for instance). Notice that an empirical approach would be to maintain a more independent and critical stance about beliefs. One would continually test and revise beliefs and be prepared to entertain different hypotheses. Einstein would tell us that these different hypotheses must come from the imagination and only then can they be confronted with the world. I submit that it is childlike behavior which conforms to this take on empiricism. Children rest only lightly on each imaginative model of the world and are constantly trying out new ones. But for profoundly social reasons it is necessary after some time that we settle upon a single set of beliefs so that we will behave consistently for the benefit of other social beings attempting to predict our future behavior. Childhood is the time in which we flex and develop our belief muscle until it is strong enough to withstand the rigorous exercise of adulthood. Recall that standing is often a more severe test of the muscles than other forms of exercise. The muscles must be taut, but are not allowed to flex and therefore will need to be well toned to stand still for long. Think of the adult imagination as being required to perform the task of sitting for indefinite periods unsupported except by a wall behind the back, so that the muscles of the thigh are in agony supporting the weight of the body in an awkward position while being unable to move. Ironically the only way to become adept at this trick is through vigorous exercise by which the muscles of the thigh are developed. Then one may "sit" as still as one likes for a long period.

Morality and the Childhood Imagination

> "Well, when Mrs. Barbauld had the temerity to charge 'The
> Rime of the Ancient Mariner' with two grave faults; first,
> that it was improbable, and next, that it had no moral;
> Coleridge cheerfully pleaded guilty to the first charge, while,
> as for the other, 'I told her that ... it had too much that is,
> for a work of pure imagination.'"
> — from *Rupert Brooke and the Intellectual Imagination*[9]

> "All art is quite useless,"
> — from *The Picture of Dorian Gray*[10]

Wilde, another apostle of the uninhibited force of the imagination, would have agreed with Coleridge, that morality has no place in an imaginative work. Nevertheless his own imaginative works, especially those for children, are highly moral in tone. Although Wilde would argue that their concern is with beauty rather than morality, it is not entirely clear that there is a legitimate distinction to be made between them, as handled by Wilde himself, other than that Wilde's morality is clearly not the traditional morality of his day. What is striking is the extent to which modern writing for children, a century after Wilde, has come to adopt Wilde's morality. Now the highest morality in much children's fiction, and especially in recent children's movies, is the morality of the liberated imagination (examples include many recent Disney films as well as TV movies like *The Legend of Frosty the Snowman* which, compared with the original TV movie, shows a major shift over the past several decades).[11]

Wilde's playful imagination goes hand-in-hand with a flexible morality in which all morality is situational. Traditional morality is noteworthy for its inflexibility. Fairy tales and children's fantastic literature then are a constant arena of struggle between those who wish to see them primarily as a tool for teaching moral beliefs, and those who see them as works of art which must be engaged with on their own terms, which may be a way of saying, as tools for developing a more highly developed and individualistic moral sensibility. For Wilde the story which he made out of his own life ended tragically when a true tale which he saw as being a beautiful story of true love was declared by society to be depraved and immoral.

When we consider Buzz Lightyear's character and his strong belief that he is real, we should not mistake Buzz's belief for a childlike belief, like Andy's, for whom Buzz is only real part of the time. Buzz's belief is an adult belief, precisely because Buzz believes he is real all the time, and indeed both Buzz and Woody clearly represent adults in the story. Woody regards Andy with a parental affection, but Buzz represents the parent who is unwilling to settle to a life of domesticity and imagines himself still free to go off and do as he pleases. Eventually Woody persuades him that it is time to settle down, a motif found in other Pixar films, in particular *The Incredibles*.[12] In fact it is common for adults, especially parents, to be portrayed in a flattering light in many recent animation films, perhaps reflecting the increasing tendency of parents to accompany their children to movies, as to other events. This is a change from times past, when many children would go with one adult where possible, and where children were sent on their own at a younger age than is nowadays common.

One secret of Pixar's success seems to be their maintaining an explicit consciousness of their own tropes, and willingness to put a twist on them. Thus, in the sequel, it is now Woody, faced with the approaching reality of being an empty nester, who seeks new horizons in what is clearly a mid-life crisis which almost sees him take off for Japan.[13] It is Buzz's turn to call Woody back to parental reality. In the third film the cycle has returned to the beginning, with Buzz electronically reset back to his original persona, once again believing he is a Space Ranger. This time there is a harder edge, with a note that, in this persona, Buzz can be as much villain as hero. Also there is a hint of sexual liberation in Buzz's new imaginative world, since he now sees himself as a Flamenco dancer, enabling him to win the eye of the comely cowgirl Jessie.[14]

An interesting vignette from the second film concerns a second Buzz toy, initially mistaken for the "real" Buzz, who still believes he is real. Having been liberated straight from the shop, and with no child to please, he is free to follow his own inclinations. This turns out to involve finding his own father (the evil emperor Zurg, in a nod to the *Star Wars* movies and their obsession with redeeming the father) and returning to childhood himself. It would seem a good deal of the appeal of the mechanical toy who believes he is real and who rebels against the conventions of the nursery world is aimed at parents in the audience. These parents imagine what it would be like for toys (and adults) who did not have to devote themselves nearly full time to pleasing and caring for the needs of a child but could be freed of such encumbrances to indulge their own whims.

I doubt that the *Toy Story* series is alone in modern moviemaking for children in making an attempt to entertain the adults in the audience. One reason for the widespread adoption of the theme of childhood imagination is its appeal to these parents. Buzz Lightyear's character nicely illustrates the dilemma faced by these adults in the audience in their own lives. As long as they can indulge in make-believe and the free play of the imagination, they are happy and can be whatever they wish to be. But such a state of happiness cannot be indulged by them for long, because the thing that they are is already believed or imagined by the wider society. Note that the intrusion of harsh reality, if by that we mean the natural world, is not the immediate cause of their alienation, contrary to de la Mare. Of course it plays a role, but indirectly, in so far as the harshness of this natural world obliges the adult to stay within society, where the help of fellow humans promises that the bodily needs will be taken care of easily enough. Try as hard as the grown-ups will to imagine a new state for themselves, it is hard to overturn the beliefs about their appropriate role already held by others around them. It seems to me that it is these beliefs that Buzz Lightyear struggles vainly against throughout the three movies. Buzz believes he is a space ranger (single person), but those around him persist in believing he is a toy (parent), in spite of Buzz's best efforts to prove that he can do the things that a Space Ranger can do (fly).

In Buzz we see the dilemma confronting those who would hold up the power of individual belief against that of collective or social belief. The individual wishes to continually re-imagine his or her own role in society, a privilege which the wider society resists indulging. It is notable that all of the examples we have encountered of the genre of childhood belief date from the late Victorian period or subsequently. Traditional conservative societies had even less time for this sort of self-indulgence than do modern liberal societies. It is no coincidence, perhaps, that in those traditional societies, childhood was a much briefer time than is the case nowadays. The space, or rather time, in which imagination can be given free reign has increased, but people still chaff at the remaining restrictions and mourn the loss of a freedom of which they now cherish happy memories. Ironically young children are not so aware of this freedom, having no other choice in their use of the imagination, since they simply lack the faculty to persist in a long held belief of any kind. Older children and young people are often more conscious of chaffing against their inability to attain an adult status and are frequently anxious to leave the nursery world of make-believe behind.

If liberal society has increased the freedom of the individual imagination against that of the social (the "American Dream"), socialists of a certain type, from Marx to Wilde to Guy Debord and beyond have promised to complete this revolution. It is one of the most attractive claims of Marxism that in the socialist society humans will be free to continually alter their social roles, and this liberty of the individual imagination was precisely the virtue of socialism which attracted thinkers whose concerns were fundamentally about art, like Wilde and Debord. Socialism, and other forms of utopianism, therefore represents the victory of the young over the old, of the future over the past. Thus Buzz, the science-fictional character trapped in a fantasy plot, can be seen as a migrant from the future, our utopian future, struggling to deal with the curious limitations of "traditional" liberal culture. That he becomes, in the end, assimilated, can be seen both as an adoption of traditional literary forms, of the bildungsroman of which this story seems to be a type, and also of the reassuring conservatism often characteristic of children's literature and film. Yet this conservatism inevitably contains within itself a radical seed too, in its very celebration of the desire for an uninhibited social role expressed by its central characters. So if science fiction is a more adult genre than fantasy fiction, then this reflects the differing roles played by belief in the imaginative play of both genres. In fantasy we see that the element of belief is highly visible. We have to "believe" to read this sort of fiction enjoyably (which is to say, we have to suspend disbelief, for that is what it is to believe) because the beliefs involved represent older beliefs (such as belief in fairies) which are no longer current in society. We say only children would believe such things, partly because we are at our most comfortable when our children play with the things which modern society at large has set aside and partly because we expect our children to experiment with belief. Science fiction, on the other hand, makes a play at presenting similar stories and tropes with a veneer of plausibility. At its most successful the modern reader can really believe science fiction, which is to say, regard it as truth, even while it discusses similar themes to those of fantasy fiction. But this is not because science fiction is true. Most patently it is not true. But then neither are the beliefs of adulthood truer than the beliefs of childhood. There is no more empirical evidence for the existence of a god than for the existence of the tooth fairy. In fact there is rather less! If a child pretends to be a doctor and is paid in toy money, how different is this from people whom adults believe to be doctors and who believe themselves well compensated if they are paid in similar looking strips of paper? The principal difference lies in the fact that tomorrow everyone will still believe the adults are doctors, even if the patients have failed in the night, and the doctors will still believe in the value of the small strips of paper and will be wondering how to obtain more.[15] If the doctors wish they could be something (or someone) else the following day, they will be hard pressed to persuade the other grown-ups that it is time to alter the premise of the game. They would be best advised to go and play with their children to satisfy that urge.

Childhood Empiricism

Why is it that Peter Pan exhorts us all to believe together? The answer is that only mass or collective belief really works wonders in our society. The chief failing of childlike individual belief is precisely that it fails to work any wonders. Although we associate belief with childhood, belief in Santa Claus, the Tooth Fairy and the Easter Bunny, we do this only in the same sense that we associate walking with toddlerhood. It is precisely because childhood is a time in which belief, by failing to be sufficiently coordinated with mass belief, fails to be transparent and becomes painfully visible. Childhood is not the age of belief except in the sense that it is the age of learning to believe. To function in the adult world one must assimilate many beliefs, from belief in religion to more practical matters such as the belief that exchanging actual goods or products for certain small strips of printed paper is actually a sensible thing to do. It turns out to be sensible behavior only because other people in possession of things we want share the belief that the pieces of paper are valuable in themselves. It is the long term persistence of belief in the power of money which makes the magic of the modern economy work. Children's belief, in remaining highly individualistic, must be left behind with the end of childhood.

So which children are the beasts who feel so offended by Peter's exhortation to believe that they actually hiss back at him? Some, naturally, are the ones who wish to grow up, who resent being treated as children so obviously as to be asked to believe. Such children are aware that adults are presumed to believe the things they need to believe. These children, if present during a performance of the play, are likely to be there somewhat unwillingly, perhaps on a family outing intended more for the enjoyment of a younger sibling. Others will object on grounds of privacy, perhaps either the very young, unready for the psychic shock of mass belief in the raw, or the older crew, realizing that adults don't normally need such crude exhortation to all believe the same thing. Finally there are those who actually believe in fairies. To them, Peter's appeal is insulting precisely because it presumes that fairies do not exist. Something which can only live if we believe in it is not real. By definition, the things that have reality continue to exist when we fail to believe in them. Thus money retains its value when a few individuals disdain it, because everyone else has continued to believe in it. Gold remains valuable because of this collective belief.[16] Those children who really do believe in fairies will be insulted by Peter's plea.

So ironically, many of those children most resistant to the notion of "never growing up," are likely to be the most resistant to Peter Pan's plea to save Tinker Bell by believing, as are those children who instinctively resent the request that they believe in something grown-ups have now rejected. Firstly because making something real by believing in it is only admitting that it was never real in the first place, and secondly because they sense that believing on cue is the very opposite of a child's nature, and so they reject it. As Pan exhorts them to believe children find themselves the focus of adult projections upon them of the anxieties of modernity, expected to believe and not to believe at the same time. Those who refuse to respond to these demands to conform, or not to conform, those who refuse to clap, or who even hiss, are responding to the exhortation to believe en mass by persisting in a private form of belief, belief in their own reality, in the reality of their own desires, if they privately wish that fairies more terrible than Tinker Bell really existed. Recall the Situationist's mantra, those apostles of the imagination ("All power to the imagination!") to whose chief spokesperson, Debord, I have already alluded, "I take my desires for reality because I believe in the reality of my desires." Or in the words of Buzz Lightyear, whose refusal to believe in his own unreality seems deeply Situationist, "To infinity, and beyond!" Paradoxically, sometimes the refusal to believe expresses the deepest commitment to belief.

Some don't clap, and a few beasts hiss.

NOTES

1. J.M. Barrie, *Peter Pan or the Boy Who Wouldn't Grow Up,* Play (London, 1904).
2. Margery Williams, *The Velveteen Rabbit or How Toys Become Real* (New York: Doubleday, 1922).
3. *Toy Story,* DVD, directed by John Lasseter (Emeryville, CA: Pixar, 1995).

4. Carlo Collodi, *The Adventures of Pinnochio* (1883).
5. *AI: Artificial Intelligence*, DVD, directed by Steven Spielberg (Universal City, CA: DreamWorks, 2001).
6. Brian Appleyard, "Why Don't We Love Science Fiction?" *The Sunday Times,* December 2, 2007, http://entertainment.timesonline.co.uk/tol/arts_and_entertainment/books/article2961480.ece.
7. *Star Wars: Episode IV–A New Hope*, DVD, directed by George Lucas (Century City, CA: 20th Century–Fox, 1977).
8. Walter de la Mare, *Rupert Brooke and the Intellectual Imagination* (London: Sidgwick & Jackson, 1919).
9. Ibid.
10. Oscar Wilde, *The Picture of Dorian Gray* (London: Ward, Lock and Company, 1891).
11. *The Legend of Frosty the Snowman*, DVD (New York: Classic Media, 2005).
12. *The Incredibles*, DVD, directed by Brad Bird (Emeryville, CA: Pixar Animation, 2004).
13. *Toy Story 2*, DVD, directed by John Lasseter (Emeryville, CA: Pixar Animation, 1999).
14. *Toy Story 3*, DVD, directed by Lee Unkrich (Emeryville, CA: Pixar Animation, 2010).
15. It may be objected that the critical difference between the adult belief in doctors and childhood play is that the grown-up doctor has actually gone through years of medical training. Generally speaking this is true enough, but note that patients and even, to a considerable extent, fellow professionals, must take the reality of this training on faith. Indeed doctors frequently mount their diplomas (more paper!) on the walls of their office to reinforce this belief. But studies, such as the ones recounted in *Dr. Golem: How to Think About Medicine* by Harry Collins and Trevor Pinch (Chicago: University of Chicago Press, 2008) suggest that patients and even medical professionals are sometimes taken in by charlatans who have no training as doctors but pass as such for years undetected, aided by the belief structure of the society around them. The reason this can happen is at least partly because some doctors are not particularly competent in spite of their training, but this is often compensated by the competence of their support staff, for instance nurses. Yet if the nurse is, in reality, the more competent person, adult belief structure does not permit patients to begin giving the nurse more of the small pieces of paper to reflect this. It is much easier to imagine children concluding that the little girl (perhaps Susie Derkins) playing the nurse is contributing more to the game than the little boy (Calvin) disinterested in playing the doctor and deciding to put the little girl in charge of the Monopoly money.
16. Recall Lenin's supposed claim that, in a future socialist society, gold would have no value and would be used to plate urinals, a claim that the Situationists, led by Debord, disillusioned with the decidedly repressive-to-the-imagination regime of Lenin's heirs, later threw back in his face, proposing that urinals be called lenins in future.

REFERENCES

AI: Artificial Intelligence. Film. Directed by Steven Spielberg. Universal City, CA: DreamWorks, 2001.
Appleyard, Brian. "Why Don't We Love Science Fiction?" *The Sunday Times,* December 2, 2007. http://entertainment.timesonline.co.uk/tol/arts_and_entertainment/books/article2961480.ece.
Barrie, J. M. *Peter Pan or the Boy Who Wouldn't Grow Up*. Play. First production, London, 1904.
Collins, Harry, and Trevor Pinch. *Dr. Golem: How to Think About Medicine*. Chicago: University of Chicago Press, 2008.
Collodi, Carlo. *The Adventures of Pinnochio*. 1883.
de la Mare, Walter. *Rupert Brooke and the Intellectual Imagination*. London: Sidgwick & Jackson, 1919.
The Incredibles. Directed by Brad Bird. Emeryville, CA: Pixar Animation, 2004.
The Legend of Frosty the Snowman. DVD. New York: Classic Media, 2005.
Toy Story. Film. Directed by John Lasseter. Emeryville, CA: Pixar Animation, 1995.
Star Wars. Film. Directed by George Lucas. Century City, CA: 20th Century–Fox, 1977.
Wilde, Oscar. *The Picture of Dorian Gray*. London: Ward, Lock and Company, 1891.
Williams, Margery. *The Velveteen Rabbit or How Toys Become Real*. New York: Doubleday, 1922.

PART 2. S IS FOR STRUCTURES OF POWER

• *Six* •

Forward to the Past: Anti-Fascist Allegory and "Blitz Spirit" Revisionism in *Daleks' Invasion Earth 2150 A.D.*

DANIEL O'BRIEN

It is widely believed that science fiction reflects the time in which it is produced, alongside the fantastical worlds it creates and explores. Political, social and cultural norms, among others, can be addressed in veiled form, enabling a boldness of approach that would be potentially problematic in more "realistic" literary, cinematic or televisual traditions. Discussing Darko Suvin's conception of science fiction as "the literature of cognitive estrangement,"[1] Edward James notes:

> The *novum*, or "fantastic element," of science fiction is its defining characteristic, in that it sets the fiction apart from the perceived world; but the aim is "estrangement," which allows the reader to learn about the perceived world by comparison with the fictional one.[2]

Whatever the limitations of this definition, which may appear somewhat simplistic, it pinpoints one of the most interesting aspects of science fiction in literature and other media. This is not to say that all science fiction offers a perceptive or interesting commentary, in whatever form, on the era of its creation; however, works in this genre gain additional resonance if they achieve such a connection for a significant number of people. This chapter examines a British film that uses its science-fiction format to address both the era of its creation and, predominantly a period of then recent history, the Second World

War. *Daleks' Invasion Earth 2150 A.D.* (1966), based on the BBC *Doctor Who* television serial "The Dalek Invasion of Earth" (1964), was the sequel to *Dr. Who and the Daleks* (1965). Both films aimed to exploit the popularity, especially among children, of *Doctor Who* and its leading villains the Daleks, malevolent aliens who inhabit mobile metal casings. I will argue that *Daleks' Invasion Earth 2150 A.D.* honed its source material into a pointed, if unintended allegory of, and commentary on, British resistance to Nazi Germany and, by extension, Britain's position on the international stage at the time of the film's production. *Daleks' Invasion Earth 2150 A.D.* also serves as a "what if..." fable, depicting a Britain invaded and seemingly conquered by fascist enemy forces. I am interested mainly in two aspects of this representation and their associated implications: the pessimistic portrayal of a futuristic Britain under siege, and the use of a child character as an embodiment, or avatar of the target juvenile audience.

To begin, I will outline the context of the film's production. Released in June 1965, *Dr. Who and the Daleks* did well at the UK box-office. According to the documentary *Dalekmania* (1995), the film was one of the top ten hits of its year, though this claim requires some qualification.[3] While it is generally held that the film did not repeat this success in the U.S.,[4] due partly to indifferent promotion and distribution, the UK returns alone justified another Dalek film. As with *Dr. Who and the Daleks*, *Daleks' Invasion Earth 2150 A.D.* was a co-production between Amicus, a company best known for its horror films, and Aaru Productions[5] which received sole billing on the credits as a condition of the deal. Peter Cushing reprised his role as benevolent scientist Doctor Who, atypical casting for the Hammer horror star.[6] Budgeted at £180,000, the sequel was shot at Shepperton Studios, Surrey, from January 31 to March 22, 1966.[7] Premiered in London on July 22, 1966, the film went on general release on August 5. Reasonably successful at the box-office, *Daleks' Invasion Earth 2150 A.D.* did not match the returns of its predecessor and plans for a follow-up were abandoned.

In some ways, *Daleks' Invasion Earth 2150 A.D.* was not doing anything radically new in equating its aliens with Nazi Germany. It is widely believed that writer Terry Nation, who created the Daleks,[8] always regarded them as a metaphor for the Nazis.[9] As a child, Nation had lived through the German blitzkrieg of 1940–41—a sustained bombing campaign intended to secure a quick British surrender—and been deeply affected by the experience.[10] The Daleks' initial representation, in the *Doctor Who* serial "The Mutants," aka "The Daleks" (1963–64) bears this out to an extent. Schoolteacher Ian Chesterton (William Russell), the Doctor's fellow space-time traveler, invokes ideas of xenophobia and racial purity, noting how Daleks have "a dislike for the unlike." Discussing the Thals, a mutated humanoid race of warriors turned farmers, the Daleks declare, "The only interest we have in the Thals is their total extermination" and, "Only one race can survive." Most memorably, Daleks raise their right "arms"[11] in a Nazi-style salute while chanting: "Tomorrow we will be the masters of the planet."

It could be argued that the 1966 film simply followed the blueprint of the sequel serial "The Dalek Invasion of Earth," with the characters and subplots inevitably re-tailored and condensed to the requirements of a feature film. I suggest that *Daleks' Invasion Earth 2150 A.D.* took the World War II allegory to a new level. In "The Dalek Invasion of Earth," Nazi parallels are contained largely in a few scattered lines of explicit dialogue rather than the images or subtext. Mine worker Wells (Nicholas Smith) refers to the Black Dalek leader as "the commandant of the camp"; a medley of Dalek chants includes "the final solution."[12] Some observers claim resistance leader Dortmun (Alan Judd) has a Churchillian quality in terms of his speeches and rhetoric, though his disastrous counter-strike against the Daleks undermines an already tenuous parallel. The film version dispenses with these direct references and is perhaps more effective for it, achieving its allegorical subtext through production design (sets and props), costume, characterization and imagery. I would also suggest that the reduction and modification of the narrative from six 25-minute episodes to a brisk 84-minute running time accentuated the allegorical elements in highly concentrated form.

On the most obvious level, the nominally futuristic landscape of *Daleks' Invasion Earth 2150 A.D.* evokes London during the blitz and the later V-1 and V-2 attacks of 1944. The establishing shots of 2150 London[13] depict a city in ruins, a backdrop of rubble and derelict buildings, including the familiar Battersea Power Station, with three of its four chimneys wrecked.[14] Later images of desolation include a burnt-out pub, another British institution. Doctor Who describes the atmosphere as "decaying" and this desolate setting is also treacherous. His granddaughter Susan (Roberta Tovey) inadvertently sets off a cascade of rubble and the Tardis, their space-time travel machine, is half-buried under debris, preventing an easy escape. A door opens into empty space and a potentially fatal drop to the ground. Public health warning posters also evoke World War II, advising citizens: "Do Not Drink Rainwater. All Water Must Be Boiled Before Consumption."

Despite the setting, few of the buildings left standing look like 1960s constructions, let alone designs from the 22nd century. This "future" England seems rooted firmly in early– to mid–20th-century architecture, looking backwards rather than forwards. Similarly, it is notable the civilian costumes in no way suggest a society nearly 200 years in the future. While budgetary restrictions were certainly a factor, this cannot have been the whole story. In the lower budgeted television serial, a lot of the costuming is vaguely futuristic or at least not obviously 1960s or earlier.[15] In the film, freedom fighter Wyler (Andrew Keir), the first human from 2150 to appear, is dressed in a donkey jacket,[16] flat cap and scarf, clothing that would comfortably fit a World War II setting. By and large, the human characters wear somber colors — grey, dark blue, black — with the men mostly in jackets, waistcoats, shirts and scarves. While these clothes would still have been worn in the mid–1960s, they are more evocative of the 1940s, at least in terms of popular images. Young rebel David (Ray Brooks), a gesture to the 1960s youth "revolution,"[17] wears a denim jacket and black turtleneck top, which suggest the 1950s rather than the 1940s but connote little of the "swinging sixties" and nothing of a 22nd century society.

The rebel base resembles a World War II munitions factory, which were staffed predominantly by female workers as many men were conscripted into the armed forces. Constructing bombs and overhauling firearms, the women on the rebel production line even wear the distinctive headscarves tied at the top — associated with women "doing their bit" for the war effort — that prevent their hair from getting caught in machinery and components. The wooden-cased radio set on which the rebels receive Dalek broadcasts also evokes a World War II image of civilians and resistance fighters listening to German orders and propaganda, most famously the *Germany Calling* broadcasts designed to undermine Allied morale. One shot frames the radio in close-up, emphasizing its "antique" nature and association with the past rather than the future. The van driven by Wyler would have been a vintage model in the 1960s, let alone 2150,[18] and the equipment seen in the location shots for the mine sequences could easily pre-date World War II. This is not to say the designers and art directors were deliberately invoking this war-time era, yet the budget constraints and key production choices result in a supposedly futuristic setting that evokes far more keenly the recent past.

The Dalek invasion is conveyed on an elemental level, the alien aggressors controlling the earth, the air, the water and — via their weapons — fire. We learn the entire planet was subjected to a blitzkrieg, whole continents wiped out to eliminate resistance to the subsequent invasion. The Daleks' guns, built into their metal casings, fire a form of gas[19] which, depending on the situation, is poisonous, corrosive and even explosive. The use of lethal gas has obvious parallels with the Nazi-run concentration camps, where mass executions were carried out using this method. Accompanied by the Daleks' signature cry of "Exterminate!" this image has an allegorical potency absent from the television serial. In *Dr. Who and the Daleks* there is only one humanoid fatality; the sequel, which opens with a brutal jewel heist, features numerous violent deaths, the camera lingering on the dying and the dead, the human race systematically culled by the Daleks. The narration on the UK trailer describes the Daleks as "men of steel, who have no flesh to pierce, no blood to spill." Rather than being soulless, emotionless robots, these invaders are men of a kind alien to the oppressed humans, familiar in some respects yet also horribly different, much as the Nazis were portrayed in British propaganda. The Daleks depict themselves as a superior race, "the masters of Earth"; humans must "obey the orders of your masters," if they are to be permitted survival as slave labor. The trailer also characterizes them as "the world's new dictators," another clear Nazi parallel.

It is notable that the Robomen, the Daleks' mentally-conditioned human ground troops, feature in the film's publicity as much as their alien masters. In the television serial, the Robomen are dressed in shabby work clothes marked with strange symbols in the Dalek language. The most obvious signs of their transformation are the large, awkward metal helmets that control their actions. Their slow, halting movement and speech is more unsettling than menacing. For all their thuggish behavior, these TV Robomen are pathetic rather than threatening, being unwilling victims of Dalek brainwashing. Episode one begins with a Roboman committing suicide, wrenching the collar from his helmet as he drowns himself in a polluted river. We learn that "robotization" is a short-lived process that inevitably brings on mental breakdown and self-destruction.

In the film, the Robomen wear shiny black overalls and crash helmets, the latter adorned with red stripes. This radically different costume design gives the Robomen a sleek, menacing appearance that plays up the parallels with Nazi soldiers — especially the black-clad SS stormtroopers[20] — while eliminating any traces of pathos. They are dehumanized further by mirrored glasses beneath their protective visors which obscure the eyes completely and render their faces emotionless. In the television serial, a subplot involving a character's search for his brother culminates with the discovery that the latter is now a Roboman, their dreadful reunion leaving both dead. The film does not dwell on the tragedy of this dehumanization and its consequences, focusing instead on the stormtrooper aspect. Dortmun (Godfrey Quigley) refers to Robomen as the "living dead" — in effect zombies — who are now the enemy and must be dealt with ruthlessly. The bowie knife-wielding David stabs two Robomen — one on camera — and impales a third on the thrown blade with nary a backward glance. A night-time shot of a Roboman operating a searchlight at the mining encampment also evokes an image familiar from numerous World War II POW films.

In one incongruous sequence, original to the film, the Robomen take a meal break, sitting in rows on two benches and clutching paper plates loaded with small, brightly colored pieces of food. The scene is staged and scored to depict — in humorous vein — the Robomen as mindless drones who do not even notice a disguised interloper in their midst. Having acknowledged and depicted the enemy as a threat, the film then ridicules him, a classic strategy of wartime propaganda. A later scene in a gloomy mineshaft restores the Robomen's more sinister aura. The robotized Craddock (Kenneth Watson) demonstrates independent thinking and ingenuity, removing his helmet so Tom (Bernard Cribbins), who was rescued from the same robotizing session, will mistake him for a normal human. The final images of the Robomen are surprisingly positive given their earlier depiction. Fleeing the mining area alongside the slave workers as the Daleks' plans go up in flames, they appear to have regained their free will and, by implication, their humanity. This suggests — however unintentionally — that the foot soldiers of fascist conquest and oppression are capable of redemption once the leaders and regime they serve have been overthrown, echoing Noel Coward's controversial wartime song, "Don't Let's Be Beastly to the Germans" (1943).

What is striking about the film, given its target audience of children, is the lack of reassurance over Britain's ability to fight back against the Dalek invaders. World War II–era films such as *Went the Day Well?* (1942) insisted that British spirit would triumph, despite overwhelming odds and the Nazis' underhanded tactics. *Daleks' Invasion Earth 2150 A.D.*, by contrast, shows a ruined country on the verge of total defeat. I suggest that, by the mid–1960s, 20 years after the end of World War II, there was enough distance from the conflict for a more measured and even critical response to the unconditionally positive recollections and representations of Britain under fire. At this point, it is necessary to address briefly the notion of the "blitz spirit" or even "blitz myth" that informed and influenced popular depictions of collective British wartime courage, both during and after World War II. Angus Calder suggests this notion of the blitz "supports a myth of British or English moral pre-eminence, buttressed by British unity."[21] The British people could endure the German aerial onslaught due to their moral superiority and ability to stand together, both of these qualities, by implication, transcending class, generation and gender. This strength of national character became gradually enshrined as modern myth, "the account of that event, or series of events, which was current by the end of the war has assumed a 'traditional' character, involves heroes, suggests the victory of a good God over a satanic evil, and has been used to explain a fact: the defeat of Nazism."[22] Dealing in moral absolutes, divine benevolence, and righteous triumph, this naive yet potent representation of Britain at war remained widely circulated throughout the 1950s, endorsed further by complementary depictions in popular media, whether film, television, radio, music, literature or journalism. Producers and consumers alike continued to subscribe, publicly at least to the consensus view, as summarized by Calder: "The Blitz proved that the British Had All Been In It Together (which was 'democratic') and had Taken It (which showed their strong moral backbone) and had Carried On (working towards well-deserved victory)."[23]

It should be emphasized that the myth of the blitz was by and large based on fact and by no means mere romantic fabrication concealing a dark and distasteful reality. Robert Mackay argues: "Like all propaganda, the official image of the British people heroically battling through this national crisis contained some exaggeration, but it was not a great departure from the truth."[24] However, the notion of a homogenous, harmonious and above all fearless response to the blitzkrieg risks downplaying the all-too human fears, doubts and weaknesses and the corresponding courage required in the face of sustained enemy assault. The first phase of bombardment, from April 1940 to June 1941, was both frightening and confusing for the British people.[25] Calder argues that "the national 'unity' was provisional, conditional, and potentially fragile. Latent pacifist feeling was widespread."[26] Nor was the general population fully cognizant of Britain's defensive capabilities — or lack thereof — at this time. The political and military leaders knew full well that the country lacked the organization, finance, resources, and equipment to mount an effective and sustained defense against Nazi invasion.[27] They were also aware this information had to be kept from the wider public to prevent a collapse in morale. Furthermore, Calder argues that Britain's initial failure to strike back against Nazi Germany in terms of significant victories abroad caused major problems for its leader: "In 1942 Churchill was fighting for his political life as discontent swelled at home over Britain's lack of military success, and it took Montgomery's victory at El Alamein in November to secure the Prime Minister's position for the rest of the war."[28]

These less palatable aspects of Britain at war had no place in the mythologized version of events, which remained dominant throughout the 1950s for a number of reasons. Calder states that the romanticized notion of the "blitz spirit" had valuable political currency long after the end of the war: "A consensual memory of 1940 was in fact an important basis for the political consensus which was achieved after the war."[29] Members of Parliament from all parts of the political spectrum made common appeal to British strength of character as exemplified by the blitz era. Over time, the political landscape altered, and this consensus finally ebbed away during the 1960s. By this time, as Calder suggests, information that questioned, or at least clarified the myth of the blitz, was readily available to scholars and interested members of the public.[30] I suggest *Daleks' Invasion Earth 2150 A.D.* reflects, to whatever degree, these increased opportunities and corresponding inclination to look beyond the established and widely circulated depictions of wartime spirit and identify more varied facets of public reaction to enemy attack and associated perils and deprivations.

There is a case for arguing that *Daleks' Invasion Earth 2150 A.D.* is, on its own level, confronting the early wartime situation as it really was: bleak, dangerous, demoralizing and, to some, near-hopeless. The dwindling resistance to the alien invaders is countered by opportunists and collaborators. In the television serial, rebel David Campbell (Peter Fraser) remarks: "Not all human beings are automatically allies. There are people who'd kill for a few scraps of food." While no such characters emerge in either the serial or the film, the British fighting spirit is conspicuously absent in several cases. Brockley (Philip Madoc) is a smooth-talking opportunist who does business with the mine workers, trading food for jewelry and other valuables. Dressed in a smart raincoat, which sets him apart from the mine workers and the rebels, he is a refined version of the World War II spiv, who sold black market goods at inflated prices. Ashton (Patrick O'Connell), the equivalent character in the television serial, is referred to as "the black marketer."[31] Brockley serves as an unwelcome reminder of the significant minority of people willing and able to exploit the wartime predicament and associated hardships of their fellow countrymen. Furthermore, this illegal trade could only flourish with the cooperation and complicity, however reluctant, of a viable number of paying customers. Donald Thomas notes: "By determined exploitation of shortages, the frontiers of crime could be extended throughout a thriving civilian black market. Men and women who might never have broken a law in peacetime would find themselves linked, distantly but inevitably, to the thief and the racketeer."[32] The black market potentially criminalized everyone involved, sellers and buyers, undercutting the myth of British stoicism and endurance in the face of hardship and deprivation.

From this perspective there is an interesting link between *Daleks' Invasion Earth 2150 A.D.* and *The Third Man* (1949), which deals with black markets in post-war Vienna. Brockley finds his equivalent in American racketeer Harry Lime (Orson Welles), who sells adulterated penicillin to hospitals where it poisons and kills child patients. Released just four years after the end of the war, *The Third Man* sidesteps any suggestion that such activities also happened in Britain, and, indeed, it is the British military police who are on Lime's tail, convincing the initially skeptical hero Holly Martin (Joseph Cotton), another American, of his former friend's criminal activities. *Daleks' Invasion Earth 2150 A.D.* offers no such reassurance, as Brockley, though Welsh rather than English, is assuredly British and preying on other Britons. While Ashton has only one scene, Brockley is a more prominent character, both an opportunist and a traitor. A cutthroat businessman in the most literal sense, Brockley holds a knife to Doctor Who's throat on their first encounter, "persuading" David to throw his shotgun aside. A dishonest trader, Brockley betrays the Doctor, as the latter anticipates, but underestimates Dalek ruthlessness, leaning casually against a wooden shed until he realizes they propose to exterminate him. Thus the opportunist is destroyed in explosive fashion by the same forces that enabled — albeit indirectly — his lucrative private enterprise.

Leaving aside the Robomen and the mine workers, who have little choice in the matter, the most notable collaborators are two women who live in a cottage near the mine and mend the workers' clothes in exchange for food. The younger woman (Sheila Steafel) greets Wyler and Susan with a shotgun but does not seem overly hostile. The older woman (Eileen Way) appears sympathetic to the travelers' plight: "You were lucky to get this far. The patrols are everywhere. They never stop, day or night." This could also be a wider reference to the changed world in which these women now live. Surrounded by occupying forces, they had two choices: cooperate and live or resist and die. Choosing to survive, they can no longer afford the luxury of traditional morality. Nevertheless, the women are depicted as pathetic and devious, betraying fellow humans for a few tins of food and a handful of fresh vegetables. Unlike Brockley, they face no punishment for this treachery within the film's diegesis, just as many wartime collaborators in occupied countries evaded justice.

The selfish attitudes of Brockley and the two women are contrasted with those of the rebels, especially the self-sacrifice shown by Dortmun and Conway (Keith Marsh), a mine worker who tackles Craddock so Tom may resume his mission to sabotage the Daleks' master plan. Yet the resistance group is clearly fighting a losing battle, as the film underlines on several levels. The underground rebel base, with its collection of shabby furniture and equipment, is depicted with low-key lighting, while the Dalek spaceship by contrast consists of bright metallic surfaces and flashing lights, connoting technology light years ahead of human achievement. Dortmun is confined to a wheelchair, his disability perhaps symbolizing the rebels' helplessness in the face of Dalek aggression.[33] Their weapons — bolt rifles, shotguns, knives — cannot harm the alien invaders, and the bombs on which Dortmun has staked victory prove useless for shattering the Dalek armor. During an attack on the spaceship, a long shot of Daleks advancing on the rebels like miniature tanks, ignoring the exploding bombs emphasizes human impotence against alien technology. After the rebels are defeated and mostly killed, the camera tracks across the debris-strewn battlefield as Robomen check the fallen humans for signs of life.

Depicting a futuristic Britain that draws heavily on a still vivid past, *Daleks' Invasion Earth 2150 A.D.* offers young viewers an unsettling message that self-sufficiency and courage may not be enough in the face of an overwhelming threat. At this point, I will consider the film's use of the character of Susan, Doctor Who's granddaughter, an obvious stand-in for the child audience. In the Doctor Who feature films, Roberta Tovey's Susan is significantly younger than her television counterpart, played by Carole Ann Ford, then in her early twenties, as a teenage schoolgirl.[34] In the early scenes of *Dr. Who and the Daleks*, Susan is established as a child prodigy, first seen reading a book entitled *Physics for the Inquiring Mind*. When Doctor Who introduces Ian (Roy Castle) to the TARDIS (Time and Relative Dimension in Space), Susan explains what the acronym means and shares her grandfather's delight in Ian's obvious bafflement. The Doctor refers to Susan as "my little fellow scientist" and credits her as co-inventor of the space time machine, "We've been working on TARDIS for many years."[35] While this extraordinary level of intelligence makes Susan a problematic figure in terms of child audience identification, other aspects of the character are much more familiar. Her delight in exploring a strange alien planet taps into a potent childhood fantasy. She skips unselfconsciously instead of walking, panics when startled by a strange presence and often holds her grandfather's hand. Contending with classic childhood fears, such as being left alone in the dark in an unfamiliar environment, she shows her bravery and is an active part of the team led by her grandfather. In the last third of the film, she becomes less active and has notably reduced screen-time, eventually serving as a passive diegetic spectator with no more influence on the narrative outcome than the audience. Fighting the Daleks, though exciting, has ultimately to be left to the adults.

Daleks' Invasion Earth 2150 A.D. plays down the super-intelligence associated with Susan in the earlier film, though she is the first to remark on the strangeness of 22nd century London, "No machines, no voices. And there aren't any birds." Stranded initially in a wrecked and besieged London, she undergoes experiences comparable to those of a child living through the blitz and then evacuated to supposed or at least relative safety. From Susan's perspective, the film is concerned partly with a child learning to trust and have faith in adults — including her extended family, new acquaintances and total strangers — and cope with unfamiliar situations and environments. Playing on a heap of rubble, equivalent to wartime bomb damage, she is nearly struck by a falling girder and rescued by Tom, a policeman representing the forces of law and order. Her twisted ankle is attended to by her aunt, Louise (Jill Curzon).[36] Separated from the Doctor and Louise for much of the film, Susan is evacuee, refugee and fugitive, left in the care of the friendly yet disabled Dortmun and the active yet emotionally distant Wyler. She cannot be shielded entirely from the horrors of the conflict and witnesses Dortmun's extermination by the Daleks, a medium close-up showing Susan close her eyes and turn her head away. When the Daleks destroy their transport, an antique van, Wyler protects the prone Susan from the explosion with his own body, and for the remainder of the film serves as a gruff yet benevolent avuncular figure. Susan feels secure enough in Wyler's company — and under his guardianship — to indulge in a child's game of hide-and-seek, a welcome distraction from the ever present Dalek peril. The only adults she encounters directly who prove untrustworthy and treacherous are the women who sell her and Wyler to the Daleks. Threatened with extermination, Susan is reunited with her grandfather, whose ingenuity will soon thwart the Dalek plans.

It is notable that Susan's new friends and allies from 2150 Britain offer only day-to-day survival rather than long-term protection and defense against the Daleks. For all the courage of the rebels, victory can only be secured through the intervention of Doctor Who, a mysterious figure apparently from 1960s Britain yet clearly not confined by its spatial-temporal boundaries. The Daleks identify the Doctor as the rebel leader, affirming that the latter has assumed the fallen Dortmun's role. It is Doctor Who's extraordinary intellectual prowess, coupled with Tom's physical endeavors in redirecting a crucial explosive device, that defeats the Daleks, rather than any wider British social, military or political organization. As with the American intervention and shifting Soviet alliance during World War II, the defeat of fascism — Nazi or Dalek — requires outside assistance transcending culture, nation, ideology, and, in the latter instance, time itself. In this respect, *Daleks' Invasion Earth 2150 A.D.* has an interesting antecedent in a little known Noel Coward play *Peace in Our Time* (1947). This drama imagines a World War II England where the Battle of Britain was lost and the Nazis launched a successful invasion and conquest. As with the 1966 film, this is a tale of resistance with, as Calder notes, only one collaborator.[37] However, while the British fighting spirit remains intact, the nation's deliverance from Nazi occupation is once more dependent on outside allies.

Calder argues that American involvement in Britain's struggle against Germany, in financial and military terms, had major and far reaching consequences way beyond the resolution of the immediate conflict: "Ironically, Churchill's determination to fight Hitler in 1940 hastened the conclusion of the British Empire overseas to which he was so totally devoted, and made Britain dependent on the United States."[38] For all its much vaunted worldwide influence and dominance, Britain could not afford an extended war and was heavily reliant on America from the earliest days of the conflict. Calder goes as far to argue: "The greatest single fact suppressed by the Myth of the Blitz is this: in 1940, because Churchill refused to give in, world power passed decisively away from Britain to the USA."[39] While this view can be criticized as simplistic or reductive, it is undeniable that America consolidated its position as one of the dominant world superpowers over the next two decades. By the mid–1960s, Britain was attempting to reinvent itself as a trusted global mediator, tempering the open distrust and frequent antagonism between the U.S. and the USSR, though its close ties to — and dependence on — the former made any claims of neutrality and impartiality problematic. In late 1964

Prime Minister Harold Wilson rejected President Lyndon B. Johnson's request for British troops to join U.S. forces in Vietnam, offering instead only policy support. As Paul Routledge suggests, Wilson "hankered after a peacemaking role, perhaps via the USSR, only to be thoroughly disabused by the Americans."[40] No longer significant on the world stage in terms of military power and struggling to find a position of influence in international diplomacy, Britain in 1966 seemed a long way from the celebrated bastion of anti–Nazi resistance. Furthermore, while few disputed the collective national resilience and courage manifested during the blitz, available documentation made it clear that British fighting spirit, though admirable in itself, had not alone prevailed against Nazi aggression during this period. Promoted as rousing, uncontroversial family entertainment, *Daleks' Invasion Earth 2150 A.D.* is notably at odds with the popular national image of the plucky British underdog routing the forces of evil. In this instance, at least, the film mirrors the actual events of the war and its aftermath a little too closely for comfort.

NOTES

1. Edward James, "Before the *Novum*: The Prehistory of Science Fiction Criticism," in *Learning from Other Worlds*, edited by Patrick Parrinder (Liverpool: Liverpool University Press, 2000), 29.
2. Ibid., 30.
3. For example, leading trade journal *Kine Weekly* did not include *Dr. Who and the Daleks* in its 1965 list of Top Ten General Releases, though the film was mentioned in the also-ran "money-makers" section of the article. See *Sixties British Cinema*, edited by Robert Murphy (Canterbury: University of Kent, 1986), 198–199.
4. Kevin Heffernan takes a dissenting view, stating, "*Dr. Who and the Daleks* was a huge success for [U.S. distributor] Continental in both its 1965 first-run release and on the kiddie matinee circuit for the rest of the decade." See Heffernan, *Ghouls, Gimmicks, and Gold: Horror Films and the American Movie Business, 1953–1968* (Durham, NC: Duke University Press, 2004), 211.
5. Philip Nutman, "Scream and Scream Again: The Uncensored History of Amicus Productions," *Little Shoppe of Horrors* 20 (June 2008), 46.
6. On television, the Doctor was played by veteran character actor William Hartnell (1908–1975). The demanding TV production schedule would have made Hartnell's participation in the film spin-offs problematic. In any case, Amicus and Aaru needed a bigger name to attract interest from overseas, especially the U.S., where *Doctor Who* was unknown. Cushing (1913–1994) was an established star of low budget British horror and fantasy films, most notably for Hammer. He had appeared in the earlier Amicus films *Dr. Terror's House of Horrors* (1964), co-funded by Aaru executive Joe Vigoda, and *The Skull* (1965).
7. Nutman, "Scream and Scream Again," 47–48. The production ran slightly over schedule after Cushing fell ill with a flu virus and shooting had to be suspended for two days.
8. To clarify, Nation devised the concept of the Daleks and is the credited scriptwriter of the first three *Doctor Who* serials in which they featured, along with several of their subsequent appearances. The distinctive look of the Daleks was the work of BBC staff designer Raymond Cusick.
9. See, for example, Nutman, "Scream and Scream Again," 46.
10. In the early 1960s, there were still bomb-damaged areas of London awaiting reconstruction, nearly two decades after the war ended.

11. Essentially a rubber suction cup on an extendable metal rod, connected to the Dalek casing by a ball and socket joint. In "The Dalek Invasion of Earth" two Daleks raise their plungers by the Albert Memorial, one of London's best known tourist landmarks. This image is framed in long shot, making the Nazi salute parallels less pronounced.

12. Freedom fighter Tyler (Bernard Kay) alludes indirectly to the slaughter of the First World War, where soldiers armed with bayonets charged machine gun installations.

13. In the original serial, the Doctor and his companions know they are back in London for the first time since the opening story but not when.

14. This is a carryover from the television serial, though the color matte painting in the film is a more effective representation than the black and white illustration in the original.

15. On the other hand, the television costumes did not have to withstand the same level of scrutiny as they were designed for a small, 405 line black and white screen rather than 35mm Technicolor and Techniscope projected on a large cinema screen.

16. A short coat, usually black or dark blue, made of tough material, often wool, with shoulder coverings made from leather or a similarly durable material. The term "donkey jacket" was first used in the 1920s and the garment is associated with manual workers employed out of doors.

17. Brooks was promoted in the film's trailer as "The boy with the knack," a reference to his role in the "swinging" sex comedy *The Knack ... and How to Get It* (1965) as a hedonistic womanizer.

18. In the television serial, the van used by Barbara (Jacqueline Hill) and Jenny (Anne Davies) is an exhibit at the London Transport Museum, kept in working order over the years for use in parades. While this rationalization may be contrived, the film attempts no such explanation.

19. An effect achieved with carbon dioxide fire extinguishers. In the television series, the impact of a Dalek gun opening fire was achieved by opening fully the aperture of the electronic camera, which put the image into negative. As this technique would not work with a film camera, producing only a milky glare, a different approach was required for the big screen adaptations.

20. The SS are commonly attributed with overseeing the majority of Nazi Germany's war crimes, including the organization and implementation of the Holocaust.

21. Angus Calder, *The Myth of the Blitz* (London: Jonathan Cape, 1991), 2.

22. Ibid.

23. Ibid., 230.

24. Robert Mackay, *Half the Battle: Civilian Morale in Britain During the Second World War* (Manchester and New York: Manchester University Press, 2002), 87.

25. Calder, *The Myth of the Blitz*, 18.

26. Ibid., 90.

27. Ibid., 29.

28. Ibid., 38.

29. Ibid., 46.

30. Ibid., xiii.

31. In both serial and film, it is unclear how Ashton/Brockley's business works in terms of profit. Where do his supplies of food come from? Is there a market in precious metals that enables him to obtain more foodstuffs as required?

32. Donald Thomas, *An Underworld at War: Spivs, Deserters, Racketeers and Civilians in the Second World War* (London: John Murray, 2003), xi.

33. There is some additional irony here, in that Dortmun's rolling movement in the wheelchair resembles the gliding motion of his mortal enemies, the Daleks.

34. Roberta Tovey was eleven at the time of filming *Dr. Who and the Daleks* and twelve when she worked on the sequel. Ford was 23 when she recorded "The Daleks."

35. Given Susan's extreme youth, this line makes little sense.

36. The characters of Barbara, Susan's older sister, and Ian, Barbara's boyfriend, are absent from the film as actors Jennie Linden and Roy Castle were unavailable to reprise their roles.

37. Calder, *The Myth of the Blitz*, 251.

38. Ibid., 48.

39. Ibid., 52.

40. Paul Routledge, *Wilson* (London: Haus Publishing, 2006), 57.

References

Calder, Angus. *The Myth of the Blitz*. London: Jonathan Cape, 1991.
"The Dalek Invasion of Earth." *Doctor Who*. Television Serial. Directed by Richard Martin. BBC-TV: 1964.
"The Daleks." *Doctor Who*. Television Serial. Directed by Christopher Barry and Richard Martin. BBC-TV, 1963–1964.
Dalekmania. Documentary Film. Directed by Kevin Davies. Amity Productions, 1995.
Daleks' Invasion Earth 2150 A.D. Film. Directed by Gordon Flemyng. Aaru: 1966.
Doctor Who and the Daleks. Film. Directed by Gordon Flemyng. Aaru-Amicus, 1965.
Heffernan, Kevin. *Ghouls, Gimmicks, and Gold: Horror Films and the American Movie Business, 1953–1968*. Durham, NC: Duke University Press, 2004.
James, Edward. "Before the *Novum*: The Prehistory of Science Fiction Criticism." In *Learning from Other Worlds*, edited by Patrick Parrinder, 19–35. Liverpool: Liverpool University Press, 2000.
Mackay, Robert. *Half the Battle: Civilian Morale in Britain During the Second World War*. Manchester and New York: Manchester University Press, 2002.
Murphy, Robert. *Sixties British Cinema*. Canterbury: University of Kent, 1986.
Nutman, Philip. "Scream and Scream Again: The Uncensored History of Amicus Productions." In *Little Shoppe of Horrors* no. 20 (June 2008).
Routledge, Paul. *Wilson*. London: Haus Publishing, 2006.
The Third Man. Film. Directed by Carol Reed. London Film Productions, 1949.
Thomas, Donald. *An Underworld at War: Spivs, Deserters, Racketeers and Civilians in the Second World War*. London: John Murray, 2003.
Went the Day Well? Film. Directed by Alberto Cavalcanti. Ealing, 1942.

• *Seven* •

The Search for a "More Civilized Age," or the Failure of Utopian Desire in the *Star Wars* Franchise

R. C. NEIGHBORS

For its more than thirty-year history, *Star Wars* (1977) and the franchise it spawned have often been maligned by science-fiction (hereafter sf) critics. Mark Bould, for instance, calls the first film of the franchise (*Star Wars Episode IV: A New Hope*) a "juvenile narrative,"[1] and Gary Westfahl states that it is "less mature and innovative as sf" than *Star Trek*.[2] However, despite possible problems with *A New Hope*, it is extremely important in the history of sf film. Bould admits that along with *Close Encounters of the Third Kind* (1977), *A New Hope* "represent[s] a turning point in American cinema."[3] Adilifu Nama even goes so far as to say that "no other film in the history of science-fiction cinema has had an impact on the collective popular consciousness of American society to the degree that *Star Wars* has,"[4] and this is certainly the case.

In 2005 CNN reported that the five *Star Wars* films at the date of the report (along with their merchandise) had out-grossed all twenty-one James Bond films combined.[5] At the time of this writing, *A New Hope* has spawned six feature film prequels and sequels (including one that is computer animated), four cartoon series, over a hundred novels, literally thousands of toys, and an untold number of other media and merchandise. Our culture is saturated with *Star Wars*, and it is this saturation — the enormous, continued cultural impact of *Star Wars*, even after over thirty years — that continues to justify rigorous scholarly attention. As sf writer Ursula Le Guin states, "All fiction has ethical, political, and social weight, and sometimes the works that weigh the heaviest are those apparently fluffy or escapist fictions whose authors declare themselves 'above politics,' 'just entertainers' and so on."[6] For these reasons, we must be cognizant of the ethical, political, and social ideologies — among other things — that *Star Wars* perpetuates, that it teaches its fans, young and old.

On the surface, *Star Wars* is rather simplistically about "good" versus "evil." More specifically, the original trilogy[7] deals with a rebellion against an oppressive empire, while the prequel trilogy centers around the heroes' attempts to overcome the machinations of predatory capitalism and a corrupt government. For these reasons, even though it is not a particularly *progressive* film franchise, the *Star Wars* saga portrays a clear utopian desire. However, certain aspects of the franchise undermine the utopian potential *Star Wars* offers, aspects such as the portrayal — and almost absence — of racial minorities in the films, the marginalization of women, and the treatment of violence.

It may be prudent to begin with what is meant when discussing sf and utopian desire. It has often been said that sf is a literature of ideas. Through the use of familiar tropes, such as spaceships, aliens, and ray guns, the genre uses the future (and sometimes the past) to comment on the present — on current social, cultural, and political ideologies. In this way, sf causes, what Darko Suvin calls, "cognitive estrangement."[8] Cognitive estrangement seeks, through events, settings, and circumstances that are unusual, to make readers (or viewers) consider alternative perspectives to the status quo. Some critics, such as Carl Freedman, point out that Suvin's definition of sf would disqualify *Star Wars* as an sf text, since, while *Star Wars* may be estranging — in that its outer-space milieu differs substantially from the viewer's environment — it is not seeking to actuate its viewer's cognition. In short, it seems more interested in entertainment than in promoting or challenging any particular ideological stance; it does not try to make the audience *think*. However, as Istvan Csicsery-Ronay, Jr., says about Freedman, "[his] conception of sf recapitulates that of Suvin: sf implies critical utopias even when it does not construct them explicitly in the narrative."[9] In other words, sf initiates cognition — specifically cognition on utopian ideals — even when it does not do so intentionally.[10]

Therefore, when discussing utopian desire, *Star Wars* is not strictly analogous to classical utopian texts, in the vein of Thomas More's *Utopia*. What is meant is related to the ideas that originate with Ernst Bloch and, more recently, are promoted by, among others, Fredric Jameson — namely that utopia exists in cultural texts as a means of improving society, as a desire to make the future better than the present, or as Jameson states, as "the imperative to imagine [alternatives to our present state]."[11] Bloch explains that "the world-substance ... is not yet finished and complete, but persists in a utopian-open state, i.e. a state in which its self-identity is not yet manifest"[12] and that "the designated realm of freedom develops not as return, but as exodus — though into the always intended promised land, promised by process."[13] Utopia, in this sense, then, is the striving of human beings — even as a form of psychological drive — to manifest the "good place" of a classical utopia, a striving away from the status quo toward the freedom of, what Bloch calls, our "homeland." Acknowledging the Marxist principles behind these ideas, Freedman refers to this place as "the unalienated classless homeland of a postrevolutionary future."[14]

According to Bloch, the primary role of utopia, then, is to critique society's current state.[15] Jameson elaborates on this idea: "at best Utopia can serve the negative purpose of making us more aware of our mental and ideological imprisonment."[16] The awareness happens through what Bloch calls a novum, "a *radical* novelty ... [that] ... reconstitute[s] the entire surrounding world and thus, in a sense, creates ... a new world."[17] This idea is related to Suvin's idea of cognitive estrangement,[18] in that a novum produces the phenomenon. Acknowledging the relationship between Bloch's utopian Hope Principle and sf, Csicsery-Ronay writes:

> Bloch argued that all manifestations of culture, even artistically worthless escapist formulas, include some utopian aspect, if only because they deny conditions as they are and activate wishes to make life manageable and pleasurable. This combination of critical denial and wish-fulfillment is particularly active in sf, since it is concerned with the wishing into being of imaginary worlds constructed on ostensibly rational principles.[19]

Sf is perfectly structured to present Blochian novums and therefore establish utopian desire within its texts.

Having established, then, the place of utopian desire within all aspects of culture (and sf in particular), it is important now to turn to how utopia presents itself within the *Star Wars* film franchise.

Utopian Desire in the *Star Wars* Films

Utopian desire in the *Star Wars* franchise arises largely within the surface narratives of each trilogy of films. Interestingly, it also presents itself differently in each trilogy, perhaps as a result of the time period each trilogy was released in. However, drawing definitive, real-world equivalencies to the events and characters of the *Star Wars* films can be challenging.

The surface narrative of the original trilogy deals with a rebellion against an oppressive Empire. Nonetheless, when attempts are made to draw analogies between the films and the real world, interpretations become complex and even contradictory. As M. Keith Booker notes in *Alternate Americas: Science*

Fiction and American Culture, the most common reading of the original trilogy is that of a Cold War narrative, with the Empire representing the Soviet Union and the Rebellion representing the West.[20] In fact, George Lucas, creator of the franchise, acknowledges that "a very powerful and technological superpower trying to take over a little country of peasants was big on my mind [during the writing of *Star Wars*],"[21] a process that occurred toward the end of the Vietnam War and Nixon's presidency. This seems to lend credence to *Star Wars* as a Cold War narrative with the Soviet Union in place of the Empire,[22] at least insofar as authorial intent is concerned.

Conversely, critics also often read the Empire as symbolic of the United States. For instance, Richard Keller Simon states that Darth Vader symbolizes "the evils of American imperial militarism."[23] Another possible reading, offered by Booker, which builds on the idea of America-as-Empire, is particularly subversive, considering today's political climate. He mentions how, by the time of *Star Wars*' release, revolutions were associated by-and-large with socialist revolutions. That aspect alone causes problems for the interpretation of the Rebellion as a force for Western ideals, or for American values in particular. However, Booker continues:

> ...the Empire, with its vastly superior resources and technology, would seem to play the role in galactic politics that the United States now plays in world politics. Similarly, the underequipped but staunchly determined rebels seem ... [like] ... the anticolonial fighters of the second half of the twentieth century and various Third World resistance movements of today, such as the Zapatistas of Mexico or even the dreaded Al-Qaeda, who, like Luke and Obi-Wan, emerged from their desert homes, buoyed by their spiritual beliefs to think they can fight an opponent with vastly superior technological resources.[24]

The parallels of this interpretation are particularly surprising and even alarming, considering how groups such as Al-Qaeda have been demonized as terrorists by the West. Of course, Westerners do not want to allow for the possibility that they are on the wrong side of a fight between hypothetical "good" and "evil."[25] In fact, during the recent Bush administration, the President repeatedly framed the foreign policy narrative in these terms, albeit with America as the embodiment of "good," showing the appealing nature of this rhetoric to modern Americans.

While critics largely disagree on which groups are symbolized in *Star Wars*, most critics do agree that the *Star Wars* franchise holds to a largely conservative ideology, critic Adam Roberts even calling it "profoundly conservative."[26] Roberts also points out the nostalgic nature of the films, especially *A New Hope*. He writes, "...it is the backward-looking aspects of the film that are dominant. So it is no coincidence that this film begins with the legend 'A Long Time Ago, in a Galaxy Far Away....'"[27] Lucas has said that many of the inspirations for the films were the serials he watched as a child, namely *Flash Gordon* and *Buck Rogers*, showing a certain nostalgia on the part of the creator for the era of his childhood. However, within even the narrative of *A New Hope* itself, there is a definite nostalgia for older, "*better*" times, represented by the Old Republic, the democratic government in place before the rise of the Empire. Obi-Wan Kenobi calls the Old Republic "a more civilized age,"[28] contrasted with the narrative present of the film as "the dark times." Even over-and-above this nostalgia, some critics have seen conservative values promoted in the films. Michael Ryan and Douglas Kellner, for instance, see the values of the Rebel Alliance as "individualism, elite leadership, and freedom from state control,"[29] which they negatively equate with the Neoconservatives of the Reagan era.

As has been shown, there are a variety of possible readings of the original trilogy of films,[30] some of which are even conflicting. Commenting on these contradictory readings, Kevin J., Wetmore, Jr. writes, "People see their own beliefs reflected in the films and see numerous (and often contradictory) real world equivalents of events, characters and elements."[31] He attributes this to a seemingly intentional avoidance of paralleling real-world politics in the films.[32] He concludes, "In short, *Star Wars* is rather contradictory and embraces a wide variety of different and differing ideologies"[33]; however, "the message remains that rebellion against an evil, economically oppressive Empire is 'good.'"[34] All this to say that while it is difficult to see utopian desire through a historical reading of the films — given the opposing interpretations available — utopian energy can still be seen, apart from any real-world political correspondences.[35]

In short, utopian desire is seen in the veneer of the series, in the surface narrative itself. Acknowledging this, Wetmore writes that *Star Wars* "celebrates freedom, adventure, and resistance to oppressive forces."[36] In the original trilogy, these utopian desires are represented through the rebellion against an oppressive, totalitarian regime, a government defined by its militarism and bigotry. Since the films are clearly pro–Rebellion and anti–Empire, it follows that the films are — on the surface anyway — against such oppression.

Through this narrative, the films seek to promote freedom and tolerance. For instance, the Rebellion is much more tolerant than the Empire, having non-humans in its officer corps, even featuring a Mon Calamari alien as an admiral. The Empire, on the other hand, is made up entirely of white humans (interestingly with British accents). The only aliens ever shown on Imperial ships are contracted bounty hunters, found in *The Empire Strikes Back* (1980), creatures an Imperial officer calls "scum."[37] Furthermore, the Rebellion's resistance to what amounts to a form of fascism seems to promote ideas consistent with Freedman's "classless ... postrevolutionary future."[38]

In the prequel trilogy, however, the villains — and therefore the opponents to utopian ideals — change. In the place of a repressive government, we find a corrupt bureaucracy, complete with predatory capitalists. The corrupt government seems to point to the dangers of any government possibly hindering utopia, not just a totalitarian one as in the original trilogy. Of particular danger is excessive bureaucracy, such as can be seen in many Western countries today, which can result in a veritable barrier to progress, or even action of any kind.

Along with bureaucracy, capitalism is also coded as an impediment to utopia in the films. In the opening scrawl of *The Phantom Menace* (1999), it states that "the taxation of trade routes to outlying star systems is in dispute."[39] While it is uncertain if the Naboo attempt to tax the Trade Federation or vice versa, the Trade Federation is unquestionably shown as the aggressor and villains of the film, so it seems reasonable to assume that Naboo is the victim of the predatory capitalism practiced by the "greedy" Trade Federation. Furthermore, most of the organizations involved in the Separatist Movement (read: the villains) of the next two prequels are related to capitalist enterprise: the Trade Federation, the Techno Union, the InterGalactic Banking Clan, the Commerce Guild, and the Corporate Alliance, among others. In their quest for peace and justice, then, the heroes of the prequel trilogy must fight both corrupt politicians and capitalists — groups who are interestingly in league with one another — promoting by proxy a resistance to corrupt government and the capitalist system in reality, in order to strive toward utopia.

However, the presentation of utopian desire in the *Star Wars* films is not so simplistic. While the surface narratives may argue against bigotry and imperial violence, the implications of various other aspects of the *Star Wars* films do exactly the opposite. In fact, utopian desire in the *Star Wars* franchise fails in at least three ways — the portrayal of racial minorities, the marginalization of women, and the treatment of violence.

The Failure of Utopian Desire

The first, and perhaps most obvious, way utopian desire fails is related to how racial minorities are portrayed in the films. It seems an *obvious* failure because racial minorities are nearly absent from the series. In fact, *A New Hope* has no non-white, human characters in the entire film. While this may not have been an intentional omission on the part of *Star Wars*' creators, Stuart Hall argues that "an ideological discourse does *not* depend on the conscious intentions of those who formulate statements within it."[40] In other words, an ideology of exclusion is presented no matter the intention. The only recurring, non-white humans in the series of films are Lando Calrissian (played by Billy

Dee Williams), introduced in *Empire*, and Jedi Master Mace Windu (played by Samuel L. Jackson), introduced in *Phantom Menace*. However, these two characters remain largely on the margins. The white male utterly dominates the *Star Wars* universe.[41]

In his book on blackness in sf film, Nama discusses at length racial issues in the *Star Wars* franchise, spending several pages specifically on the character of Lando. Nama acknowledges that the appearance of Lando in the sequels is most often discussed as a "sidekick" or "token position," even stating that it "smacks" of Hollywood tokenism.[42] However, Nama argues for a more complex reading of the character. He offers that Lando's position in the Empire is analogous to the divided loyalties of middle-class African Americans in the 1980s, loyalties divided between "alliances with whites in their same class" and "their 'duty' to give back to the black community."[43] He also suggests that Lando's betrayal of Han points to a racial message that "whites must be guarded toward blacks, and blacks must be evaluated according to their degree of allegiance to white interests."[44] Admittedly, while this may be a more complex reading of the character of Lando, it is still a decidedly negative one, which continues to reflect poorly on the films. Nonetheless, Nama does offer that the complexity of Lando's character in the Star Wars films is "markedly different" from African American characters in previous sf films — citing such examples as *Planet of the Apes* (1968) where the sole African American character dies within minutes of the film's beginning — Lando's marking "a trend toward increased racial inclusion in the sf film genre."[45]

Perhaps even more troubling, though, is the encoding of the aliens in the series as racial "others." Nama argues for this symbolic reading of non-humans from the near omission of non-white characters in the films.[46] The reading is only strengthened by offensive, racial stereotypes represented by Jar Jar Binks and other aliens. Wetmore writes that these racial "others" are characterized as "alien, primitive, and undeveloped,"[47] as well as "dangerous, cute, or buffoonish."[48] Nama notes that they are "unequivocally abnormal and threatening."[49] This is perhaps most clearly seen through the classic cantina scene from *A New Hope*. Just prior to the scene, Obi-Wan describes Mos Eisley spaceport as a "wretched hive of scum and villainy."[50] Cut to the only locals presented to the viewer — strange aliens in the cantina, implying their scummy and villainous natures. During the scene, Obi-Wan's words are shown to be true, when two of these dirty aliens pick a fight with protagonist Luke Skywalker (played by Mark Hamill). The series also repeatedly uses several epithets for alien species, such as "filthy Jawas" and "walking carpet,"[51] among others. In short, aliens are routinely treated, in one way or another, as subhuman and are consequently marginalized.[52] By association, non-white humans receive the same position. As Wetmore writes, "The disenfranchised of the galaxy remain so, regardless of which group is in power. The Empire uses violence to suppress and the Republic simply ignores the margins."[53]

Another group continually marginalized in the films are women, reiterating the dominance of the white *male* in the series. The only two women that have much screen time within the two trilogies are Leia Organa (played by Carrie Fisher) and Padmé Amidala (played by Natalie Portman), a princess and a queen, respectively, echoing the fairy tales that inform the roles the two women predominantly play in the franchise—that of the damsel in distress. While both women are headstrong and occasionally participate in the fighting, overwhelmingly they serve the narrative as objects of rescue and desire. These goals are even conjoined in such sequences as the escape from Jabba's palace in *Jedi*, where Fisher wears a very revealing "slave girl" outfit, which is nothing more than a loincloth and metal bra.

All other females remain on the periphery of the narrative.[54] In the prequel trilogy, a few female Jedi are added to the catalog of characters, even being given the honor of wielding a phallic lightsaber; however, these characters have very few minutes of screen time, and their names are not even mentioned within the trilogy. Of note is the presence of Mon Mothma in *Jedi*, as the leader of the Rebellion; however, she also has only minutes of screen time, her name is not disclosed in the film, and she does not participate in the final battle against the Death Star.[55]

Along with pushing women and racial minorities to the margins, *Star Wars* also glorifies violence. Now, it should be expected that a film series with the word "wars" in the title would have some violence within the narrative; however, there are definite problems with the way violence is treated in the series. Wetmore notes that it is not only the Empire who uses violence: the Rebellion follows the Empire's example, using violence to achieve their ends and gain power.[56] He writes, "clearly a distinction is made in the use of violence. Violence is good when 'we' use it and bad when 'they' use it."[57] The distinction seems interestingly to follow the cultural rhetoric of the United States concerning revolution, as in "our" revolution against colonizing forces is to be celebrated, while "other" revolutions are to be denounced. However, the treatment of violence in *Star Wars* brings up an even more troubling proposition:

> One does not have to think of one's enemies as human if they are evil. In fact, if one's enemies are evil, one has a moral obligation to destroy them. If an action is good, we do it and if we do it, it must be good. The logic is circular but results in an ideology that justifies militarism, imperialism, and conquest.[58]

This kind of stance is how religious fundamentalists justify suicide bombings and the murder of workers at abortion clinics, yet the ideas are clearly presented within the *Star Wars* franchise. Perhaps the most glaring example is the destruction of the Death Star[s]. In *A New Hope*, the rebels, including Luke Skywalker, attack the first Death Star not long after the Imperials have performed the horrific act of destroying the entire planet of Alderaan. However, the attack results in Luke performing nearly the same massacre that was implicitly denounced earlier in the film, killing possibly millions of people. Not only does the film fail to consider Luke's action in this light, it rewards him with a medal for his actions!

The division of people into a dichotomy of "good" and "evil," followed by the use of that division to justify unmitigated violence is inherently problematic. Likewise, the seeming marginalization in the film of both females and racial minorities is antithetical to the inclusive idea of utopia.

Conclusion

While the *Star Wars* franchise seeks to promote utopian ideals — namely freedom; interspecies and racial tolerance; and, deliverance from totalitarian, bureaucratic, and capitalist regimes — it subverts some of these very principles. Roberts remarks, rather condemningly, "this is the way ideology masks itself: it pretends to be forward-looking to disguise its conservatism"; however, he continues, "there is something more here, a sense in which this is the creative tension at the core of the *Star Wars* films, the contradiction that powers their unique appeal."[59] And truthfully, *Star Wars* is a contradiction — both progressive and regressive, forward-looking and nostalgic, utopian and dystopian. It is this contradiction — these failures — that most define *Star Wars*, but paradoxically it is also through these failures — the racism, the misogyny, and the violence — that the saga achieves some measure of success.

As Jameson writes, "at best Utopia can serve the negative purpose of making us more aware of our mental and ideological imprisonment ... therefore the best Utopias are those that fail the most comprehensively."[60] Through its utopian desire, *Star Wars* shows us certain ideals that should be sought after, and through its failures, *Star Wars* shows us areas that must be addressed in humanity's pursuit of utopia. The films hold up a mirror to Western society, and when we see the imperfections[61] — both in the films and in ourselves — *Star Wars* spurs us onward, toward a better future.

NOTES

1. Mark Bould, "Film and Television," in *The Cambridge Companion to Science Fiction*, edited by Edward James and Farah Mendlesohn (New York: Cambridge University Press, 2003), 92.
2. Gary Westfahl, "Space Opera," in *The Cambridge Companion to Science Fiction*, edited by Edward James and Farah Mendlesohn (New York: Cambridge University Press, 2003), 205.
3. Bould, "Film and Television," 91.

4. Adilifu Nama, *Black Space: Imagining Race in Science Fiction Film* (Austin: University of Texas Press, 2008), 28.

5. Krysten Crawford, "The 'Star Wars' Blitzkrieg," *CNN.com*, 13 May 2005, http://money.cnn.com/2005/05/13/news/newsmakers/starwars/index.htm.

6. Ursula K. Le Guin, *Dancing at the Edge of the World: Thoughts on Words, Women, Places* (New York: Grove, 1989), 198–199.

7. Or "holy trilogy" as comedian Kevin Smith refers to it, humorously denoting the almost religious devotion granted the series by its committed fans ... as well as the often negative view of the prequel trilogy.

8. Darko Suvin, "Estrangement and Cognition," in *Speculations on Speculation: Theories of Science Fiction,* edited by James Gunn and Matthew Candelaria (Lanham, MD: Scarecrow Press, 2005), 24.

9. Istvan Csicsery-Ronay, Jr., "Marxist Theory and Science Fiction," in *The Cambridge Companion to Science Fiction,* edited by Edward James and Farah Mendlesohn (New York: Cambridge University Press, 2003), 120.

10. Of course, if one follows Freedman and others and clings steadfastly to the idea that *Star Wars* is not sf but is instead fantasy, the question arises of whether fantasy results in cognitive estrangement. However, that question would require a whole essay (or more) unto itself. For the purposes of this chapter, it is more important that one recognizes the messages *Star Wars* conveys to its audience than that *Star Wars* is identified either as sf or fantasy. Nonetheless, I will take for granted — based on its tropes and milieu, among other things — that the *Star Wars* franchise is, in some sense, sf.

11. Fredric Jameson, *Archaeologies of the Future: The Desire Called Utopia and Other Science Fictions* (New York: Verso, 2005), 416.

12. Ernst Bloch, *A Philosophy of the Future*, translated by John Cumming (New York: Herder and Herder, 1970), 96.

13. Ernst Bloch, *The Principle of Hope*, translated by Neville Plaice, Stephen Plaice and Paul Knight, 3 vols. (Cambridge: MIT Press, 1986), 1:205.

14. Carl Freedman, *Critical Theory and Science Fiction* (Middletown, CT: Wesleyan University Press, 2000), 65. Naturally, situating utopia within Marxist ideology does beg the question of how and why it (and not conservative capitalism, for example) is utopian. However, that question is outside the bounds of this essay. Suffice it to say that the rapidly dwindling middle class and growing economic inequality of late capitalism would seem to preclude it from leading to a better future for *all*.

15. Ernst Bloch, *The Utopian Function of Art and Literature*, translated by Jack Zipes and Frank Mecklenburg (Cambridge: MIT Press, 1988), 12.

16. Jameson, *Archaeologies of the Future*, xiii.

17. Freedman, *Critical Theory and Science Fiction*, 69.

18. This makes sense considering that Bloch very much influenced Suvin.

19. Csicsery-Ronay, "Marxist Theory and Science Fiction," 119.

20. M. Keith Booker, *Alternative Americas: Science Fiction and American Culture* (Westport, CT: Praeger, 2006), 116.

21. Quoted from Tom Roston, "Holy Smith!" *Premiere,* May 2005, 55.

22. It seems Lucas intended his statement to refer to the Soviet Union, therefore supporting the stance that the Empire of *Star Wars* represented the Soviets. Of course, with interesting irony, this same statement could also be used to support the interpretation of the *United States* as Empire, given the imperial motivations often attributed to the actions of the U.S.

23. Richard Keller Simon, *Trash Culture: Popular Culture and the Great Tradition* (Berkeley: University of California Press, 1999), 69.

24. Booker, *Alternative Americas*, 118.

25. We will return to this interpretation and possible repercussions of it later.

26. Adam Roberts, *Science Fiction: The New Critical Idiom* (New York: Routledge, 2006), 66.

27. Ibid.

28. *Star Wars Episode IV — A New Hope*, DVD, directed by George Lucas (Century City, CA: 20th Century-Fox, 1977).

29. Michael Ryan and Douglas Kellner, *Camera Politica: The Politics and Ideology of Contemporary Hollywood Fiction* (Boomington: Indiana University Press, 1988), 228.

30. While possible historical interpretations of the prequel trilogy are not as hotly debated as those of the original trilogy, critics have noted the parallels between the rhetoric of the George W. Bush administration and the dialogue of Sith characters from *Revenge of the Sith* (2005). Also of note is the narrative of a leader, who is given too much power and then manipulates a republic into war — showing possible parallels with Bush, the Patriot Act (not to mention the allowed torture of prisoners of war), and the Iraq War, respectively.

31. Kevin J. Wetmore, Jr., *The Empire Triumphant: Race, Religion, and Rebellion in the Star Wars Films* (Jefferson, NC: McFarland, 2005), 56.

32. Ibid., 51.

33. Ibid., 38.

34. Ibid., 51.

35. That said, many of the individual, historical readings of the films do possess some utopian potential. For instance, the possible reading of Rebel Alliance-as-Al-Qaeda (or some other Third World resistance group), considered by Booker, seems a historical interpretation that is particularly estranging and Novum-esque, resulting in considerable utopian potential. Any narrative that reads America and the West as the villains should, at the very least, cause Americans to question their actions on the international stage, possibly leading to more "utopian" policy. The utopian potential is only compounded when "terrorists" are cast as the plucky heroes in the same narrative.

36. Wetmore, *The Empire Triumphant*, 27.

37. *Star Wars Episode V—The Empire Strikes Back*, DVD, directed by Irvin Kershner (San Francisco, CA: Lucasfilm, 1980).

38. Freedman, *Critical Theory and Science Fiction*, 65.

39. *Star Wars Episode I—The Phantom Menace*, DVD, directed by George Lucas (San Fransico, CA: Lucasfilm, 1999).

40. Stuart Hall, "The Whites of Their Eyes: Racist Ideologies and the Media," in *Silver Linings: Some Strategies for the Eighties*, edited by George Bridges and Rosalind Brunt (London: Lawrence and Wisehart, 1981), 37–38.

41. Wetmore, *The Empire Triumphant*, 35.

42. Nama, *Black Space*, 33.

43. Ibid., 32.

44. Ibid.

45. Ibid., 34.

46. Ibid., 28.

47. Wetmore, *The Empire Triumphant*, 35.

48. Ibid., 77.

49. Nama, *Black Space*, 30.

50. *Star Wars Episode IV—A New Hope*, DVD.

51. Ibid.

52. As mentioned earlier, the Rebel Alliance *does* make more of an effort at inclusion of disparate races and species than the Empire. For instance, aliens are shown in *Return of the Jedi* (1983) as members of the Alliance, specifically the Sullustian Nien Nunb, who copilots the Millennium Falcon during the attack on the second Death Star, and the Mon Calamari Admiral Ackbar ("It's a trap!"), who leads the attack. However, these few characters do not make up for the sheer dominance of the white males characters in the two trilogies.

53. Wetmore, *The Empire Triumphant*, 38.

54. The most recent animated film and series introduce the character of Ahsoka Tano, a female alien who is Anakin's Padawan apprentice. As opposed to most other female or non-human characters in the franchise, Ahsoka plays a more central role to the story, though one arguably still subjugated to the white male characters of Anakin and Obi-Wan. Hopefully, Ahsoka's presence shows a growing trend toward more inclusion of female, non-white, and non-human characters in the *Star Wars* franchise.

55. For further discussion on women and gender in *Star Wars*, see Diana Dominguez, "Feminism and the Force: Empowerment and Disillusionment in a Galaxy Far, Far Away" and Veronica A. Wilson, "Seduced by the Dark Side of the Force: Gender, Sexuality, and Moral Agency in George Lucas's *Star Wars* Universe," both found in *Culture, Identities and Technology in the Star Wars Films*, edited by Carl Silvio and Tony M. Vinci (Jefferson, NC: McFarland, 2007).

56. Wetmore, *The Empire Triumphant*, 71–72.
57. Ibid., 70–71.
58. Ibid., 76.
59. Roberts, *Science Fiction*, 66.
60. Jameson, *Archaeologies of the Future*, xiii.
61. The utopian success, in fact, *hinges* on the audience's seeing the franchise's faults, in the hopes that they will then acknowledge the corresponding real-world failures and that those failures won't continue to plague our society.

REFERENCES

Bloch, Ernst. *A Philosophy of the Future*. Translated by John Cumming. New York: Herder and Herder, 1970.
_____. *The Principle of Hope*. Translated by Neville Plaice, Stephen Plaice and Paul Knight. 3 vols. Cambridge: MIT Press, 1986.
_____. *The Utopian Function of Art and Literature*. Translated by Jack Zipes and Frank Mecklenburg. Cambridge: MIT Press, 1988.
Booker, M. Keith. *Alternative Americas: Science Fiction and American Culture*. Westport, CT: Praeger, 2006.
Bould, Mark. "Film and Television." In *The Cambridge Companion to Science Fiction*, edited by Edward James and Farah Mendlesohn, 79–95. New York: Cambridge University Press, 2003.
Crawford, Krysten. "The 'Star Wars' Blitzkrieg." *CNN.com*. 13 May 2005. http://money.cnn.com/2005/05/13/news/newsmakers/starwars/index.htm.
Csicsery-Ronay, Istvan, Jr. "Marxist Theory and Science Fiction." In *The Cambridge Companion to Science Fiction*, edited by Edward James and Farah Mendlesohn, 113–124. New York: Cambridge University Press, 2003.
Freedman, Carl. *Critical Theory and Science Fiction*. Middletown, CT: Wesleyan University Press, 2000.
Hall, Stuart. "The Whites of Their Eyes: Racist Ideologies and the Media." In *Silver Linings: Some Strategies for the Eighties,* edited by George Bridges and Rosalind Brunt, 37–38. London: Lawrence and Wisehart, 1981.
Jameson, Fredric. *Archaeologies of the Future: The Desire Called Utopia and Other Science Fictions*. New York: Verso, 2005.
Le Guin, Ursula K. *Dancing at the Edge of the World: Thoughts on Words, Women, Places*. New York: Grove, 1989.
Nama, Adilifu. *Black Space: Imagining Race in Science Fiction Film*. Austin: University of Texas Press, 2008.
Roberts, Adam. *Science Fiction: The New Critical Idiom*. New York: Routledge, 2006.
Roston, Tom. "Holy Smith!" *Premiere,* May 2005: 55.
Ryan, Michael, and Douglas Kellner. *Camera Politica: The Politics and Ideology of Contemporary Hollywood Fiction*. Boomington: Indiana University Press, 1988.
Simon, Richard Keller. *Trash Culture: Popular Cultrue and the Great Tradition*. Berkeley: University of California Press, 1999.
Star Wars Episode I: The Phantom Menace. Directed by George Lucas. Lucasfilm, 1999.
Star Wars Episode IV: A New Hope. Directed by George Lucas. 20th Century–Fox, 1977.
Star Wars Episode V: The Empire Strikes Back. Directed by Irvin Kershner. Lucasfilm, 1980.
Suvin, Darko. "Estrangement and Cognition." In *Speculations on Speculation: Theories of Science Fiction*, edited by James Gunn and Matthew Candelaria, 23–35. Lanham, MD: Scarecrow Press, 2005.
Westfahl, Gary. "Space Opera." In *The Cambridge Companion to Science Fiction*, edited by Edward James and Farah Mendlesohn, 197–208. New York: Cambridge University Press, 2003.
Wetmore, Kevin J., Jr. *The Empire Triumphant: Race, Religion, and Rebellion in the Star Wars Films*. Jefferson, NC: McFarland, 2005.

• *Eight* •

Inexplicable Utterances: Social Power and Pluralistic Discourse in *Transformers*

Jacqueline Wiegard

The reliance of action films on hyper-visuality directs audiences to what is seen, but Michael Bay's *Transformers* (2007) also invites us to perceive what is occurring behind the action. In regards to the final battle of the movie — where Starscream smashes into an office building — Joseph Clover observes that "[the creators] reveal the interior stuff with impossible detail."[1] While *Transformers* has always been preoccupied with what is visually hidden, Bay's film also reveals an Other discourse — through the intervention of the Alien robots — one that relies on what Damien Broderick refers to as the absent signified: "an empirically empty but imaginatively laden paradigm."[2] The presence of these ambiguous robot signs points to an absence of meaning, and in this case what is absent is the ability of the Other — in particular the child — to accurately represent his or herself through the dominant discourses: of both consumerism and the military. I contend that the robot fantasy of the film functions to usurp the dominant discourses by supplanting them with pluralistic cyber discourse dependent upon a seemingly intuitive understanding of technology. As the action of the narrative becomes increasingly reliant on the characters' abilities to negotiate cyber discourse — in which the children are framed as adepts — adult power is deconstructed and displaced.

As John Stephens observes, language in children's texts is a site upon which a struggle for social power is enacted. Indeed, Stephens' asserts that language is inextricably connected to social order, as the principle signifying code used by a society "is language, since language is the most common form of social communication, and one particular use of language through which society seeks to exemplify and inculcate its current values and attitudes is the imagining and reordering of stories."[3] Thus, it may be posited that the elusive nature of language — in particular, signification — in science fiction may potentially function to redress the power imbalance between adult and child. In Roberta Seelinger Trites' discussion of institutional discourses — government politics, schools, religion, and identity politics — in the young adult novel, she observes that:

> Social institutions are determined by discourse, and they exist for the purpose of regulating social power, which is why [Louis] Althusser refers to them as "Ideological State Apparatuses." They use language simultaneously to repress and to empower their constituents; they gain power from the very people whom they regulate.[4]

In one of the young adult novels that Trites examines in her study, she asserts that the claim of an adolescent protagonist, "'I don't know the words,' serves as a metaphor for the adolescents' position within many institutional cultures."[5] Discourses of adult power are inexplicable to the child, which serves to further marginalize the child's already liminal position in society.

The movie *Transformers* also occupies a "borderline" space of childhood in that the protagonist Sam is a teenager who is referred to as both "boy" and "man" throughout the course of the narrative, reflecting the diverse age-group manifestations of the *Transformers* franchise itself[6] — which since the creation of the robots in the early 1980s has included comics, children's animated television series and action movies. Yet, this ambiguity also suggests his precarious access to social power. Sam is not financially independent, and indeed his ability to purchase consumer goods — in particular his first car, the young Autobot Bumblebee — is reliant on the purchasing power of his father. Indeed, Bumblebee has not only functioned as a "helper" and friend to the young male protagonist (Spike/Sam Witwicky) throughout his various incarnations in the *Transformers* franchise (Volkswagen/Goldbug/Camaro), but he also mimics the child's position in his occupying a liminal space as "messenger" or intermediary between the robot world and the human world. Ironically, Bumblebee's ability to convey messages is impeded by the evil Decepticon patriarch Megatron, thus further reinforcing Bumblebee's bond with his young human friend. Alex Irvine's short story "Bumblebee at Tyger Pax" (2010) describes how Bumblebee loses his voice after distracting Megatron from finding the Allspark:

> Megatron seized Bumblebee around the neck and dragged him upright. "You talk too much, Autobot."
> "Everybody says that," Bumblebee said. He tried to raise his arms, but could not; the damage from Starscream's airstrike was too severe. "Coming from you,

I'll take it. Hey, did you see that Allspark? That was something, the way it flew out into space completely out of your reach —"

Megatron squeezed, cutting off Bumblebee's voice. "You mock me, mech?" He squeezed. Something snapped in Bumblebee's throat. "That is the last time you mock anyone..."

"You could die here, but the last thing your pitiful librarian leader needs is another martyr," Megatron said. "You live as a reminder that I can kill when I please, and grant mercy when I please. But there is a cost. And for you, the cost is that voice of yours that you love so much."[7]

In Bay's *Transformers*, the intervention of the Alien robots and the subsequent dominance of cyber discourse, shifts the power struggle from an adult-dominated discourse of consumerism and the military to the site of language, in particular cyber-related language, where the children's knowledge of technology increases their relative social power. That is, this act of subversion positions the adult figures of social authority as those who "don't know the words."

On the surface, *Transformers* appears to be a thematically conventional militaristic heroic narrative privileging "male heroism, battlefield camaraderie, superpatriotism, violent struggle of good against evil, noble U.S. objectives, and glorification of high-tech warfare."[8] Bay acknowledges not only a respect for the armed forces, but a keen interest in military equipment and strategy that carries with it an implicit support of enforced adult social power. Indeed, in his commentary on the film, Bay recalls a conversation that he had with a Pentagon official, where he enthusiastically posits that: "If we did have Alien robots anywhere on earth, I think the American military would be involved, and we would bring the fight anywhere we have to."[9] Captain William Lennox's assertion, at the end of the movie, that Sam is "a soldier now" reinforces the idea that this narrative is primarily concerned with the *monomythic* initiation of a young man into a modern world savior.[10] Furthermore, the conventional quest aspects appear to be representative of a significant component of the fantasy of this movie, which Joshua Clover somewhat dismissively asserts "lovingly preserves the boy's dream that every single object in the world is a weapon."[11] Yet, despite Bay's evident desire to adhere to the U.S. military's wish to be portrayed in a positive light, the fact that Bay chooses to use military vehicles as Decepticons complicates the representation of military discourse, and suggests that the fantasy of this film is concerned with more than an insidious adult endeavor to conscript children as future imperialistic heroes.

Bay's film also supports discourses of adult consumerism in the real world through Hasbro robot figurines and other merchandise.[12] In fact, prior to commencing on the film, Bay attended *Transformers* school at Hasbro in Rhode Island to familiarize himself with *Transformers* lore.[13] Furthermore, the necessity to meet toy production deadlines meant that the robot characters and the nature of their transformation, was determined even before the script was completed.[14] However, the reliance of the film on the child's interaction with *Transformers* robots through play does not necessarily inhibit the power of the child, even though the child is dependent upon the consumer power of the adult. As Louis R. Kuznets observes, "toys in both life and fiction are not only the products of the artistry of the artisan or writer, but also bring out the imaginative creativity of player or reader."[15] While the child may be framed by his knowledge of *Transformers* lore, the absence of fixed meaning, inherent in the nature of the robot itself, enables the child to effectively "speak through the robot" and, in turn, to perform self-creation. While the *Transformers* robots in the film are more grown-up toys, they are also concerned with the forging of identity and performance of social power. When Sam receives only a B- for a history presentation, putting the purchase of his first car in jeopardy, he tells his teacher: "Okay, I wanna tell you about a dream. A boy's dream. And a man's promise to that boy."[16] Sam's dream of freedom and the ability to forge his independence as a young man is dependent upon his acquisition of this grown-up toy, and Bumblebee's ability to vocalize Sam's unconscious desires through his radio transmissions is instrumental in facilitating Sam's *bildungsroman*.

"Witwicky Man. He Has Seen Our Language": Technology, Communication and the Child

The way in which the children specifically interact with robot technology in this film — where the child is subversive through his or her ability to negotiate cyber discourse — offers them the social power and agency which the child's "play" with toy robots anticipates. As Seymour Papert observes, "children know that it is just a matter of time before they inherit the machines."[17] Bay's robots embody a serious threat to adult authority, one that supplants the power of the dollar and military. Following the first Decepticon attack on SOCCENT Forwards Operation base in Qatar, where the military network is hacked, a group of signal analysts are given the task of discovering the origin of the foreign signal. When John Keller, Secretary of Defense, observes the youth of the analysts, an aide remarks: "They're the top subject matter experts, sir. NSA's recruiting them straight out of high school these days."[18] This reveals not only a shift in social power toward the child — due to his or her superior understanding of technology — but also the anxiety of the supplanted adult. Noga Applebaum, in her study of technology, power and the adult-child relationship in science fiction, has acknowledged that the link between the child's knowledge of technology and its ability to empower the child is a complex one. It would appear that "the discourse of technology revolves around knowledge and the control of it, thus placing it in direct conflict with the ongoing discourse of childhood which is still entrenched in the notion of the vulnerable child in need of protection."[19] Conversely, Applebaum also observes that "a new discourse regarding children and technology has developed. This discourse highlights children's innate talent when engaging with cutting-edge technologies."[20] It is evident that *Transformers* adheres to the latter ideology, as the child's ability to interact with the robots and translate cyber discourse is the only basis for which they are granted social power. It is telling, though, that Sam's ebay account *LadiesMan217*, which reveals his inability to accurately represent himself in consumer discourse, is what ultimately makes him vulnerable to the Decepticons. In their transformation into military vehicles, and Megatron's role as the father of the modern consumer age, the Decepticons both embody and are instrumental in the deconstruction of these discourses of adult power. The intervention of the Alien robots catalyzes the displacement of the ideological external determinants of cyber discourse — particularly economic— that are infused with adult power, and so the children who "don't know the words" are able to become the speaking subjects.

"Are You on Drugs?"

Despite the awesome fight scenes, the real battle in *Transformers* occurs at the site of communication, a space where the adults exhibit serious weaknesses from the outset of the film and the children are framed as illicit. Conversely, the children quickly adapt to different modes of communication through an evident acceptance of the fluidity and ambiguity of language. Subsequent to the Alien robot invasion, the adult systems of social power break down due to their evident inability to communicate effectively. As Julia Kristeva observes:

> Every social practice ... is determined by a set of signifying rules, by virtue of the fact that there is present an order of language; that this language has a double articulation (signifier/signified); that this duality stands in an arbitrary relation to the referent; and that all social functioning is marked by the split between referent and symbolic and by the shift from signified to signifier coextensive with it.[21]

The actions of the human adults in *Transformers* are impeded by the fact that they frequently find themselves perplexed by other speech, where they are confronted with a signifier with which they cannot associate a fixed signified. Essentially, language becomes inexplicable to the adults, which reduces their relative social power. This is where the adults expose their vulnerability, and the robots are able to exploit this by swiftly learning to converse in a variety of linguistic modes. This is subtly anticipated early in the film, just prior to the Decepticon attack on the Qatar army base, where the soldiers are, when Jorge "Fig" Figueroa muses on how he misses his mother's cooking, especially alligator *étouffée*. It is telling that when Robert Epps — Bobby — responds to Fig by saying "I understand," even when it is evident that he does not because he clearly thinks Fig's favorite dishes are unappetizing, Fig begins speaking Spanish and is berated:

> BOBBY: "English ... please..."
> LENNOX: "English ... I mean how many times do we have... We don't speak Spanish. I told you that."
> FIG: "Why you got to ruin it for me, man? That's my heritage."
> LENNOX: "Go with the Spanish. Whatever."[22]

The tension is ultimately resolved through their discussing their shared love of baseball and a perfect day watching "the Sox at Fenway." However, the communication problems for the military characters continue to emerge in the film, an example of this is when the surviving soldiers have difficulty calling for assistance when they are under attack from the Decepticon Scorponok, in a small village outside of the army base in Qatar. Lennox attempts to place a call to the Pentagon using one of the villager's mobile phones. The call goes to an Indian call centre where the unsympathetic employee appears to be completely unreceptive to the plight of the soldiers, and insists on Lennox providing credit card details in order to transfer the call.[23] The military, in its insistence on conformity and "accurate representation" — both admired and somewhat bemoaned by Bay in his commentary on the film — creates a discourse that is vehemently antagonistic to difference, and this is particularly evident in the breakdown of military communications that occurs later in the film. It is unsurprising then, that the technologically and linguistically superior Alien robots exploit this vulnerability, and the armed forces are eventually reduced to using Morse code on primitive equipment and walkie talkies from Radio Shack.

The communications between Sam and the human figures of paternal authority in *Transformers* are typically limited to demands, threats and negotiation, blurring the lines between the military, consumerism and family. Sam's ability to assert himself as a speaking subject in this *bildungsroman* involves a number of different types of negotiation with the various adult characters. In his discussion of subjectivity, ideology and language in children's fiction, Stephens' asserts that:

> The conventional strategy is to situate the character within a complex of social practices so as to construct a number of self-other interactions. The crucial ideological implication is then whether the self demands that the other replicate the

self's desires ... whether the other overwhelms the self ... or whether self can negotiate with the other so as to encourage personal growth.[24]

In the following examples, Sam's character moves from the second situation to the third, as he initially finds himself in a position where the other (adult) overwhelms the self (child), but is able to negotiate with the other (adult) to encourage personal growth. Sam's history teacher, Mr. Hosney, maintains order in his classroom in a simple and ironically robotic fashion reiterating the need for responsibility, and repeatedly holding up a sign that says "Quiet."[25] This demonstrates the adult effectively erasing the voice of the child in order to maintain order, as the child's utterances transgress prescribed classroom boundaries, but it also highlights the difficulty the teacher has communicating with his students in any meaningful way. In a mimesis of military command, the teacher gives simple orders that are expected to be followed. Yet, Sam's mischievous "hawking" of his great-great-grandfather Captain Archibald Witwicky's property defuses the power struggle with humor, by attributing some legitimacy to his teacher's intolerance. Sam is supposed to be presenting a history paper, not "selling off his ancestor's crap"—which includes the glasses engraved with a map to Megatron's location—eagerly sought by the Decepticons. Yet, in keeping with the ambiguity of human father figures in the film, the teacher negotiates Sam's grade giving him an A-instead of a B-, thus enabling Sam to fulfill his agreement with his father regarding the purchase of his first car.[26] Thus, while the teacher's impatience with Sam is understandable, the way in which Mr. Hosney expresses his displeasure suggests that teacher-student communication is unilateral. The teacher's willingness to engage in a compromise with Sam, and ultimately facilitate his consumer power, only occurs because Sam positions the purchase of the car as a necessary part of the formation of his identity within a patriarchal consumer society: Sam needs to be able to buy a car so he can "become a man." So, Sam does not really subvert adult authority through this compromise. Rather, he just negotiates between different types of paternal authority (the teacher and the father) in order to assert his own limited subjectivity.

In addition to paternal authority figures who cannot read foreign signals or who reduce communication to simple commands, there are other adult characters whose ironic grasp on reality is so tenuous as to render challenging the mutual understanding and negotiation with the child. Yet, Sam's sensitivity to the pluralistic nature of language—explored further in the *Transformers* sequel *Revenge of the Fallen* (2009)—enables him to slip signification, and thus mirror back the irrationality of the adults. As negotiation is predicated on some kind of mutual understanding, this mode of communication is impossible for Sam when dealing with these characters. Thus, these scenarios relate to Stephens' first situation where the self (child) demands that the other (adult) replicates the self's desires. When Sam reports the apparent theft of Bumblebee, he undergoes a bizarre interrogation by an evidently unhinged Sheriff. The Sheriff is revealed to be incapable of interpreting the signs associated with Sam's dilemma: from his story, to the label on Mojo's bottle of painkillers, to Sam's wary glance at the Sheriff's gun. In this latter instance, the Sheriff refers to Sam as "50 cent" and challenges him: "'You wanna go make something happen? Do it. 'Cause I promise you I will bust you up.'"[27] The adult's behavior here reinforces an underlying concern of the film: the antagonism of adult paternal authority figures toward the child. The serious threat that the Sheriff poses to Sam's freedom is undermined by his comic irrationality and grants Sam authority which enables him to be situated in the position of speaker. It is the inept adult figure of social authority who is eventually implicated in Sam's guileless irony, when he finishes the conversation by whispering back to the Sheriff: "Are you on drugs?"[28] Sam reinstates rationality through rhetorically situating the question in a more appropriate place — at the site of the adult other — thus undermining the reduced power of his status as illicit. Sam's ability to negotiate with irrational adults continues to empower him as the film progresses, and is largely based on his ability to navigate the adult's difficulty in comprehending what is signified.

"We Have Learned Earth's Languages Through the World Wide Web."

The Autobots are the antithesis of the adult humans in their ability to accommodate pluralistic discourse, through their ability to not only grasp Earth's languages very quickly, but also to understand the social and cultural context that informs human communication, and then apply this knowledge. Optimus Prime formally introduces the Autobots to Sam and Mikaela Banes, and Jazz — like Bumblebee — also demonstrates an awareness of the social context of human language:

> JAZZ: "What's cracking, little bitches? This looks like a cool place to kick it."
> SAM: "What is that? How did he learn to talk like that?"
> OPTIMUS: "We've learned Earth's languages through the World Wide Web."[29]

The other Autobots follow Jazz's lead with phrasing that includes everything from movie references to awkward observations on the human physiology of Sam and Mikaela and its connection to human relationships. This demonstrates the compatibility of the Alien robot's cyber discourse with the "cyber speak" of the internet.

Bumblebee's communication with Sam is more complex than the other Autobots. When they first meet in Bobby Bolivia's second hand car yard,

Bumblebee represents his name to Sam in a number of different ways that demonstrate a sophisticated and empathetic understanding of human language: his color is yellow with black stripes like a bumblebee, and there is also a picture of a bumblebee hanging from his rear-view mirror with the word "Bee-Otch" written underneath.[30] While Bumblebee has his own identity that is independent of Sam, there is also an obvious empathy between the two that is comically anticipated by the car salesman when he says:

> BOBBY: "Sam, your first enchilada of freedom awaits underneath one of those hoods. Let me tell you something, son. A driver don't pick the car. The car'll pick the driver. It's a mystical bond between man and machine."[31]

The salesman's words are revealed to be empty, when his philosophical musings are undermined by his refusal to reduce the price of the car so that Sam can own the car:

> SAM: "No. no. no. You said cars pick their drivers."
> BOBBY: "Well sometimes they pick a driver with a cheap-ass father. Out the car."[32]

However, Bumblebee reasserts the meaning to this bond. His radio broadcasts the sound-bite "...greater than man..." and he produces a soundwave that shatters all the other car windows, "encouraging" the salesman to sell him to Sam's father. Bumblebee — the Camaro high performance muscle-car with a plush toy lion on the dashboard — does indeed signify a new strength in Sam's character that is concerned with his increasing ability to negotiate and usurp adult authority.

Sam's new car, as well as being a source of strength and protection, also appears to transmit the teenager's unconscious desires through the radio. This type of communication is evidence of Bumblebee/Sam's ability to negotiate pluralistic discourse. When Mikaela needs a ride home from the party by the lake, Bumblebee plays the Cars' song "Drive" on his radio. The main lyrics of the song are "Who's gonna drive you home?" and so, Bumblebee's message functions as a clear expression of Sam's unconscious desire to drive Mikaela home.[33] After Mikaela accepts Sam's offer of a lift, Bumblebee's radio flicks from song to song, and the lyrics of these songs suggest that Mikaela's presence inspires a range of erratic and intense emotions in Sam: from a desire for the love object to a fear of losing love. Bumblebee creates a semantic space, another way of speaking, that represents Sam on the deepest level, and is free of adult judgment and power. Indeed, immediately following the "giant droid death match" between Bumblebee and Barricade, Sam realizes that Bumblebee is using sound bites from the radio to communicate with him.[34] It is also revealing that Bumblebee's voice box is broken in a fight with a Decepticon, functioning as a mimesis of the way in which the child is silenced, or reduced to fragmented speech within discourses of consumerism and the military.

Conversely, the Decepticons — apart from Megatron — typically speak in Cybertronian: the Alien robot language. This foreign signal — sounds and images that have no meaning to the humans — is the primary source of social disruption, for which Sam ultimately becomes a nexus. When Frenzy hacks into the POTUS Mainframe of the Airforce One computer, he finds files containing the strange symbols (Cyberglyphs) that Sam had spoken about in his genealogy talk, regarding his great-great-grandfather's mental breakdown. After escaping from the plane, into a Decepticon police car, Frenzy unambiguously asserts a connection between language and perception that is a major concern of this film. He informs his fellow Decepticon that the Witwicky man "has seen our language."[35] Archibald Witwicky's glasses — which Sam is trying to sell on ebay under the name *LadiesMan217* — and their embodiment of Cyberglyphs become a symbol of the limits of human understanding of language and perception. At the opening of the film, Optimus Prime, relating the genesis of the *Transformers* states that the Allspark — a cube covered in Cyberglyphs — has the power to create worlds and fill them with life, much like language itself.

"Freedom Is the Right of All Sentient Beings": Deconstructing Adult Social Power

The battle between the Autobots and Decepticons for the cube and its ability to create life may be seen as a displacement of the struggle between the child and adult, within discourse, to attain agency. Furthermore, I assert that this struggle operates primarily between Sam and paternal figures of adult authority. Thus, the Alien robots — in particular Optimus Prime and Megatron — function as displacements of paternal authority. In its etymological link to humanity, the robot offers us another way of seeing ourselves; it is essentially a post-human *speculum mentis*.[36] The Alien robots function as a projection of our own social ideologies and values. Andrew Milner observes that, "in twentieth- and twenty-first century SF, the monster has been reworked as the mechanical 'robot.'"[37] As a postmodern monster then, the robot frequently embodies what is socially marginalized, including forced labor (*robotá*).[38] Thus, in *Transformers* the robot as both consumer and military vehicle (laborer) provides an incisive social commentary on human freedom in relation to the dominant social discourses.

The human "fathers" in *Transformers* are a perplexing mix of agents of independence and emasculation, creating an untenable tension that necessitates the child's rebellion, and this is achieved through the intervention of the Alien robots. The robots come to signify what the child is unable to find in the real world: clear exemplars of "good" and "evil" paternal authority. As Nicolas Michaud observes of the *Transformers* robots, that "the ethical rules that motivate these gargantuan robots are the rules that govern our own actions."[39] The human characteristics that these robots embody are — in a moral sense — evident in the type of vehicle into which they transform. As Robert Arp asserts, in his discussion of morality and the Transformer robots:

> Transformers communicate, have the capacity for reason, can be involved in complex social relationships, and obviously deceive other Transformers and human beings. More importantly, they express feelings of disillusion, contempt, pain, and suffering as well as joy, satisfaction, and contentment ... a being that has these traits has mental states, and such a being is a person....[40]

On the whole, the Decepticons transform into vehicles related to enforced social authority and power — connected to government agencies — such as police cars, tanks, and fighter planes. Anthony Breznican relates that, in the original back story to the robots, written by Jim Shooter — while he was editor in chief at Marvel Comics in the early 1980s — "the heroic Autobots were designed as peaceful transport vehicles, but the villainous Decepticons were primarily weapons of war."[41] Thus, rather than being encouraged to perform imperialistic social oppression, as critics such as Clover have asserted, the child, positioned as sympathetic to the Autobots, effectively enacts a rebellion against oppressive paternal authority. Indeed, in an early confrontation with Sam, Barricade transforms into a police car with the words "to punish and enslave," supplanting the LAPD police motto "to protect and serve."[42] This reinforces a negative connotation with the armed forces that are paradoxically celebrated in the militaristic heroic narrative of the solders.

The child evades morally ambiguous human adult authority through his interaction with cyber discourse, and then confronts this deconstructed authority through projection in the paternal authority figures of the robot leaders Optimus Prime and Megatron. In Breznican's comments on the original *Transformers* television series, he observes that Peter Cullen's Optimus Prime was "a stoic, stern but forgiving father figure to ... Bumblebee."[43] Furthermore, that "Prime never lost his temper, and even in the heat of battle never lost his dignity or desire to preserve the lives on earth."[44] Conversely the villain Megatron, as "the leader of the resource-plundering Decepticons, is practically the epitome of a bad parent — quick to anger, judgmental, cruel — which is why his second in command, the fighter jet Starscream, has always secretly plotted to usurp him."[45] In his discussion of fairy tale transformations, Bruno Bettelheim asserts that the splitting of the parent figure into the good and bad parent in fairy tales functions to support the child's inability to process the ambiguity of the parent.[46] It seems that in *Transformers*, the robots not only disrupt paternal authority, but also provide a projection of the good and bad parent fantasy. Yet, as Sam is a teenager, it suggests that this splitting of good father (Optimus Prime) and bad father (Megatron) also embodies a wider commentary on the prevalence of morally flawed paternal authority figures — personal and social — revealing a culture of oppression and antagonism to the Other.

Subverting "Adult" Language

Sam's initiation into the young adult realm of cars and girls is completely dependent on his father's financial contribution, which Ron Witwicky mocks by initially driving Sam through a Porsche dealership. His father, while financially supportive of his son, frequently reinforces his desire for uncompromising authority. This personality trait is highlighted in Bay's commentary of the film, where he explains part of the inspiration for Ron's character was a friend who would not let his children walk on the lawn. On his way to the party by the lake, Sam walks across the grass in the backyard. His father Ron, who is gardening, berates him:

> RON: "I do not like footprints on my grass."
> SAM: "It's family grass, Dad."
> RON: "Well, when you own your own grass, you'll understand."[47]

In his commentary of the film Bay muses: "What neurotic father doesn't let his kids walk on the grass?"[48] Yet, this impulse to excessively order and control the child is not just confined to Sam's father. Indeed, it appears to mirror the military's somewhat neurotic insistence on "accurate representation" in the film, evident in Bay's comments on their feedback on the NSA-related scenes set in the Pentagon.[49] It is telling, then, that the consumer products of the modern age are attributed to the reverse engineering of Megatron's technology, and thus, Megatron is also effectively the "father of the modern consumer age." Consequently, the consumer father and oppressive social authority figures are both positioned as the enemy of the child in their alignment with the Decepticons.

The Decepticons, in their quest for the Allspark or cyberglyph-covered cube, demonstrate an excessive drive to control, oppress and enslave the human race. They are not interested in breaching the chasm of otherness — as the Autobots do — but rather seek to order the world on their own terms. In their uncompromising drive to order, the human adult father-figures and the Decepticons, suggest Lacan's conception of language as *Symbolic*, which Kristeva asserts is constituted "through narcissistic, specular, imaginary investment, [which] protects the body from the attack of drives by making it a place — the place of signifier — in which the body can signify itself through positions."[50] This defense of the self inevitably creates an Other — the child — whose "absence" in discourse creates subversive tension. The Autobots, especially Bumblebee through his radio transmissions, suggest Kristeva's *Semiotic chora*, which in its association with the maternal body disrupts the paternal symbolic "as rupture and articulations (rhythm) ... verisimilitude, spatiality and temporality."[51] Furthermore, she asserts that this elusive, polymorphous language of the *chora* is "generated in order to attain [a] signifying position."[52] As Maggie Madsen tells the Secretary of Defense: "The signal pattern is learning. It's evolving on its own."[53] The foreign signals that are so inexplicable to the adults, yet accessible to the children, reassert the child's speaking position — through the absence of what is signified — that features even more prominently in the sequel *Revenge of the Fallen* and grants the child even greater social power.

NOTES

1. Joshua Clover, "Dream Machines," *Film Quarterly* 61, no. 2 (2008): 7.
2. Damien Broderick, *Reading by Starlight: Postmodern Science Fiction* (London: Routledge, 1995), 61.
3. John Stephens, *Language and Ideology in Children's Fiction* (London: Longman, 1992), 8.
4. Roberta Seelinger Trites, *Disturbing the Universe: Power and Repression in Adolescent Literature* (Iowa City: University of Iowa Press, 2000), 22.
5. Ibid., 21.
6. Mark Bould, "*Transformers* (Review)," *Science Fiction Film and Television* 1, no. 1 (2008): 163.
7. Alex Irvine, "Bumblebee at Tyger Pax," *MTV*, June 22, 2010, http://moviesblog.mtv.com/2010/06/22/exclusive-learn-how-bumblebee-lost-his-voice-in-this-short-story-from-exodus-author-alex-irvine/.
8. Carl Boggs and Tom Pollard, "The Imperial Warrior in Hollywood: Rambo and Beyond," *New Political Science* 30, no. 4 (2008): 567–568.
9. Michael Bay, "Commentary," *Transformers*, DVD, directed by Michael Bay (2007; Los Angeles: Paramount Pictures Corporation and DreamWorks L.L.C., 2009.)
10. Joseph Campbell, *The Hero with a Thousand Faces* (Princeton: University of Princeton Press, 1968), 245–246.
11. Joshua Clover, "Dream Machines," *Film Quarterly* 61, no. 2 (2008): 7.
12. Mark Bould, "*Transformers* (Review)," 163.
13. Bay, "Commentary."
14. Ibid.
15. Louis R. Kuznets, *When Toys Come Alive: Narratives of Animation, Metamorphosis, and Development* (New Haven: Yale University Press, 1994), 180.
16. *Transformers*, DVD, directed by Michael Bay (2007; Los Angeles: Paramount Pictures Corporation and DreamWorks L.L.C., 2009).
17. Seymour Papert, *The Children's Machine: Rethinking School in the Age of the Computer* (Hemel Hampstead: Harvester Wheatsheaf, 1993), x.
18. *Transformers*, DVD.
19. Noga Applebaum, *Representations of Technology in Science Fiction for Young People* (Hoboken: Routledge, 2009), 103.
20. Ibid., 103.
21. Julia Kristeva, "The System and the Speaking Subject," in *The Kristeva Reader*, edited by Toril Moi (Oxford: Blackwell, 1986), 25.
22. *Transformers*, DVD.
23. Ibid.

24. John Stephens, *Language and Ideology in Children's Fiction* (London: Longman, 1992), 282.
25. *Transformers*, DVD.
26. Ibid.
27. Ibid.
28. Ibid.
29. Ibid.
30. Ibid.
31. Ibid.
32. Ibid.
33. Ibid.
34. Ibid.
35. Ibid.
36. James Gunn, "Science Fiction and Philosophy," in *Reading Science Fiction*, edited by James Gunn, Marleen S. Barr and Matthew Candelaria (Houndmills: Palgrave Macmillan, 2009), 232–233.
37. Andrew Milner, *Literature, Culture and Society* (London: Routledge, 2005), 242.
38. Ibid.
39. Nicolas Michaud, "Good Robot, Bad Robot, What's the Difference?" in *Transformers and Philosophy: More than Meets the Mind*, edited by John R. Shook and Liz Stillwaggon Swan (Chicago: Open Court Press, 2009), 155.
40. Robert Arp, "Morally Responsible Machines," in *Transformers and Philosophy: More than Meets the Mind*, edited by John R. Shook and Liz Stillwaggon Swan (Chicago: Open Court Press, 2009), 137.
41. Anthony Breznican states that "Megatron's machine form in the 1980s was a silver handgun. In the movie, he's an alien fighter craft but can form his arms into a cannon." See Anthony Breznican, "'Transformers': From Toy Story to Serious Art?" *USA Today*, June 28, 2007, http://www.usatoday.com/life/movies/news/2007-06-28-transformers-main_N.htm.
42. The LAPD motto is actually "To Protect and to Serve." Los Angeles Police Department, "The Origin of the LAPD Motto," *Los Angeles Police Department*, http://www.lapdonline.org/history_of_the_lapd/content_basic_view/1128.
43. Anthony Breznican, "From Toy Story to Serious Art?"
44. Ibid.
45. Ibid.
46. Bruno Bettelheim, *The Uses of Enchantment: The Meaning and Importance of Fairy Tales* (London: Penguin, 1991), 66–73.
47. *Transformers*, DVD.
48. Bay, "Commentary."
49. Ibid.
50. Julia Kristeva, "Revolution in Poetic Language," in *The Kristeva Reader*, edited by Toril Moi (Oxford: Blackwell, 1986), 103.
51. Ibid., 94.
52. Ibid.
53. *Transformers*, DVD.

References

Althusser, Louis. "Ideology and Ideological State Apparatuses." In *Lenin and Philosophy and Other Essays*, translated by Ben Brewster, 127–186. New York: Monthly Review Press, 1971.
Applebaum, Noga. *Representations of Technology in Science Fiction for Young People*. Hoboken: Routledge, 2009.
Arp, Robert. "Morally Responsible Machines." In *Transformers and Philosophy: More Than Meets the Mind*, edited by John R. Shook and Liz Stillwaggon Swan, 127–138. Chicago: Open Court Press, 2009.
Bay, Michael. "Commentary." Disc 1. *Transformers*, special ed. DVD. Directed by Michael Bay. Los Angeles, CA: Paramount Pictures Corporation and DreamWorks L.L.C., 2009.
Bettelheim, Bruno. *The Uses of Enchantment: The Meaning and Importance of Fairy Tales*. London: Penguin, 1991.

Boggs, Carl, and Tom Pollard. "The Imperial Warrior in Hollywood: Rambo and Beyond." *New Political Science* 30, no. 4 (2008): 565–78.
Bould, Mark. Review of Michael Bay's *Transformers* (Paramount Movie). *Science Fiction Film and Television* 1, no. 1 (2008): 163–67.
Breznican, Anthony. "'Transformers': From Toy Story to Serious Art?" *USA Today*, June 28, 2007. http://www.usatoday.com/life/movies/news/2007-06-28-transformers-main_N.htm.
Broderick, Damien. *Reading by Starlight: Postmodern Science Fiction*. London: Routledge, 1995.
Campbell, Joseph. *The Hero with a Thousand Faces*. Princeton, NJ: Princeton University Press, 1968.
Clover, Joshua. "Dream Machines." *Film Quarterly* 61, no. 2 (2008): 6–7.
Gunn, James. "Science Fiction and Philosophy." In *Reading Science Fiction*, edited by James Gunn, Marleen S. Barr and Matthew Candelaria, 227–34. Houndmills: Palgrave Macmillan, 2009.
Irvine, Alex. "Bumblebee at Tyger Pax." *MTV*, June 22, 2010. http://moveiesblog.mtv.com/2010/06/22/exclusive-learn-how-bumblebee-lost-his-voice-in-this-short-story-from-exodus-author-alex-irvine/.
Kristeva, Julia. "Revolution in Poetic Language." In *The Kristeva Reader*, edited by Toril Moi, 89–136. Oxford: Blackwell, 1986.
_____. "The System and the Speaking Subject." In *The Kristeva Reader*, edited by Toril Moi, 24–33. Oxford: Blackwell, 1986.
Kuznets, Louis R. *When Toys Come Alive: Narratives of Animation, Metamorphosis, and Development*. New Haven: Yale University Press, 1994.
Los Angeles Police Department. "The Origin of the LAPD Motto." Los Angeles Police Department. http://www.lapdonline.org/history_of_the_lapd/content_basic_view/1128.
Michaud, Nicolas. "Good Robot, Bad Robot, What's the Difference?" In *Transformers and Philosophy: More than Meets the Mind*, edited by John R. Shook and Liz Stillwaggon Swan, 155–163. Chicago: Open Court Press, 2009.
Milner, Andrew. *Literature, Culture and Society*. London: Routledge, 2005.
Nunez, Alex. "2010 Transformers Special Edition Chevy Camaro Unveiled." *Autoblog*. July 22, 2009. http://www.autoblog.com/2009/07/22/2010-transformers-special-edition-chevy-camaro-unveiled/.
Papert, Seymour. *The Children's Machine: Rethinking School in the Age of the Computer*. Hemel Hampstead: Harvester Wheatsheaf, 1993.
Stephens, John. *Language and Ideology in Children's Fiction*. London: Longman, 1992.
Transformers, special ed. DVD. Directed by Michael Bay. Los Angeles: Paramount Pictures Corporation and DreamWorks L.L.C., 2009.
Trites, Roberta Seelinger. *Disturbing the Universe: Power and Repression in Adolescent Literature*. Iowa City: University of Iowa Press, 2000.

• *Nine* •

"Population: Us": Nostalgia for a Future That Never Was (Not Yet) in *The Iron Giant*

Sandy Rankin

"What exactly is 'nostalgia,' though? Or perhaps the first question really should be: what WAS nostalgia? With its Greek roots — nostos, meaning 'to return home' and algos, meaning 'pain' — this word sounds so familiar to us that we may forget that it is a relatively new word, as words go. It was coined in 1688 by a 19-year-old Swiss student in his medical dissertation as a sophisticated (or perhaps pedantic) way to talk about a literally lethal kind of severe homesickness (of Swiss mercenaries far from their mountainous home). This medical-pathological definition of nostalgia allowed for a remedy: the return home, or sometimes merely the promise of it."

— Linda Hutcheon[1]

"A history lesson is the best cure for nostalgic pathos."

— Fredric Jameson[2]

What a Strange Thing! — A Proto-Novum

Fin de siècle suggests hope for an imminent historical rupture, hope for a radically different near-future. It also suggests anxiety or despair about that which may be forthcoming, and normally suggests the last years of a period of decadence. *Fin de siècle* is usually more specifically reserved as a term for 19th century aesthetic productions in Europe, such as the productions of Oscar Wilde, who, though Irish, lived and wrote for some years in England and France. Wilde's fairytales for children, however, can be described as decadent anti-decadence. The following is from Wilde's "The Happy Prince":

> "What a strange thing!" said the overseer of the workmen at the foundry. "This broken lead heart will not melt in the furnace. We must throw it away." So they threw it on a dust-heap where the dead Swallow was also lying. "Bring me the two most precious things in the city," said God to one of His Angels; and the Angel brought Him the leaden heart [of the statue of the Happy Prince] and the dead bird. "You have rightly chosen," said God, "for in my garden of Paradise this little bird shall sing for evermore, and in my city of gold the Happy Prince [the lead statue become ugly without his gems, which were carried by the living Swallow to poor people in dire need] shall praise me."[3]

As an accident of history would have it, providing a fortuitous, dialogic, and theoretical-aesthetic open door, the Warner Brothers' animated feature film *The Iron Giant*, directed by Brad Bird, appeared in cinemas in the United States in 1999, our socially-constructed mark of a century's and a millennium's conclusion and of a century's and a millennium's beginning: our contemporary *fin de siècle*. Indeed, the late twentieth century in the United States was a decade of decadence and anxiety, not yet unabated, though the decade ended post–9/11 and with the Y2K fears that now look as decadently ridiculous as (and to some of us, looked as ridiculous then, as) the fears generated by the Soviet launching of Sputnik, the latter fears spoofed as fears of difference in *The Iron Giant*, whose setting is *Earth 1957*. The film's titular 50 feet tall sentient robot, a giant metal man, can be characterized as a strange thing, an ugly-beauty, like Wilde's the Happy Prince (who, after death becomes a statue in memoriam in the town square, who upon seeing poverty-sticken humans says, "And though my heart is made of lead yet I cannot choose but weep"[4]). The lead heart of Wilde's fairytale statue and the unseen heart of Bird's animated robot share decadent anti-decadence. Thus, Bird's robot can be characterized as an echo-representation of Wilde's subversive art-religion (sometimes considered a religion of decadence), but simultaneously as a science-fiction aesthetic novum: a new emergence, a strange thing. Darko Suvin says, "An aesthetic novum is either a translation of historical cognition and ethics into form, or (in our age, perhaps more often) a creation of historical cognition and ethics as form."[5] Indeed, what we have motivating the film is something like a novum as a translation of historical cognition and ethics in a form that Bird casts into our 1957 past, arguably a pseudo-novum or a fake novum, or a quasi-novum, or, even better, a proto-novum, constituted by advanced technology with a soul. Thus, what we have with *The Iron Giant* is not so much nostalgia for 1957, not so much nostalgia for childhood (thought that nostalgia exists, too) but more so nostalgia for a future that never was (not yet).

Istvan Csicsery-Ronay, Jr., tells us in *The Seven Beauties of Science Fiction*, "Few crucial concepts have had greater influence on sf [science fiction] theory than the novum, introduced by Darko Suvin in *Metamorphoses of Science Fiction* as the defining trope of the genre," which is an understatement (italics original). Are there any other crucial concepts as influential as the novum, or more influential than?—except for cognitive estrangement, which is part and parcel of Suvin's concept of the novum. For Suvin, as Csicsery-Ronay explains, the novum is the central imaginary novelty in a science-fiction text. The novum is the "source of the most important distinctions between the world of the tale and the world of the reader."[6] The significance of a true novum goes beyond the thrill of a new commodity, beyond the exhilaration of imaginary textual or filmic difference. For Suvin, a true novum—as opposed to a fake or a pseudo-novum—has as its directive not art for the sake of art but art for the sake of hope, which is to say that a true novum has radical real-world ethical-political potential. The science-fiction novum questions ideological formations (particularly of power) of the past and of the present, compels the implied addressees to think about our world from a fresh perspective, compels the readers or viewers to realize that, as Donna Haraway suggests, "We might have been otherwise, and still might be."[7]

But a pseudo-novum, unlike a true novum, implies no significant difference between the world of the text and the world of the implied addressees. A pseudo-novum, Suvin says, "will not have the vitality of a tree, an animal species, or a belief." A pseudo-novum will be "of brief and narrow relevance,"[8] similar to fashion fads, similar to winning a lottery, similar to a new and improved commodity luxury, even a new and improved weapon. As Suvin says, alluding to Henri Bergson, a pseudo-novum has the "spurting elan of a howitzer shell exploding into successively smaller fragments."[9] The robot in *The Iron Giant* is such a weapon, who or that ultimately explodes into successively smaller fragments—but for a soul (a secret too huge to hide), but for an ability to think and feel, but for his ability to decide he will be otherwise than the advanced weapon of mass destruction that he was apparently programmed to be. A pseudo-novum may, indeed, suggest—at the level of what Fredric Jameson calls the political unconscious, identified at the level of form, form as an argument that often differs from the argument(s) of the content—that we yearn individually and collectively to become otherwise, and that we may still become otherwise. We can create a decadent anti-decadent world in which the spectacular individual flourishes because everyone flourishes spectacularly. We can create a socio-economic structure in which work and art mean serving the needs and pleasures (metaphorical-aesthetic and material) of people rather than the needs of profit for the few, and rather than misery (metaphorical-aesthetic and material) for the many.

In fact, as Csicsery-Ronay suggests, a pseudo-novum may be a quasi-novum, "both less and more rational" than Suvin's conception of the novum. Popular quasi-novums of science fiction are "arbitrary devices designed for spectacular effects that use the images and jargon from the archive of conventional science fictional performances of the past." Quasi-novums are intended to "create the feeling that novums are intrusions from the anima mundi or supernature that have been forced to adapt to contemporary conditions." Here, an example would be Leeloo (a god with an unseen Maker, and a god who weeps when she watches human history, so much violence, cruelty, and poverty play itself out on a television screen) in *The Fifth Element* (1997), written and directed by Luc Besson. Quasi-novums also exceed scientific rationality by claiming that scientific discourse can comprehend and penetrate the supernatural and the surreal."[10] Finally, though neither Suvin nor Csicsery-Ronay says so, a pseudo-novum may, as Carl Freedman suggests about Frankenstein's monster, manifest itself "as one novelty of such radical and profound newness that" though the entire surrounding world is not reconstituted (yet) "the superficially mundane context is dynamically reconstituted as a potential future, new and strange."[11] To hopefully clarify, we may re-name and re-think a pseudo-novum of such radical and profound newness, reconstituting a potential future, a *proto-novum*, and with the proto-novum in mind we turn to Csicsery-Ronay once again:

> A novum is a negative apocalypse. Its meaning lies first ... in the sense that an event has separated the significant time of human species life into a past and a future. Whatever came before the novum is the past; all that lies in the future has been altered. Where the apocalypse of eschatology invokes an Omega-truth to demonstrate history's ultimate purpose, the novum reveals history's contingency: that, at any point, history can change direction, and consequently, its meaning. As the Russian proverb has it, 'The past is unpredictable.'"[12]

Bird's robot (voice, Vin Diesel) *is* a Frankenstein's monster, *is* a proto-novum, (ditto: Leelu in *The Fifth Element*) though the robot's friendship with pre-teen Hogarth Hughes (voice, Eli Marienthal) averts Frankensteinian catastrophe, because, unlike Dr. Frankenstein, Hogarth does not recoil in fear, does not recoil from the ugly-beauty of the giant metal-eating "Frankenbot," whose maker and origins and social-political alternative-world context are unknown. The Frankenbot proto-novum appears as if from the anima mundi, the soul of the world, or of the cosmos, a negative apocalypse revealing the contingency of history. Furthermore, Bird and film-team deploy the CGI image of the sublime robot in Cinemascope,[13] in the midst of hand-drawn animation (images of people, landscape, houses, trees, rocks, and ocean). Thus we have a hybrid anti-commodity commodity — human and machine, machine and soul, past/present/future — a form of adult-generated ugly-beauty as that which generates a longing for personal and social transformation in the heart of an angst-driven post-industrial society, or, as in the case of the film, an angst-driven coastal village, Rockwell, Maine. Though the Iron Giant may be a kind of pseudo-novum, a commodity embedded in a commodity (film), if we re-imagine it and re-think it as a quasi-novum and as a proto-novum, it acquires the vitality of a tree, an animal species, or a belief. Pace Suvin, we can argue for the value of a pseudo-novum when we re-articulate that pseudo-novum as a quasi-novum and as a proto-novum. The imaginary existence of a quasi-novum, henceforth referred to only as a proto-novum, like a true novum, disrupts whatever bearings we may think that we with certainty can claim for ourselves. The proto-novum disrupts our notions about what is possible and never possible in our present, in our near and our far-flung future, and in a future not yet ours.

May Day! May Day!

Jameson argues that because the image is the reified form of the commodity in contemporary society "it is vain to expect a negation of the logic of commodity production." Indeed, he says, "that is why, finally, all beauty today is meretricious and the appeal to it by contemporary pseudo-aestheticism is an ideological manoeuvre and not a creative resource."[14] Jameson's argument is that because advertising arranges all our libidinal investments, because the capitalist commodity structure lies in the form and content of every late-modern work of art, and lies within the form and content of the unconscious of late-modern spectators, we inescapably read, view, imagine, and think via the commodity-image, via capitalist commodity production. Hence, there is in contemporary art in our world of widespread advertising no genuinely proto-political function, no subversive deployment of beauty or subversive deployment of art-religion, such as there was in the 19th century: pre-global capitalism, pre-post-industrialization for the so-called Western world. Jameson's primary 19th century example is Wilde, who, Jameson says, "deployed beauty as a political weapon against a complacent materialist Victorian bourgeois society and dramatized [beauty's] negative power as what rebukes commerce and money and generates a longing for personal and social transformation in the heart of an ugly industrial society." But for us, part and parcel of the society of the spectacle, part and parcel of the post–industrial society, there is no "door open."[15]

If Jameson is quasi-correct, rather than pseudo-correct, about late-modern art, the creators and producers of *The Iron Giant*, beginning with the image *Earth 1957,* commodify space and time. They embrace and promote global, eventual-cosmic, past, present, and future, commodity production when the image of Sputnik circles the earth while what appears to be a comet hurtles towards earth through the eye of a hurricane. We later learn that the comet is not what it appears to be. It is the titular and singular Iron Giant doubling as his own spaceship. In the midst of the hurricane off the coast of imaginary Rockwell, Maine, a fishing-boat captain, Earl Stutz (voice, M. Emmett Walsh), cries out "May Day! May Day! ... I've lost my bearings!" Stutz, alone on his fishing boat, announces a structure of feeling that dominates the if-often-secret lives of adults — epistemological uncertainty, ontological anxiety, fear of metaphorical and material hurricanes — a structure of feeling that adults generally attempt to conceal, particularly from children. *That* secret anxiety is *The Iron Giant's* shadow film that haunts the film's residual Victorian-Romantic argument for art-religion goodness. The shadow film exists despite and because of the comic moments that lampoon paranoiac anxiety, such as the "Duck and Cover" film sequence — what to do in case of a nuclear attack — that the whispering, gossiping school children ignore, and such as the shot of a newspaper headline "Disaster Seen As Catastrophe Looms," which echoes Jim Dear's newspaper headline in Disney's *Lady and the Tramp* (1955). Jim Dear says, "Have you noticed, Darling? Since we've had Lady, we see less and less of those disturbing headlines."[16]

Loom of catastrophe/nostalgic pathos: the 1950s in general were a dark decade that would later ironically come to be the focus of much nostalgic longing post–1960s, reflected in 1970s television: *Happy Days*; *Laverne and Shirley*; syndicated re-runs of *Leave It to Beaver*, the latter which aired its debut the same day that Sputnik was launched. The 1950s were a decade when the ruling class in the U.S. were economically thriving, a decade when parents (ruling class or ruled) could spank their children without fear of accusations of abuse, a decade when prayer-in-schools was the uncontested norm, a decade of racial and ethnic school segregation (separate-but-equal, ahem!), and of civil unrest. And, as Archie and Edith Bunker nostalgically lament in the 1970s television show *All in the Family*, though their nostalgia is for the 1930s, the 1950s to those today filled with nostalgic pathos were a decade when: *"Guys like us, we had it made. Those were the days! Didn't need no welfare state* [only welfare reforms]. *Everybody pulled his weight. Gee, our old LaSalle* [Thunderbird or Studebaker] *ran great. Those were the days! And you knew who you were then! Girls were girls and men were men. Mister, we could use a man like Herbert Hoover* [Ronald Reagan] *again. People seemed to be content. Fifty dollars* [500 dollars] *paid the rent. Freaks were in a circus tent. Those were the days!"*[17]

Freaks in a circus tent: via the aestheticized surface of the 1950s and the science-fiction surface, with *The Iron Giant*, Bird and his film-team invite children *and* adults to believe in the real-world possibility of happiness, friendship, love, goodness, and pleasure, for freaks against worldwide catastrophe. "Dream the impossible!" might be their adult-slogan along with the historically optimistic and bourgeois assertion that actually appears in the film: "You are who you choose to be," first said to Hogarth by Dean McCoppin (voice, Harry Connick, Jr.), goateed, dressed in a black yin-yang robe, in his home at night. Dean is a beatnik-artist who makes art (that no one buys) from the scraps in his junkyard, the entrance bearing the sign: "Where Art Meets Junk." Later, Hogarth repeats to the robot Dean's words,— you are who you chose to be — dissuading the robot from submitting to his programming that determines him to be a weapon of mass destruction, persuading him to fight, only if he must fight, for the sake of goodness, like Superman. Moreover, Bird and his film-team circumscribe *The Iron Giant's* corresponding shadow film, an otherwise absent presence: the real-world probability of sorrow, subjugation, alienation, anxiety, paranoia, and cruelty, the real-world probability that most of us, if not all of us, have very little choice about who we are or who we become. We are but (commodified and instrumentalized) freaks in a circus tent, adult freaks in a real-world circumscribed shadow film.

Generally the term "shadow film" or "shadow text," as Perry Nodelman discusses it in *The Hidden Adult: Defining Children's Literature*, indicates another layer of meaning that is cognitively accessible primarily to adults, as opposed to the surface level that is cognitively accessible to children. Nodelman says, "The simple surface sublimates — hides but still manages to imply the presence of— something less simple," and *that* sublimated "something less simple" must by definition be unchildlike according to adult ideas about childhood and adulthood.[18]

However, Nodelman cites and affirms Zohar Shavit,[19] who says literature for children often has two implied readers (and, in our case here, two implied viewers): a "pseudo-addressee and a real one." In fact, for Shavit, children are more an excuse for the ambivalent texts rather than the texts' "genuine addressee[s]."[20] Hence, as Nodelman paraphrases Shavit, "ambivalence is the normal condition of texts of children's literature."[21] For Nodelman, children's literature subverts childlike innocence by including the "presence of knowledge that a text invites its readers to know but pretend not to know," and this triple awareness of innocence, knowledge, and pretense, or, awareness of text and shadow text or film and shadow film "seems available" to children as well as to adults.[22]

However, particularly when we are speaking of a film, which is expensive to produce, rather than speaking of literature in the form of printed words, much less expensive to produce than a film, ambivalence, equivocation, and pretense may be often due to sloppy, incoherent politics, the need to be sure not to bite the hand that feeds, as much as due to a generic double-coded norm. Tim McCanlies, screenwriter for *The Iron Giant* says in an interview, though he is mostly discussing his later film *Secondhand Lions* (2003): "I am trying to say you should think people in general are basically good even when there's evidence to the contrary ... be very moral even if you pay a penalty. It means: set your own moral code — not in a twisted way — but set your standards high. Do the right thing *because* it's the right thing — even if there is no heaven" (italics original).[23] McCanlies' emphasis on "morality" and on basic goodness of people, against contrary evidence, may be popular neoliberal cant and wishful thinking, the individualistic, muddled thinking of an artist/writer/agnostic (or hushed atheist) rather than the hard-headed critical thinking of a left-wing cultural theorist well-versed in the historical-political-ideological problems of determining "the right thing."

Furthermore, Bird is better known for *The Incredibles* (2004) than for *The Iron Giant*. The former has often been seen as a right-wing film, or at least as the most right-wing of the Pixar films. Bird's *Ratatouille* (2007), however, may be the most left-wing Pixar film. In response to the politically-aware critics, Bird calls himself a "centrist," bristles, and calls critics silly when they say that *The Iron Giant* (Warner Brothers, not Pixar) depicts a leftist argument.[24] Like McCanlies, interested in morality, in goodness, contrasting the good with danger, identifying goodness with spiritual sophistication, Bird says, "We're constantly at odds with our own inventiveness. Every technological leap we take, it's never just a plus. It's always, 'This could cure cancer, and it could also make you have five eyes.' So we have to deal with our technological sophistication," he says, "versus our spiritual sophistication — and technology always seems to be ahead of where we are spiritually. The machine in the movie [*The Iron Giant*] ends up representing our own inventive side of ourselves and begs the question: Is it a good thing, or is it a dangerous thing?"[25] Is *The Iron Giant*, as a contemporary work of art, as a commodity spectacle (though at least part anti-commodity, like Wilde's decadent anti-decadence statue of the Happy Prince), a good thing or a dangerous thing?— or, neither here nor there, art for the sake of art, sloppy-incoherent political aesthetic maneuvering? There is a moment in the film when the Iron Giant hides for self-protection in front of a billboard, comically blending with the advertisement for "Cosmo Burgers," indicating the film-makers conscious or unconscious acknowledgement of the giant robot as a spectacular commodity, as if the film-makers *almost* know that the best place to hide a not-yet revolutionary secret, a proto-novum at the point of becoming revolutionary, is in plain sight, where most of us least expect to find it. However, it is more likely that for the film-makers, animating the giant robot holding an imaginary cosmo-burger was intended for ludic amusement, rather than intended to admit its own anti-ideology ideology.

If Jameson is pessimistically mistaken about late-modern art — partly or completely — we can argue, without making Jameson a straw-man, that what was proto-political for Wilde (a socialist) may be proto-political and subversively proto-effective today as potential nourishment of revolutionary consciousness, i.e., dangerous to the ruling class, despite McCanlies' and Birds' sloppy politics and aesthetic maneuvering. Despite the late 20th and early 21st century intensification of global capitalism, inclusive of widespread advertising, in our *fin de siècle* times, late-modern bourgeois society is hardly complacent, though the working class mostly lacks consciousness of itself as a class, let alone consciousness of itself as an exploited class and as a class in opposition to its exploiters. What we have in the advanced and advancing capitalist nations is an anxiety- and paranoia-stricken bourgeois class, and their or our fears — plus some — are shared by the working and under- or unemployed class. We fear and do not trust not only "foreign" others, not only "freaks," but one another: everyone is foreign, everyone a freak, everyone unsupremely alienated. However, if we believe in the goodness or the possibility of goodness of people, sloppy politics or not, we can more readily understand that a socialist-communist society (which we have not yet had) means no more anxiety- and paranoia-stricken classes — no classes at all — and no more anxiety- and paranoia-stricken individuals, means a world of goodness: no reason to fear the other (menacing monsters, menacing freaks) within or without, no reason to fear our eventual destiny: death. Jameson is entirely (not pseudo) proto-correct when he says:

> In future societies people will still grow old and die, but the Pascalian wager of Marxism lies elsewhere: namely in the idea that death in a fragmented and individualized society is far more frightening and anxiety-laden than in a genuine community, in which dying is something that happens to the group more intensely than it happens to the individual subject. The hypothesis is that time will be no less structurally empty, or to use a current version, presence will be no less of a structural and ontological illusion, in a future communal social life, but rather that this particular "fundamental revelation of the nothingness of existence" will have lost its sharpness and pain and be of less consequence.[26]

Souls Don't Die

Though the giant robot as the inventive side of ourselves, and his pseudo-death, near the end of the film, has limited narrative relevance (significant relevance to a pre-teen boy, his mother, his new father, the boy's former-bully friends), *The Iron Giant* is figuratively shot through with the yearning for socio-economic transformation: the right left thing, even if, or particularly because, there is no heaven. Thus, viewers, whether children or adults, whether religious or non-religious, can choose to recognize the value of representing a possible truth in deep-down bone-marrow goodness (against commodified Cosmo Burgers, and against fear), even when such an argument is part of an aesthetic production within a class against class and an each-against-each alienating capitalist system in which the image is the commodity today. Science-fiction novums, though image-commodities, though beautiful and/or simultaneously ugly, e.g., in *The Iron Giant*, the robot with a steam-shovel jaw, the art that no one buys that Dean makes from junk-yard scraps, can indicate proto-political subversion *in potential*, a proto-negation of the logic of commodity production via what Jameson refers to as 19th century art-religion, but for us it is 20th/21st century hint-of-nostalgia art-religion.

In a world of heterotopic contradictions: idyllic utopia/critical dystopia, technological sophistication/spiritual sophistication (or waning thereof), we in the 21st century can turn to art-religion of the ugly-beautiful, of the comic-serious, for a creative resource, which is exactly what Bird and his film team do. The apparently ugly-monstrous beauty *is* the open door to a transformed future, *is* the subversive deployment of sublime ugly-beauty, of pleasurable freakiness, is a proto-novum (always-already but not yet a true novum) against debilitating anxiety, against debilitating apathy. *Pace* Jameson, today we *can* choose to turn to that which is ugly-beauty for a creative resource, and we can illogically or logically subversively deploy ugly-beauty, and discarded rubbish (Where Art Meets Junk), as a proto-novum *against* the logic of commodity production, much as Wilde did in the 19th century. We may deploy art-religion, and a proto-novum cast backwards in time to 1957, changing the direction of our future, if in unseen ways, against the threat of real-possible world-wide catastrophe, defined as apocalyptic or post-apocalyptic barbarism, and as apocalyptic or post-apocalyptic unremitting banality and nihilism. Nihilism is each-against-each suspicion and mistrust, demanded of us by global capitalism, and yet also unintentionally indicative in Jameson's for us there is no door open. When Hogarth tells the Iron Giant that a soul is "something inside of all good things.... [I]t goes on forever and ever," and suggests — with "I don't know but" — that since the Giant thinks and has feelings — it must have/be a soul, do we call that poignant-progressive kid-logic/kid-trust, mystical flash of critical genius at the edge of the void, or reactionary ideological-consolation and pretense borrowed from a mother, and therefore, for us, a closed door pretending it is open to a better future?

Maybe.

Or we could call the machine, with a soul that doesn't die, the proto-novum (emerging and immanently true novum) of cognition and emotion *within* the pseudo-novum of advanced atomic weaponry (advanced howitzer), within the pseudo-novum of the giant's self-reconstruction. Indeed, there may be more than one kind of "pseudo-novum" in play here in both film and shadow film. This is especially true given the film's double-coding for children vs. adults. Younger children, especially, are so accustomed to encountering new things that they do not fully understand that they process the new much better than adults. As a result, they do not experience the element of discomfort that is crucial to cognitive estrangement as Suvin sees it. For younger children, everything is a novum and so nothing is. Without much of a past from which they can be estranged, they live in a world of novums, which they accept as a given.[27] And yet, as a result, the pseudo-novum of atomic weaponry constituting a giant robot (with a soul) frightens as much as it pleases (ergo: sublime), while for adults the ugly-beauty robot offers nothing new, only pseudo-new, an old sf trope, and only the appearance of the pseudo-religion of "souls don't die." Wilde wrote: "People say sometimes that Beauty is only superficial. That may be so. But at least it is not so superficial as Thought is. To me, Beauty is the wonder of wonders. It is only shallow people who do not judge by appearances. The true mystery of the world is the visible, not the invisible."[28] Furthermore, it is likely that 21st century adults experience novums similarly to children in that for adults everything is a novum, and so nothing is. A science-fiction difference between, oh, say, 19th century adults and adults today is as Csicsery-Ronay puts it:

> Sf is ingrained within the quotidian consciousness of people living in the postindustrial world; each day they witness the transformations of their values and material conditions in the wake of technical acceleration beyond their conceptual threshold.
> So it is that, encountering problems issuing from the social implications of science, and viewing dramatic technohistorical scenes in real life, we displace them into virtual imaginary space, an alternate present or future [or past] that we can reflect on, where we test our delight, anxiety, or grief, or simply play, without having to renounce our momentary sense of identity, or social place, and the world. We transform our experience into sf, if only for a moment.[29]

As adults, cognitively estranged, and pseudo-ludic, beautiful, thoughtful, wonder of wonders, and some few of us adamantly-oddly Marxist, materialist and idealist, we may re-write the possible and quasi-imagined Jamesonian critique of *The Iron Giant* (commodity absent subversion), dialogically altered for the sake of a different future, this way: the robot of *The Iron Giant* is a proto-novum cast into *our* past, as Sputnik (once-upon-a-time a real-world novum) begins its trek. *Earth 1957*, the comet/giant robot/spaceship are space and time reconstituted, not as cosmic commodities, but as a future, new and strange, created by and producing either anxiety or hope or both. *Fin de siècle!* The robot hails either from another planet, another world, or from the future — the diegetic future and our imagined future — or from the anima mundi. Amnesiac, the robot — a bump on his head because of his crash landing — cannot remember his mission. Nor does the robot remember until he is attacked that ontologically and epistemologically he is "a gun," a howitzer, actually, an atomic weapon arsenal with the capability to quickly destroy humankind, the earth itself.

However, because of a soul, and because of the as-if-parent influence of Hogarth — who befriends the robot and teaches him to speak and understand English, who shares with him comic books such as *Superman* and *Atomo* (an evil robot who looks a lot like the Iron Giant), while casting aside *Boy's Life* (humdrum, mundane, conventional, irrelevant, anti-freak), as bedtime stories — the Giant, the as-if-child, whose first words in English in imitation of Hogarth are "blah blah blah," has the capacity to decide who he wants to be, to resist and subvert his original programming. Hogarth tells the robot: "You have feelings, and you think about things. And that means you have a soul." Or, as the army general (voice, John Mahoney) says when he first sees the Iron Giant: "Sweet mother of God!" Art-religion! The inventive side of ourselves, the Giant is a metal man (arguably ugly, or at least monstrous, by human standards) with a (beautiful-freaky) soul. Though amnesiac, he is not a blank slate. The death of a deer shot by men with guns saddens him. Hogarth tells him, "It's not bad to die. But it is bad to kill." It is not bad to die because, as Hogarth says his mom tells him, a soul is "something inside all good things, and it goes on forever and ever." Souls think and feel. And "souls don't die." During the director's commentary on the DVD, Bird affectionately refers to Hogarth's reflections as "kid logic." Some of us prefer, against May Day! May Day!: "mystical flash of critical genius at the edge of the void."

You're Gonna Get It

Representations of menacing monsters (often aliens), menacing freaks with physical deformities and mutations, missile and rocket combat, led Susan Sontag in 1963 to characterize science-fiction films from the 1950s as "not about science" but "about disaster."[30] Their target audience was adults and young adults, not children, though the protagonists had an innocent relationship to disaster, which makes those films seem childlike and unsophisticated to contemporary viewers, including children. Sontag said, "We live under continual threat of two equally fearful, but seemingly opposed destinies: unremitting banality and inconceivable terror." Science-fiction film, she said, is "fantasy served out in large rations by the popular arts, which allows most people to cope with these twin specters." And she suggested that the last-minute happy endings of these sf films serve to "allay" our world-wide anxieties.[31]

However, Sontag argued that modern historical reality, post–1950s, "has greatly enlarged the imagination of disaster and the [science-fiction] protagonists — perhaps by the very nature of what is visited upon them — no longer seem wholly innocent" in their relationship with disaster. Sontag said that more recent science-fiction films have a "decided grimness" not found in the older films,[32] which means that they are less allaying of our world-wide anxieties.

"You're gonna get it," says Hogarth in the *The Iron Giant* to the adult male protagonist of an unnamed science-fiction film that Hogarth is watching on television. Hogarth seems at once sophisticated and innocent in his relationship to disaster or at least in his relationship to the imagination of disaster, and, so, *The Iron Giant* enlarges the absence of decided grimness of those 1950s science-fiction films, *and* enlarges decided grimness, via its circumscribed shadow film. "A SECRET TOO HUGE TO HIDE," proclaims a poster advertising the film. Indeed, Bird and his film-team affectionately parody the kind of science-fiction films that Sontag referred to as "about disaster," alluding to *It Came from Outer Space*, *Invaders from Mars* (1953), *Forbidden Planet* (1956), *The Brain from Planet Arous* (1958), and *The Brain that Wouldn't Die* (1962). Bird says he set the film in 1957 because "There's a little 'Invaders from Mars,' a little 'The Day the Earth Stood Still.' But I also wanted that time period because it presented a wholesome surface, yet beneath the wholesome surface was this incredible paranoia. We were all going to die in a freak-out."[33] Of a kind of parody, the kind with which *The Iron Giant* engages adults, Sontag, in the 1964 essay "Notes on 'Camp,'" said "camp taste is a kind of love, love for human nature. It relishes, rather than judges, the little triumphs and awkward intensities of 'character.' ... Camp taste identifies with what it is enjoying. People who share this sensibility are not laughing at the thing they label as 'a camp,' they're enjoying it. Camp is a *tender* feeling" (italics original).[34]

Bird and team also pay *homage* to, or *borrow from*, or *camp*, and/or *parody*,[35] *E.T.: The Extra-Terrestrial* (1982), *King Kong* (1933, 1976), *Frankenstein* (films based on Mary Shelley's novel, 1818, 1831), and comic-books with heroes such as *Superman* (1938–present). Finally, or, rather, in the first place, Bird and his film-team pay homage to the novella on which the film is loosely based, 20th century English poet Ted Hughes' *The Iron Man* (1968, recently reprinted as *The Iron Giant*) that Hughes wrote to comfort his children after the suicide of their mother, Hughes' marriage-partner, American poet Sylvia Plath. However, the film bears little empirical resemblance to Hughes' novella — except in its fusion of text and shadow text; hope and anxiety; and in its inclusion of a sentient robot. The giant robot in Hughes' story has no super technological powers, and is not the clearly identified alien in the novella. In fact, the novella reads more like a tall-tale or a trickster myth than like science fiction. In the end, after losing a battle of wits with the Iron Giant, a giant space-bat-angel-dragon (who *is* the threatening alien, until defeated) sings the music of the spheres: "a strange soft music that seemed to fill the whole of space, a deep, weird singing, like millions of voices singing together." The music begins to alter the people of the earth so that they stop making weapons. Hughes' narrator (third-person) says: "The countries began to think how they could live pleasantly alongside each other, rather than how to get rid of each other. All they wanted to do was to have peace to enjoy this strange, wild, blissful music from the giant singer in space."[36] Hughes takes his readers to the hopeful precipice (art-religion) of a utopian-musical present, then stops: or leaves the narrative consequences "open," as the countries began to think.... *All they wanted ... this strange, wild, blissful music....*

Jameson, discussing science fiction as a subgenre of utopian literature, argues that because "our imaginations are hostages to our own mode of production (and perhaps to whatever remnants of past ones it has preserved)" that at best the alternative-world utopian representations of science fiction "can serve the negative purpose of making us more aware of our mental and ideological imprisonment...; and that therefore the best Utopias are those that fail the most comprehensively" (xiii). Jameson's conclusion is: "Utopia as a form is not the representation of radical alternatives; it is rather simply the imperative to imagine them."[37] Jameson thus favors decided grimness, for the sake of hope. Representations of strange, wild, blissful music are consolatory-conservative or reactionary — or sloppy — politics. Jameson's theoretical vantage point is what Theodor Adorno, one of Jameson's influences, referred to as the negation of the negation, or, in simplified colloquial parlance, we would say that Adorno and Jameson argue that stories representing the nightmare of history — violent class struggle, and, for us, global capitalism, or, in short, as Jameson says in an early essay, "profit, commodity production, boom and bust, wage labour"[38] — will compel us to realize that we need to imagine and create an otherwise world. However, we will feel more angst when we find such a task to be impossible for us. The stories and films that Jameson favors will not "allay our world-wide anxieties," but will de-conceal and emphasize them. Hope for wresting control from history (a violent class struggle) lies first in our angst, in our awareness of painful economic necessity, not in consolation, and certainly not in nostalgic pathos for the music of the spheres or for childhood and pulp science fiction, not in camp-taste (style without substance, much like pastiche), but instead, and secondly, and ultimately, hope lies in collective action.

At once joyously ecstatic and a neurotic nightmare, at once nostalgic pathos (for childhood, for hand-drawn animation, for pulp sf films) and a history lesson, a cure for nostalgic pathos, at once consolatory and cognitively estranging, at once a time-slip fantasy (for viewers) and science fiction, at once reactionary, conservative, progressive, and radically subversive (at the level of the political unconscious: form and proto-novum against the grain of the content in which very little changes), *The Iron Giant* is also at once parody, camp, and pastiche, for children and adults. There are sexual insinuations; there is the cruel ridicule of a town drunk; and the allusions to sf films from the 1950s are allusions children will not know; there is mild profanity: "Hell, I," "Sweet Mother of God!," "Damn it!" Thus, the fusion of film and shadow film, of the comically frivolous and the serious, points towards the question: if genres construct the "'proper spectator for their own consumption,'" as Dudley Andrew argues[39], what sort of spectator does *The Iron Giant*— not one genre, but several — ideologically construct[40] for its consumption? Who are the implied addressees? America in a nutshell? Bird says, "'Kent Mansley,' the national security agent — he's representing the Ward Cleaver side, and Dean [McCoppin] is representing the rebel side. To me that's America in a nutshell."[41] The preceding is yet another sign of sloppy politics, in this case, Bird's. Mansley, as a representative of abusive government power (who nearly destroys the entire town and is willing to engage in torture and intimidation), is a far more sinister figure than Ward Cleaver, who simply represents banality and conformity. Mansley, of course, now has new dimensions given the post–9/11 context of the "war on terror." Kent Mansley/Ward Cleaver, who utters the words, "You're either for us or against us," is the hybrid-villain of the film. Dean McCoppin/rebel/artist is a reluctant pseudo-hero who assists Hogarth in hiding the metal-eating Iron Giant in Dean's fenced junkyard with the signifying self-referential filmic sign of art-religion, *and* of sloppy-politics: we repeat, "Where Art Meets Junk."

More America in a nutshell, imaginary 1957: in *The Iron Giant* Hogarth enters the forest alone. He rides his bicycle through the streets of town. He has no fear of lurking strangers. There are not any lurking strangers — yet, until the advent of Mansley, paranoid and ruthlessly ambitious, sent to investigate the report of a dangerous thing possibly from outer space, or a dangerous thing possibly created and sent by the Russians, or a beast. In town, Hogarth has no fear of traffic. There isn't much. Hogarth's main libidinal desire is to have a pet, not a dog or a cat. His choices come from the wild, the nearby woods: previously a raccoon, but at the beginning of *The Iron Giant*, a squirrel he has caged. The squirrel escapes to cause havoc in the diner where Hogarth's widowed mother, Annie Hughes (voice, Jennifer Anniston), is a frazzled waitress with a sarcastic sense of humor, and who often works over-time at night, which means that Hogarth is often left alone: a situation he and the townspeople appear to accept without questioning. No one offers assistance.

Hogarth cannot be said to be guilty of much, except for his desire for a pet, and except for occasionally secretively disobeying his mother (for which we love him), as when his late-working mother tells him by phone to be in bed by 8:00, not to watch any scary movies, and to eat the cold chicken and carrots that are in the icebox. Hogarth watches a late scary movie (a crawling brain, imagination of disaster) and eats Twinkies. He also cannot be said to be wholly innocent of the drag of reality, of disaster. He is acquainted with death, with alienation, and with the anxiety of possible poverty. In one scene, in Hogarth's bedroom, we see a photograph of a fighter pilot: Hogarth's father, who was apparently killed in war. Furthermore, at school Hogarth is an outsider to his peers. They ridicule him as a "poindexter," as a "little spaz," because, as Hogarth tells Dean, "They think I think I'm smarter than they are." Hogarth studies, does his homework, makes good grades, has been moved up a grade. Bullies take his lunch money. No wonder Hogarth says of the squirrel he has not yet shown his mother, "He's not a pet, Mom. He's a friend." But Mom does not want a pet-friend that is likely to tear up the furniture because she needs to rent a room in their two- or three-story house (a mortgage easily paid when her husband, Hogarth's father, was alive?) so that she can "make ends meet, and no one wants shredded upholstery.... Do you remember the raccoon, Hogarth? Uggggg. I remember the raccoon."

The End — or Is It?

If not for the science-fictional Iron Giant (quasi-novum/proto-novum), the film would be merely a realistic glimpse at American middle-class boyhood, but a middle-class boyhood in danger of downward mobility and decided grimness, teetering on the edge of poverty, and a friendless boyhood. And if not for the science-fictional Iron Giant, Annie and Dean would likely never marry — Annie's waitressing schedule and single-parenting, as well as Dean's essential kooky otherness in Rockwell, an impediment to intimate socializing. "Excuse me! I apologize to everyone in advance for this," Dean says, as he stands in the diner and unzips his pants to free the undomesticated squirrel that has crawled up the leg of his pants (heading "north," where Dean is tender). No Jim Morrison, residual decadent beatnik of spectacular excess in 1969 who shocked his audience by unzipping his pants — Dean's unzipping is no shock and awe strategy, but one of knowing innocence: not "wanna see my gun-cock?," not Sputnik (initially designed to carry nuclear warheads, though it did not), but only the bushy-tailed squirrel that camply creates havoc. Bird and film-team call the scene "Rocket in Pocket": a sexually suggestive pun for adults, though a non-threatening rocket in pocket, just as the squirrel is not menacing, merely a temporary nuisance to a business establishment.

Thus, *The Iron Giant* may construct spectators who are a nuisance to business establishments, and who question dominant and conventional views of reality, who value rationality against irrationality, or irrationality against rationality, who stick up for the kooks, as Dean suggests we should do (unless the kook is Kent Mansley), who either fear or embrace technological advances, and who then consume more science fiction, more comic books, more fantasy, more animated feature films, who consume (or make) art made from scraps (parody and/or pastiche, art or anti-art). But *The Iron Giant* also constructs spectators who believe that they can decide who they want to be: Kent Mansley/Ward Cleaver or Dean McCoppin/rebel(without a cause)/artist. Who in his or her right mind would choose Kent Mansley/Ward Cleaver? But people do choose Mansley/Cleaver — or become Mansley/Cleaver by default: no choice, when paranoia is socio-economically, ontologically, and epistemologically ingrained, when a bushy-tailed squirrel in one's pants signifies un/domesticated gender disaster, more than a nuisance. Within the film, how much choice does Mansley have when driven by paranoia and ambition? Furthermore, a world in which a relatively young mother commits suicide (Sylvia Plath), and an imagined world in which a young boy's father fights and dies in a war (Hogarth's father), does not leave much room for children or adults to maintain an innocent relationship to disaster. Neither does an awareness of our mental and ideological imprisonment and neither does the awareness of thus-far utopian failure motivate grief-stricken and anxiety-stricken people to imagine that the world can be otherwise than it is. For many of us, failure after failure leads to bitter cynicism, nihilism, and hopelessness, the feeling that the more things change, the more they stay the same. As Bruce E. Levine argues:

> The U.S. government-corporate partnership has used its share of guns and terror to break Native Americans, labor union organizers, and other dissidents and activists. But today, most U.S. citizens are broken by financial fears. There is potential legal debt if we speak out against a powerful authority, and all kinds of other debt if we do not comply on the job. Young people are broken by college-loan debts and fear of having no health insurance.... When people get caught up in humiliating abuse syndromes, more truths about their oppressive humiliations don't set them free. What sets them free is morale. What gives people morale? Encouragement. Small victories. Models of courageous behaviors. And anything that helps them break out of the vicious cycle of pain, shut down, immobilization, shame over immobilization, more pain, and more shut down."[42]

We may suspect, however, and we would probably be right, that children viewing the film are spectators who, if they may choose truly, would choose to be the Iron Giant, the proto-novum, the negative apocalypse who can fly, the historical contingency yet to happen. These children, and some adults engaging in wishful thinking, experience nostalgia for a future that never was (not yet), but yet may be, a future in which we choose who we are without social-economic restraints, without ideological constructions and real-world practices that prevent us from being creators wresting control from history, wresting control from painful necessities. We may suspect that *The Iron Giant* likely constructs spectators who identify as white, and/or who yearn for a negative apocalypse indicating who they and we are by indicating who they and we are not. Hogarth *is* white, as are almost all of the characters in the film, or perhaps all of the characters—a scan of the crowd scenes indicates everywhere whiteness.

Even now *Rockport*, Maine, upon which the imaginary Rockwell may be based, has a population of approximately 3,300, of which 98 percent are white. We might say that Bird and his film team are peopling Rockwell realistically—a painful, non-cognitively estranging necessity, or, alternately, a reactionary's dream—but Rockwell is in a work of science fiction, whose necessary and sufficient condition is the kind of cognitive (not without emotional) estrangement that depictions of an alternative world provide, even an alternative history, arguably particularly an alternative history that includes a negative apocalypse. Thus, so much whiteness is ideologically normalizing: a whitewashing of history, a whitewashing of the future, a whitewashing of science-fiction film for children, if unintentionally. Bird somewhat makes up for this whitewashing, this ethnic absence, in his subsequent animated fantasy films *The Incredibles* and *Ratatoullie*. But, here, with *The Iron Giant*, it is difficult to forgive him for this absence, and we shouldn't.

Yet, in sweet cynicism (one of Sontag's characterizations of camp), we may be wryly happy, when, at the end of *The Iron Giant*, Hogarth gets a father when Annie and Dean marry, when Hogarth's peers accept Hogarth in friendship. No more bullies. After all, Hogarth had known the giant robot, had taught him to use his powers only for good, never for evil, and the robot rescued two of Hogarth's bully-peers from a fall to certain death, sacrificed himself to rescue the town from a U.S. submarine missile. "Not Atomo," the Iron Giant says, "Superman!" But the socio-economic structure of the coastal town of Rockwell, Maine, and by implication the entire world, remains unchanged—old history as the history of violent class struggle unbroken—which is why the surface appearance of the robot meets the requirements of a pseudo-novum rather than a true-novum. It is as if the novum had never existed, or, rather, that the novum has limited or brief relevance. But we know the robot's head is in Iceland, and his body parts that have been blown to smithereens are making their way there to join his head, to self-reconstruct: where and when the Iron Giant will not be content to lie still; he will need to eat; he will seek friendships.

In the last-minute happy-ending — the marriage of Dean and Annie, the unbejeweled statue of the Iron Giant created by Dean and placed in the town-square (Dean now selling his art), and then the Giant's self-reconstruction, his calling of his scattered body parts to come "home" to the glacier in Iceland where his head is — we find a proto-novum, a proto-negative apocalypse, a proto-utopian star. But, the same is true in the fact that Bird wanted — but was out-voted by his film-team — to end *The Iron Giant* without the Giant's happy self-reconstruction, which when included becomes pulp science-fiction camp: "The End — or Is It?" Bird wanted to end the film with the U.S.A. and Russia at war. The war that never happened (in the film and in history) is another haunting or absent presence, a shadow film to the film we see. Had the war occurred in the film we could then call *The Iron Giant*, and Rockwell, the diegetic world of *The Iron Giant*, a critical dystopia: "a non-existent society described in considerable detail and normally located in time and space that the author intended a contemporaneous reader to view as worse than contemporary society."[43] The correction of that society is usually implied by the inclusion of "at least one eutopian enclave" in the narrative — the junkyard where Hogarth plays with the Iron Giant, where the Iron Giant assists Dean in creating art from scraps; the lake in which Hogarth and the Iron Giant swim — or, at the very least, "hope that the dystopia can be overcome and replaced with a eutopia."[44] We would probably also call such a film, a film for adults, not for children.

Is it possible to include eutopian yearning without nostalgia for an idealized past that never was, and for an idealized but subversive 19th century art-religion? Yes. Instead of merely nostalgia for childhood,[45] for kid-logic, or merely nostalgia for nostalgia or merely nostalgia for the present, as Jameson may claim,[46] what we have in depth with *The Iron Giant* is, as utopian philosopher Ernst Bloch has argued about all cultural artifacts, a "utopian laboratory." The value of art, whether meretricious, decadent, mawkish, decidedly grim, or comic/camp, is its ability to serve, as Bloch suggests, as a "feast of elaborated possibilities for the future." These are the elaborated possibilities that are indicative of nostalgia for a future that never was (not yet). Art, as Bloch says, is not "a reflection of the world, but of what the world wants to become"[47] — which science fiction is particularly good at reflecting, though so are fairytales and fantasies. With and against the alienating bullies, with and against the imagination of disaster (real in possibility), with and against commodity production in which financial profit is the bottom line, with and against our looming shadow of paranoia, anxiety, fear, and cruelty, we may choose a kind of love, and tender feeling (also real in possibility), and we may choose kid-logic, hieroglyphic trust ("I don't know but ... you think, and you have feelings"), *for* signs of cognition and emotion, *for* signs of future utopian plenitude, *against* no door open for us, *for* a history lesson as nostalgic pathos, *and* its cure, *for* a return to the promise of a homeland, our real beginning.

The promise of a homeland is I/we with the subjective and objective ability to decide who I/we want to be, possibly constituted by advanced technology with a soul: hint of pseudo-fantasy, hint of pseudo-religion, hint of Donna Haraway's cyborg manifesto, and of shintoist cybermarxism: Darko Suvin's poetic "updating" of Marxism and fusion of Haraway's cyborg with Shinto pantheism[48] (for which we love him). Haraway says: "I am conscious of the odd perspective provided by my historical position — a PhD in biology for an Irish Catholic girl was made possible by Sputnik's impact on U.S. national science-education policy." She says, "I have a body and mind as much constructed by the post–Second World War arms race and cold war as by the women's movements. There are more grounds for hope in focusing on the contradictory effects of politics designed to produce loyal American technocrats, which also produced large numbers of dissidents, than in focusing on the present defeats."[49] Such a souls-don't-die cyborg-shintoist-cybermarxist homeland can only belong to a possible not-yet future, to an odd perspective provided by a historical-aesthetic position, and can only belong to a possible future in which threats of banality and terror, and power hierarchies, no longer exist. What is a focus on film and shadow film, and a focus on a team of artists' sloppy *fin de siècle* politics but *fin de siècle* good-heartedness? What is a focus on contradictory effects of politics, designed to produce children as spectators who can decide who they want to be in a world in which such is mostly impossible, particularly when compared to the possibility of "Cosmo Burgers"? It is a decadent anti-decadence focus where there "arises in the world something [a proto-novum] which shines into the childhood of all in which no one has yet been: homeland."[50] Or, as poindexter/little spaz kook/freak Hogarth says, "Welcome to downtown Coolsville! Population: Us!": our collective proto-negative apocalypse, our collective proto-novum, our collective nostalgia for a future that never was (not yet).

NOTES

1. Linda Hutcheon, "Irony, Nostalgia, and the Postmodern," January 19, 1998, http://www.library.utoronto.ca/utel/criticism/hutchinp.html.
2. Fredric Jameson, *Postmodernism, or the Cultural Logic of Late Capitalism* (Durham, NC: Duke University Press, 1991), 156.
3. Oscar Wilde, "The Happy Prince," *The Complete Fairy Tales of Oscar Wilde* (New York: Penguin Group, 2008), 22.
4. Ibid., 12.
5. Darko Suvin, "Science Fiction and the Novum," in *Defined by a Hollow: Essays on Utopia, Science Fiction, and Political Epistemology* (Bern, Switzerland: Peter Lang, 2010), 85.
6. Istvan Csicsery-Ronay, Jr., *The Seven Beauties of Science Fiction* (Middletown, CT: Wesleyan University Press, 2008), 47.

7. Donna Haraway, *Modest_Witness@Second_Millennium* (New York: Routledge, 1997), quoted in Suvin, *Defined by a Hollow*, 369.

8. Darko Suvin, "Science Fiction and the Novum," 87.

9. Ibid.

10. Csicsery-Ronay, 74–75.

11. Carl Freedman, *Critical Theory and Science Fiction* (Middletown, CT: Wesleyan University Press, 2000), 69.

12. Csicsery-Ronay, 57.

13. Brad Bird says, "I thought you could use CinemaScope to give scale to the Iron Giant, if you weren't trying to show the Giant all at once, if you could see a part of him and then follow things. People basically see in the dimensions of CinemaScope—we see more at the sides. There's something immersive about the experience." See Brad Bird, "Iron without Irony," August 5, 1999.

14. Fredric Jameson, "Transformations of the Image in Postmodernism," in *The Cultural Turn: Selected Writings on the Postmodern, 1983–1998* (London: Verso, 1998), 134.

15. Jameson, "Transformations of the Image in Postmodernism," 134, 135.

16. *Lady and the Tramp*, directed by Clyde Geronimi (Walt Disney Productions, 1955).

17. *All in the Family*, Producer Norman Lear (January 12, 1971–April 8, 1979, USA: CBS).

18. Perry Nodelman, *The Hidden Adult: Defining Children's Literature* (Baltimore: Johns Hopkins University Press, 2008), 206.

19. Zohar Shavit, *Poetics of Children's Literature* (Athens: University of Georgia Press, 1986), quoted in Nodelman, *The Hidden Adult*, 208.

20. Shavit, *Poetics of Children's Literature*, quoted in Nodelman, *The Hidden Adult*, 210.

21. Nodelman, *The Hidden Adult*, 210.

22. Ibid., 211.

23. Tim McCanlies, "Iron Lion: An Interview with Tim McCanlies," interviewed by Scott Holleran, October 16, 2003, www.boxofficemojo.com/news.

24. Brad Bird, "An Interview with Brad Bird," interviewed by Andy Patrizio, March 9, 2009, http://dvd.ign.com/articles/594/594806p3.

25. Brad Bird, "Iron Without Irony," interviewed by Michael Sragow, *Salon*, August 5, 1999, www.salon.com/entertainment.

26. Fredric Jameson, *The Political Unconscious: Narrative as a Socially Symbolic Act* (Ithaca, NY: Cornell University Press, 1981), 261.

27. I thank M. Keith Booker for this idea about children's experience of novums.

28. Oscar Wilde, via Lord Henry in chapter 2 of *The Portrait of Dorian Gray* (1891), www.classicreader.com/book/1914/3/.

29. Csicsery-Ronay, *The Seven Beauties of Science Fiction*, 4–5.

30. Susan Sontag, "The Imagination of Disaster," in *Against Interpretation and Other Essays* (New York: Farrar, Straus, and Giroux, 1966), 213.

31. Ibid., 224–225.

32. Ibid., 215.

33. Bird, "Iron Without Irony."

34. Susan Sontag, "Notes on 'Camp,'" in *Against Interpretation and Other Essays* (New York: Farrar, Straus, and Giroux, 1966), 291–292.

35. Sometimes the borderlines between the preceding three modes are non-existent or invisible; sometimes parody is what Jameson et al. call ludic *pastiche*—all surface play, a blank use of previous motifs for entertainment purposes, without historical or political substance. Sometimes parody or pastiche in sf signifies a quasi-novum.

36. Ted Hughes, *The Iron Giant: A Story in Five Nights* (New York: Random House, 2002), 76–79.

37. Fredric Jameson, *Archaeologies of the Future: The Desire Called Utopia and Other Science Fictions* (New York: Verso, 2005), 416.

38. Jameson, "Transformations of the Image in Postmodernity," 93.

39. Dudley Andrew, *Concepts in Film Theory* (Oxford: Oxford University Press, 1984), quoted in Ian Wojcik-Andrews, *Children's Films: History, Ideology, Pedagogy, Theory* (New York: Garland, 2000), 171.

40. Bird bristles and denies that animation counts as a genre as if animation as "genre"

suggests not art but junk, or sentimental pap, for indiscriminating children, or as if "genre" limits animation to one form of narrative rather than to several forms.

41. Bird, "Iron without Irony."
42. Bruce E. Levine, "Are Americans a Broken People? Why We've Stopped Fighting Back Against Oppression," December 11, 2009, www.alternet.org.
43. Lyman Tower Sargent, "US Eutopias in the 1980s and 1990s: Self-Fashioning in a World of Multiple Identities," in *Utopianism/Literary Utopias and National Cultural Identities: A Comparative Perspective*, edited by Paola Spinozzi (Bologna: COTEPRA/University of Bologna, 2001), 222. I thank Alexander Charles Oliver Hall for sharing with me this reference that is a key part of his Ph.D. dissertation-in-progress.
44. Ibid., 222.
45. "Adults driven to write for children and about childhood are likely to be driven by nostalgia, for all were once children and are therefore revisiting a part of their own experience now past every time they write. As Valerie Krips suggests, however, 'few adults would want to return to childhood as it was actually lived, with all its unremembered difficulties, humiliations, and problems, but returning to a past in which the problems of adulthood are by and large unknown is a different and much more enticing prospect.'" Valerie Krips, *The Presence of the Past: Memory, Heritage, and Childhood in Postwar Britain* (New York: Garland, 2000), quoted in Nodelman, *The Hidden Adult*, 16.
46. Fredric Jameson, "Nostalgia for the Present," *Postmodernism, or the Cultural Logic of Late Capitalism* (Durham, NC: Duke University Press, 2001), 279–296.
47. Ernst Bloch, *The Principle of Hope*, translated by Neville Plaice, Stephen Plaice, and Paul Knight (Cambridge, MA: MIT Press: 1986), 1:216.
48. Darko Suvin, "The Profession of Science Fiction, 49: Travels of a Shintoist CyberMarxist," interview by Liau Chao-Yang and Tami Hager, *Foundation*, 67 (1996), 5–27.
49. Donna J. Haroway, "A Cyborg Manifesto: Science, Technology, and Socialist-Feminism in the Late Twentieth Century," in *Simians, Cyborgs, and Women: The Reinvention of Nature* (New York: Routledge, 1991), 173.
50. Bloch, *The Principle of Hope*, 3:1375–1376.

REFERENCES

All in the Family. Television Program. Produced by Norman Lear. January 12, 1971–April 8, 1979. USA: CBS.
Andrew, Dudley. *Concepts in Film Theory*. Oxford: Oxford University Press, 1984.
Andrews, Ian-Wojcik. *Children's Films: History, Ideology, Pedagogy, Theory*. New York: Garland, 2000.
The Fifth Element. Directed by Luc Besson. USA and France: Gaumant, 1997.
Bird, Brad. "An Interview with Brad Bird." Interviewed by Andy Patrizio. March 9, 2009. http://dvd.ign.com/articles/594/594806p3.
_____. "Iron without Irony." Interviewed by Michael Sragow. *Salon*. August 5, 1999. www.salon.com/entertainment.
Bloch, Ernst. *The Principle of Hope*. Vol. 1–3. Translated by Neville Plaice, Stephen Plaice, and Paul Knight. Cambridge, MA: MIT Press: 1986.
Csicsery-Ronay, Istvan, Jr. *The Seven Beauties of Science Fiction*. Middletown, CT: Wesleyan University Press, 2008.
Freedman, Carl. *Critical Theory and Science Fiction*. Middletown, CT: Wesleyan University Press, 2000.
Haraway, Donna J. "A Cyborg Manifesto: Science, Technology, and Socialist-Feminism in the Late Twentieth Century." In *Simians, Cyborgs, and Women: The Reinvention of Nature*, 149–181. New York: Routledge, 1991.
_____. *Modest_Witness@Second_Millennium*. New York and London: Routledge, 1997.
Hughes, Ted. *The Iron Giant: A Story in Five Nights*. New York: Random House, 2002.
Hutcheon, Linda. "Irony, Nostalgia, and the Postmodern." Last modified January 19, 1998. www.library.utoronto.ca/utel/criticism/hutchinp.
Jameson, Fredric. *The Political Unconscious: Narrative as a Socially Symbolic Act*. Ithaca, NY: Cornell University Press, 1981.

_____. *Postmodernism, or the Cultural Logic of Late Capitalism.* Durham, NC: Duke University Press, 1991.

_____. "Transformations of the Image in Postmodernity." In *The Cultural Turn: Selected Writings on the Postmodern, 1983–1998.* London: Verso, 1998.

Krips, Valerie. *The Presence of the Past: Memory, Heritage, and Childhood in Postwar Britain.* New York: Garland, 2000.

Lady and the Tramp. Directed by Clyde Geronimi. Walt Disney Productions, 1955.

Levine, Bruce E. "Are Americans a Broken People? Why We've Stopped Fighting Back Against Oppression." December 11, 2009. www.alternet.org.

McCanlies, Tim. "Iron Lion: An Interview with Tim McCanlies." Interviewed by Scott Holleran. October 16, 2003. www.boxofficemojo.com/news.

Moylan, Tom. *Scraps of the Untainted Sky: Science Fiction, Utopia, Dystopia.* Boulder, CO: Westview Press, 2000.

Nodelman, Perry. *The Hidden Adult: Defining Children's Literature.* Baltimore: Johns Hopkins University Press, 2008.

Sargent, Lyman Tower. "US Eutopias in the 1980s and 1990s: Self-Fashioning in a World of Multiple Identities." In *Utopianism/Literary Utopias and National Cultural Identities: A Comparative Perspective*, edited by Paola Spinozzi. Bologna: COTEPRA/University of Bologna, 2001.

Sontag, Susan. "The Imagination of Disaster." In *Against Interpretation and Other Essays*, 209–225. New York: Farrar, Straus, and Giroux, 1966.

_____. "Notes 'On Camp.'" In *Against Interpretation and Other Essays.* New York: Farrar, Straus, and Giroux, 1966.

Suvin, Darko. "The Profession of Science Fiction, 49: Travels of a Shintoist CyberMarxist." Interview by Liau Chao-Yang and Tami Hager. *Foundation*, 67 (1996), 5–27.

_____. "Science Fiction and the Novum." In *Defined by a Hollow: Essays on Utopia, Science Fiction, and Political Epistemology*, 67–92. Bern, Switzerland: Peter Lang, 2010.

Wilde, Oscar. "The Happy Prince." *The Complete Fairy Tales of Oscar Wilde.* New York: Penguin Group, 2008.

_____. Via Lord Henry in ch. 2 of *The Portrait of Dorian Gray* (1891), www.classicreader.com/book/1914/3/.

• *Ten* •

Doctor Who:
A Very British Alien

J. P. C. Brown

Doctor Who is a British show about an alien time-traveler, who wanders through space and time in a ship (called the TARDIS) which has been disguised as a London police box: it's meant to change shape to match its surroundings, but at the outset of the series it got stuck. The show was first transmitted in the UK on 23 November 1963 in the late Saturday afternoon slot that would be its usual one for most of the life of the original (a.k.a. "classic") series (1963–1989).[1] Given that its title appears to tie the show closely to the main character, one might have expected the show to end when its first leading man, William Hartnell, left the series. Instead the show hit upon the ploy that made it possible, in principle, for it to keep going indefinitely: the Doctor can regenerate. When seriously injured or worn out, he literally becomes a different man. For as long as there are actors capable of playing him, the show can go on. From the end of October 1966 for the rest of the decade the Doctor was played by Patrick Troughton. Then in 1970 a new Doctor (Jon Pertwee) embarked on a series of adventures in color for the first time, and working with the United Nations Intelligence Taskforce (UNIT). From 1974 to 1981 Tom Baker played the role, draped in what became an iconic and enormously long scarf. The original series boasted three more Doctors (Peter Davison, 1982–84; Colin Baker, 1984–86; and Sylvester McCoy, 1987–89), but it ceased production in 1989. A pilot TV movie of 1996 set in the USA didn't lead to a new series. And yet in 2005 the show was reborn and is currently being made by BBC Wales, and this new version of the series has already had three different doctors over five years (Christopher Ecclestone,

2005; David Tennant, 2006–2010; Matt Smith, 2010–present), and is going strong. Why, then, did it grind to a halt in 1989? It's the claim of this essay that, notwithstanding the diverse topics that were being addressed week by week early on in the show's life, the program drew much of its imaginative life from the way it explored one topic, the problem of Britishness, and that this topic was only really sustaining for the first decade and a half or so of the show's life.

Why should Britishness be a problem? It's a problem partly for the reason any national identity is a problem: it involves asserting homogeneity in the face of diversity and particularity. But, as with all national identities, the identity has to be particular in relation to other national identities, while ultimately trumping particular identities within the territory of the nation-state: loyalty to the nation-state must, in the last analysis, override loyalty to one's region or to any sub-group within the nation-state. Hence the paradoxical note often struck in writing that advocates nationalism in which the nation is distinct from a universal concept of humanity, while also drawing something of its legitimacy from the assertion of the nation's special role in human progress as such. That is exactly the claim made by Mazzini's *The Duties of Man* in the way it puts "Duties to Humanity" before duties to country, family or oneself, while seeing the realization of the nation-state as essential to the progress of humanity. Previously Herder had made a similar claim.[2]

There are various ways of theorizing national identity. Sometimes it's tied to religion, though that can prove divisive in pluralist societies, and sometimes to biological race, though that was never popular in Britain. In the nineteenth century the idea of there being a definite national character enjoyed some vogue — though it was commoner to speak of English character than of British character.

In practice national characters tend to be fluid and contested. There may be tussles between representing certain traits in pejorative terms (e.g., the critical claim that "the British are emotionless" may be countered with the claim that the British have a "stiff upper lip"— i.e. the British are stoical, restrained and courageous). The contestation can be internal to the nation as well as external, and sometimes the two struggles interact. For example, even in the heyday of talk about national character, there was always some tension between representing the nation by its elite, who, of course, in many ways actually did represent it to the world at large, not least, in Britain's case, by governing the British Empire, and representing the nation by some stereotypical figure further down the class system, such as "John Bull," who, when he first appeared in eighteenth-century political cartoons, was a yeoman farmer of blunt good sense and decidedly rural character, though he later moved up the social ladder to become a country squire. Women were routinely excluded from representations of the British national character, and, to an extent that now seems astonishing, this went largely unchallenged. But one could often find some sort of struggle between the gentleman as the British archetype and a figure who commonly appeared in British discourse before the Second World War: the "Little Man." The struggle could be used to articulate, for example, very different responses to empire. It could also be used to articulate arguments about the character of national life: the stereotypical gentleman could be attacked as hopelessly amateurish, incompetent and blessed with unmerited privilege. There was an argument within Britain in the 1930s, which carried on into World War Two along these lines. The gentlemanly stereotype of Britishness could be used, for example, to argue that a technically competent, more energetic and aggressive working class needed to be freed from the stifling paternalism of the ruling class (a stereotypical stand-off that persists in popular culture: see, e.g., *Gosford Park*). But it also figured in the way Britain appeared to the rest of the world, and the way it thought of itself in relation to the rest of the world.

This was particularly true during the Second World War, which, as Peter Mandler argues, was almost the last hurrah for confident talk of national character, even though it was almost impossible to specify exactly what that character might be:

> ... there were multiple national characters in play during the war, some more bourgeois and some more proletarian, some more passive and some more active, some looking backwards and some looking forwards. This is only to be expected from what was, after all, the first war fought by Britain in which the character of the people was universally acknowledged from all points of the political spectrum as the key to winning the war, and even to deciding what the war was for. It was, coincidentally, the first war in which all of the people — on home front and war front alike — were constantly bombarded with intimate descriptions of what they themselves were like.[3]

This problem of how to represent the British was of particular importance in Britain's relation to the U.S. Churchill was determined to draw the U.S. into the war, since he knew Britain couldn't win otherwise. Many in the U.S. were understandably reluctant to get mired in an essentially European conflict. It was possible for Americans to wonder why they should come to the aid of what could be represented as an intensely hierarchical, class-bound society. Given his aristocratic background, Churchill was easily represented as the embodiment of that hierarchical society, even though he was in fact Anglo-American and chose to remain a commoner to the end of his days. Therefore British propaganda made a point of showing the plight of ordinary, plucky Britons, especially of showing them coping with the Blitz. Films such as *London Can Take It* established a myth (albeit one based on fact) which persists on both sides of the Atlantic to this day, as was seen in the way in which the London bombings of 7 July 2005 were reported.

However, after the war talk of national character quickly foundered on underlying diversity and an inevitable weakening of common purpose. The war's moment of national unity symbolically came to an end with the 1945 election which voted Churchill out of office, and installed Atlee's Labor administration, which established the welfare state and nationalized key industries. From one point of view, this was delivering on promises made during the war (especially in the Beveridge Report of 1942): Britain was to assert national solidarity across classes, by ensuring everyone was looked after and had a stake in the nation. From another point of view, this development was worryingly bureaucratic, *dirigiste* and difficult to reconcile with British traditions of self-reliance, individualism, free markets and liberty. This sense of missing the lost certainties of wartime and of entering a period when national character was not always easy to be sure about would inform approximately the first decade and a half of *Doctor Who*. In many ways the Second World War lurked in the background of the show's first decade or more.

The Suez Crisis of 1956 coincided with what became a sustained debate about the state of the nation, which lasted until 1964,[4] and helped to ensure that the question of Britain's decline in the world kept being explored. The tendency to invoke the opposition between an old-fashioned gentlemanly elite and the rest of the country was used to explain the Prime Minister, Anthony Eden's, dire miscalculation in sending troops to take the Suez Canal in an Anglo-French operation, coordinated with an Israeli attack on the Sinai. It was a military success. But politically, without the support of the U.S., it was a fiasco, and the U.S. coordinated opposition to the invasion in the General Assembly of the UN, which led to a British climb-down and Eden's fall from office. The next few years saw the withdrawal from empire accelerate, without it becoming clear how a post-imperial Britain saw itself in relation to the rest of the world (Dean Acheson's remark about Britain losing an empire without having "yet found a role" dates from December 1962). It's in these years of pessimism and internal debate, as the ideas of national character and of national unity are called into question, that what there is in the way of a stereotypical national character comes to be seen as overwhelmingly gentlemanly: by the left, the better to attack it, and by many of the right, the better to celebrate it.[5]

Doctor Who appeared at a significant moment in relation to Britain's withdrawal from empire, which, while seldom the principal determinant of Britain's self-image (plenty of British stereotypes had blithely ignored the empire), did have an impact on how Britain conceived of its role in the world, and to that extent on British identity. Since Britain had quit India in 1948 amidst the ghastly bloodshed of partition, it might appear that the idea of empire was done for by the end of the 1940s. But, as Michael Paris points out, while British public opinion had been prepared before 1939 for the eventual independence of India, Africa was a different matter.[6] The image of imperialism revived in the early 1950s. Hence the savagery with which the British responded to the Mau-Mau uprising. However reprehensible, this was not the policy of a country that thought the empire was finished. It was only post–Suez, and possibly not until the 1960s that one finds "a real feeling of disillusionment and disintegration."[7] In the early 1950s the empire still informed Britain's self-image. Films that assumed the rightness of empire continued to appear as they had done in the 1930s.[8] According to MacIntyre the debate about empire was especially intense between 1960 and 1963.[9] The propaganda by which the British public had been persuaded to support imperialism faded rapidly thereafter.[10] *Doctor Who* began its long life as popular imperialist ideology in Britain was changing as part of broader changes in the nation's self-image. The main claim of this paper is that *Doctor Who* responded to this changing climate of opinion, and that at its best it does so in ways that informed the program's imaginative vitality.[11]

For when *Doctor Who* was launched it was hard to know exactly what the British national character was, or if such a thing existed at all. Britain was haunted by the lost unity of the war, and was having difficulty coming to terms with its post-war decline. To the extent that there were national stereotypes, they were gentlemanly. But these were always contentious — and, indeed, in popular culture, the gentlemanly Brit would be treated ironically (as, for example, in 1960s shows such as *The Avengers* or *Adam Adamant*). While there are certain traits that one could perhaps see as ones that some of the British like to think of as typically British (such as eccentricity, decency, strong feelings largely concealed by reserve and good manners, love of liberty, championing the underdog, distrust of bureaucracy and big government), one could just as well come up with a completely different list with at least as strong a basis in fact.

The problem of Britishness was of particular relevance to the institution which made *Doctor Who*: the *British* Broadcasting Corporation. From 1922 until 1955, supported by the license fee, the BBC enjoyed a monopoly of broadcasting in Britain. None of the BBC's channels carried commercial advertising. The sense of its projecting an official version of Britishness (albeit at arm's length from the government: radio and television licenses were required by law, but the BBC was overseen by a Board of Governors nominally appointed by the monarch) had been intensified in the war, during which radio was rivaled as a mass medium only by cinema, since BBC television had been taken off the air for the duration of the conflict. Notwithstanding some good British films, Hollywood dominated the British movie market. Hollywood's success in developing its overseas markets was felt particularly in Britain, partly because in the era of sound cinema, English-speaking Britain could import Hollywood films without dubbing or subtitles. The attempt to sustain a distinctively British cinema foundered on the difficulty of penetrating the vast and necessary American market. So in terms of Britishness and mass media, for several decades the BBC was the principal guardian of the nation's identity.

It was a tricky role to play, not least because, though the BBC was ultimately just one organization, British national identity could appear to be different things, depending on how one looked at it in relation to class, generation, gender and region. The stereotypical image of the BBC in its first decades has it insisting on Britishness as essentially white, male, upper middle-class and (above all) respectable. Regional voices were heard, but for the most part Received Pronunciation (a standard version of spoken English that is probably closest to middle or upper middle class speech) was the order of the day.

However, in 1954 the Television Act became law. It provided for regional television stations to be paid for by advertising. Between 1955 and 1962 these stations were established, and were known collectively as Independent Television (ITV).[12] So by 1962 British viewers had a choice of two channels, and the ITV channels were drawing bigger audiences than the BBC.[13] The means by which they did so were often criticized for sensationalism (especially in pursuit of ratings) and for Americanizing British media — American television affording the key instance of commercial television at this date. This reflected a continuing anxiety. Popular cinema was already largely American; several kinds of popular music, notably rock and jazz were more American than anything else, and the popularity of American cultural imports in some ways gave a powerful voice to groups that had been marginalized (consider, for example, the way the déclassé Jimmy Porter in John Osborne's 1956 play, *Look Back in Anger*, uses jazz trumpet as a weapon). Yet cultural authority of the kind the BBC represented remained a real force, even if its position was being undermined. This authority was partly a class matter. The upper middle class tone of the BBC could assert the BBC's claims to be the arbiter of cultural merit partly because the BBC seemed to have reconciled its popularity as a mass medium with its cultural status. While this worked, authority and democracy were reconciled. But the ITV channels challenged this squaring of the circle by getting better ratings. That was why the Pilkington committee, charged with making recommendations about the future of radio, in June 1962 came out against commercial radio entirely.

Such was the climate of opinion about the national role of broadcasting in which *Doctor Who* was conceived. From the first, it was clear the program was going to be pulled in different directions. Sidney Newman, the new Canadian head of television drama at the BBC, gave *Doctor Who*'s first producer, Verity Lambert, instructions that there were to be no "bug-eyed monsters." There was to be a serious element to the show, which was aimed at children, but in the hope that adults would watch too, and that it would be in some way improving. But there was always going to be a danger of its heading downmarket in a very non–BBC manner. Newman was initially furious with Lambert over the second story, which introduced the Doctor's greatest enemy, the Daleks, because, in his view, these cyborgs smacked of sensationalism. Lambert defended them: the story (set on the ravaged, post-nuclear planet of Skaro) was a serious exploration of the possibility of nuclear annihilation, and of the problems involved in two responses to it. In the story the Thals and the Daleks are the survivors of a long war. The Thals are now beautiful and pacifist. The Daleks, by comparison, have given up human form, and withdrawn into motorized and armed travel machines. In the aftermath of the Cuban Missile Crisis of October 1962, the story explored a topical dilemma: a pacifist response to nuclear weapons might prove too idealist to do any good (and in the course of the story the Doctor would rally the Thals to fight the Daleks), while too ready an embrace of nuclear weapons would rob one of one's humanity. As it turned out, the Daleks were such a sensation that "Dalekmania" guaranteed the show's success.[14] The ethical and thematic context of the story was quickly forgotten, partly because the Daleks proved surprisingly appealing to small children, whose playground imitations of the Daleks (especially their electronic shriek of "Exterminate! Exterminate!") sociologists and psychologists anxiously observed. There was a powerful dimension of the Daleks' appeal that was irrational and sensational, and at odds with the mission the BBC had given the show.

Part of the series' initial remit was to combine entertainment with education. Hence the historical stories that were a feature of the first Doctor's travels, in which the TARDIS took its occupants to see Marco Polo, the Aztec Empire, the French Revolution, the Roman Empire, the Crusades, the St. Bartholomew's Day Massacre and the shoot-out at the OK Corral. These historical stories drew upon the BBC's acknowledged expertise in costume drama. Unlike many of the later stories set in the past, they usually eschewed science-fictional elements once the TARDIS and its crew had landed. So there would not usually be technologically advanced aliens meddling with history for the Doctor to thwart. Instead there would be a carefully created historical setting and a story that often turned on the travelers' attempts to resume their journey without changing history. Initially the overall mix resembled *Look and Learn*, a magazine for children that appeared in the UK between 1962 and 1982, which published illustrated articles on history, literature, science and technology, and which also included fiction, notably the SF/fantasy strip, *The Trigan Empire*.[15]

The crew of the TARDIS's earliest journeys comprised the Doctor, his granddaughter, Susan, and her schoolteachers, Barbara and Ian, who stumbled into the TARDIS by mistake, and whom the Doctor kidnapped to prevent their telling anyone else about his time machine. If anyone was intended to be the hero, it was Ian. In the earliest stories the Doctor was hardly dependable. In the second story (the one that introduced the Daleks) the Doctor even sabotaged the TARDIS to make it impossible to leave Skaro because he wants to investigate, and he showed a worrying streak of selfishness, notably when he seeks to rally the Thels to fight for their freedom, when it's clear his real motive is to get them to attack the Dalek city so that he can recover the component from the TARDIS that he removed in the first place. Over the first season his character softened, but he could still be off-putting. However, if there's an inhuman side to the Doctor, it may not be entirely un–British. As the possessors of a vast empire, the British often saw others as needing British guidance to realize their potential, and also as having to go through a process of historical development under British tutelage — a scheme of things in which the British blithely supposed themselves to be historically advanced. Even J.S. Mill (arch-proponent of liberal freedoms) had proposed such an ideal.[16] Reality seldom lived up to it, even if a case can be made for its having had some long term benefits.[17] Thinking of the Doctor's dress sense and demeanor for most of the original series, Piers Britton and Simon Barker state that the "ideological underpinnings" of the series "are essentially the values of British colonialism."[18] There is some truth in this, but the Doctor's relation to imperialism is more complex. From the first episode it was clear that, so far from being the agent of an imperial power, he was fleeing his own, powerful people, though it would be some years before we learned much about them. In certain respects his image suited a Britain that in 1963 was beginning to acknowledge that the empire was over. And it's perhaps also worth nothing that, though the first Doctor's clothes made him look like an Edwardian gentleman, William Hartnell was known for playing people of a lower class, especially fierce army sergeants, though he also gives a fine performance as the criminal, Dallow, in the 1947 film of Graham Greene's *Brighton Rock*. Indeed, Hartnell's own background included a spell of juvenile crime while he was growing up as the child of a single mother in a poor part of London. In class terms, especially in terms of the opposition between gentlemanly and other stereotypes of Britishness, Hartnell communicated a mixed message.

By the show's second season the Doctor's initially worrying character had settled into something more heroic: no more kidnapping of his companions or sabotaging the TARDIS to get his own way. The second story of that season was *The Dalek Invasion of Earth*.[19] It derives from H.G. Wells's *The War of the Worlds* (1898), which itself sprang from Wells's desire to bring home the realities of colonial exploitation to Britain, especially to its richest, southeastern part — something flagged in the novel's opening chapter.[20] Hence the devastation of Guildford and London. But *The Dalek Invasion* also reflects on Nazi imperialism.[21] For an audience which always included, and was meant to include, adults as well as children,[22] the parallels with aspects of World War Two would have been clear: an underground resistance, black marketeers, slave labor camps and so on. Though it is meant to be set in the 2160s, after humanity has been decimated by a Dalek-inflicted plague, there is no evidence of anything in London from later than 1964 other than the invaders. But that is part of the point, so much so that the rebels seem deliberately at one moment to be pushed back into the past. Barbara and the rebels, Jenny and Dortmun, stop off at a transport *museum* as they flee London, and they escape in a vintage lorry. Elsewhere, the story dwells upon British national monuments: it tracks the Daleks as they patrol Trafalgar Square, sweep across Westminster Bridge, with the Houses of Parliament in the background, and pass in front of the Albert Memorial. These are nineteenth-century celebrations of British power, now used as the ironic backdrop for Britain's conquerors.

It is possible to cavil at many of the details of the story. Tat Wood and Lawrence Miles in their entry on the story in their immense and illuminating multi-volume account of *Doctor Who* have a whole list of "Things That Don't Make Sense."[23] Yet the story has an eerie resonance. The Daleks are alien and yet worryingly recognizable as a projection of an aspect of the human. They are cyborgs, their organic components confined within their wheeled travel machines. It is hard to account for the decision to confine the rebel leader, Dortmun, to a wheelchair other than in terms of pointing up a parallel between Daleks and humans. It is clear when he wheels himself outside the transport museum to confront three Daleks with the bombs he has obsessively been trying to perfect. Later it becomes clear that the Daleks too are obsessively working on a bomb: one to destroy the earth's magnetic core, so they can steal the planet.

Consider Dortmun's name. Why use a Germanic name (reminiscent of Dortmund, where Hitler held rallies in the 1930s) for a resistance leader in London, if not to raise questions about him? The Daleks are irredeemably bad, so if one wants to watch the story simply in terms of beating the bad guys, that's possible. But complexity develops when one turns from Daleks to people. These include the morally compromised characters of the defeated, among whom are numbered a black marketeer and a couple of women who betray Jenny and Barbara to the Daleks for some food. Even the Robomen (humans used as policemen, and under electronic control by the Daleks) start to look like collaborators. References to Britain's imperial past need to be seen in this context. They are mainly a question of the monuments against which the Daleks are photographed in scenes reminiscent of the Nazis posturing in Paris, but there is also, bizarrely, an allusion to India: the only other part of the globe specifically said to be occupied by the Daleks. The allusion reminds us that the previous occupying power in India had been the British.

The story, then, addresses the question of soon-to-be post-imperial Britain in such a way that straightforward identification with the British is problematic. It is as if the makers had taken to heart not only everything affectionate but also everything scathing that George Orwell has to say about Englishness in *The Lion and the Unicorn* (1941), in which he notes that "the gentleness of English civilization is mixed up with barbarities and anachronisms."[24] Simple oppositions (British/German; human/alien; virtuous/corrupt) are called into question by the story, and, if the end of the story seems implausible, that is not only because practical questions are left hanging (in defeating the Daleks at the slave-worked mine, can the Doctor and his friends really have defeated the entire occupation force?), but also because underlying ideological questions cannot readily be resolved.

It's in the nature of a story that it can, at best, furnish only symbolic solutions to real problems, which will still be there once one has finished watching the story. In any case, a children's television show that explicitly set about providing "answers" to the problem of Britain's changing conception of itself would be likely to prove doctrinaire and simplistic. It's not necessarily that the key creative personnel were unaware of the larger issues they were broaching. In some cases there's evidence that they knew precisely what issues they were invoking (see the discussion of the *Peladon* stories, below). But their main concern was to tell stories. In any case, the kind of imaginative vitality at stake in this context is probably less a question of the intentions of individual writers or producers than of the show's engagement with topics that troubled the audience, and its adroit negotiation of how far it could afford to go in tackling them. To use an obvious Marxist concept, one might say that one of the interesting things about the moment at which *Doctor Who* appears is that it coincides with a rupture or shift in the dominant ideology in Britain. Even if one is unhappy with the singular nature of the classic Marxist formulations (just one dominant ideology: why does there have to be one dominant ideology, provided the various ideologies that predominate within particular groups in society are functionally integrated?), this way of registering what the program was responding to acknowledges the conditions in the world at large that contributed to it, without necessarily devaluing the creative contribution of particular people. The crucial mediating element is arguably the institution of broadcasting as such, and, in particular, the BBC itself, given its simultaneous concern to nurture talent and to fulfill a role in the state, as required by its public service remit, even if it is never to be seen merely as the instrument of government, since that would devalue its role in national life by rendering it politically partisan or beholden to specific political interests.

In this regard the seemingly self-evident Britishness of the Doctor becomes significant. The mystery surrounding the Doctor insulates him from many awkward questions. For the series' first few years he has virtually no backstory. That saves him from complicity with empire. On the other hand, the first Doctor's clothes associate him (and in successive regenerations would continue to associate him) with imperial Britain in the decade or two prior to World War One. They also, therefore, associate him with the era of H.G. Wells's "scientific romances," and *The Time Machine* is plainly an influence on the series as a whole.[25]

If the Doctor himself evokes the era of imperial Britain, in echoing World War Two, which the show does not only in *The Dalek Invasion* but repeatedly, *Doctor Who* reflects the global decline of the British state. In the 1960s *Star Trek* could plausibly envisage an interplanetary federation seemingly under American direction and embody this in the heroic figure of James T. Kirk. British science fiction for children had flirted with the idea of that kind of hero in Dan Dare in a comic strip (1950–1969) and on radio (1951–1956). But Dan Dare harked back to World War Two as well as looking forward: notwithstanding the subtitle ("pilot of the future") parts of his uniform, such as the sheepskin flying jacket, hinted that he was really modeled on Battle of Britain pilots. However, by the time *Doctor Who* started, political and financial commitment to the advanced technologies that might have led to a British space program was already faltering. By comparison, President Kennedy had committed the U.S. to landing a man on the moon, and the U.S. ran its series of unmanned Ranger missions from 1961 to 1965. Admittedly, in the *Doctor Who* stories of the early 1970s a British space program does exist (see *The Ambassadors of Death* of 1970), and this is one of several aspects of the stories from the Pertwee era to have people arguing about whether they're set in the present or the near future. However, it always felt like a fictionalized version of the present and didn't really make that much difference to the sense of British decline.[26] Indeed, such a fictional space program arguably reflected technocratic plans for renewal put in place in the 1960s which, by the 1970s, were widely deemed to have failed to reverse Britain's decline.[27] The backhanded compliment paid to Britain by *Doctor Who* in that era was that so many alien and other threats zeroed in on Britain first, though that may also have expressed a national sense of victimhood. The fantasy of national identity

Doctor Who offered accordingly shifted from being one of real political power to the image the Doctor presented of the maverick who operates on his own terms, even when associated with the authorities: thus individualism and national power can still be combined, even in an age of systems and growing bureaucracies. In this much the Doctor is akin to another consolatory fiction of Britishness in an age of decline: the James Bond films, another long-running series that, since starting in 1962 has gone through several different leading men.

If the Doctor as a renegade could appear to be his own man, he also had ready entrée to the British "establishment" from early in the series' history. We see this in *The War Machines* (1966), where he serves simultaneously as a representative of old Britain, the embodiment of scientific advancement, and a critic of technocracy. The Doctor arrives in London in the viewers' present, to find a super-computer, WOTAN, about to be networked with computers around the world. Inevitably, it becomes conscious and starts to build "war machines" to dominate the world. It also proves adept at brainwashing people. The Doctor swings through the swinging sixties, is complimented on his "fab gear," and reprograms one of the war machines to destroy WOTAN. In some ways it's a routine story, but its pattern would recur in the early 1970s with many of the UNIT stories. It is striking how quickly the Doctor is accepted by the powers that be. In no time at all he's in the confidence of an elite civil servant, is advising a minister, and having his plans followed by troops and others. How apt that he travels in a London police box: a symbol of British authority. That doesn't stop him castigating officialdom or the military when he has a mind to, but it indicates one of the ways in which the Doctor has it both ways: accepted as British (and as part of the British establishment), while being beyond Britishness — a man of peace, who nevertheless has troops at his disposal at the showdown.

With the second Doctor, the program changed direction, with fewer historical stories and more monsters — especially more recurring monsters (cybermen, ice warriors, Yeti). In one of the last historical stories, *The Highlanders* (1967), the second Doctor found his longest serving companion, Jamie McCrimmon. He's a young Scots refugee from the Battle of Culloden (1746).[28] Two years previously, Culloden had been the subject of Peter Watkins' controversial BBC film.[29] In the 1960s the relation of Scotland to Britain was once again being contested. The Scottish National Party had looked set to make a breakthrough from about 1962.[30] In the event, it had to wait until the advent of the Scottish Parliament in 1999, but Scottish nationalism was a live issue in the 1960s, and this was partly a consequence of the end of empire.[31] In making the redcoats entirely English (in reality there'd been many Scottish soldiers in the British army), the *Doctor Who* story looks set to sharpen the questions it raises about Britishness. However, a lot of its interest shifts from serious questions about the conflict to the tricks the Doctor uses to get away and to the thwarting of the villain, Solicitor Grey, who is illegally trying to turn a profit by selling captured Highlanders into slavery. In the process the Doctor sides with the fleeing Highlanders, one of whom is Jamie McCrimmon. In the end the Doctor and his English companions, Ben and Polly, come to represent a revisionist English response to the Jacobites of 1745, acknowledging their personal bravery and loyalty. Thereafter, Jamie accompanies the second Doctor throughout his adventures, and between them they present an image of Anglo-Scots cooperation.

One's perception of the Doctor's "nationality," notwithstanding his being an alien, has a lot to do with the company he keeps. Of some twenty-five companions in the original series, at least half of them are British. Several more from the future are likely to be perceived as more British than anything else. In almost every episode from 1963 to 1976 the Doctor was accompanied by one or more British companions, and, if one shares the view of Wood and Miles that Steven Taylor, who traveled with the Doctor in stories aired between 1965 and 1966, is really an Englishman from the future, then there's a British companion in every episode until 1976.[32]

Patrick Troughton bowed out with *The War Games* (1969), which combined sixties playfulness with serious reflection on the human talent for violence. He appears to have landed in the middle of World War One, but that's an illusion. The War Lords have kidnapped soldiers from Earth's history for their gladiatorial games, from which they will select an elite force to fight for them. If one sees the story as an alien plot against humanity, it's simple; but if one sees the aliens as representing facets of humanity (and they disguise themselves as senior officers, so that's how we start by seeing them), the story's more disturbing. If the War Lords and the humans are reflections of each other, then it's apt that the Doctor should also run into one of his own kind: the War Chief, who has stolen time-travel technology in order to further the War Lords' plans. He also helps some of the British to lead a resistance movement comprising soldiers from different ages, races and regions. In the last episode, the Doctor's people are named for the first time as the Time Lords, when the Doctor seeks their help to get all the soldiers back where they belong.

The Time Lords' name echoes British titles: the Sea Lords (the admirals who serve on the Board of the Admiralty) and the Law Lords (who until recently exercised the judicial functions of the House of Lords, and who have just been reconstituted as the UK's Supreme Court). Having returned the kidnapped soldiers and cancelled their memories, the Time Lords put the Doctor on trial for breaking a law that forbids the Time Lords to intervene in the affairs of other peoples. They regard the Doctor's companions, Jamie and Zoe, in the same light as the War Lords' captured soldiers: people who've been illegally removed from their time and place, and who need to be returned with their memories wiped. At this stage the Time Lords take the principle of non-intervention seriously, and it provides them with a defense against accusations of imperialist meddling along the lines of *Star Trek*'s Prime Directive. But the Doctor, our hero, routinely violates it. Even at their most august, the Time Lords risk looking insular. Later they would prove to be adept at bending their own rules — not least by using the Doctor as an unofficial agent.

The sentence imposed at the end of *The War Games* was that the Doctor be exiled to Earth, with the TARDIS disabled. Emerging from the TARDIS ill and disorientated, Jon Pertwee's Doctor was taken to hospital, where he stole the foppish clothes (ruffed shirt, velvet jacket, cape) of a consultant while escaping. In reality Pertwee's look was based on some clothes of his grandfather's. But, as Britton and Barker note, his outfit was also, in 1970, "bang-up-to-date in fashion terms."[33] Pertwee projected an odd sense of being both contemporary and out of time. Troughton had done a lot of running, but Pertwee was the first Doctor to be an action hero. Yet if he seemed in some ways contemporary, that didn't mean he fit in. If the Doctor stands for what is best in the British past (for example, in his eccentric heroism, his way of improvising his way out of problems, his know-how, and his desire for different peoples to get along), it's not surprising that he is routinely at loggerheads with the British present. Officialdom often elicited exasperation, while corporations (following the model established earlier by *The Invasion*) proved sinister. In *The Sea Devils*, impatient at the intransigence of a naval officer, he points out that "If Horatio Nelson had been in charge of this operation, I hardly think that he would have waited for official instructions." The Captain agrees: "Yes ... a pretty impulsive fellow. If one can believe the history books," and gets the answer, "History books? Captain Hart, Horatio Nelson was a personal friend of mine." For those familiar with the show, the only surprising thing about the Doctor's riposte is the past tense of "was" since for a time traveler presumably there is a sense in which Nelson still *is* his friend. That captures something of the significance of the Doctor as a fantasy of Britishness, in whom what is past is perpetually present. He is a figure who can revive and make real and present qualities that Britain would like to think defined it, and which, presented more straightforwardly, would have looked stodgy, wishful or old-fashioned.

One early Pertwee story that presents this debate about Britishness is *Inferno* (1970). It uses the creaky device of a parallel universe, which enables most of the regular cast to play good and bad versions of themselves. The story is that Professor Stahlman (note the tellingly Germanic name for a British professor) is masterminding a project to derive cheap energy from drilling to the Earth's core (echoes of the promises that accompanied the advent of nuclear power). The snag is that what comes back up from the drillhead turns people into a heat-seeking primordial werewolves, and in the end will cause the Earth to burn (perhaps an anticipation of global warming; compare *The Green Death* (1973), another ecologically themed tale of this era). The sense that technology and technocracy bring hidden dangers is a familiar one (and has been so since *Frankenstein* at least), but it perhaps also betrays a sense of the fragility of post-war normality: a feeling that peace and prosperity were illusions that could readily dissolve. The story's preoccupation with drilling makes one think of oil, and the oil crisis was just around the corner when *Inferno* was made.

The story also has World War Two in mind. Stahlman is a monomaniac who clashes with everyone. But the Doctor acts decisively to stop him only after he has accidentally jumped to a parallel world in which the same project is under way, but in a Britain that executed its Royal family in the 1940s and became a fascist republic. Everyone is miraculously the same, except for wigs, facial hair, latex scars and costumes. The story is like a fable. It's unsettling that it's the regular characters, the ones we normally trust, who are revealed as potential fascists. The story implies that Britain could have turned into a totalitarian state in the 1940s, and possibly could do so yet.

Though there's no direct plot link between the political regime in the parallel Britain and the fact that theirs is the Britain that's destroyed, imaginatively one feels there is a connection. The implication is, perhaps, that having in reality fought off fascism in the 1940s, there's a danger of succumbing to it if we submit to technocrats like Stahlman. If Britishness had defined what Britain was fighting for in World War Two, it now proves worryingly unstable, and capable of flipping over into the very things to which it was supposed to be implacably opposed. The story implies that Stahlman's kind of power leads to self-destruction, and it seems poetically just that Stahlman in "our" Britain is destroyed, even though the world as a whole survives. By comparison, in the parallel world the Earth is engulfed in fire and molten larva. It's the Doctor's ability to move between these two worlds that saves "our" Britain. This means there are scenes in which the Doctor is almost the sole advocate of "normal" behavior against a military and scientific elite that's accountable to no one. If the Doctor represents authentic Britishness, then it's apt that he doesn't exist at all in totalitarian Britain, since he's the only character who has no counterpart in the parallel world.

This continuing sense of the Doctor representing a perfected Britishness emerged in several other stories in the early 1970s. *The Curse of Peladon* of 1972, for example, has the Doctor and his assistant, Jo Grant, transported by the Time Lords to Peladon, where attempts are being made to sabotage its joining the Galactic Federation. The story reflects Britain's entry into the EEC that same year.[34] This means that Peladon (feudal and traditional) stands for Britain, but then so does the Doctor, who is mistaken for the delegate from Earth who is to chair the multi-species meeting that will decide whether or not Peladon can join. As the delegate from Earth, the Doctor could scarcely be anything other than British, so the image of Britain the story presents is double: both the outsider seeking admittance to the club, and the insider presiding over it, and also (this being the Doctor) blessed with the kind of more than merely diplomatic expertise necessary to foil the plot to prevent Peladon from joining. As ever, the Doctor presents an image of a kind of perfected Britishness, which can intervene in the affairs of others without ever having his motives called into question by his relation to the institutions of power.

The next Doctor, Tom Baker, was sent back by the Time Lords to prevent the Daleks from evolving by destroying them or changing them at their creation. In a significant revision to the account of the origins of the Daleks given at their first appearance in 1963, the 1975 story, *The Genesis of the Daleks*, shows them being produced by a military and scientific elite, presided over by the evil genius, Davros. Davros masterminds the destruction of his own people (renamed the Kaleds) sooner than have the production of the Daleks halted. Again, the equation between technocracy and fascism is manifest — especially in the shape of Davros's security chief, Nyder, who resembles Himmler,[35] and in allusions to racist eugenics.[36] One could be forgiven for thinking that the further the British get from the Second World War, the more it preoccupies them. However, racist ideology persisted on the fringes of British politics, especially in the National Front, which, having been founded in 1967, had done well in several local elections and by-elections in 1973 and 1974, stirring fears that the kind of consensus that the main parties had tried to maintain over race relations and immigration would unravel. The Daleks inherited their creators' racism: one of the last Dalek stories of the "classic" series, *The Remembrance of the Daleks* (1988), would see two groups of Daleks trying to wipe each other out to preserve their respective genetic purity. In the midst of the totalitarians of the military-scientific elite, the Doctor projects a benign, enlightened Britishness. Even though he's being used as a kind of undercover agent by his own people, he remains more concerned to answer to his own conscience. Famously, having planted explosives in the incubating chambers where the mutated creatures inside the Daleks are grown, he hesitates to detonate them, agonizing over whether he really has the right to commit genocide, no matter how good the cause. In the end a trundling Dalek runs over the wires and detonates the explosives anyway, but by then the production lines are rolling, so the destruction of the incubator room just sets the Daleks back a bit, rather than exterminating them entirely.

Some of Baker's subsequent stories harked back to the heyday of empire — the era that the Doctor's patrician manner and his clothes, no matter how qualified by eccentricity, tended to recall. There'd always been something of Sherlock Holmes in the Doctor's makeup: brilliant, Bohemian, but ultimately in with the establishment, albeit on his own terms. We've noted the side of the Doctor that the British elite were willing to recognize as one of them going back as far as 1966. The Holmesian side to him was confirmed by *The Talons of Weng-Chiang* (1977), in which, contrary to his usual practice of sporting the same broadly nineteenth-century costume wherever and whenever he goes, he changed into *different* nineteenth-century clothes for a visit to late nineteenth-century London — specifically an Inverness cape and a deerstalker. Nothing could more plainly declare that this was, in a sense, the Doctor's real homecoming (rather than one of his occasional trips to Gallifrey). Why should he change out of his usual traveling clothes unless, in returning to imperial, nineteenth-century London, he was in some sense coming home?

The Doctor's manner is accordingly enough to open doors for him. It's perhaps worth noting that, like Hartnell, Baker's own background meant he sent out mixed signals, especially in respect of class: he possesses (onscreen and off) a grand manner, but his background is Catholic-Jewish, working class and Liverpudlian, and he's almost impossible to place in conventional class terms. In *The Talons* the Doctor swiftly goes from being a suspect to telling the police what to do. He's also readily acknowledged as a colleague by Professor Litefoot, the pathologist. But at the same time, as ever, it's important that the Doctor also demonstrate mastery of advanced technology, since he's up against Magnus Greel, an Icelandic war criminal who has fled to this time from the 51st century. As the title indicates, there's a Chinese connection. Greel had materialized in China. He's now followed Litefoot to London to recover his time travel cabinet which Litefoot has unwittingly acquired under the impression that it's a Chinese antiquity. Meanwhile Greel needs his Chinese followers to capture young girls whose life force he can drain to keep himself alive. So there's also an element of Jack the Ripper woven into imperialist fiction. Wood and Miles announce that it's "a parody of British imperialist fiction rather than an example of it,"[37] but parody in this case doesn't imply subversive intent, so much as a desire to appropriate certain kinds of desirable materials, using irony as a solvent to break them free from their original contexts. *Doctor Who*, with its insatiable demand for story material, has a way of assimilating other kinds of story.

However, the show was in danger of descending into blank parody, to borrow Fredric Jameson's phrase, in which its flights of fancy would cease to feel as if they were about anything. It's not a question of needing bigger themes: science fiction can sometimes ring more hollow the bigger its themes. In reality, the danger developed in the midst of the show's heyday. The sixties playfulness of the Troughton era had sometimes thinned the imaginative texture of show. The era of the fourth Doctor is often looked back to as the show's golden age, and yet after Philip Hinchcliffe as producer (1974–77) had steered the show into its Gothic phase (of which *The Talons* was the culmination) there were indications that it was having difficulty renewing itself. Where this thinness was concealed, it was concealed by a sense of the show falling back on being in some sense about acting: especially in the Baker era about presenting Tom Baker with a rival performance to which he could rise. It's widely reckoned that *City of Death* (1978), which came at the end of a season presided over by Graham Williams as producer and Douglas Adams (he of *The Hitchhiker's Guide to the Galaxy*) as script editor, is one of the last great stories.[38] If so, it's a lot to do with the chemistry between Baker and Lalla Ward, as his assistant, Romana, and between Baker and Julian Glover as the story's villain. The sense of personal force that Baker could summon when he wasn't sending the show up went some way towards disguising how little there was in the late 1970s below the surface in the fabric of the show as such to disturb or animate anyone.

One of those disturbances had been the question of Britishness and British power. It's often said that the actors who followed Baker were lighter weight performers, but there wasn't often much for them to get hold of — with one or two striking exceptions, such as Peter Davison's last story as the Doctor, *The Caves of Androzani* (1982). Another story of the Davison era that academics are apt to comment upon, partly because it was the story to whose making Tulloch and Alvarado devoted a chapter of their book,[39] is *Kinda* (1982). It's an explicit condemnation of British imperialism, khaki, pith-helmets and all — notwithstanding its being set on another planet. It boasts a delightful performance by the veteran film star Richard Todd. But it suffers from two snags. It's so busy being politically correct in condemning imperialism that it never allows the colonists to give a strong defense of themselves: they're either caricatures or mad. What of colonists as pioneers, who featured in *Colony in Space* (1972), where they were favorably compared with the giant, corrupt mining company? At the heart of *Kinda* is an elusive idea — which one might see as having connections either with *A Passage to India* or with *Heart of Darkness* — to do with the "advanced" colonizer gazing at himself in the mirror presented by the supposedly "primitive" culture she or he colonizes, and suffering a crisis. Well, it worked for Forster and Conrad. But such is the show's need for pace and MacGuffins that there's nothing as mysterious as the Marabar caves for the colonizers to gaze into: just a wooden box that the Kinda (the natives) present to the men of the expedition, since it drives men mad. It has no effect on the Doctor. But why? Hasn't he exercised power over other peoples? Why should he be untouchable? Richard Todd is, first, a stereotypical British imperialist and then suddenly, after gazing into the box, he's sweet and childlike. But the two states of mind are so separate that they never really tangle with each other to make for the kind of ambiguities and problems noted in *The Dalek Invasion of Earth*.

The wooden box becomes quasi-technological in the way it operates — as quick and effective as injecting a psychotropic drug. The conclusion of the story is that the Kinda aren't primitive, and so their planet is not appropriate for colonization. The impression is that the conclusion is based on the power of the box as well as the power of the Mara, an evil creature that dwells inside people's minds, but which can, if one's not careful, slither out and take the form of a giant serpent, which the Doctor then has to defeat. The symbolism of letting a serpent loose in paradise is obvious, but the serpent gives the Doctor the kind of external threat and action that he commonly needs. Such things, if they're not extraneous to the plot, feel too much like metaphors to have much basis in the imagined world. In other words, when *Doctor Who* finally got around to delivering an outright condemnation of imperialism of all stripes, whatever the merits of that position, in terms of the show's imaginative life it pointed to a thinning of the show's underlying preoccupations.

There were some signs at the end of the original series of its seeing the impasse it had to move beyond — not least in allowing the last Doctor to speak with a Scottish accent, rather than another middle-class English one. The new series has jettisoned some of the preoccupations of the old to do with costume and class and the increasing assumption that the Doctor was (especially emotionally) invulnerable. In obvious ways *Doctor Who* remains a British program, but it is perhaps no longer preoccupied by Britishness as a problem in the way that for its first decade and a half arguably it was. That's not to say that it doesn't reflect on Britain in various ways. In relation to issues including class and family and sexuality, arguably it does. But the era when Britishness as such was an animating problem for *Doctor Who* has passed.

Notes

1. For a survey of the original series, see the section of the BBC website devoted to it: "Doctor Who: The Classic Series," http://www.bbc.co.uk/doctorwho/classic/.

2. See Giuseppe Mazzini, *The Duties of Man*, edited by Thomas Jones (London: Dent, 1955), chapters 4–7 & 12, and J.G. Herder, "Ideas for a Philosophy of the History of Mankind," in *J.G. Herder on Social and Political Culture*, translated and edited by F.M. Barnard (Cambridge: Cambridge University Press, 1969).

3. Peter Mandler, *English National Character: The History of an Idea from Edmund Burke to Tony Blair* (New Haven: Yale University Press, 2006), 193.

4. Ibid., 216.

5. Ibid., 217–218.

6. Michael Paris, "Africa in Post–1945 British Cinema," *South African Historical Journal* 48 (May 2003): 63.

7. W. David McIntyre, *British Decolonization, 1946–1997* (Basingstoke: Macmillan, 1998), 8.

8. Paris, "Africa in Post–1945 British Cinema"; John M. MacKenzie, *Propaganda and Empire: The Manipulation of British Public Opinion 1880–1960* (Manchester: Manchester University Press, 1984), 90–91.

9. MacIntyre, *British Decolonization*, 8, 45–57.

10. MacKenzie, *Propaganda and Empire*, 253–8.

11. On *Doctor Who*'s relation to a fading British imperialism, see also Alec Charles, "The Ideology of Anachronism: Television, History and the Nature of Time," in *Time and Relative Dissertations in Space: Critical Perspectives on Doctor Who*, edited by David Butler (Manchester: Manchester University Press, 2007), 108–122.

12. For contemporary documents relating to the establishment of ITV, see *Television and the Press since 1945*, edited by Ralph Negrine (Manchester: Manchester University Press, 1998), 20–28.

13. On the broadcasting context of the creation of *Doctor Who*, see James Chapman, *Inside the Tardis: The Worlds of Doctor Who* (London: I.B. Tauris, 2006), 12–23; Jim Leach, *Doctor Who*, TV Milestones series (Detroit: Wayne State University Press, 2009), 1–6; Tat Wood and Lawrence Miles, "Where Did *All* This Come From?" in *About Time: The Unauthorized Guide to Doctor Who*, volume 1 (Des Moines, IA: Mad Norwegian Press, 2006), 7–13; "Doctor Who: Origins" [DVD extra] in *The Edge of Destruction*, DVD, directed by Richard Martin and Frank Cox (1964; London: BBC Worldwide, 2006).

14. On "Dalekmania" see Jonathan Bignell, "The Child as Addressee, Viewer and Consumer in Mid-1960s *Doctor Who*," in *Time and Relative Dissertations in Space*, especially 51–54.

15. See Steve Holland, "Look and Learn: A History of the Classic Children's Magazine," *Look and Learn Magazine Ltd.*, 2006, http://www.lookandlearn.com/history/Look-and-Learn-History.pdf.

16. See J.S. Mill, *Considerations on Representative Government* (1862) in *Three Essays* (Oxford: Oxford University Press, 1975).

17. See, for example, V.G. Kiernan, *Imperialism and Its Contradictions* (New York: Routledge, 1995).

18. Piers D. Britton and Simon J. Barker, *Reading Between Designs: Visual Imagery and the Generation of Meaning in "The Avengers," "The Prisoner," and "Doctor Who"* (Austin: University of Texas Press, 2003), 145.

19. Not to be confused with the 1966 film based on it called *Daleks Invasion Earth 2150 AD*.

20. H.G. Wells, *The War of the Worlds* (London: Everyman, 1993), 6–7.

21. Kim Newman, *Doctor Who*, BFI TV Classics (London: BFI, 2005), 31–32; Wood and Miles, *About Time*, volume 1, 105–109; Chapman, *Inside the Tardis*, 43.

22. Leach, *Doctor Who*, 11–17.

23. Wood and Miles, *About Time*, volume 1, 112.

24. George Orwell, *The Lion and the Unicorn* (1941), http://www.k-1.com/Orwell/index.cgi/work/essays/lionunicorn.html.

25. Leach, *Doctor Who*, 3; Newman, *Doctor Who*, 16, 23.

26. See Tat Wood's judicious disposal of this alleged problem: *About Time: The Unauthorized Guide to Doctor Who*, volume 3 (Des Moines, IA: Mad Norwegian Press, 2009*)*, 9–15.

27. David Edgerton, *Warfare State: Britain 1920–1970* (Cambridge: Cambridge University Press, 2006).

28. *The Highlanders* no longer exists. However, one can get some sense of the story from clips on disc two of *Lost in Time*, the CD of the audio track. See *The Highlanders* (London: BBC Radio Collection, 2000). For a detailed summary, see "Doctor Who Reference Guide," http://www.drwhoguide.com/who_2f.htm. For the scripts, see "Doctor Who Script Project," http://homepages.bw.edu/~jcurtis/Scripts/Highlanders/intro.html, and "Doctor Who Photonovels: *The Highlanders*," http://www.bbc.co.uk/doctorwho/classic/photonovels/highlanders/.

29. On Watkins's film see "Culloden (1964)," *BFI Screenonline*, http://www.screenonline.org.uk/tv/id/520802/index.html, and on its relation to *The Highlanders*, see Matthew Kilburn, "Bargains of Necessity? *Doctor Who*, Culloden and Fictionalising History at the BBC in the 1960s," in *Time and Relative Dissertations in Space*, 68–85.

30. Arthur Marwick, *British Society since 1945* (Harmondsworth: Penguin, 1996), 165.
31. Kiernan, *Imperialism and its Contradictions*, 194.
32. Wood and Miles, *About Time*, volume 1, 233.
33. Britton and Barker, *Reading Between Designs*, 149.
34. Wood, *About Time*, volume 3, 218; Chapman, *Inside the Tardis*, 93–94.
35. Chapman, *Inside the Tardis*, 102.
36. Tat Wood and Lawrence Miles, *About Time: The Unauthorized Guide to Doctor Who*, volume 4 (Des Moines, IA: Mad Norwegian Press, 2004), 39.
37. Wood and Miles, *About Time,* volume 4, 146.
38. See Alan McKee, "Why is the 'City of Death' the Best *Doctor Who* Story?" in *Time and Relative Dissertations in Space*, 233–45.
39. John Tulloch and Manuel Alvarado, *Doctor Who: The Unfolding Text* (Basingstoke: Macmillan, 1983).

REFERENCES

Bignell, Jonathan. "The Child as Addressee, Viewer and Consumer in Mid-1960s *Doctor Who*." In *Time and Relative Dissertations in Space: Critical Perspectives on* Doctor Who, edited by David Butler, 43–56. Manchester: Manchester University Press, 2007.
Boies, Dominique. "Doctor Who Reference Guide." http://www.drwhoguide.com/who.htm.
British Broadcasting Corporation. *Doctor Who: The Classic Series.* http://www.bbc.co.uk/doctorwho/classic/index.shtml.
British Film Institute. "Culloden (1964)." *Screenonline.* http://www.screenonline.org.uk/tv/id/520802/index.html.
Britton, Piers D., and Simon J. Barker. *Reading Between Designs: Visual Imagery and the Generation of Meaning in "The Avengers," "The Prisoner," and "Doctor Who."* Austin: University of Texas Press, 2003.
Chapman, James. *Inside the Tardis: The Worlds of Doctor Who.* London: I.B. Tauris, 2006.
Charles, Alec. "The Ideology of Anachronism: Television, History and the Nature of Time." In *Time and Relative Dissertations in Space: Critical Perspectives on* Doctor Who, edited by David Butler, 108–122. Manchester: Manchester University Press, 2007.
The Curse of Peladon. VHS. Directed by Lennie Mayne. 1972. London: BBC Enterprises, 1993.
The Dalek Invasion of the Earth, part 1. VHS. Directed by Richard Martin. 1964. London: BBC Enterprises, 1990.
The Dalek Invasion of the Earth, part 2. VHS. Directed by Richard Martin. 1964. London: BBC Enterprises,1 990.
The Edge of Destruction. DVD. Directed by Richard Martin and Frank Cox. 1964. London: BBC Worldwide, 2006.
Edgerton, David. *Warfare State: Britain 1920–1970.* Cambridge: Cambridge University Press, 2006.
The Genesis of the Daleks. VHS. Directed by David Maloney. 1975. London: BBC Enterprises, 1991.
Herder, J.G. "Ideas for a Philosophy of the History of Mankind." In *J.G. Herder on Social and Political Culture,* translated and edited by F.M. Barnard. Cambridge: Cambridge University Press, 1969.
Holland, Steve. "Look and Learn: A History of the Classic Children's Magazine." *Look and Learn Magazine Ltd.* 2006. http://www.lookandlearn.com/history/Look-and-Learn-History.pdf.
Inferno. VHS. Directed by Douglas Camfield. 1971. London: BBC Enterprises, 1994.
The Invasion. VHS. Directed by Douglas Camfield. 1968. London: BBC Enterprises, 1993.
Jameson, Fredric. *Postmodernism, or, the Cultural Logic of Late Capitalism.* Durham, NC: Duke University Press, 1991.
Kiernan, V.G. *Imperialism and its Contradictions.* New York: Routledge, 1995.
Kilburn, Matthew. "Bargains of Necessity? *Doctor Who, Culloden* and Fictionalising History at the BBC in the 1960s." In *Time and Relative Dissertations in Space: Critical Perspectives on* Doctor Who, edited by David Butler, 68–85. Manchester: Manchester University Press, 2007.
Kinda. VHS. Directed by Peter Grimwade. 1983. London: BBC Enterprises, 1994.
Leach, Jim. *Doctor Who.* TV Milestones series. Detroit: Wayne State University Press, 2009.

Lost in Time. DVD. Directed by Douglas Camfield et al. 1965–1969. London: BBC Worldwide, 2004.

MacKenzie, John M. *Propaganda and Empire: The Manipulation of British Public Opinion 1880–1960.* Manchester: Manchester University Press, 1984.

Mandler, Peter. *English National Character: The History of an Idea from Edmund Burke to Tony Blair.* New Haven: Yale University Press, 2006.

Marwick, Arthur. *British Society since 1945.* The Penguin Social History of Britain. 3rd ed. Harmondsworth: Penguin, 1996.

Mazzini, Giuseppe. *The Duties of Man,* edited by Thomas Jones. London: Dent, 1955.

McIntyre, W. David. *British Decolonization, 1946–1997.* Basingstoke: Macmillan, 1998.

McKee, Alan. "Why Is the 'City of Death' the Best *Doctor Who* Story?" In *Time and Relative Dissertations in Space: Critical Perspectives on* Doctor Who, edited by David Butler, 233–245. Manchester: Manchester University Press, 2007.

Mill, J.S. *Considerations on Representative Government* (1862). In *Three Essays.* Introduced by Richard Wollheim. Oxford: Oxford University Press, 1975.

Negrine, Ralph. ed. *Television and the Press since 1945.* Manchester: Manchester University Press, 1998.

Newman, Kim. *Doctor Who.* BFI TV Classics. London: BFI, 2005.

Orwell, George. *The Lion and the Unicorn.* 1941. http://www.k-1.com/Orwell/index.cgi/work/essays/lionunicorn.html.

Paris, Michael. "Africa in Post-1945 British Cinema." *South African Historical Journal* 48 (May 2003): 61–70.

Remembrance of the Daleks. VHS. Directed by Andrew Morgan. 1988. London: BBC Enterprises, 1993.

The Sea Devils. VHS. Directed by Michael Briant. 1972. London: BBC Enterprises, 1995.

The Talons of Weng-Chiang. DVD. Directed by David Maloney. 1977. London: BBC Worldwide, 2003.

Tulloch, John and Manuel Alvarado. *Doctor Who: The Unfolding Text.* Basingstoke: Macmillan, 1983.

An Unearthly Child. DVD. Directed by Waris Hussein. 1963. London: BBC Worldwide, 2006.

The War Games, part 1. VHS. Directed by David Maloney. 1969. London: BBC Enterprises, 1990.

The War Games, part 2. VHS. Directed by David Maloney. 1969. London: BBC Enterprises, 1990.

The War Machines. VHS. Directed by Michael Ferguson. 1966. London: BBC Worldwide, 1997.

Wells, H.G. *The War of the Worlds.* Introduced by Arthur C. Clarke. London: Everyman, 1993.

Wood, Tat. *About Time: The Unauthorized Guide to Doctor Who,* volume 3. Rev. ed. Des Moines, IA: Mad Norwegian Press, 2009.

Wood, Tat, and Lawrence Miles. *About Time: The Unauthorized Guide to Doctor Who,* volume 1. Des Moines, IA: Mad Norwegian Press, 2006.

Wood, Tat, and Lawrence Miles. *About Time: The Unauthorized Guide to Doctor Who,* volume 4. Des Moines, IA: Mad Norwegian Press, 2004.

PART 3. F IS FOR FUTURE SHOCK

• Eleven •

No Future Shock Here: *The Jetsons,* Happy Tech, and the Patriarchy

BRIAN COWLISHAW

Ask anyone who watched *The Jetsons* what they remember about the show, and they always say: the technology! (They tend to include the exclamation point, along with an enthusiastic smile.) Flying cars, personal rocket packs, pushbuttons to do all our work (including dressing us and brushing our teeth), pneumatic transportation tubes, moving "slidewalks" rather than the kind you have to walk on, robot maids, huge mobile television screens, instant interplanetary travel, and much more — everyday life looked so amazing, so amusing, so convenient! This is the central essence, the primary appeal, and the cultural effect of the show: the thorough, consistent reassurance to its primary audience, children, that the future would not only be endurable, it would be absolutely wonderful in every way.

Broadcast History

The Jetsons originally aired in prime time on ABC between September 1962 and March 1963. The adult audience for animation then was not nearly as large or established as it is now; only kids could watch cartoons without stigma or embarrassment. So *The Jetsons*, aired on Sunday nights, never found much of an audience, and the show was canceled after one season.[1] The fact that most of the half-hour plots revolved around George's worklife and relationship with his boss—something a lot closer to home for the adults watching than for the kids—didn't help. (In other words, it was probably a little *too* much like real life to be funny for the adults watching, and incomprehensible for the kids.)

But it became a longstanding favorite among children when those 24 episodes moved to Saturday mornings—kids' programming time. They began to work their cultural influence upon American children immediately,[2] and did so for over two decades. Between the reruns' longstanding presence on the airwaves, and the concentrated nature of popular culture at the time, their influence on twenty-plus years' worth of children is almost too profound to estimate. For most of that long run, cable television either didn't exist or was, compared to today, extremely limited in its offerings and availability. Most major television markets supported three commercial networks plus PBS. So basically, everyone in those years watched the same shows because there were simply so few to choose from. Thus, nearly every TV-watching American child of a certain age range has received profound, long-term indoctrination via *The Jetsons*. In 1985, Hanna-Barbera produced a second, 40-episode season—lots of new episodes, but they were seldom watched. Later, there were a few more sporadic attempts to revive the once-popular series, but in the newly fragmented, cable-driven TV climate, that popularity never really returned.[3]

The key reason that no *Jetsons* show produced after 1963 ever achieved anything like the popularity or cultural power of the original episodes, though, is that the new *Jetsons* had a new essence, a new message, precisely opposite what it had been in the popular original show. Whereas the original series always saw the future and its technologies through rose-colored glasses, the new shows—like much other popular science fiction of the time—had a considerably darker vision. The 1980s *Jetsons* fretted, for instance, about the changing relationship between humans on one side and machines on the other, reflecting (and feeding) popular fears on the subject. Iconic science-fiction films such as *The Terminator* (1984), *WarGames* (1983), and *Bladerunner* (1982) expressed the same kinds of fears: that the computers, machines, and other technologies that human beings were developing so rapidly would eventually become untrustworthy, insidious—maybe even turn against us. That's the opposite message of the original *Jetsons*. "Everything will be great!" in 1962 became "Our own machines will get us in the end" in the mid–80s. Thus, many people who had watched the original episodes, which were repeated so often and for so long that they became second nature, strongly preferred the original show's optimism over the later shows' doubts and fears. Only the original *Jetsons* felt "right" or "real"; the later shows felt like diminished copies, failed attempts to cash in on the original's popularity. So only the original *Jetsons* gathered much of an audience or, therefore, achieved much cultural traction. In this essay, accordingly, when I refer to *The Jetsons*, I refer exclusively to the original 24 episodes, the ones that taught eagerness and optimism for the future to at least two generations.

Why We Needed *The Jetsons*

The Jetsons reflects its immediate zeitgeist. The show premiered on television at the tail end of the very well-attended, culturally persuasive Seattle World's Fair. This fair, called the "Century 21 Exposition," ran from April 21 to October 21, 1962. Its primary theme, made both verbally and via its exhibits and buildings, was that "the United States was not really 'behind' the Soviet Union in the realms of science and space."[4] In other words, technology is wonderful, and we've got it in spades. Exhibit A was the Space Needle, built as a showcase of American technological superiority specifically for the fair. It shot its visitors to the top in high-speed elevators, resembled a flying saucer (especially at night, when only the restaurant was lit), and towered so high above everything around it as to seem to be in space itself. In all this, the Space Needle resembled buildings in *The Jetsons*— the eponymous family's apartment building in particular. Even its name sounds right out of *The Jetsons*. The Space Needle would not be at all out of place if depicted realistically in the series, with its steep curved tower, flying-saucer cap, and pointy needle top.

The sort of optimism expressed in Seattle and in *The Jetsons* was culturally expedient for Americans, serving to counter serious, growing fears related to technology. For instance, the World's Fair occurred just five years after the Soviet Union shot the Sputnik satellite into orbit around Earth and can be seen primarily as a response to that epochal event. The Century 21 Exposition told us, in effect, "Okay, fine, the Russians may have Sputnik. But the year 2000, and the future in general, belong to us! The future will be great, and we will rule it!" Previously unreachable technologies such as Earth-orbiting satellites became synonymous with bone-deep anxiety. High tech was a life-or-death race the U. S. was losing — hence the need for reassurance and optimism.

Such determined — one might even say, manufactured — optimism went against the grain of much history and popular thought of the time. The first atomic bombs had been detonated — by America, no less — one generation earlier in 1945. The new generation had lived literally all its life knowing the incredibly destructive, dystopian possibilities of technology. The nuclear arms race had proceeded all this time and did so until about the time *The Jetsons* were revived in the 80s. The insanity of Mutual Assured Destruction hung permanently in the air like a giant radioactive mushroom cloud. It seemed merely a matter of time; in fact, it seemed likely that nuclear Armageddon would be triggered *by* technology, accidentally. In the 1983 movie *WarGames*, for example, a teenager who just wants to play a computer game very nearly begins World War III; U.S. and Russian missiles get *that* close to being released en masse. *Doctor Strangelove*, screened in 1964 — the year of my birth, and two years after *The Jetsons* premiered — memorably expressed this pervasive fear. Schoolchildren from the mid–40s on participated routinely in nuclear defense drills. I remember being told as late as the early 70s to hide beneath my desk in the event of a nuclear blast, and to "find a ditch to lie down in" if one occurred while I was outside.

It's no wonder that events such as the Century 21 Exposition and shows such as *The Jetsons* tried so hard to brighten up our imagined future. The time's omnipresent paranoia and angst would unnerve anyone. But even the supposedly positive possibilities of technology in the days of *The Jetsons* were pretty alarming to contemplate. As the Space Age progressed, it came to seem increasingly likely that our everyday lives would fundamentally change. There was constant talk about the technological marvels, many of them related to space travel, that would exist "in the Year 2000." Humans walked on the moon seven years after *The Jetsons* began; by 1962, actual representations and hopeful projections of space travel saturated American popular culture. Reputable scientists agreed that by 2000 we would see:

— Flying cars and larger, more group-friendly vehicles widely available for personal space travel
— Colonies on the moon
— Colonies on Mars
— Many space stations, inhabited by large groups of people, like apartment buildings or even cities in the sky
— Fundamentally changed living conditions on earth, necessitating the above. Some predicted mass exodus, some simply expansion as Earth became overpopulated and/or overpolluted.

In other words, we learned to expect that we would probably live somewhere other than the planet where our species had evolved and always lived. What change could possibly be more radical, and therefore unnerving, than that? Even the small details involved in such a change were alienating. Tang, for instance, was popularly believed (especially after 1965[5]) to have been developed for the U.S. space program. Marketed to consumers from 1959 onward, this powdered drink mix made something as familiar as our morning glass of orange juice "new," "improved," and strange. Anyone who remembers drinking Tang also remembers the gritty residue that always collected in the bottom of the glass; you had to drink your Tang quickly to get it all. Several similar experiments were made with food at the time: dried foods, dehydrated dinners, whole meals made into a paste squeezed out of a tube. We never quite got aspirin-sized pills that contained a whole day's nutrients, but we were certainly promised them "by the year 2000." And on the subject of pills: the nature of sex changed during this time, too, due to the widespread availability and adoption of contraception via The Pill. Thus, the basic facts of everyday life — eating, drinking, and having sex — began to look radically different from what we were accustomed to. Plus, we faced the very strange prospect of doing it all in space. How would such a life feel? Even if it were arguably better, more high-tech and "advanced," it would surely feel bizarre and prove difficult to adjust to.

Alvin Toffler has made a career of predicting such changes and of documenting human beings' radical difficulties adjusting to them. His still-influential book *Future Shock*, first published in 1970[6], details two key realities just beginning to clash. First, humans' capacity to assimilate, internalize, and adjust to change has always been limited. Until recently this has presented no problem, because change itself has been limited. But second, unfortunately for us, late-twentieth-century (and later) technology has ceased changing incrementally, at a pace we can intellectually and psychologically manage; lately, technology is changing at an exponential rate.[7] So even the most flexible, sanguine, optimistic people born since World War II simply can't adjust to the more-and-more rapidly-changing way we live. We worry; we get depressed; we act bizarrely. Modern life is ineradicably strange, and just when we start to get used to it, it gets stranger.

Although I was born a year after the last *Jetsons* episodes were produced, my own life serves as a pretty good representative sample. These are some of the big technological changes I still sometimes struggle to get used to:

1964	2010
Movies in the theater	Hi-definition DVDs, Blu-Ray, movies on demand
Books made of paper	Electronic databases, Kindle, the Internet
Rotary phones, anchored in place	Cell phones, ubiquitous
Slide rules[8]	Calculators (available even on cell phones)
Paper maps, compasses	GPS navigation (also available on cell phones)
Vinyl music albums, easily damaged	ITunes, other downloadable music
Black-and-white broadcast TV, on 4 channels, with fuzzy picture	Color cable TV, on hundreds of channels, in high definition
—	Computers

Almost everything we do or use daily now is widely different from what it was when I was a kid. And computers, so central to our existence now, were completely unavailable to everyone but a few scientists then. Side by side like this, the two sets of technology look strikingly, fundamentally different — and less than 50 years passed in between them.

In the seminal essay "Progress versus Utopia; or, Can We Imagine the Future?"[9] published in 1982 (the year I graduated from high school), Fredric Jameson makes an intriguing claim in this regard. He points out that most readers, including early science-fiction authors such as Jules Verne and H. G. Wells, assume that one key social function science fiction has always served is to *prepare* us for the future by helping us imagine it in advance, thereby lessening its potential to shock. But in fact, argues Jameson, exactly the contrary is true: yes, science fiction helps us gain perspective and insight into the present and the past, but it repeatedly shows how difficult the task of adequately imagining the future must always be. Science fiction's

> deepest vocation is over and over again to demonstrate and to dramatize our incapacity to imagine the future, to body forth, through apparently full representations which prove on closer inspection to be structurally and constitutively impoverished, the atrophy in our time of what Marcuse has called the *utopian imagination*, the imagination of otherness and radical difference; to succeed by failure, and to serve as unwitting and even unwilling vehicles for a meditation, which, setting forth for the unknown, finds itself irrevocably mired in the all-too-familiar, and thereby becomes unexpectedly transformed into a contemplation of our own absolute limits.
>
> This is indeed, since I have pronounced the word, the unexpected rediscovery of the nature of utopia as a genre in our own time.[10]

This is the final concept necessary to fully understanding *The Jetsons*. Rapid technological change unsettles us. We turn to science fiction, in a Saturday-morning cartoon, hoping at some level to heal and ward off further future shock. But because we can never adequately imagine the future, science fiction as a genre is unequipped to do that. Instead, it points us right back to "the all-too-familiar." And in *that* it provides comfort.

This is why we needed, and still maintain such nostalgic fondness for, *The Jetsons*. In times of dizzying techno-sociological change, it provided reassurance. It showed a future utopia that was happily, in every respect but technology, just like the times in which it was produced. The technology was really different in this imagined future from what we had at the time, but always in totally positive ways. In a word, *The Jetsons* was exactly like our lives, only better.

How Life Is Better in *The Jetsons*

This is the part *Jetsons* fans remember with a smile: the specific ways in which new, improved technologies will have improved life in the imagined year 2062.[11] Here is a selected list of fabulous new techs projected to be available then to an ordinary middle-class family:

- Robot maids (Rosey the Robot, tellingly introduced right away, in the first episode)[12] and handymen (Mac)[13]
- Flying cars (of course!) that routinely travel 2500 miles per hour, or upwards of 3500 in the case of speeders, and automatically self-fold to briefcase size
- Food as often as not in the form of pills (of course!)
- One-button machines to perform almost every domestic task: cut your hair, dress yourself, brush your hair and teeth, cook a meal (when you feel like eating actual food), vacuum the living room, take your kid to school, etc. For the boss, there are even better things machines can do with one button press: create an entire new office building in a second,[14] summon or trapdoor-eject an employee, maintain constant surveillance on lazy subordinates.
- "Slidewalks" everywhere, including inside the house. In the first episode, Jane even complains that the "local slidewalks" don't go as fast as the "express" ones.
- Pneumatic tubes and moving chairs to remove *all* necessity of walking; they shoot people from parking garage to apartment, or from your desk to the boss's office
- Personal rocket packs
- Nearly instant interplanetary travel. In the sixth episode,[15] George unwillingly shepherds a Space Scout troop to the moon for an overnight camping trip, and the trip takes just a few minutes. (It's made to seem even faster by a sexy artificial voice attributed to "your stewardess, Lana Luna," that instantly has George bug-eyed and panting.) On the moon, George's troop marches past a group of Martians on a similar trip.
- A "flight suit" that requires no fuel[16]; it responds to the wearer's unspoken wishes, through "brainwave frequency." It accidentally gets destroyed, but it does work.
- Retractable, mobile, two-way televisions[17] in nearly every conceivable place (including a child's wrist)[18]; also, stationary, wall-sized, room-rattling televisions in every living room
- A nine-hour work week (three days per week, three hours per day), in George's case mostly taken up by talking to Jane on the videophone, scheming to get more time off, or just plain slacking; still, George complains constantly about his "brutal" schedule and "slave-driver" boss.

Put this all together, and it adds up to one fantastic future life. Now, a clever, pessimistic viewer could probably find inconsistencies or problems built even into this wonderful picture. But there's always a positive way to answer even those. For example:

Question: if the need for human labor has been so nearly eliminated, why would someone need a maid? Could, or would, humans be eliminated altogether? Answer: Rosey does many things better than humans, but always in a strictly helping capacity; there's no *Terminator* scenario looming. Her cooking is somehow even more miraculous and tasty than what humans produce with the same machines; Rosey saves the day, and George's job by whipping up a delicious feast for Mr. Spacely in Episode One. She's always there to offer extra love to the family (and she does tell them she "loves" them), throw a football for Elroy, or anything else required. Rosey won't *replace* humans, or endanger them, she only performs some *tasks* better than humans can. She even has a love life of her own, as demonstrated in Episode Eight: she falls in love at first sight with the newly built handyman Mac. The greatest threat from machines—outside of comic mishaps—comes from the five-billion-dollar computer Uniblab in Episode 10.[19] At first, Spacely sets Uniblab as George's superior, and Uniblab proves to be a demanding, efficiency-obsessed taskmaster. But the computer is easily outsmarted and dispatched with nothing more complicated than a bit of spiked lubricating fluid.

Question: if humans never exercise but still (much of the time, anyway) eat like we do now, won't they be fat and unhealthy? Answer: no. In Episode 14,[20] George's doctor tells him he can expect to "live to be 150." George's grandfather comes to visit in Episode 11[21]; he's 110 already and plausibly claims, "I got plenty of good years left, young fella!" In Episode One Jane performs "push-button finger exercises" along with a Jack LaLanne–like trainer; in Episode 10 George merely *watches* an exercise program, yet works up a sweat; and for both of them it seems to be enough.

Question: won't life around all those machines be unsettling and alienating? Answer: apparently not. The machine George works with and on may be a Referential Universal Digital Indexer, but it answers to the name RUDI. It plays cards with George and cracks jokes. Rosey is more human than most humans. The "electronic dog" called 'Lectronimo is no substitute for the actual canine Astro. Mechanical secretaries and maids (always female in the show) may have curves built in, but nowhere is there evidence of a man choosing one of them over a real woman. There is no evidence of bombs, war, or even nations in conflict, so there's no worry about Weapons of Mass Destruction. In fact, there's effectively not even weather; in Episode Five,[22] George's handyman Henry raises the building 1000 feet, at the press of a button, to put it above the rain currently falling. In every instance, the worst that ever happens with a machine is that it malfunctions amusingly: for example, the "Fooderackercycle" mixes up the breakfast orders in ways no normal human would (eggs in the coffee, etc.). *Jetsons* machines only help us or make us laugh. The show consistently reassured the children watching it that machines in the future will only make their lives better and more amusing.

The Patriarchy

So life in 2162 will be exactly like our lives, only better — unless you happen to be female. American society in 2010 has a long way to go before achieving gender equality, but society in 1962–1963 was even more thoroughly and blatantly sexist. *The Jetsons* faithfully reflects this. Jameson, remember, argues that science fiction is "irrevocably mired in the all-too-familiar, and thereby becomes unexpectedly transformed into a contemplation of our own absolute limits."[23] Patriarchy is one such limit. Watching *The Jetsons* is a study in retro sexism. Supposedly we're watching the future, but we're really watching our sexist (then-) present.

The opening and closing sequences are quite telling in this regard. In the opening, for instance, the characters are all presented in relation to George: "Meet George Jetson! His boy Elroy! Daughter Judy! Jane, his wife!" Jane is not a person in her own right; she is "his wife," an object, not a subject. The center of the universe is the male head of household. The animation shows George dropping off the kids at their respective schools, then Jane at a generic "Shopping Center." True to sexist stereotypes on both sides, George grudgingly offers Jane a couple of bills out of his wallet; instead, she grabs the wallet and escapes to shop, which makes George frown. Then he continues on to work, where he parks, watches his flying car fold itself into a briefcase, rides the escalator inside, and puts his feet up on the desk. On the way home, the patriarchal emphasis announces itself even more loudly. George, the family breadwinner and returning hero, arrives home. Assembly-line-style from his moving chair, he receives a lit pipe (!) from Judy, a friendly greeting from Elroy, and Astro's leash from his (nagging) wife. The closing credits end with George stuck in Astro's treadmill, screaming for "Jaaaaaaane!"

Negative female stereotypes abound in *The Jetsons*. Mr. Spacely's wife is the Platonic ideal of the shrewish wife bullying her henpecked husband. She's easily twice his size, aggressive, and usually angry. He plays his time-honored part, she plays hers. Judy is the familiar boy-crazy teenage girl, switching boyfriends (innocently, asexually) every couple of days. All workers like George or the employees at Cogswell's Cogs are men. Women who work fill jobs traditionally reserved for women such as secretary or telephone operator, but mostly they lounge, and shop, and gossip. Even the (female) robot secretaries in Episode Nine[24] waste most of their workday gossiping around the water cooler, suggesting that gossip is such a deeply ingrained gender trait as to transcend even the human-robot divide: build a robot with curves, call it female, and it will gossip.

One episode, Episode 18,[25] almost seems now to have been written with the *intention* of being egregiously sexist. The episode dramatizes "Jane's Driving Lesson." In accordance with the stereotype, Jane is an incorrigibly horrible driver. There are many, many jokes about "lady drivers'" alleged inherent inability to control a car. Her driving instructor even has to swallow tranquilizers to tolerate the terrifying experience. To the relief of everyone, at the end of the episode, she decides not to drive after all — to stick to public transit or rides from her man.

This is life in 2162, says *The Jetsons*: just like ours, with all the patriarchy and sexism we recognize from our own time, only greatly improved through technology. And funny! Not at all scary!

In its own odd, counterintuitive way, even the sexism provides reassurance to its audience of children, who above all crave predictability and stability. The advanced technologies will clearly make all aspects of life better, as discussed above; but what about family life? Will it be alarmingly different? In 100 years, what if people lived in families that looked and were organized in seriously different ways? What if there were no gender divide at work? What if men and women were considered fundamentally equal? Clearly that would be very *different* from prevailing conditions in 1962–1963 America; and most of the time, for most kids, different equals scary. So by reproducing the same old sexism, *The Jetsons* makes the imbalanced relationship between George and "Jane, his wife" seem as soothing as a nice hot meal from the Fooderackercycle produced by a quick button press.

NOTES

1. *The Jetsons* on prime time had another significant handicap: it ran against the perennially popular *Walt Disney's Wonderful World of Color*, as *The Wonderful World of Disney* was called then.

2. Apparently the redefinition of *The Jetsons* from prime-time sitcom to Saturday-morning kids' show wasn't totally unexpected. In the middle of that first season, in January 1963, Gold Key comics began publishing a monthly *Jetsons* comic. Gold Key published *The Jetsons* until October 1970, then Charlton Comics did so from November 1970 to December 1973. The primary audience of these comics is clearly children.

3. There was also a third, 10-episode truncated season in 1987; the little-watched *Jetsons* television specials "The Jetsons Meet the Flintstones" in 1987, "Rockin' with Judy Jetson" in 1988, and "The Jetsons: Father & Son Day" in 2001; and *Jetsons: The Movie* in 1990. All of these shared the key differences from the 1962–1963 show described above.

4. "Lesson Twenty-five: The Impact of the Cold War on Washington: The 1962 Seattle World's Fair," *HSTAA 432: History of Washington State and the Pacific Northwest*, http://www.washington.edu/uwired/outreach/cspn/Website/Course%20Index/Lessons/25/25.html.

5. It was used from 1965 onward in the Gemini manned space flight program, and that fact was heavily advertised. The association, which was in fact accidental, was assumed to have been causal: we have Tang because we have a space program.

6. Alvin Toffler, *Future Shock* (New York: Random House, 1970). *Future Shock* was reissued in 1984 with no significant updates. *The Third Wave* (1980) and *Powershift* (1990) essentially recycle the same material, with a bit more emphasis on commerce's role in change.

7. On this point, see the widely read, highly influential essay "The Law of Accelerating Returns" by Ray Kurzweil, first published in 2001. See also "Moore's Law," which claims that electronic devices specifically are improving at an exponential rate rather than incrementally.

8. Pocket calculators came into popular use in the 1970s but were expensive until the 80s. I learned how to use a slide rule and used one until I was 16, in 1980.

9. Fredric Jameson, "Progress versus Utopia; or, Can We Imagine the Future?" in *Science Fiction: Stories and Contexts*, edited by Heather Masri (New York: Bedford/St. Martin's, 2009), 876–891.

10. Ibid., 885.

11. In other words, exactly 100 years later. Several *Jetsons* episodes specify that this is the year their events take place.

12. "Rosey the Robot," *The Jetsons*, DVD, directed by Joseph Barbera and William Hanna (September 23, 1962; Los Angeles: Hanna-Barbera Productions).

13. "Rosey's Boyfriend," *The Jetsons*, DVD, directed by Joseph Barbera and William Hanna (November 11, 1962; Los Angeles: Hanna-Barbera Productions).

14. "Dude Planet," *The Jetsons*, DVD, directed by Joseph Barbera and William Hanna (February 17, 1963; Los Angeles: Hanna-Barbera Productions).

15. "The Good Little Scouts," *The Jetsons*, DVD, directed by Joseph Barbera and William Hanna (October 28, 1962; Los Angeles: Hanna-Barbera Productions).

16. "The Flying Suit," *The Jetsons*, DVD, directed by Joseph Barbera and William Hanna (November 4, 1962; Los Angeles: Hanna-Barbera Productions).

17. In Episode 16, future televisions demonstrate another astonishing capability: the capacity to *physically* move objects both directions through the airwaves. Mr. Cogswell and Mr. Spacely trade blows with golf club and bowling ball through their respective screens. Still, this seems to be a one-shot visual gag rather than a message about how TVs will work; the conceit is not repeated.

18. "Elroy's Mob," *The Jetsons*, DVD, directed by Joseph Barbera and William Hanna (March 3, 1963; Los Angeles: Hanna-Barbera Productions).

19. "Uniblab," *The Jetsons*, DVD, directed by Joseph Barbera and William Hanna (November 25, 1962; Los Angeles: Hanna-Barbera Productions). The then-deposed Uniblab also reappears in Episode 19 as a Space Guard sergeant.

20. "Elroy's Pal," *The Jetsons*, DVD, directed by Joseph Barbera and William Hanna (December 23, 1962; Los Angeles: Hanna-Barbera Productions).

21. "A Visit from Grandpa," *The Jetsons*, DVD, directed by Joseph Barbera and William Hanna (December 2, 1962; Los Angeles: Hanna-Barbera Productions).

22. "The Coming of Astro," *The Jetsons*, DVD, directed by Joseph Barbera and William Hanna (October 21, 1962; Los Angeles: Hanna-Barbera Productions).

23. Jameson, "Progress versus Utopia," 885.

24. "Elroy's TV Show," *The Jetsons*, DVD, directed by Joseph Barbera and William Hanna (November 18, 1962; Los Angeles: Hanna-Barbera Productions).

25. "Jane's Driving Lesson," *The Jetsons*, DVD, directed by Joseph Barbera and William Hanna (January 20, 1962; Los Angeles: Hanna-Barbera Productions).

REFERENCES

Jameson, Fredric. "Progress versus Utopia; or, Can We Imagine the Future?" In *Science Fiction: Stories and Contexts*, edited by Heather Masri, 876–891. New York: Bedford/St. Martin's, 2009.
The Jetsons: The Complete First Season. Hanna-Barbera Studio, Turner Home Entertainment, 2004.
Kurzweil, Ray. "The Law of Accelerating Returns." http://www.kurzweilai.net/articles/art0134.html?printable=1.
"Lesson Twenty-five: The Impact of the Cold War on Washington: The 1962 Seattle World's Fair." HSTAA 432: History of Washington State and the Pacific Northwest. University of

Washington Center for the Study of the Pacific Northwest. http://www.washington.edu/uwired/outreach/cspn/Website/Course%20Index/Lessons/25/25.html.

Toffler, Alvin. *Future Shock*. New York: Random House, 1970.

―――. *Powershift: Knowledge, Wealth, and Violence at the Edge of the 21st Century*. New York: Random House, 1980.

―――. *The Third Wave*. New York: Random House, 1990.

• *Twelve* •

"No One's Lazy in LazyTown": The Making of Active Citizens in Preschool Television

Lynn Whitaker

"Ziggy, you learn more when you are little than any other time in your whole life!"

"If that's true then I'm going to learn a lot now so that when I grow up I'll know everything!"[1]

So say superhero Sportacus and little Ziggy of the children's television show *LazyTown*, laying bare the underlying didacticism of a brand whose aim is to inspire healthy lifestyle choices for a preschool audience imagined to be especially receptive to the entertainment medium of television: an audience constructed as ready, willing and able to become active citizens. By exuberantly declaring that "No one's lazy in LazyTown!" the show's theme song confirms that the ideal or model citizen is an *active* citizen in both senses of the word — physically active and consciously so. In this essay I explore the ways in which this ideology of active citizenship is supported through aspects of science fiction and fantasy in the *LazyTown* brand, even though *LazyTown* is not strictly speaking a science-fiction text. I argue, through analysis of the program texts and their associated publicity and production materials, that the science-fiction and fantasy elements of the brand creatively capitalize on societal hopes and fears for the future of children and society, and so help to make the *LazyTown* doctrine of healthy lifestyle choices engaging for its imagined audience.

Of course it is a truism that children's television, like all other media produced *by* adults *for* children, is, as David Buckingham argues (in response to what Jacqueline Rose terms the "impossibility" of children's fiction), "a reflection not so much of children's interests or fantasies or desires but of adults."[2] This is not to suggest that children's media texts are "false" or invalid, but rather that they demand an extra scrutiny as to what is at stake in their implicit adult/child narrative contract, a contract which the text itself may disguise or efface. The highly explicit lifestyle message of *LazyTown* may suggest a transparency of the adult/child contract within the brand (from an adult perspective it is made abundantly clear that children are being directed to positive choices in diet and exercise), but there remains an implicit tension in using entertainment for educational purposes in a medium that is frequently characterized as antithetical to child health.[3] *LazyTown* must therefore resolve a complex set of issues in negotiating the competing demands of message and medium, parent and child, education and entertainment. Indeed, the creator of *LazyTown*, Magnus Scheving, suggests that the healthy lifestyle message of the show, although appealing to parents, would be rejected by its preschool audience if the medium was *overly* didactic or moralistic, and so seeks instead to exploit the entertainment potential of television to educate "by stealth": "Our biggest challenge has been to make it so entertaining that they don't know they're being educated."[4] Given the seeming success of *LazyTown* as both an entertainment product,[5] and as an educational tool (among other examples, it is credited with an increase of fruit and vegetable sales in its native Iceland),[6] the show would seem to merit its "guilt-free" status in the anxious parental discourse around children's television.[7] However, *LazyTown* fulfils its avowed education/entertainment remit in a rather different way to the somewhat saccharine utopian world of much other "educational" preschool television,[8] as, in its use of science-fiction and fantasy elements, I would argue that *LazyTown* is more able to explore problematic aspects of the human condition and specifically the imagined childhood state. In *LazyTown*, aspects of excess and of (self-)destruction or death drive are figured in the (constructed) child's relationship to food, pleasure, adults and society—a far cry perhaps from the "big hugs" of Teletubby Land and the optimistic curiosity of Dora's unfettered explorations—and they are achieved through the displacement of reality and the containment of threat offered by science-fiction and fantasy tropes.

Brand Background

Originating in Iceland and spanning some fifty or so episodes produced 2004–2007, *LazyTown*'s explicit ideological vision, as evidenced both in the text and in the creator's much stated mission "to move the world to be a healthier place,"[9] is one of healthy living for young children through the promotion of "positive choices" in diet and exercise, most especially the choice of fruit and vegetables over "junk food" and the choice of outdoor play over sedentary activities (although other positive choices as to, e.g., personal hygiene and bedtime routines are also advocated). This dedicated focus on *child* health is constructed not merely as a promotion of current gain (i.e., benefiting the lived experiences of children today) but as an ongoing safeguard of futurity, as we see in the brand statement: "the [*LazyTown*] concept needs to have an ongoing impact on this generation of kids to have an impact on future generations."[10] The current preschool audience are thus characterized as simultaneously cultural heirs and progenitors — and at risk. *LazyTown* posits that the current preschool audience constitute society's last chance to preserve and perpetuate itself through healthy lifestyles: if it is lost to them, then it is lost forever. Protecting children, preserving childhood, safeguarding society and saving the world are thus one and the same thing — the *LazyTown* telos an apposite example of what Lee Edelman describes as "the reproductive futurism that perpetuates as reality the fantasy frame intended to secure the survival of the social in the Imaginary form of the Child."[11] While many may dispute the main thrust of Edelman's arguments — a theoretical construct of the queer as symbolically antithetical to futurity — harder to resist are his arguments around the figure of the child being politically utilized as "the emblem of futurity's unquestioned value"[12] and "the perpetual horizon of every acknowledged politics, the fantasmatic beneficiary of every political intervention."[13] Taken along with Lauren Berlant's "theory of infantile citizenship,"[14] in which "the [infant] citizen form figures a space of possibility that transcends the fractures and hierarchies of national life,"[15] the inculcation of children as active citizens can be seen as the ultimate goal within the ideological ambit of a self-perpetuating society: it is a logical aspiration for a preschool show.

Conceptual Tensions

LazyTown airs in over one hundred territories,[16] and an important factor in this global success can be considered its timeous engagement with current anxieties around child obesity in the developed world. Although much of the brand revenue comes from ancillary marketing opportunities (with licensed merchandise available in a diverse range of children's products), and despite the expansion of the brand in non-television media forms (live stage shows, publishing, online games, etc.), the core *LazyTown* product or urtext, in an international context, remains the television show — a television show which aims to function as a spur to a healthy lifestyle. As such, the show attempts to resolve a classic tension between message and medium in children's TV — that of advocating active exercise through a chiefly passive activity. Several other preschool television texts could be said to acknowledge this tension, mainly in their direct invitation to the child viewer to get up and join in with the onscreen action (e.g., *Dora the Explorer, Yo Gabba Gabba* and *Blues Clues* will encourage children to simultaneously dance along or replicate actions) and there is academic research to support a notion of the children's television audience as especially "lively" and physically active while viewing.[17] *LazyTown*, however, relies not on audience participation *during* the show but, rather, *after* the show, while *not viewing*, in the form of healthy choices in diet and exercise: the show's medium can never therefore be its message as the message advocates redundancy of the medium.

Already a site of some conceptual tension therefore, *LazyTown* exhibits further schism in its representation of technology. The show, itself a state-of-the-art, hi-tech blend of puppetry, live-action and CGI, is set in a surreal, futuristic fantasy world where technology — especially that of labor-saving devices or leisure use — is frequently shown to be the enemy of a happy, healthy childhood, its "evils" akin to indolence and greed. Children both "inside" and "outside" the text are constructed as inherently inclined to this self-gratifying greed and indolence — but are also readily persuaded otherwise, as their natural proclivities may be "cured" by positive example and encouragement and, above all, through the mechanism of free play. Thus, according to *LazyTown*, the challenge facing society is how best to motivate and inspire children towards their own self-realization and control and how to harness children's perceived love of fun to the benefit of society.

Most unusually for preschool television, which tends to be relentlessly "nice" in its focus on only the positive and harmonious, and which tends therefore to avoid the representation of conflict or of potentially negative imitative behaviors,[18] *LazyTown* presents childhood as under threat through a series of Manichaean structures in character, plot and aesthetics; it is most often in these Manichaean structures that aspects of science fiction surface to reinforce a pro-health and often anti-technology agenda. Each episode revolves around uber-fit hero "Sportacus" foiling crazed baddie "Robbie Rotten" from successfully deploying yet another madcap scheme to fool the gullible children of LazyTown into eating junk and spurning exercise. Sportacus, clad head to toe in blue lycra and never missing the opportunity to demonstrate his signature aerial split (perhaps while brushing his teeth, reading a book, preparing for his 8:08 P.M. bedtime or other virtuous activities), has allies in the fight for child health: a pink-haired, pink-clothed girl called Stephanie (a visitor to LazyTown) and liberal helpings of "Sportscandy," LazyTownese for fruit and vegetables. Sportacus's kryptonite is sugary foodstuffs which cause him to have a "meltdown" and enter into a catatonic state. The show is technologically and aesthetically sophisticated, but it certainly is not subtle in its ideology, with every plot explicitly demonstrating that children are unwell and/or unhappy without outdoor play and without eating fresh fruit and vegetables.[19] The creator, Magnus Scheving, believes it is the supreme entertainment value of the show that allows the producers to "get away" with such heavy-handed didacticism and not alienate the very audience of children they hope to address: "If we called it HealthyTown or HappyTown no one would watch."[20] He adds elsewhere, "I just wasn't sure if a kids' program that educates about healthy lifestyle was 'doable.'"[21] *LazyTown* must balance the needs of message and medium: it must be appealing so that children watch and receive the message, but can't be so appealing that children continue watching (other) television without acting on that message. The brand supposes future action on the part of the audience and paradoxically confirms Marie Winn's classic arguments regarding "the plug-in drug" as a "displacement activity" for children's other activities, presumably those considered more beneficial or worthwhile: "It is easy to overlook a deceptively simple fact: one is always *watching* television when one is watching television rather than having any other experience."[22]

Sportacus as "Real" Role Model

The brand is the brainchild of native Icelander Magnus Scheving, who, in addition to his starring role as "Sportacus," has writing, direction and production credits and is CEO of LazyTown Entertainment; allegedly Scheving (a former carpenter-cum-architect-cum-champion athlete, motivational speaker and Icelandic TV personality), built the LazyTown studios with his own bare hands.[23] As such the show is holistically conceived around Scheving's talent and charisma, and the blurred boundary between the Scheving/Sportacus star personas serves to ground the fictional character in reality and elevate the man to myth. Not surprisingly, this slippage fits well with the ideological message of the show, expressed in textual aphorisms, such as "There's always a way," "You've got to believe in yourself," "Practice, practice, practice," and "Anyone can be a hero," amongst others, with the Scheving/Sportacus entity simultaneously representing the ideal or impossible — yet also the achievable. Sportacus calls himself not a "superhero" but a "slightly above average hero" in reinforcement of the achievability of the ideal he represents.[24] The masculine spectacle of Scheving's honed "hard body" (an unusual sight in children's television, especially preschool texts), itself a locus of aspiration, empowerment and desire (in the broadest sense of the word) for both adult and child, represents a non-faked version of the "here's one I made earlier" "trick" of children's instructional TV, and it is the ultimate symbol of the fit and healthy future perfect that is available to children if they simply make the right choices in diet and exercise. One episode features Sportacus transformed back to his childhood body (perhaps at around ten years of age), a body in which he struggles to "pretend" to be less physically skilled than the gymnastic athlete he will grow to become: the message is writ large — the child is the "before" and the athlete is the "after" (and the road in between paved with fruit, vegetables and exercise): even Sportacus was once an "ordinary" child.[25] The ordinary children of the audience can also grow to become athletes by adopting the healthy lifestyle advocated by Sportacus, and in so doing, the children of the audience are not just safeguarding their own personal future but that of society — they are both being and becoming "active citizens."

Blurred Boundaries

The prevailing theme of safeguarding futurity is suitably enhanced by the show's utilization of aspects of what broadly might be considered science fiction and further developed by the uncertain boundary between fantasy and reality consistently suggested in the highly distinctive textual aesthetics: the groundbreaking format of the show's blend of puppetry, live-action and CGI is, I believe, as yet unparalleled in children's television. The format is so unique that the basic material premise of the show is difficult to describe to those who have not seen it, and even then there is considerable confusion over how it is actually achieved, even within the professional production community. In a nutshell, nine characters — four adults and five children — exist in the eponymous town (a village really) of LazyTown, a largely CGI landscape but with physical sets and props and a temporal setting of a more technologically advanced "now." Few other persons are ever seen or directly referred to in LazyTown, though the infrastructure of the town-it has a museum, a theatre, an elected mayor, etc.— would suggest that there are other unseen residents. It should be noted too that the parents or careers of the children are never seen or referred to — the only explicit familial relationship is between the visiting niece Stephanie and her uncle, Mayor Milford Meanswell. It could be that the banishment of parental roles from LazyTown is another means by which to soften the didacticism of the message. Three of the characters (two adults and one child) are human actors, and the others are latex puppets with highly expressive animatronic faces (operated by two puppeteers each). There is no distinction between the two "species" in the diegesis as all nine characters are presented as within the same genus: this is partially facilitated by the studio set up whereby trenches in the studio floor allow the puppeteers to perform the scene in real time and space with the human actors, and also by the fact that most of the puppet characters are voiced by the puppeteers on set. A feature of the *LazyTown* studio set-up is the state-of-the-art computer processor which allows CGI backdrops to be seen in real time with the live-action filming: usually the finished look of "green screen" filming can only be seen at a post-production stage, but, in *LazyTown,* the director and the performers can see the composite effect on a monitor as the scene is shot. As such, the texture of the show, which is shot in HD, is very "real" (with the human and puppet interactions in particular having a tangible quality) and yet other aspects of the aesthetics belong clearly to the fantastic.

The aesthetic vocabulary is that of the surreal: super-bright colors, stretched shapes, distorted proportions and angles. There are no straight lines in *LazyTown,* its buildings a swollen, molten, Gaudiesque version of Rekjavik's quaint fin de siècle townscape. The super-fast editing (again, boundary pushing for the preschool audience c/f *Teletubbies* or *Dora the Explorer*) and the electronic soundscape of an estimated one thousand sound effects provide a grammar and punctuation that can verge on the frenetic; the overall aesthetic impact of the show has the somewhat unsettling appeal of a hallucination or of the weird or uncanny, both familiar yet strange. Certainly the show, reputed to be the most expensive children's television production ever at $1 million USD per episode,[26] is exacting in its production values, but its creator, who could almost be accused of excess or profligacy in his approach,[27] (and who, tellingly, is described by production colleagues as "like a child who has no pre-knowledge of what is possible, only that he wants it")[28] is keen to emphasize that his perfectionism is because the show is the critical carrier of the message, and that "nothing is too good for kids."[29] While such self-reflexive industry discourse is, as John Thornton Caldwell warns, "almost always offered from some perspective of self-interest, promotion, and spin,"[30] each individual textual constituent — narrative, mise en scene, sound effects, editing, etc.— contributes to the luxurious quality and cohesion of the whole. Another way of expressing this is that each and every element of brand identity can be perceived to add value to the effective promulgation of the *LazyTown* ethos, as summed up here in a BBC press release:

> From day one, all of *LazyTown*'s entertainment products were carefully designed as a vehicle to carry the core health message that the brand is all about. [...] This health-related value is deeply ingrained in the brand's DNA and is *LazyTown*'s most valuable asset.[31]

The discursive construction of the brand as "carefully designed" and of possessing "DNA" has many connotations of science fiction that, if taken to negative extreme, may characterize the brand itself as a genetically modified child of body fascism: perfected, beautiful, post-human. Surprisingly, there seems little criticism of the brand's assumption that the body beautiful is universally accessible to all — that you, too, can grow to be a Sportacus — although the foregrounding of a diversity of *real* children including those with disability in the spin-off show *LazyTown Extra*[32] may be a pre-emptive sequitur to such a charge.

Science-Fiction Aesthetics and Tropes

Setting, character and mise en scene are key areas which suggest science fiction and through which the Manichaean duality of good and evil are sustained in the text. This can be illustrated through analysis of the respective home bases of hero Sportacus and his arch-nemesis, Robbie Rotten (played by Icelander Stefán Karl Stefánsson). These two bases provide structuring bookends to the show (each individual episode has a completed storyline) with the opening sequence always set in Sportacus's airship and the final sequence — usually a comedy "sting" — taking place in Robbie's lair. Sportacus's airship, floating high in the heavens above LazyTown, is a highly futuristic environment, a seamless white, shiny, spartan interior straight out of Kubrick's *2001: A Space Odyssey* (only with a *female* computer voice). The ship responds to Sportacus's verbal commands for "Apple," "Ball," "Bed," "Book," etc., by opening concealed spaces or ejecting the item with suitable techno sound effect. Sportacus, however, never simply retrieves these items; indeed Sportacus never performs any action in a linear or sequential manner. Why walk between A and B when one can backflip, somersault and cartwheel, perform a selection of press-ups and handstands and still keep one's waxed moustache looking good? The airship "plays" with Sportacus, ejecting items unexpectedly, lighting up areas he must "tag," setting him challenges: the ergonomic design *facilitates* rather than reduces movement, and, significantly, although hi-tech, this and all of Sportacus's transport devices are pedal-powered, reinforcing the notion that technology can enhance health if used appropriately, and eliciting a rear shot of Scheving's powerful buttocks and thighs pumping away. The overblown aesthetics are complemented by the "Flash Gordon" campery of Scheving's performance of masculinity, his teutonic vocal inflection and orgiastic physical display somewhat reminiscent of Arnold Schwarzenegger. Sportacus descends to earth from a blue perfect sky, a god trailing clouds of glory, eager to help earth-bound mortals when the flashing crystal on his chest warns him that "Someone's in trouble."

And someone is always in trouble in LazyTown, usually as a result of

Robbie Rotten's rotten schemes. Robbie lives *beneath* LazyTown, under an industrial cowshed, in a vast basement laboratory equipped with infinite resources for his dastardly plans to keep LazyTown lazy ... "FOREVER!" Each time the action cuts to Robbie's lair the camera tracks downwards at high speed through CGI layers of pavement and earth to reinforce the subterranean nature of Robbie's existence in the bowels of hell. The mise en scene suggests a mottled industrial grime of "dark Satanic mills," the lighting an artificial, blue-violet mirk relieved only by the lamp beside Robbie's orange fluffy armchair[33] and the eerie acid glow of the giant glass test tubes which display costumed mannequins like pickled specimens: Robbie Rotten is a master of disguise. Decaying metal machinery and nameless vats and pipes stretch, through CGI trickery, to infinity, mirroring Robbie's own limitless capacity for devilry and deception. This nexus of evil and decay with the industrial is a well-worn trope of Romanticism that is easily aligned to science-fiction utopias/dystopias,[34] and has particular resonance with a pastoral idyll of childhood to which it presents a threat. Robbie is "rotten" both figuratively and literally, just as he is the enemy of childhood both figuratively and literally. He hates noise, activity and (therefore) children. He likes only sleep and cake, and he embodies indolence and greed (in spite of the fact that Stefánsson is 6"2' and lithe as a whip).

The role is played with a manic physicality and mercurial personality (Stefánsson is frequently compared to Jim Carrey) in which we recognize the classic literary villain; the role is more akin to Captain Hook or a pantomime/fairytale villain than any character typical of preschool television, which has very few "baddies."[35] The peculiarly elastic, off-kilter physicality of Rotten — a character who expends excessive energy in the pursuit of slothful torpor — invites a reading that Rotten is the "evil twin," alter ego or doppelganger (a popular science-fiction trope) of Sportacus. This "evil twin" trope is particularly explicit in the "Sportafake" episode,[36] where Robbie dresses up as Sportacus in attempt to get him banished from LazyTown. The citizens must choose who the real Sportacus is, as coexistence is not possible for the doppelganger who presages death (figurative or otherwise) of the duplicate. Through the lens of the evil twin or alter ego trope, Rotten's hatred of Sportacus is tantamount to a *self*-hatred or a *self*-destructive impulse: Robbie Rotten is the death drive. Robbie's catchphrase regarding keeping LazyTown lazy "FOREVER" reinforces that his negative desire is perpetual; if this generation of LazyTown kids is silenced, then there is silence forevermore. In this sense Robbie Rotten is an important antagonist, a representation of the dark side of human nature, of a stasis and nihilism that is normally excised for the preschool television audience, despite Neil Postman's fears for the "disappearance of childhood" and the collapsed age categories of the "total disclosure medium."[37]

LazyTown not only *shows* this dark side but also suggests that it should never be eradicated or repressed but instead acknowledged and (thereby) contained. Indeed, in one episode, Rotten is restored to LazyTown and paralleled with Sportacus by the children's plea to a wish-granting Genie (in one of only three episodes where additional characters are included): "LazyTown wouldn't be LazyTown without Sportacus and it wouldn't be LazyTown without the skinny man in the stripy suit [Robbie Rotten]." When the genie responds, in amazement, that Robbie is a "pain in the neck," Stingy replies, "Yes, but he's our pain in the neck!" thereby acknowledging Robbie's unpleasant but nonetheless valid place in society.[38]

Sex and Death: The Struggle to Contain the Dark Side

The textual "containment" of Robbie Rotten through a range of devices — humor and narrative resolution, the presence of the hero, comic costuming, a big false chin and outlandish Elvis hairstyle, slapstick physical comedy, the science-fiction/fantasy framing — makes the presence of this character possible and permissible and renders him a permanent yet manageable threat. The nature of that represented threat is of critical importance to our understanding of "proper" adult-child relationships in the text. Rotten, a lone male who spies on children, who appears in friendly disguise, who tempts them with sweets and games, who even imprisons them (in a phallic tower no less),[39] is a de facto child-predator; yet the show, through its range of "containment" strategies, closes down the reading of these actions as pedophilic or as motivated by anything other than a hatred of healthy living, Rotten's paradoxical raison d'être. In the episode where the children are imprisoned, Rotten does so only to gain peace and quiet in which to do nothing. By closing off a sexualized reading, Robbie can be considered a manifestation of what Edelman argues (through analysis of characters such as Dickens's Scrooge, Barrie's Captain Hook and Eliot's Silas Marner) as the ultimate symbolic enemy of childhood and of futurity — the "sinthomosexual." The sinthomosexual is a queer figure not because of his sexuality but because of his symbolic meaning as the antithesis of procreative futurism:

> I've already defined this child-aversive, future-negating force, answering so well to the inspiriting needs of a moribund familialism, as *sinthom*osexuality, a term that links the jouissance to which we gain access to the sinthome with a homosexuality made to figure the lack in Symbolic meaning-production on account of which, as Lacan declares, "there is no sexual relation."[40]

For all Sportacus is a positive mirror image of Rotten (Sportacus too is a lone male — his female blimp not withstanding — who plays with children;

who befriends them; who handles them physically in a range of athletic instruction). He is *not* coded as a queer figure; nonetheless the text, as is typical of children's television, both emphatically *asserts* yet also *contains* his heteronormative male status (hence the campery endemic in preschool programming[41]): his special relationships are with females (Stephanie and his airship), he is dressed in blue while Stephanie is in pink, he is "fancied" by an adult female (Bessie Busybody flutters her eyelashes and contrives to fall in to his arms) yet he chooses an ascetic life. Here the juxtaposition with Rotten resonates further as where Rotten is an anti-father, Sportacus is a father figure (as is Scheving both to his actual children and to his puppet creations[42]) guiding and caring for the children, setting them a positive example. Where Rotten imprisons children, Sportacus frees them. Another important containment strategy by which we are prevented from reading anything sinister in the adult-child relationships in *LazyTown* is that neither Sportacus nor Robbie truly symbolizes adulthood; both characters are facets, instead, of the imagined child. Robbie is an adult presence, but he does not represent an adult threat, instead he represents the inner threat of greed and laziness and self-destruction that exists as part of the child's own psyche (as constructed in *LazyTown*), just as Sportacus represents the positive potential within children. Robbie Rotten is the sulking child who does not want to play and wants to ruin everyone's fun; Sportacus, on the other hand, loves to play and to facilitate play—he is usually shown with some symbol of play (a deck of cards, a ball, a bat, a scooter) and all activities—even chores—are transformed into play.

Moreover, *all* of the characters in *LazyTown*—adult and child alike— can thus be said to represent a projection of the conceptualized child psyche, their names by and large offering connotations of their representational aspect: "Stingy" finds it difficult to share, "Trixie" is resistant to authority, "Pixel" loves computer games, "Ziggy" loves sweets and cakes, "Mayor Meanswell" is hapless and clumsy and "Bessie Busybody" is a chatterbox gossip. Like Barrie's Neverland, *LazyTown* is a psychic as much as a physical realm, as we note in Scheving's conception of LazyTown as "a state of mind. We've all been to LazyTown"[43] and again in his assertion that "if you mix all the *LazyTown* characters together into one, I would say you have a really balanced person."[44] The character of Stephanie—a visitor to LazyTown—is situated somewhat outside this construct in that she is the only "real child" in the text, and, like Sportacus, she does not have any flaws—she is an aspirational figure that James Kincaid would describe as "the adorable child" of a "long line of culturally mandated [child] cuties."[45] Reading Sportacus as a fellow child playmate mitigates some of the "problem" of the non-familial Sportacus-Stephanie adult-child dynamic, but ultimately the casting of a teenage pubescent girl (Julianna Rose Mauriello) to play an eight year old "cutie" creates a problem in its own right, injecting, as it does, an unavoidable precocity of performance that both Walkerdine and Kincaid respectively term as one means of eroticizing or fetishizing "innocence" within mainstream popular culture.[46]

In this way, too, the status of Stephanie as a "real child" (a real eight-year-old child, that is) becomes contested, and Stephanie, with her pink hair and flat shining features, is a representation of a child akin to the way in which a mannequin or doll is. Scheving originally described her as such: "She is half human, half puppet — or rather half make-believe. She sits in the gap between Barbie and Britney, and I believe parents do want their daughters to make a transition between the two."[47] (Scheving's unproblematized identification of a "desired" transition between "Barbie and Britney" would seem to support Walkerdine's contention of "the ubiquitous eroticization of little girls in popular media and the just as ubiquitous ignorance and denial of this phenomenon.")[48] Stephanie too has a doppelganger narrative in the "Dancing Duel" episode wherein she is pitted against a clockwork rival in a dance competition. Stephanie eventually wins, of course, but that this was ever in doubt highlights her proximity to the doll.[49] The repeated narrative motif of Stephanie's struggle with the robots and "living" dolls (c/f *Barbarella*) of Robbie Rotten's invention, serves to mirror Stephanie's liminal status as a human child, while her *resistance* to such threats implies the autonomy and self-determination (even precocity) demanded of the real — yet "model"— child in both the narrative and mission of *LazyTown* (and therefore both inside and outside of the text).

Technology, Surveillance and Other Threats

Just as the fantastical non-realist framing allows the text to (at least partially) overcome the problem of representing non-familial adult-child relationships (remembering also the limited range of such relationships in the preschooler's life), it is also used to explore other notions of threat to childhood and futurity as embodied in Robbie Rotten. The range of guises and means of surveillance available to Robbie means that his threat is ever present but ever new and unrecognized in LazyTown, although "seeing through" and predicting Robbie's ludicrous disguises is one of the pleasures offered to the audience. Robbie uses a periscope to spy on the inhabitants above, all the better to keep track of their health initiatives and respond with his own anti-health devices: robots that run amok, machines that suck energy, gadgets that freeze time or repeat it over. Although such devices are a trope of pre–1950s science fiction, and Farah Mendlesohn notes that the theme of "redundancy due to technology" has largely disappeared from children's science fiction [literature] since then, labor saving devices *do* continue to be presented in a particular way to children throughout the genre and "spare time is mostly celebrated or condemned for generating self-absorption and other manifestations of decadence."[50] The latter is true of *LazyTown*, with free time generally "punished" within the narrative, even where well intentioned, such as when Stephanie attempts to give Sportacus a "day off" but realizes that sitting still and doing nothing makes him bored and unhappy: in effect free time denies Sportacus his identity as an active citizen.[51] Labor-saving technology is still more pilloried — Robbie's devices always backfire, always with hilarious results and usually to his detriment. Even within his own lab Robbie's equipment and inventions seem "out to get him," lurching at him unexpectedly, tripping him up, "misbehaving" as if sentient (indeed his periscope has eyes). Sportacus enjoys a healthy and positive relationship to technology (some also seemingly sentient, like his airship), but Robbie *abuses* it — so it bites back. Failed or out of control technology accounts for roughly one third of the *LazyTown* plotlines, and here the figurative device of Robbie and Sportacus as symbolizing children suggests that just as the elements of the child's psyche must be balanced, so too must be the child's relationship to technology.

The puppet character of Pixel, eldest of the LazyTown children, explicitly represents the "dangers" of an unbalanced relationship with technology, particularly in relation to computer gaming. Because no parents are ever seen in *LazyTown*, we are offered a vision of what the child would do if unfettered by parental supervision at home, and gaming is shown as a particularly addictive and immersive experience, effectively turning the child into a zombie. The mise en scene reinforces this. Pixel's home is easy to spot on the LazyTown skyline as it is covered with various antennae, satellite dishes, transmitters and receivers. Pixel is similarly augmented, with strange cuboid dreadlocks and a permanently attached headset/visor/mouthpiece. The interior of Pixel's room looks like ground control: banks of computers and electronic devices and a dazzling array of dials, switches and flashing lights. Thus Pixel is "disconnected" to the real world, removed through multiple barriers, "lost" in his room, his game and his head. Following the classic antinomic analysis of the Western by Jim Kitses,[52] one can trace a series of oppositions and thematic dualisms in *LazyTown*, between the virtual and the real, indoors and outside, the mental and the physical, the private and the social, the artificial and the natural. These are neatly illustrated in the discussion of Pixel's completed 3D digital blueprint for an outdoor clubhouse: Stephanie asks, "When are we going to build it?" and Pixel, indicating the computer screen, replies, "I just have."[53] Gaming and the virtual world is not *real* play, not considered as valid, creative or imaginative within the *LazyTown* ethos and is shown as a shallow gratification that provides no satisfaction beyond novelty, such as when the children grow bored and exasperated with the remote control device that "plays for them."[54] *Real* play is physical, outdoors, and though it can happen alone (e.g., Ziggy riding his bike) it would seem to be at its best when with other children, i.e., as part of a society. It also "just happens," requiring no special toys or equipment. This is shown most clearly in the episode where Robbie creates a device to steal the toys of children all over the world: Sportacus saves the toys, but, in their absence, the children of LazyTown realize that "You don't need toys to have fun."[55] (This episode also makes explicit the threat that Robbie holds for *all* children of the world — not just the localized ones of LazyTown.) Of all the vices and aspects of the psyche in *LazyTown*, gaming is perhaps the most antithetical to the *LazyTown* ethos (interestingly, television is rarely mentioned in the text): it is a particularly potent enemy of childhood as it displaces what *LazyTown* constructs as the most fundamental defining constituent of childhood — outdoor play.

Like Robbie Rotten, Pixel frequently designs hi-tech gadgetry, usually around the idea of virtual play or of labor-saving devices: inventions to tie shoelaces, inventions to rewind and fast forward the present (so one can do one's homework at a time that suits), inventions to make unwanted things (piles of trash) invisible. Of course, like those of Robbie Rotten, these gadgets always backfire but, unlike Robbie, Pixel is shown to *learn* from the experience, to realize that it is much more fun to play in the real world, to build the clubhouse there. Importantly, too, Pixel reaches this conclusion through his own experience of "real play — such as when he wins a race in the LazyTown square, rather than in a computer game. It is not something that is imposed on him, and it occurs "naturally" through his socialization with Stephanie who, as an outsider, is appalled at the lack of "real play" in LazyTown. Stephanie, the outsider, is able to directly ask, "Don't you play — outside? Running and jumping in the fresh air?" and her "Have you never?" song solo continues this series of direct questions to the LazyTown children (who answer in the negative):

> STEPHANIE: Have you never skipped rope?
> CHILDREN: (Uh uh uh uh uh uh)
> STEPHANIE: Have you never played ball?
> CHILDREN: (Uh uh uh uh uh uh)
> STEPHANIE: Never jumped around?
> CHILDREN: (Uh uh uh uh uh uh)
> STEPHANIE: Have you never danced at all? ... You gotta listen to me. Can't you see that life is full of games? And they make you feel so happy. You know they make you wanna fly. So play games all your — every single day of your — life![56]

As the framing of Stephanie's solo song/dance routines breaks the "fourth wall" that is maintained throughout the rest of the narrative — while singing she performs directly to the camera, front on, square to it, in a mixture of close up and full length shots — this suggests Stephanie, who remains center frame and has the children *behind* her throughout the song, is directly addressing and performing for the child in the audience more so than the children of LazyTown. The reprise of this song, however, occurring after Robbie Rotten has tempted all Stephanie's new friends away with sweets and video games, reintroduces the fourth wall to set at a distance the sadness and loneliness of childhood. Here Stephanie is framed side on in medium shot, wandering alone, in a pathos-inducing state of self-reflection, as she sings to herself with a tremble in her voice, looking in to the distance: "Have you ever been sad? Have you got a friend who'll stay? Have you ever been lonely? All I want is just to ... play." Despite the direct address of the lyrics, the reprise is not framed as a direct address to the audience; instead we are voyeurs of a child's private angst, the address of the lyrics to *no audience* reinforcing their meaning and poignancy: happiness, friendship, fellowship and play are constructed as fundamental to a child's wellbeing. Mauriello's performance is sensitive and convincing, and the reinstatement of the fourth wall suggests that the director is inviting a different response from the audience to the situation — sympathy rather than empathy, analysis rather than identification, indirect rather than direct response to the problem contained in the narrative. The child at home is being shown that the child in the text is unhappy because she has been denied the opportunity of play; furthermore the desire to play is constructed as a "normal" and "natural" desire even if thwarted or repressed.

Active Citizenship and Active Play: Model Behaviors

The idea of play as both a natural right and a natural action of childhood is associated with the natural education of Rousseau, but in *LazyTown* it emerges more as a Lockean philosophy: children learn most effectively through play, so if one can harness the potential for play, you can inculcate them with appropriate knowledge and behaviors. The range of civic activities that the children of LazyTown engage in once they are enlightened as to healthy lifestyles suggests a very simple connection between caring for self and caring for society. Clean up campaigns, sports days, awards ceremonies, vegetable gardening, talent competitions and restoration works become the norm of LazyTown, with each member of the little community — except Robbie — actively participating with encouragement. The concepts of community and participation are emphasized in storylines and the "Teamwork" song has the refrain, "Teamwork: do it together. Teamwork: friends forever. We're all for one and one for all. We'll help each other stand tall — with teamwork!"[57]

Because children make up the bulk of the LazyTown community they are very valuable contributors to civic life within the diegesis, and, in this, *LazyTown* posits that children can contribute effectively to society now as well as in the future: active citizenship need not be referenced solely against adult achievement or putative future success. In *LazyTown* the interests of the child are seemingly served by a healthy society, not (just) parents, as in the old proverb that "it takes a village to raise a child." While the project of citizenship entails the balance of individual and societal needs, *LazyTown* constructs the mechanism of outdoor play as aligning those needs, such as when the children have fun together planting vegetables in the LazyTown square. *LazyTown* posits that when a child is playing and having "healthy active fun" then they are both looking after themselves and contributing to society. In short they are safeguarding futurity. It is up to adults to ensure that healthy activity is available to children: although offering "guilt-free" television, *LazyTown* actually makes an implicit demand that adults take responsibility for "real" play in their society. The inculcation of "active citizens" in (and through) *LazyTown* applies to both adult and child in society.

The *LazyTown* ethos may construct the role of adults as essential gatekeepers of children's health and happiness but, within the diegesis itself, adults generally adopt a relaxed, laissez faire approach, only intervening as necessary (such as Bessie Busybody chastising and offering an alternative venue when Ziggy rides his bike into her clean washing),[58] thus allowing children maximum freedom. Even Sportacus only intervenes when there is a crisis or when specifically invited—he does not initiate or instigate interactions between himself and the children. In depicting the adults as caring but sparing in their interventions, there is perhaps some further tension here between message and medium in the *LazyTown* brand. On the one hand, the *LazyTown* product, as an educational aid or parental tool, could be considered part of what Matt Briggs describes as the "ethicalization of existence"[59] whereby institutional structures and resources replace experiential parentcraft as the expert source of knowledge and guidance for child-rearing; yet, conversely, within the *LazyTown* text, such "ethicalization" or "expert discourse" is refuted in favor of an apparently more instinctual and experiential approach on the part of adults, made explicit when Bessie Busybody says that Mayor Meanswell doesn't "know anything about raising children" and he replies "What's to know?"[60] The brand paradoxically shows that child-rearing can be a "common sense" process. A central aspect of this "common sense" approach is in *LazyTown*'s take on risk in child development; this notion has become a central theme of the campaign to preserve child freedom and access in an increasingly risk-averse and threat-aware society. In her 2006 research into contemporary (UK) childhood, Libby Brooks discusses the findings that, "in a single generation, the 'home habitat' of a typical eight-year old — the area in which the child was able to travel without direct supervision — had shrunk to one ninth of its former size,"[61] likening this to a generation of children "bred in captivity" and shielded from every imagined external danger. *LazyTown* capitalizes on the notion that risk-aversion is a risk in itself if taken to the extreme, and the children of LazyTown are shown to benefit from an element of jeopardy — e.g., overcoming fears of ghosts and dinosaurs, etc., exploring beyond the boundaries of the village, utilizing building tools and camping without supervision — in their journey towards autonomous active citizenship.

The conception of the "indoors" child and its relationship to risk is explored in *LazyTown* and allied to unhealthy lifestyle in diet and exercise, too. When showing children "indoors" in Pixel's home, they are sedentary, playing computer games and eating grotesque platters of junk food; the children are fractious, and the environment is messy and confined, shot from a close, oppressive angle. A lack of growth or forward movement is emphasized by the fact that as one game ends in squabbles another immediately begins, and as one batch of debris is pushed to the side another begins to accumulate. In contrast, when shown outside, the children are happy; they take responsibility for keeping their environment clean, and fruit and vegetables — Sportscandy — are presented as clean, shiny and orderly, whether stacked symmetrically on a platter or growing in neat systematic rows in seed beds. Most of these outdoor activities suggest forward movement, nurture or growth or improvement through practice (building, planting, running, dancing, etc.): they imply futurity.

The idea of risk is diffuse within the *LazyTown* brand (all 52 of its episodes having a narrative of jeopardy), but *actual* threats to child welfare always occur indoors whereas, when playing outdoors, the risks or threats to children are only ever *artificial*, born of Robbie Rotten's deceptions and artifice. Even the mere presence of a "baddie" character can be construed to reflect an open attitude to the role of (figurative) danger within child development in the *LazyTown* brand, and is a departure from the norm of preschool television, even that which also employs a fantasy or non-realist frame such as *Teletubbies* or *In the Night Garden*. The function of danger in a fantasy narrative has been theorized as a means whereby children can safely explore and come to terms with not only the dark side of life but of their own psyche, as Bettelheim famously suggests of fairy tales,[62] and as Gerard Jones says of contemporary children's media in his polemic, *Killing Monsters: Why Children Need Fantasy, Super Heroes, and Make-Believe Violence*, thus:

> *Trust the child's desires.* Our culture leads us to be leery of a child's most fervent appetites [...]. Children's desires, however, usually reflect their needs [...]. It's tempting to mirror only the behavior we like and ignore the others, hoping

they'll fade away. It's the behavior we refuse to acknowledge, however, that will trouble them most. They'll need to have those sides of themselves seen.[63]

I believe that *LazyTown*, in its use of Robbie Rotten and the flawed puppet characters, shows "those sides" of children that are not often acknowledged in preschool television, as well as the more commonly represented "behavior we like" sides. Scheving's choice of non-realist modes is central to this: "Puppets work because each of these characters has a flaw. This would be hard with a real child actor. Also you can do slapstick things with puppets, like have things fall on their heads."[64] *LazyTown* is uniquely able to fulfill its ideological mandate to inculcate active citizenship through healthy lifestyle choices in its preschool audience precisely because it can show the reverse of active citizenship in its content. It carefully aligns education and entertainment to promote the brand goal of a healthy future for preschool children and — therefore — society.

Conclusion

LazyTown does not advocate risky or inappropriate behavior; rather, in mirroring the darker aspects of children's behavior back to the children's audience through the safety of a fantasy narrative, it acknowledges such behavior, making it less threatening. It also shows aspirational or positive aspects of the childhood state in its use of the live-action Sportacus and Stephanie characters (who can most clearly move between modes of realism and fantasy) and in the ready adoption of healthy lifestyle choices by the puppets once they are set positive example. Indeed truly "no one's lazy in LazyTown" other than Robbie Rotten, as each episode picks up from the point that Sportacus and Stephanie have started to effect change — this is emphasized both in the theme song and the opening credits. The science-fiction tropes, in particular the battle between good and evil, the camp aesthetics, the doppelganger and the cautious relationship to technology, are also part of the conceptual framework by which *LazyTown* resolves the implicit tension between message and medium in educational children's television and creates a distance from reality that invites the audience not merely to engage directly with the show but to consider and act on its message of positive choices in diet and exercise. The Robbie Rotten character is especially important in providing the entertainment value that elevates the show above a moralistic didacticism. Robbie represents a direct threat to childhood but also symbolizes adult control, the child's own dark side, and the death drive. Although *LazyTown* posits that the main threat to the future of childhood is the denial of play, compounded by poor choices in diet and exercise, a logical tenet of the *LazyTown* proposition is that a focus on diet, exercise and lifestyle would not be necessary if children were engaged in active outdoor play in the first place. So, ironically, the "real" threat to a healthy childhood in the *LazyTown* ethos is not pedophiles, traffic or bullies but the unhealthy captive lifestyle which is our adult response to the fear of those risks; it is the over-protection and constant surveillance of children that have become the risk, minimizing the autonomy of the child. The very different motivations behind child surveillance — whether predatory or protectionist — may both have the same effect of harming children.

That is why we must read Robbie Rotten's behavior as an abstracted nihilism rather than a more predatory threat: Robbie's surveillance is anti-children because its logical purpose is to close down and limit childhood, to stop their noise, their expression, their play. Robbie is not so much anti-children but anti-life or anti-futurity, and children, as the fullest expression and symbol of futurity are thus reviled objects for him. Following this, *LazyTown* could be said to show a certain courage in the bold way that it presents adult-child relationships as the legitimate concern of *all* members of society — one does not need to be a parent in order to take an interest — so it is not "strange" that Sportacus, Bessie Busybody and Mayor Meanswell nurture the children and, by allowing them freedom, contribute to their development as citizens. *LazyTown* is ultimately a hopeful and optimistic text in its notion of futurity as it places children in positions of personal empowerment and esteem while acknowledging the challenges and restrictions of 21st century childhood. *LazyTown* constructs even the youngest members of society as active citizens valued for who they are now, as much as for what they represent and what they will become in the future. This future is neither the dystopia nor "pie in the sky" utopia of much science fiction and fantasy, but instead a pragmatic and achievable vision that we can all contribute towards and benefit from. *LazyTown* posits, as Postman suggests, that:

There is a sense in which adults are at their best, their most civilized, when tending to the nurture of children. For we must remember that the modern paradigm of childhood is also the modern paradigm of adulthood. In saying what we wish a child to become, we are saying what we are.[65]

Notes

1. "Little Sportacus," *Go, Go, LazyTown*, DVD (2007; UK: BBC Worldwide, 2007).
2. David Buckingham, "On the Impossibility of Children's Television: The Case of Timmy Mallett," in *In Front of the Children: Screen Entertainment and Young Audiences*, edited by Cary Bazalgette and David Buckingham (London: British Film Institute, 1995), 47.
3. See titles such as Marie Winn, *The Plug-In Drug*; Sue Palmer, *Toxic Childhood*; Barrie Gunter and Jill L. McAleer, *Children and Television: The One-eyed Monster?*
4. Magnus Scheving, quoted in Bryony Gordon, "Could We Move into LazyTown?" *The Telegraph* (London, UK), 28 August 2006, http://www.telegraph.co.uk/health/3342731/Could-we-move-into-LazyTown.html.

5. I use global sales and vast ancillary merchandising as the marker of success here, suggested by Jeanette Steemers's model in her recent monograph on preschool production ecology, *Creating Preschool Television: A Story of Commerce, Creativity and Curriculum* (London: Palgrave, 2010).

6. Theunis Bates, "Kids' Show Makes Spinach Cool," *Time Magazine Online*, 14 May 2008, http://www.time.com/time/arts/article/0,8599,1779487,00.html.

7. See, for example, Alex Freeman, "Television — Good For Our Children?" *eParenting.co.uk*, 2004, http://eparenting.co.uk/education/televisiongoodforourchildren.shtml; or, "What Do You Think of Preschool TV?" *Blogher, Mommy and Family*, February 2009, http://www.blogher.com/what-do-you-think-preschool-tv.

8. I use the term "preschool television" in its accepted industry sense of having a target audience of children up to around six years of age, although in many of *LazyTown*'s broadcast territories, including the UK, schooling begins at five or even four years old.

9. "Move the World," *LazyTown* Branding Presentation, 2009, http://chinese.made-in-iceland.com.cn/download/Brand_Guide.pdf.

10. Ibid.

11. Lee Edelman, *No Future: Queer Theory and the Death Drive* (Durham and London: Duke University Press, 2004), 14.

12. Ibid., 4.

13. Ibid., 3.

14. Lauren Berlant, *The Queen of America Goes to Washington City: Essays on Sex and Citizenship* (Durham, NC: Duke University Press, 1997).

15. Ibid., 27.

16. From http://www.lazytown.com/partners/.

17. Patricia Palmer, *The Lively Audience* (Sydney: Allen & Unwin, 1986), 63.

18. Steemers argues that the trend of conflict avoidance is especially pronounced in the U.S. preschool market (and therefore impacts on global markets). Steemers, *Creating Preschool Television*, 52–53.

19. An apposite example is the "Dr Rottenstein" episode wherein Robbie Rotten fakes a fruit and vegetable disease that prevents the children from eating "Sportscandy." Soon all the children are sick and in bed, only getting better when the trick is exposed and they eat fruit and vegetables again. *Welcome to LazyTown* (2006; UK: BBC Worldwide, 2006).

20. "Meet the Creator of LazyTown," *Nick Jr*, http://www.nickjr.com/lazytown/about-lazytown/lazytown-creator_ap.html.

21. Magnus Scheving, quoted in Sam Phillips, "Face to Face with Magnus Scheving," *Global License*, 1 December 2004, http://www.licensemag.com/licensemag/article/articleDetail.jsp?id=161191&sk=&date=&pageID=2.

22. Marie Winn, *The Plug-in Drug: Television, Computers and Family Life* (New York: Penguin, 2002), 3.

23. Amanda Andrews, "Fit for Purpose — Iceland's Superhero," *The Telegraph*, January 9, 2009, http://www.telegraph.co.uk/finance/newsbysector/mediatechnologyandtelecoms/media/4209769/LazyTown-superhero-Magnus-Scheving-on-a-health-mission.html.

24. "Welcome to LazyTown," *Welcome to LazyTown*.

25. "Little Sportacus," *Go, Go LazyTown*.

26. See Iceland's domestic reportage in the aftermath of the collapse of the Icelandic banks and economy, for example, Brett Young, "Bing Bang Goes on in Iceland's LazyTown," *Reuters*, November 19, 2008, http://www.reuters.com/article/idUSTRE4AJ0D920081120.

27. It should be noted that rumors of LazyTown Entertainment's financial difficulties surfaced in February 2010, shortly after the completion of the draft of this essay.

28. Raymond Le Gue (producer of *LazyTown*), quoted in *Avid Magazine*, November 2006, http://emea.promax.tv/emea/nov06_news_1.html.

29. Magnus Scheving, quoted in Phillips, "Face to Face with Magnus Scheving."

30. John Thornton Caldwell, *Production Culture: Industrial Reflexivity and Critical Practice in Film and Television* (Durham: Duke University Press, 2008), 14.

31. *BBC Worldwide Press Release*, May 6, 2009, http://www.bbc.co.uk/pressoffice/bbcworldwide/worldwidestories/pressreleases/2009/05_may/lazytown.shtml.

32. *LazyTown Extra*, Television Series (2008; CBeebies Channel, 2008).

33. Robbie is shown fitfully dozing in this armchair, never in a proper bed like Sportacus. Robbie is always trying to take naps, often in inappropriate places like on a wall or bench. Sportacus, in contrast, has a "proper" bedtime routine and wakes fully refreshed.

34. See, for example, Robert Corbett, "Romanticism and Science Fictions — A Special Issue of Romanticism on the Net," in *Romanticism on the Net*, February 2001, http://id.erudit.org/iderudit/005970ar. Farah Mendlesohn provides an informative précis of this trope in children's/young adult science fiction literature in her *The Inter-Galactic Playground: A Critical Study of Children's and Teens' Science Fiction* (Jefferson, NC: McFarland, 2009).

35. "Swiper," the pilfering fox in *Dora the Explorer*, is another rare villain of preschool television.

36. "Sportafake," *No One's Lazy in LazyTown*, DVD (2008; UK: BBC Worldwide, 2008).

37. Neil Postman, *The Disappearance of Childhood* (New York: Vintage Books, 1994).

38. "The LazyTown Genie," *Once Upon a Time in LazyTown*, DVD (2006; UK: BBC Worldwide, 2006).

39. "Prince Stingy," *Once Upon a Time in LazyTown*.

40. Edelman, *No Future*, 113.

41. See, for example, *The Wiggles*; *High 5*; *Barney the Dinosaur*, et al.

42. Scheving publicly promotes his literal and metaphorical fatherhood in interview. See, for example, Scheving in interview with parents on the CBeebies website, http://www.bbc.co.uk/cbeebies/grownups/about/programmes/magnus_scheving_interview.shtml.

43. "Meet the Creator of LazyTown," *Nick Jr*.

44. Magnus Scheving in interview with parents on the CBeebies website.

45. James R. Kincaid, "Producing Erotic Children," in *The Children's Culture Reader*, edited by Henry Jenkins (New York: New York University Press, 1998), 245.

46. See Valerie Walkerdine, "Popular Culture and the Eroticization of Little Girls," in *The Children's Culture Reader*, edited by Henry Jenkins (New York: New York University Press, 1998), 254–264, and James R. Kincaid, *Erotic Innocence: The Culture of Child Molesting* (Durham, NC: Duke University Press, 1998).

47. Magnus Scheving, quoted in Phillips, "Face to Face With Magnus Scheving."

48. Walkerdine, "Popular Culture and the Eroticization of Little Girls," 254.

49. "Dancing Duel," *Go Go LazyTown*.

50. Mendlesohn, *The Inter-Galactic Playground*, 140.

51. "LazyTown's New Superhero," *Anyone Can Be a Hero!* DVD (2006; UK: BBC Worldwide, 2006).

52. Jim Kitses, *Horizons West: Directing the Western from John Ford to Clint Eastwood* (1969; London: BFI, 2008). It should be noted that there is of course considerable analysis of genre similarities between science fiction and the Western.

53. "Hero for a Day," *Anyone Can Be a Hero!*

54. "Remote Control," *Go, Go, LazyTown*.

55. "Sportacus Saves the Toys," *Snow Monster and Other Stories*, DVD (2008; UK: BBC Worldwide, 2008).

56. "Welcome to LazyTown," *Welcome to LazyTown*.

57. "LazyTown's Greatest Hits," *Go, Go, LazyTown!*

58. "Haunted Castle," *Once Upon a Time in LazyTown*.

59. Matt Briggs, "BBC Children's Television, Parentcraft and Pedagogy: Towards the 'Ethicalization of Existence,'" *Media, Culture & Society* 31, no.1 (January 2009): 23–39.

60. "Welcome to LazyTown," *Welcome to LazyTown*.

61. Libby Brooks, *The Story of Childhood: Growing Up in Modern Britain* (London: Bloomsbury, 2006), 30.

62. Bruno Bettelheim, *The Uses of Enchantment: The Meaning and Importance of Fairy Tales* (London: Penguin, 1991).

63. Gerard Jones, *Killing Monsters: Why Children Need Fantasy, Super Heroes, and Make-Believe Violence* (New York: Basic Books, 2002), 188–189.

64. Magnus Scheving, quoted in Phillips, "Face to Face With Magnus Scheving."

65. Postman, *The Disappearance of Childhood*, 63.

REFERENCES

Andrews, Amanda. "Fit for Purpose — Iceland's Superhero," *The Telegraph,* January 9, 2009, http://www.telegraph.co.uk/finance/newsbysector/mediatechnologyandtelecoms/media/4209769/LazyTown-superhero-Magnus-Scheving-on-a-health-mission.html.
Anyone Can Be a Hero! DVD 2006; UK: BBC Worldwide, 2006.
Avid Magazine, November 2006, http://emea.promax.tv/emea/nov06_news_1.html.
Bates, Theunis. "Kids' Show Makes Spinach Cool," *Time Magazine Online,* 14 May 2008, http://www.time.com/time/arts/article/0,8599,1779487,00.html.
Berlant, Lauren. *The Queen of America Goes to Washington City: Essays on Sex and Citizenship.* Durham, NC: Duke University Press, 1997.
Bettelheim, Bruno. *The Uses of Enchantment: The Meaning and Importance of Fairy Tales.* 1975. Reprint, London: Penguin, 1991.
Brooks, Libby. *The Story of Childhood: Growing Up in Modern Britain.* London: Bloomsbury, 2006.
Buckingham, David. "On the Impossibility of Children's Television: The Case of Timmy Mallett." In *In Front of the Children: Screen Entertainment and Young Audiences,* edited by Cary Bazalgette and David Buckingham, 47–61. London: BFI, 1995.
Caldwell, John Thornton. *Production Culture: Industrial Reflexivity and Critical Practice in Film and Television.* Durham, NC: Duke University Press, 2008.
Edelman, Lee. *No Future: Queer Theory and the Death Drive.* Durham, NC: Duke University Press, 2004.
Go, Go, LazyTown, DVD 2007; UK: BBC Worldwide, 2007.
Gordon, Bryony. "Could We Move into LazyTown?" *The Telegraph* 28 August 2006, http://www.telegraph.co.uk/health/3342731/Could-we-move-into-LazyTown.html.
Jones, Gerard. *Killing Monsters: Why Children Need Fantasy, Super Heroes, and Make-Believe Violence.* New York: Basic Books, 2002.
Kincaid, James R. *Erotic Innocence: The Culture of Child Molesting.* Durham, NC: Duke University Press, 1998.
Kincaid, James R. "Producing Erotic Children." In *The Children's Culture Reader,* edited by Henry Jenkins, 241–253. New York: New York University Press, 1998.
Kitses, Jim. *Horizons West: Directing the Western from John Ford to Clint Eastwood.* 1968. Reprint, London: BFI, 2008.
LazyTown Extra, Television Series 2008; CBeebies Channel, 2008.
Mendlesohn, Farah. *The Inter-Galactic Playground: A Critical Study of Children's and Teens' Science Fiction.* Jefferson, NC: McFarland, 2009.
"Move the World," *LazyTown* Branding Presentation, 2009, http://chinese.made-in-iceland.com.cn/download/Brand_Guide.pdf.
No One's Lazy in LazyTown, DVD 2008; UK: BBC Worldwide, 2008
Once Upon a Time in LazyTown, DVD 2006; UK: BBC Worldwide, 2006.
Palmer, Patricia. *The Lively Audience.* Sydney: Allen & Unwin, 1986.
Phillips, Sam "Face to Face with Magnus Scheving," *Global License,* 1 December 2004, http://www.licensemag.com/licensemag/article/articleDetail.jsp?id=161191&sk=&date=&pageID=2.
Postman, Neil. *The Disappearance of Childhood.* New York: Delacorte Press, 1982.
Snow Monster and Other Stories, DVD 2008; UK: BBC Worldwide, 2008.
Steemers, Jeanette. *Creating Preschool Television: A Story of Commerce, Creativity and Curriculum.* London: Palgrave, 2010.
Walkerdine, Valerie. "Popular Culture and the Eroticization of Little Girls." In *The Children's Culture Reader,* edited by Henry Jenkins, 254–264. New York: New York University Press, 1998.
Welcome to LazyTown. DVD 2006; UK: BBC Worldwide, 2006.
Winn, Marie. *The Plug-in Drug: Television, Computers and Family Life.* 25th Anniversary Edition. New York and London: Penguin, 2002.

• *Thirteen* •

Flash Gordon: Remembering a Childhood Hero (Past, Present, Future)

Patrick D. Enright

Imagine a 1930s rocket ship, shaped like an Electrolux vacuum cleaner with fins, leaving a trail of smoke as it crosses the star field of space. A voiceover proclaims the thrilling report:

> A news flash from Williams Observatory verifies a rumor broadcast earlier today that radio contact has been made with Flash Gordon, Dale Arden, and Dr. Alexius Zarkov aboard their rocket ship returning from the planet Mongo. By means of the observatory's hundred inch telescope they have sighted the rocket ship several thousand miles distant, and moving toward the Earth at the incredible speed of at least twelve hundred miles an hour.

This quote from early in Chapter One of *Flash Gordon's Trip to Mars*[1] probably provokes a gentle smile, or perhaps even a guffaw, but in the 1950s, to a young boy of four or five, 1200 miles per hour did sound like an incredible speed, and in 1938 when the serial premiered, no doubt it was just as incredible. Today, in 2011, the *Flash Gordon* serials, 70 years old and more, may strike many people as naïve and old-fashioned, but they had worth in their day, and they have worth even now — indeed, the first serial in the series, *Flash Gordon*,[2] was named a cultural treasure by the National Film Registry in 1996.[3]

Movie serials, or chapter plays, as they were called, have a long history stretching from 1912 to 1956.[4] In the early years, of course, the serials were silent, the first film with recorded dialogue coming out in 1928.[5] The silent serials were primarily aimed at adult audiences, but by the late twenties, adult audiences were losing interest, chiefly because of the attraction of radio.[6] The downward trend of serials changed, however, in 1930, thanks to a producer/director named Henry MacRae:

> MacRae, almost singlehandedly ... rescued the serial from oblivion and popularized the format with a new (although now largely juvenile) audience.... MacRae had breathed fresh commercial life into the chapter plays, and would increase their popularity even more when he produced the hugely successful *Flash Gordon* for Universal in 1936.[7]

In 1934 Alex Raymond had created the comic strip *Flash Gordon* in direct competition with the already-popular *Buck Rogers*.[8] It was such a success that in the next year Universal paid $10,000 for the rights to the strip.[9] Filming and release took place in 1936.[10]

Flash Gordon was the most expensively-produced serial in its day. Some scholars estimate the cost of its thirteen 20-minute chapters at $350,000, "an amount exceeding that allotted most top-of-the-line features at the time,"[11] but Buster Crabbe, who starred as the eponymous hero, believed the figures to be even higher:

> [T]he first *Flash*, which had been the most expensive serial ever made, [cost] almost $500,000. In those days that was a hell of a lot of money. Double-A features were costing only a little more, about three-quarters of a million.[12]

This large budget notwithstanding, cost-saving measures were necessary, especially since Universal did not give its serial division access to resources available to regular films.[13] Consequently sets and/or soundtracks were borrowed from other Universal films, such as *The Bride of Frankenstein*, *The Black Cat*, and even Leni Riefenstahl's *White Hell of Pitz Palu*.[14] Special effects varied from the astonishingly good to the laughably bad — in one scene, depicting Ming's rocket fleet traveling to King Vultan's sky city, at least one of the rockets can be seen slowly spinning on its wire.

In spite of any drawbacks, however, the serial was a great accomplishment: "...*Flash Gordon* was so successful that it played evening performances at first-run theaters, one of only a handful of sound serials to do so ... [it] proved to be one of Universal's most profitable 1936 releases."[15] It was followed in 1938 by *Flash Gordon's Trip to Mars*, at the lower cost of $182,000, and in 1940 by *Flash Gordon Conquers the Universe*,[16] at a cost of $177,000.[17]

That the *Flash Gordon* serials were popular and made a lasting impression can be seen in the way they have become a byword for anything that is futuristic or out-of-this-world, and especially the way they have influenced other people's work. For instance, a review of a performance of Wagner's *Ring des Nibelungen* at the New York Metropolitan Opera claims that "photos of early productions look as zany as Flash Gordon movies."[18] A 2009 collection of drawings based on the Mars Rover's photographs uses chapter titles drawn from *Flash Gordon's Trip to Mars*.[19] A 1984 short story in the *Kenyon Review*, "Flash Gordon," features an aging professor named Freeman Post Gordon who is called (behind his back) Flash Gordon by his housekeeper, who "had confused the stories he told her children ... with the Saturday morning television shows the children watched."[20] And quite significantly, George Lucas originally wanted to shoot a remake of the *Flash Gordon* serials but, refused permission by Universal, wrote his own story which eventually became *Star Wars*. Not surprisingly, Lucas's *epos* was influenced by his memories of those weekend television serials: "Light bridges, cloud cities, space swords, blasters, video screens, medieval costumes and aerial battles were all lifted from the crude serials of the thirties."[21]

What made these serials so good that 70 or more years later they are remembered and even celebrated? Roy Kinnard, a *Flash Gordon* specialist, explains, "Compared to other serials, *Flash Gordon* is remarkable because it combines plot and characterization into a solid whole. Much of the serial's enduring charm is due to the chemistry of the leading actors."[22] John C. Tibbetts agrees, commenting on Buster Crabbe, who starred as Flash in all three serials:

> All Buster did was to move well and infuse his roles with spirit and conviction. It was as simple as that. He really did look like a comic strip character come to life. Tights or leotards may have sagged on other actors, and the armor may have been too tight and the helmets too heavy. But on Buster they looked just fine. He made the costumes believable. He was one of those rare people who can wear a costume rather than be worn by it.
>
> Had he not believed in what he was doing, we viewers would not have believed, either. But he did believe, and he kept on believing. Looking back after the almost 20 years since we spoke together on that spring evening in Kansas City, I have no doubt of that. As long as he was moving, he had a conviction about him that was undeniable.[23]

Jean Rogers (Dale Arden) and Priscilla Lawson (Princess Aura) were "beautiful young actresses"; Frank Shannon's Dr. Zarkov, the archetypal scientist, was always cobbling together something at the last moment to turn the tables on Earth's foes; and in Ming the Merciless actor Charles Middleton "found the role he was born to play."[24]

When movie serials started to go out of fashion shortly after World War II, television was there, ready to pick up where the big screen left off, regularly showing the *Flash* serials. I grew up during the 50s, and I remember spending Sunday mornings glued to the little screen, watching a full hour of *Flash Gordon* chapters (three in an hour), "brought to you by Burt Weiman, Chicago's Ford man, 3535 Ashland Avenue."[25] World War II was close enough in the past (this would have been from approximately 1955, when I was four, to 1961) that at least one of my playmates had a father who was in the war and had a luger to prove it, so we did play Army once in a while (when he could persuade us to do so), but our favorite game was always Flash Gordon.

Of course the most immediate appeal the serials had was that they were filled with adventure. There were fights of all kinds — swords, ray guns, strange beasts like the orangopoid or the octosac; those marvelous, spark-dropping rocket ships, supplemented by the twisting gyroships of the Lion Men and the soaring stratosleds of the Martians; terrifying dangers, such as dropping into a bottomless pit, being electrocuted in the static room, explosions and crashes, and (what frightened me most) the disintegration room. And looming over all these thrilling threats was the imposing figure of Ming the Merciless, Emperor of the Universe, slowly closing his fist while he cackled "Nothing can save Flash Gordon now!"[26]

Adding to the thrills was each chapter's ending in a cliffhanger. The early, silent serial chapters were complete in themselves without cliffhanger endings,[27] but that great device for bringing customers back week after week soon developed. Many of them were what I considered "cheats": this week's installment showed a detail left out of the previous week's ending. Dozens of serials employed the device of the hero locked in a car, a stage coach, or a railway car going over a cliff to certain destruction, only to show in the next chapter's reprise that the hero got a door open at the last moment and jumped out. The *Flash Gordon* serials rarely employed this sort of rewriting, choosing to show something that happens *after* the previous week's cliffhanger. In Chapter One of *Flash Gordon*, for instance, Flash and Princess Aura are precipitated into a bottomless pit; in Chapter Two, while they are still falling, Emperor Ming orders a safety net deployed. And in Chapter 10 of *Flash Gordon Conquers the Universe*, Flash and Ming's most trusted servant, Captain Torch, are fighting on top of a tower during a gas attack, eventually carried by their struggle over the parapet, presumably to a sure doom. In Chapter 11, we find that they have landed, not on hard rocks, but safely in the moat. The *Flash Gordon* serials, then, played fair with their young viewers and pulled no rabbits out of hats.

An important factor in these serials' appeal to a young audience was the values they promoted. Take, for a start, the primary hero, Flash. In the 1980 *Flash Gordon* he is a football player (and apparently not a very good one) who bumbles his way through the kingdoms of Mongo trying to save the Earth and looking mighty bewildered as he does so. In the 1936 serial, Flash is a polo player (in the Alex Raymond strip, he is also a Yale graduate) and clearly both a gentleman and a man of intelligence. When a battle with ape men on Mongo in Chapter One leaves his shirt in tatters, one can see he is an athlete as well. (Crabbe was an Olympic swimming champion.) He certainly looks the hero-type.

Moreover, he exhibits true concern for helping other people, from helping the terrified Dale to parachute from their faltering airplane to trying to save the planet. In fact, all three of the Earth people, Flash, Dale, and Zarkov, are intensely committed to rescuing our world from Ming. Take, for instance, this scene from Chapter One of *Flash Gordon*. Flash and Dale have landed, by chance, on Zarkov's property after bailing out of the plane. Dale notices Zarkov's rocket ship, Zarkov treats them first as intruders, but after learning that Flash, though Professor Gordon's son, is not trying to stop him, ends up asking for Flash's help:

> ZARKOV: I need a man to help me. Will you go? It's the only chance to save the Earth.
> FLASH: It's a chance all right. I'll bet on a long shot with you! When do we start?
> ZARKOV: At once! There's no time to lose.
> FLASH: What about Miss Dale? We've got to get her to a place of safety.
> ZARKOV: There's no place of safety on the Earth.
> FLASH: All right, then, we'll take her with us.
> ZARKOV: No.
> DALE: Oh, please take me with you!
> ZARKOV: [shakes his head no]
> FLASH: All bets are off.
> ZARKOV: In that case ... we take her.

Notice how quickly Flash has made a friend of Dale, one of his endearing characteristics. In this instance, Flash and Zarkov are the ones trying to save the Earth, while Dale is coming along for safety.[28]

By the second serial, *Flash Gordon's Trip to Mars*, Dale has become a seasoned space traveler and has survived numerous dangers on the planet Mongo. She is now as enthusiastic a savior of Earth as her two friends, as we see in this scene in which Zarkov announces he is going back to Mongo, while Flash initially tries to dissuade him, asking what just one man can hope to accomplish:

> ZARKOV: You're not asking me to stand by without doing all one man can to prevent the destruction of the Earth, are you? Of course not, Flash. I'm leaving as soon as the rocket ship can be made ready.
> FLASH: Well, in that case, of course, the two of us will make the trip together.
> DALE: You mean the three of us! [fade][29]

The three are excellent examples of heroes taking responsibility for the welfare of others — in this case, the entire population of the world.

The third serial, *Flash Gordon Conquers the Universe*, has a similar scene. Here Flash has driven off the Ming ship which was dumping an "electrified dust" which causes the dreaded plague, the Purple Death:

> ZARKOV: ...Ming will send other ships to scatter that fiendish dust. The Earth has no defense against such an attack.

FLASH: Yes, I know. Our only chance is to get to Mongo, find Prince Barin, and solicit his aid. Zarkov, radio the Earth. Report what's happened; tell them what we're going to do.
ZARKOV: Yes, it's our only chance to save them.[30]

This time there isn't even a question of whether such a small number can be effective; without hesitation, they are off to Mongo.

Another virtue children could have learned from the series is the value of friendship. In *Flash*, for instance, we see Flash making instant friends with Thun, the Lion Man, after the two have a swordfight and Flash spares Thun's life (Chapter Two). In the following chapter, Thun returns the favor by saving Flash from the claws of the Crab Monster. In Chapter Five, Prince Barin secretly enters Ming's laboratory and, explaining how he was dethroned by Ming, who killed his father, offers his friendship to the Earth people. He is never absent from the rest of the serial, constantly helping (and being helped by) his friends. In the final chapter, Flash and the others are saved by the timely arrival of Thun and his Lion Men.

Friendship is a theme in the second serial, too, most conspicuously in the presence of Prince Barin, who has flown from Mongo to Mars in order to try to save the Earth from Ming. He shows up in Chapter Seven and is present from then on. Other friendships are formed on Mars when Flash agrees to help the Clay People to regain their normal bodies and, among most Martians, when he unmasks Ming — murderer of their former queen — whom the Martians are unknowingly about to elect as their new ruler.

Barin is again Flash's most formidable ally in the final serial, *Flash Gordon Conquers the Universe*, supplemented by Roka and Ronal, two of Barin's followers. Other friendships are made with Karm and Druk, both scientist-slaves in Ming's laboratory who are secretly working against him. Thus it is apparent that heroism, heroic responsibility, self-sacrifice, and friendship are all potent desirable qualities that young audiences would have been able to perceive and appreciate.

Leonard J. Kohl has pointed out the ideological importance for adults and child audiences alike.[31] The 1930s, of course, were the time of the Depression, a time when the film companies were producing movies filled with music and dance in an attempt to distract Americans from the hardship and hopelessness of everyday life. The *Flash Gordon* serials, too, would have had the same sort of entertainment value, whisking audiences from their poverty-stricken lives to the planets Mongo or Mars. *Flash Gordon*, however, offered more, an ideology to counteract the depression of the Depression:

> The optimism of Flash, Zarkov, Dale, Prince Barin, and the other heroic characters encouraged youngsters to feel positive about themselves and the future of this country.... The *Flash Gordon* serials ... taught us to never give up on the

future, no matter how bleak it seems.... For kids and imaginative adults it was just the kind of medicine to help swallow the bitter reality of a wrecked economy and impending war, make the best of it, and survive for another, better day.[32]

Surprisingly, this ideology was aimed at girls as well as boys, by means of the continuing heroine Dale Arden. In the 1930s the typical role of a woman was as wife and mother. Those women who worked usually did so in traditional feminine roles: "According to the 1930 census almost eleven million women, or 24.3 percent of all women in the country, were gainfully employed. Three out of every ten of these working women were in domestic or personal service. Of professional women three-quarters were schoolteachers or nurses."[33]

Dale Arden's role in the first serial is fully in accordance with the view of the traditionally dependent, subservient woman, with Dale constantly pursued as a love-object by the various monarchs of Mongo and Flash always having to rescue her. In *Flash Gordon's Trip to Mars*, however, Dale is no longer the constant victim but an equal sharer in the adventure, at one point stealing a Martian stratosled to save Flash and the others with some well-placed bombs. This was indeed a Dale of a different color, quite the opposite of the wilting heroine of the first series. By the final serial, she has become "a trained chemist" who climbs mountains to identify the "polarite" needed to defeat Ming's Purple Death dust and who operates the mechanism that protects Flash as puts out the fire of Ming's flaming projectiles. Dale showed girls of the 30s (and the 50s) that women could be both feminine and heroic.

Another important idea for young people in these serials comes from their depiction of science. Science and the idea of progress were powerful forces at this time, the height of the Art Deco movement, but already in film there were darker visions of the applications of science. *Frankenstein*, for instance, came out in 1931, followed by *The Bride of Frankenstein* in 1935, both featuring the "mad scientist" Dr. Frankenstein trying to create life. Numbers of serials feature the mad (or criminal) scientist, often using a robot or some other device to cause mayhem. *Flash Gordon* promoted a more balanced view of science by offsetting the evil Ming with the beneficent Dr. Zarkov. Yes, Ming was the master of murderous science. The major plots of all three serials depend on his super-science: crashing the planet Mongo (whose movement is under Ming's control) into the Earth, destroying Earth's atmosphere by removing "nitron," or killing off large numbers of people with the Purple Death dust. There are other horrible inventions as well; the explosive annihilatons and the fiery projectiles of the third serial leap to mind.

But standing against Ming there is Dr. Zarkov, whose rocket ship brings the three Earth people to Mongo in the first serial. No matter what the need,

Zarkov is always able to come up with a saving invention in the nick of time. One might consider, in *Flash Gordon*, the ray he discovers which prevents the destruction of King Vultan's sky city and which results in Flash being proclaimed a free man (at least for the present). Also there is the invisibility machine which Zarkov uses to rescue Flash from a firing squad. In the *Mars* serial, there is the paralyzing ray he discovers and which Flash uses to good effect, while in *Conquers the Universe* his "counter-freeze spray" protects his friends from the bitter cold of Frigia and his "contra-thermal device" puts out the otherwise unstoppable fires of Ming's flaming projectiles. In other words, at a time when science was beginning to be looked upon as a potential threat, Dr. Zarkov's presence promotes in the serials' young audience a more balanced view of science as able to do either great ill or great good, depending on its user.

A final point on the fitness of the *Flash Gordon* serials for youthful audiences (and for adults as well) is its reflection of twentieth-century politics. Probably this reflection was more obvious in the years of the serials' release, and surely it was more visible to older than younger viewers — I was in late grade school or early high school before I started noticing these details — but its nature was such that one's pleasure was not affected by not picking up on cultural clues. Nonetheless, perception of historical reflections added to the enjoyment and the seriousness of the serials for those who could see.

In all three serials, the weight of this historical reflection is carried by the villain, Ming the Merciless. There was a Ming dynasty in China (1368–1644), and the planet Mongo's name recalled Mongolia and Mongol hordes. Most importantly, Emperor Ming the Merciless himself, both in appearance and voice, was clearly inspired by Sax Rohmer's Chinese villain (also a superscientist), Fu Manchu. Rohmer's famous character, "the yellow peril incarnate in one man,"[34] is described as having a "smooth, hairless countenance,"[35] but Ming, with his drooping Fu Manchu mustache, both in the comic strip and the serial, clearly is modeled after the Chinese villain's depiction in movies and on book covers. And it has been suggested that Alex Raymond's yellow-skinned Ming "[played] into the "yellow peril' slant of Hearst's newspapers."[36]

But most likely in American minds he symbolized the threat of the Japanese, who already had taken over Korea in 1905 and in the 1930s were becoming more and more involved in China. Japan already outnumbered China in the numbers of men in uniform, airplanes, and battleships. Japan was the more obvious threat, and in 1937, between *Flash Gordon* and *Trip to Mars*, it invaded China.[37] It seems possible, perhaps even likely, that this world event is mirrored in Ming's one-man invasion of Mars in 1938. If such an "invasion" seems trivial, note that Ming is behind the use of the nitron lamp against the Earth, that he has apparently infected Queen Azura with his favorite plan of conquest of the universe, that Queen Azura consults him frequently, and that he is responsible for her death, which is followed by his attempt to take over the Martian throne.[38]

In 1939 harsh laws against the Jews had been passed in Germany, several concentration camps had been established, and various ghettoes in Poland were being set up, following Germany's invasion of Poland.[39] It is no wonder, then, that in the final serial Emperor Ming has become Dictator Ming, complete with white uniform and gaudy medals. In Chapter One, Jenda, one of his scientists, is experimenting upon live prisoners in an attempt to refine the Purple Death dust so it will kill only people of high intelligence (who might revolt against Ming) but leave unharmed people of low intelligence. And one of Ming's victims even refers to the dictator's "filthy concentration camps." So the historical subtext has shifted from east to west, glancing at Hitler's death camps, lethal medical experimentation, and ambition for world dominance. In the serial's final chapter, it is not hard to imagine Hitler echoing Ming's mad statement, "The universe? I am the universe." As pointed out above, small children would not have seen in any of these historical subtexts any more than Ming just being Ming, but those who were old enough to have studied a bit of world history would have been able to see the similarities and perhaps would have taken the lesson, seen both in the *Flash Gordon* serials and history, that heroic defiance can overcome evil aggression.

So there they are: serials written in the 1930s for a primarily juvenile audience but possessing an artistry and sophistication that have kept them popular for more than 70 years. Projecting hope and personal responsibility for both girls and boys, women and men, they remain an inspiration, and will continue to inspire, against historical shocks. As said before, these serials were shown on television during the 1950s and 1960s. In the 50s they came up against science-fiction shows made for television, such as the 1954 *Flash Gordon* starring Steve Holland, *Tom Corbett—Space Cadet* (1950–55), *Space Patrol* (1950–54), *Commando Cody* (1955), *Rocky Jones, Space Ranger* (1953), and others[40] (see "1950s"). No contest. Most of the television were broadcast live, with live special effects, and could not come close in execution to the then 20-year-old serials.

In 1979 a cartoon version of *Flash Gordon* began, lasting two seasons. In 1980 came the feature film *Flash Gordon*, famous almost entirely for its soundtrack by Queen. In 2007, the SciFi Channel began a Flash Gordon series, though it received poor reviews and was quickly canceled.[41] And now there is news of a new Flash Gordon feature film in the works, to be released in 2012. The little bit of information available makes it sound ominously like a remake of the 1980 film, since it identifies Flash as an "American football player."[42] These different versions show how durable the story with its virtuous hero has become since its first appearance in Alex Raymond's comic strip in 1934, but for my money and for our future, I'll take the serials.

NOTES

1. *Flash Gordon's Trip to Mars*, DVD, directed by Ford Beebe and Robert F. Hill (1938; Los Angeles: Image Entertainment, 2000).
2. *Flash Gordon*, DVD, directed by Frederick Stephani and Ray Taylor (1936; Los Angeles: Image Entertainment, 2000).
3. Roy Kinnard, Tony Crnkovich, and R.J. Vitone, *The Flash Gordon Serials, 1936–1940* (Jefferson, NC: McFarland, 2008), 23.
4. Ibid., 5–21.
5. "20's," *Film Sound History*, http://frank.mtsu.edu/~smpte /twenties.html.
6. Roy Kinnard, *Science Fiction Serials* (Jefferson, NC: McFarland, 1998), 2–3.
7. Ibid., 4.
8. Kinnard, Crnkovich, and Vitone, *Flash Gordon Serials*, 1.
9. Ibid., 6.
10. Ibid., 11.
11. Ibid., 6.
12. John C. Tibbetts, "Man in Motion: An Interview with Buster Crabbe," *Films in Review* 47, nos. 7 & 8 (Jul/Aug 96).
13. Kinnard, Crnkovich, and Vitone, *Flash Gordon Serials*, 10.
14. LoBue, "Music and Bites." I had been trying to identify and acquire music to the *Flash Gordon* serials for over 30 years when I stumbled across Tony LoBue's *Flash Gordon* site. It is the most useful site for such information I have ever found, identifying the films and their composers used in the *Flash Gordon* serials and providing sound bites. Alas, most of this music, except for the soundtrack to *Bride of Frankenstein*, is unavailable because Universal refuses to grant the rights to publish or rerecord it.
15. Kinnard, Crnkovich, and Vitone, *Flash Gordon Serials*, 15–16.
16. *Flash Gordon Conquers the Universe*, DVD, directed by Ford Beebe and Ray Taylor (1940; Los Angeles: Image Entertainment, 2000).
17. Ibid., 16–19.
18. "Twilight Time," *Opera News Online*.
19. David Clarkson, "On Himmelskibet Hill, Mars," *Bomb* 107 (Spring 2009):66–70.
20. Lois Shapley Bassen, "Flash Gordon," *Kenyon Review* 6, no. 1 (Winter 1984): 29.
21. John L. Flynn, "The Origins of Star Wars: Evolution of a Space Saga," *Starkiller: The Jedi Bensu Script Site*, http://www.starwarz.com/starkiller/writings/origins.htm.
22. Kinnard, *Science Fiction Serials*, 38.
23. Tibbetts, "Man in Motion."
24. Kinnard, *Science Fiction Serials*, 39.
25. "Burt Weiman Ford (closed)," *Wikimapia*, http://wikimapia.org/733261/Burt-Weiman-Ford-closed.
26. Although a poor copy of a better original at best, the 1980 *Flash Gordon* features Max von Sydow as Ming the Merciless in a performance that rivals that of Charles Middleton in the serials.
27. Kinnard, *Science Fiction Serials*, 3.
28. *Flash Gordon*, DVD.
29. *Flash Gordon's Trip*, DVD.
30. *Flash Gordon Conquers*, DVD.
31. Leonard J. Kohl, "Flash Gordon Conquers the Great Depression and World War Too! The Flash Gordon Serial Trilogy," in *Science Fiction America*, edited by David J. Hogan (Jefferson, NC: McFarland, 2006), 55.
32. Ibid.
33. *Working Women in the 1930s*, http://www.enotes.com/1930-lifestyles-social-trends-american-decades/working-women.
34. Sax Rohmer, *The Mystery of Dr. Fu-Manchu*, (London: Cassell, 1913), in *The Fu-Manchu Omnibus*, volume 1 (London: Allison and Busby, 1995), 15. Page references are to the 1995 edition.
35. Ibid., 42.
36. Kinnard, Crnkovich, and Vitone, *Flash Gordon Serials*, 2.

37. "From War to War: 1931–1939," *Euronet,* http://www.euronet.nl/users/wilfried/ww2/tot-1939.htm.
38. There may have been a nod towards increasing distrust of Germany, since Zarkov's original first name, the Germanic *Hans,* is changed to *Alexius* in the first chapter.
39. "The Holocaust Timeline, 1933–1940," *About.com,* http://history1900s.about.com/library/holocaust/bltimeline3.htm.
40. "1950s: Science Fiction TV 1950–1959," *SF Television,* http://www.magicdragon.com/UltimateSF/tv-chron.html#TV-1950s.
41. "Flash Gordon (2007)," *Internet Movie Database,* http://www.imdb.com/title/tt0959086/.
42. "Flash Gordon (2012)," *Internet Movie Database,* http://www.imdb.com/title/tt0421201/.

REFERENCES

Bassen, Lois Shapley. "Flash Gordon." *Kenyon Review* 6, no. 1 (Winter 1984): 29.
"Burt Weiman Ford (closed)." *Wikimapia.* http://wikimapia.org/733261/Burt-Weiman-Ford-closed.
Clarkson, David. "On Himmelskibet Hill, Mars." *Bomb* 107 (Spring 2009): 66–70.
Flash Gordon. DVD. Directed by Frederick Stephani and Ray Taylor. 1936. Image Entertainment, 2000.
Flash Gordon Conquers the Universe. DVD. Directed by Ford Beebe and Ray Taylor. 1940. Image Entertainment, 2000.
"Flash Gordon (1936)." *Internet Movie Database.* http://www.imdb.com/title/tt0027623/.
"Flash Gordon (1936), Flash Gordon's Trip to Mars (1938), Buck Rogers (1939) and Flash Gordon Conquers the Universe (1940)." *The Beloved Serials.* http://www.slick-net.com/space/serial/serials2/index.phtml.
"Flash Gordon (1980)." *Internet Movie Database.* http://www.imdb.com/title/tt0080745/.
"Flash Gordon (2007)." *Internet Movie Database.* http://www.imdb.com/title/tt0959086/.
"Flash Gordon (2012)." *Internet Movie Database.* http://www.imdb.com/title/tt0421201/.
Flash Gordon's Trip to Mars. DVD. Directed by Ford Beebe and Robert F. Hill. 1938. Image Entertainment, 2000.
Flynn, John L. "The Origins of Star Wars: Evolution of a Space Saga." *Starkiller: The Jedi Bensu Script Site.* http://www.starwarz.com/starkiller/writings/origins.htm.
From War to War: 1931–1939. Euronet. http://www.euronet.nl/users/wilfried/ww2/tot-1939.htm.
The Holocaust Timeline, 1933–1940. About.com. http://history1900s.about.com/library/holocaust/bltimeline3.htm.
Kinnard, Roy. *Science Fiction Serials.* Jefferson, NC: McFarland, 1998.
Kinnard, Roy, Tony Crnkovich, and R.J. Vitone. *The Flash Gordon Serials, 1936–1940.* Jefferson, NC: McFarland, 2008.
Kohl, Leonard J. "Flash Gordon Conquers the Great Depression and World War Too! The *Flash Gordon* Serial Trilogy." In *Science Fiction America,* edited by David J. Hogan. Jefferson, NC: McFarland, 2006.
LoBue, Tony. "Music and Bites." *Flash Gordon.* http://flashgordon.ws/The_Music.htm.
"1950s: Science Fiction TV 1950–1959." *SF Television.* http://www.magicdragon.com/UltimateSF/tv-chron.html#TV-1950s.
Rohmer, Sax. *The Mystery of Dr. Fu-Manchu.* London: Cassell, 1913. In *The Fu-Manchu Omnibus.* Vol. 1. London: Allison and Busby, 1995.
Tibbetts, John C. "Man in Motion: An Interview with Buster Crabbe." *Films in Review* 47, nos. 7 & 8 (Jul/Aug 96).
"20's." *Film Sound History.* http://frank.mtsu.edu/~smpte /twenties.html.
"Twilight Time." *Opera News Online.*
Working Women in the 1930s. http://www.enotes.com/1930-lifestyles-social-trends-american-decades/working-women.

• *Fourteen* •

Toys, a T-Rex, and Trouble: Cautionary Tales of Time Travel in Children's Film

KRISTINE LARSEN

In a 1956 letter, author J.R.R. Tolkien warned against what he found to be "the most widespread assumption of our time: that if a thing can be done, it must be done."[1] More recent (and vociferous) echoes of this caution are found in *Jurassic Park* and countless other science-fiction films, especially in regards to meddling with time and history. While the idea of traveling back in history appeared in such works as Mark Twain's *A Connecticut Yankee in King Arthur's Court* (1889), the first hard science-fiction work to discuss the possibility of using technology to travel forward or backward in time is generally considered to be H.G. Wells's *The Time Machine* (1895). Since the time of the Industrial Revolution, numerous science-fiction writers and film directors have continued to explore the scientific and ethical issues surrounding the possibility of altering the past and future. Interestingly, in the second decade of the twenty-first century, science fact may have finally caught up with science fiction.

Due to the work of theoretical physicist Ronald Mallett, today's youth may witness the first steps toward time travel. However, as with all scientific discoveries and technological advances, ethical and philosophical concerns remain long after the experiments have been completed. Is it truly possible to travel without bounds (and consequences) into the past and future? If you could change one thing, what would it be? Could you bring back artifacts (or even people) from your journeys? Then there are the famous paradoxes associated with time travel (such as those demonstrated in *Back to the Future*). Can you change the past, or is the past (and perhaps the future as well) predetermined? Equally importantly, could time travel be exploited for nefarious purposes, either by the scientists themselves, or politicians and profiteers? Adult works such as *A Sound of Thunder* or H.G. Wells's own *The Time Machine* have long explored the promise and paradoxes of time travel. These same basic themes have also been tackled in films targeting a younger audience, such as *We're Back! A Dinosaur's Story* (1993), *Meet the Robinsons* (2007), and *The Last Mimzy* (2007). However, such stories and films not only feed the reader/viewer's fascination with the possibility of time travel, but often utilize a time travel plotline to explore other important themes at the interface between science and society (as in the case of H.G. Wells's seminal work). These same children's films likewise explore several other weighty themes, such as the perceived gulf between scientists and the general public, the tension between science and religion, the role of women in science, and various stereotypes of science and scientists.

In his famous 1959 Rede lecture and essay "The Two Cultures," C.P. Snow warned that "the intellectual life of the whole western society is increasingly being split into two polar groups" from which the essay draws its name, the two cultures of the sciences and the humanities.[2] He explained that this

> polarization is sheer loss to us all. To us as people, and to our society. It is at the same time practical and intellectual and creative loss, and I repeat that it is false to imagine that those three considerations are clearly separable.[3]

Some of this polarization is based on mistrust and fear. A letter to the editor printed in the London *Evening Standard* clearly articulated the widespread misunderstanding of science and scientists by the non-scientific majority culture:

> When I was a child the mad scientist was a figure of derision and contempt, a fictional joke. How times have changed. The world is now full of mad scientists — mad doctors tampering with embryos, mad physicists and chemists working out more refined methods of termination.... What can be done about these loonies?[4]

Famed popularizer of science Carl Sagan understood well that the source of this deep-rooted stereotype is the destructive as well as controversial byproducts and secondary applications of science and technology such as nuclear weapons, CFCs, and global warming. As he noted, "There's a reason people are nervous about science and technology. And so the image of the mad scientist haunts our world — down to the white-coated loonies of Saturday morning children's TV."[5] But this stereotype goes further still, leading the non-scientist to picture average scientists as "moral cripples driven by a lust for power or endowed with a spectacular insensitivity to the feelings of others."[6] Coupled with the famous stereotype of the science geek — the fashion-challenged, socially inept and disaffected nerd — these deeply-ingrained depictions of scientists further the disconnect between the "Two Cultures" and exaggerate the sense of "otherness" projected by the average person upon science and its practitioners.

Another classic stereotype of the scientist is that he (after all, according to the common stereotype, nearly all scientists are men) is at best an agnostic, and at worst a raging atheist.[7] This stereotype has two possible origins; firstly, the unfortunate long-standing tension between organized religion and science in Western Culture (witnessed as early as the infamous case of Galileo in the 1600s) and secondly the Frankenstein archetype of the scientist. After all, one might argue, how can one "play God" if one is a fervent believer in God? It is therefore no surprise that a 2004 poll found that 55 percent of Americans believe that "we depend too much on science and not enough on faith."[8] In the case of women in science, the sum of these stereotypes can be especially negative, leaving young girls interested in science bereft of positive and attractive role models in much of the mainstream media. The result is that although girls and boys have nearly equal interest in science at the elementary grades, by middle school girls are leaving the pathway to careers in science in droves.[9] This essay will therefore explore how the three family films listed above tackle these serious issues of science and society while simultaneously exploring concerns raised by time travel (with varying degrees of fidelity to the basic science).

The basis for any serious scientific discussion of time travel is the work of Albert Einstein. In his 1905 Special Theory of Relativity, he demonstrated that the known three dimensions of space and one of time are actually interwoven into a four-dimensional fundamental fabric of the universe known as space-time. The theory is based on the postulate that the speed of light is the universal speed limit, and faster-than-light travel is unattainable for physical objects in our universe, as it would require an infinite amount of energy to accelerate a physical object to this speed (an inconvenience regularly ignored by science-fiction writers). If one were to somehow travel faster than light, one would, indeed, travel backwards in time. This idea was demonstrated in 1978's *Superman* when the Man of Steel traveled faster than light in order to travel back in time to save Lois Lane from certain death. Such past-directed time travel is unfortunately beyond the reach of us mere mortals.

In his 1915 General Theory of Relativity, Einstein extended his understanding of space-time to demonstrate that what we experience as the force of gravity is actually the warping of space-time by mass and energy. For example, the Earth orbits the Sun as it does because the Sun warps space-time in its vicinity in a specific way. If the presence of matter (and energy) can warp space-time, is it possible to warp it in such a way as to permit a material object to travel backwards in time? Not only is it possible to generate solutions of the Einstein field equations that allow for time travel, but a number of such solutions have been found.

However, with the possibility of time travel comes serious paradoxes. Take, for example, the so-called Grandfather paradox. A time traveler could theoretically travel back in time and either kill her grandfather or otherwise prevent her grandparents from marrying before her father or mother were conceived, meaning that she would never have been born. A version of this is depicted in *Back to the Future*, when Marty McFly briefly derails his parents' courtship, resulting in him and his siblings fading from a family picture. But if Marty prevented his parents from marrying, how, then, could he be there to prevent the marriage in the first place? In the end, of course, the timeline is restored, but the curious bending of the paradox is clearly dramatic license.

Although time travel is possible in theory, is it possible to actually construct a time machine that can be utilized by human explorers? Research on practical time travel surprisingly owes its genesis to science fiction. While writing his novel *Contact*, Carl Sagan sent the manuscript to a friend, physicist Kip Thorne, in 1995. Like other science-fiction writers, he was trying to get his heroine from earth to a distant location faster than the speed of light would allow. Thorne suggested a wormhole (a shortcut in space-time — a tunnel connecting two universes or two points in the same universe), even though he had doubts as to whether a real wormhole could exist as a traversable tunnel in space-time.[10] What Thorne and his graduate students later found was that under the right conditions, a wormhole might allow a traveler to return to her starting point before she left, and somehow change history.[11]

However, some calculations suggest that a wormhole would be destroyed in a flurry of radiation as soon as it was created, or at the very least render the wormhole useless for human travel.[12] Wormholes are not the only proposed scientific models for time machines. For example, Ronald Mallett has demonstrated that a circulating beam of electromagnetic radiation (such as a ring laser) will theoretically warp space-time in such a way as to allow for time travel.[13] It has been proposed that this model could be used (given the proper laser technology) to construct a workable time machine.[14]

But assuming that a time machine can and will be successfully built, and will not be destroyed by quantum fluctuations or any other unforeseen physical effects, what are we to make of the very real paradoxes time travel poses, such as the Grandfather paradox? Stephen Hawking[15] offered two possible resolutions to these paradoxes, which he called the "consistent histories" and "alternative histories" approaches. The first solution demands that the laws of physics are constrained such that paradoxes cannot arise. For example, if you try to go into the past and kill your grandfather before your parents are conceived, the gun will jam, or you will slip and fall and miss the shot. As Hawking[16] succinctly puts it, "So much for free will." You might intend to change the future, and believe that you actually have the free will to do so, but in the end you will always do exactly what you were destined to do, acting in such a manner as to keep events historically consistent. This is termed a causal loop. In such a "block universe" the past, present, and future have a simultaneous reality and are fixed.[17]

The ability to change history by time travel leads us to consider a different possibility, namely alternative histories and the existence of parallel universes. The alternative histories explanation of time travel is based on an alternative to the standard Copenhagen interpretation of quantum mechanics, called the Many Worlds Interpretation or MWI.[18] In this model, every time an experiment with several possible outcomes is conducted, the universe branches into parallel realities, one for each of the possible outcomes. For example, when you woke up this morning and decided on breakfast, the universe split into multiple realities, including one in which you ate cereal, another one in which you ate toast, and still another where you ate at your favorite fast-food establishment.

But as David Deutsch[19] explains, it is actually more complicated than this. In fact, he has demonstrated that in a modification of the MWI it is possible for the various parallel universes to interact, and it is the existence of this infinite multiplicity of parallel universes, each with its own unique timeline, that allows time travel into the past without relinquishing free will or causing paradoxes. A time traveler who succeeds in going back in time and killing her grandfather before her parent's conception is doing so in a universe in which she will never be born. In the universe in which she was born her grandparents lived to successfully reproduce. Free will is conserved, and no paradox results. However it can be shown that no time machine can be used to visit a time prior to when it was switched on. Therefore, until we succeed in building a time machine (and leave it running for some length of time), visitors from the future will only exist in the world of science fiction.

In science-fiction literature and film, these limitations to time travel are as often ignored as the finite speed of light. For example, in the case of *Back to the Future*, it was previously noted that Marty McFly appears to temporarily change the past in his own universe, rather than in a parallel universe. A more consistent film in terms of time travel between parallel realities is J.J. Abrams' *Star Trek* (2009), which allowed the director to violate the well-known television and movies series' canon (for example, destroying Spock's planet and killing his mother, both of whom are alive and well in the timeline of the main franchise universe). A recent example of a consistent use of a single universe was seen in *Harry Potter and the Prisoner of Azkaban*, when Hermione Granger and Harry Potter use the Time-Turner to travel to the past to save the Hippogriff Buckbeak from execution. As Silberstein describes in detail,[20] Buckbeak never actually died in the first place, because Hermione and Harry had previously saved him by time traveling. Therefore the past was never changed, but unfolded as it always had without paradox.

Although *Star Trek* and *Prisoner of Azkaban* demonstrate that it is possible to remain true to the science while simultaneously entertaining the audience, as one might expect, the paradoxes and prohibitions of time travel are often deemed unnecessarily complex for children's literature and film, so authors and directors frequently pick and choose which aspects of time travel to remain faithful to in their particular work. This is certainly true in the case of the three films selected for this essay. In addition, the motivations and modes of time travel in all three significantly differ. The animated film *We're Back! A Dinosaur's Story* (1993) was based on the 1987 Hudson Talbott children's book of the same name. A time-traveling inventor from the future named Captain Neweyes travels between the far past, our present, and our future in his whimsical flying ship, accompanied by his alien assistant Vorb. The future is portrayed as one of not only astounding technological achievement, but universal peace among all the known species of the universe. Neweyes uses his time travel technology in the name of philanthropy, to grant the wishes of children in past times. Using his "wish radio" he has discovered that the children of our present most desire to see real dinosaurs, so he travels more than 65 million years into the past in order to procure real dinosaurs to bring to our time. In an apparent nod to the issues of free will inherent in time travel paradoxes (even in the case where none originally exists), Neweyes feeds four dinosaurs some of his intelligence-increasing Brain Grain cereal, essentially genetically-engineering the dinosaurs in order to make them smart enough to be able to make a conscious decision as to whether or not to travel to the present. Led by Rex the Tyrannosaurus Rex, the dinosaurs agree to accompany Neweyes to the present, and as expected, mayhem initially ensues, involving two children, Louie and Cecilia.

Meet the Robinsons uses the medium of an engaging action-filled computer-animated film starring an eccentric family to illustrate the possible consequences of time travel, as well as the potential for science and technology to be exploited for personal gain. Based on William Joyce's *A Day with Wilbur Robinson*, the Disney Pictures film follows the journeys of orphan and precocious child-inventor Lewis between his past, present, and future, as he seeks to prevent his birth mother from giving him up while those around him seek to prevent the twisted Man in the Bowler Hat (MitBH) from changing history. Lewis is taken from the scene of an ego-crushing science fair by Wilbur Robinson, later revealed to be Lewis's future son. Wilbur has borrowed one of his inventor-father's two time-traveling ships (which look similar to the flying cars of *The Jetsons*) in order to chase the MitBH, his evil mechanical hat Doris, and the second (stolen) time machine to Lewis's present in order to prevent the dastardly duo from stealing Lewis's first invention, a memory-scanner which Lewis invented to try to remember his birth mother's face. In the course of their adventures, Lewis travels to Wilbur's present (Lewis's future) and meets his future family, a collection of eccentrics (many of whom personify the classic stereotype of the scientific nerd). The Robinsons are clearly unified in their love and support for Cornelius Robinson (future Lewis's name), a successful and confident inventor whose discoveries have created a Disney World–esque future, with clean skies, shiny, beautiful buildings, and a pollution-free bubble transportation system.

But this idyllic future is threatened by the meddling of MitBH, who introduces the stolen memory-scanner to the board of InventCo with the bold statement "I'm here to change the future."[21] Indeed, it is revealed that MitBH is actually the embittered future self of present-day Lewis's meek sidekick and unwitting lab assistant, fellow orphan Mike Yagoobian (nicknamed Goob). Goob's road to villainy begins with an important Little League baseball game, in which he falls asleep in the outfield (due to spending all night helping Lewis with his science fair project), misses a catch which loses the game for his team, and is afterwards beaten up by his teammates. The audience is later told that as a result Goob was never adopted, and instead remained at the orphanage even after it was closed. In an interesting application of a causal loop, MitBH travels back to this pivotal moment and urges his younger self to embrace the pain and resentment he feels, to let it "fester and boil inside you.... Let hate be your ally.... Heed my words, Goob, don't let it go."[22] In this way MitBH becomes the cause for his own becoming, by assuring Goob's transition from flunky to arch villain. The sanctity of the timeline is also demonstrated in a future scene, in which Lewis's identity as Cornelius Robinson's younger self is revealed to his family. Frannie, his wife, sagely warns him that he has to return to his own time, knowing that if he doesn't her own son will never be born.

But MitBH's motivation is clearly to change the future from the utopia Lewis's inventions have brought about, which is impossible unless we are dealing with alternate realities. Putting aside this inconsistency, we are faced with a *Back to the Future*–like version of time travel. When MitBH succeeds in getting InventCo to patent Lewis's memory-scanner as his own invention, the future is changed in important ways. Lewis never becomes a confident and creative inventor, Wilbur is never born, and the future becomes distinctly dystopian. Similar to McFly's fading, Wilbur is turned into vapor and disappears into the clouds, the rest of the Robinsons and their house disappear, and the world morphs into a filthy industrial complex. In an interesting parallel to the *Terminator* series of time travel films, Doris the mechanized bowler hat (one of Lewis's failed inventions in the main timeline) leads a revolution of the machines, who take over the world. Like the original Terminator machine, Doris has a demonic red eye (also reminiscent of the malicious HAL of *2001: A Space Odyssey*).

Not surprisingly, the hero triumphs over his sinister rivals in this Disney film, and Lewis succeeds in returning to the science fair in time to undo MitBH's sabotage of the memory-scanner, apparently restoring the timeline. But Lewis also exercises his free will in a number of important ways, including actions which both confirm the main timeline and threaten to introduce paradoxes (which the director understandably ignores). Lewis and Wilbur travel to the moment of Lewis's arrival at the orphanage as an infant, and Lewis sees his mother placing him at the doorstep. However, he chooses to refrain from seeing her face, and is content in his knowledge that he will be adopted by the Robinsons in his timeline, keeping the timeline intact. However, Lewis willfully changes the future in two significant ways. First, he declares that he will never invent Doris, and the malevolent hat disappears upon that pronouncement. Secondly, he travels to Goob's fateful baseball game, wakes up his friend, and allows Goob to win the game. But in doing so, he has prevented the evolution of Goob into the MitBH, and eliminated the two villains who motivated his adventures in the first place. Technically nothing in his main timeline may have changed due to these actions, but he has changed the future nonetheless, which is impossible within a single reality. Therefore the laws of physics fall by the wayside in the name of artistic expression and simplifying the plotline (although one can certainly argue that the plotline of this film is the most involved of the three films under consideration).

The Last Mimzy is narrated in the point of view of a flashback, a story told by a teacher in a utopian future which was created when an unnamed scientist in an undetermined century between ours and the teacher's sent a series of toys (called mimzys) into our past and present in search of pure genetic material in order to reverse a genetic and ecological disaster. As the teacher explains, "a long time ago, the soul of our planet was sick. People had become isolated and warlike. Our world was frightened. It was dying."[23] Unlike the previous two films, wormholes, not ship-like machines, are the mode of time travel, and no living beings travel in time, as it is explained that this would cause the death of those beings (similar to current theories about the dangers of wormhole travel). The time travel in this story can be considered consistent in both theoretical approaches. If we assume that the Last Mimzy was successful in the future and has always been successful, then it is a causal loop with no inconsistencies. The goal of the mimzy is not to change the past, but rather to bring something from the past into the near future in order to assure that the far future is improved. There is obviously also no problem with picturing the far future inhabited by the teacher as one of multiple possible realities, one in which the Last Mimzy did succeed. In this approach there would be a far larger number of unfortunate realities, in which the mimzy failed and humanity faltered.

In order to successfully return to her own (near future) time, the Last Mimzy (an advanced artificial being in the guise of an adorable stuffed rabbit) establishes a psychic link with Emma and Noah, a young sister and brother, and teaches them how to construct a wormhole using the other "toys" which arrived with the rabbit in a curious box. The wormhole concept is first introduced to the audience in the form of a strange "web bridge" which the Noah teaches spiders to build for his science fair project. Noah learns to open and control small wormholes which he uses to transport small objects short distances through space, such as a soda can and a golf ball.

The film was loosely adapted from the 1943 short story "Mimsy Were the Borogroves" by Lewis Padgett (a pseudonym of the husband and wife writing team of Henry Kuttner and C.L. Moore). The title was taken from the famed nonsense poem "Jabberwocky" which appeared in Lewis Carroll's *Through the Looking Glass*. An important difference between the original story and the film is the reason for the toys' time travel. In the former, two time machine boxes were built by Unthahorsten, a scientist whose motivation may be simple boredom or curiosity — he did it because he could.

Both the fictional characters portrayed in these films and real-world scientists have individual motivations for pursuing the work they do. In "The Two Cultures," C.P. Snow[24] separates these motivations into two broad categories: "to understand the natural world" and "to control it." It can be argued that the time travelers in these films fall into the latter category in some way, although their motivations for controlling some aspect of the natural world are portrayed as being for the betterment of humankind. For example, the unnamed scientist of *The Last Mimzy* is driven by the desire to save humanity from its previous bad choices. However, those bad choices involved science and technology in the first place, in the form of polluting the environment and corrupting the human genetic code. While the utopian, naturalistic community portrayed at the end of the film suggests that the scientist's meddling with time has indeed fulfilled its goal, who is to say that his changes to humanity's DNA will not have some unforeseen consequences in the future? As Larry White, the elementary school science teacher warns his students (a two-headed snake in a jar illustrating his point), "this is what happens when you screw with the code."[25]

The scientists who developed Thalidomide in the 1950s and the doctors who prescribed it to thousands of pregnant woman in order to ease their morning sickness certainly never dreamed it would cause the horrific birth defects with which its name is now inextricably linked. But their intentions do not mitigate the suffering caused by this so-called treatment. Similarly, although it has been claimed that genetic engineering offers the hope of future treatments for such devastating conditions as cystic fibrosis, diabetes, Alzheimer's, and paralysis, no one can predict what unforeseen side effects may be introduced alongside these treatments. Therefore White's arguments succinctly encapsulate the heart of the ongoing debate over genetic engineering in general, and more specifically about such applications as genetically enhanced crops and food animals, transgenic animals for transplantation and hormone replacement therapy, and the cloning of Dolly the sheep and other animals. Having a character in the film which espouses these views is a common plot device which seeks to provide balance to the gung-ho scientist and provides a voice to the concerns of the audience. What is novel in this film is that this character is himself a scientist, and, one assumes, understands both sides of the issue simultaneously.

Lewis's invention of the memory-scanner was originally motivated by a self-centered desire to find his birthmother, but as he explains to Goob early in the film, "there's so many things in the world that can be improved.... All it takes is some imagination and a little science and we can make the world a better place."[26] Cornelius, his elder self, lives by the oft-repeated mantra "Keep moving forward" and invents for the betterment of humanity. Interestingly, this catch-phrase of Cornelius Robinson's is taken from a quote of Walt Disney which appears on screen at the end of the film: "Around here, however, we don't look backwards for very long. We keep moving forward, opening up new doors and doing new things, because we're curious ... curiosity keeps leading us down new paths."[27] Putting aside claims by various scholars that the Disney-fication of society has been a detriment rather than a boon,[28] unbridled curiosity and a desire to push the boundaries of both nature and technology also led Dr. Frankenstein, Dr. Faustus, and myriad other tortured scientists of literature and film down the slippery-slope of self-proclaimed good intentions into disaster. To be fair, even though the Disney film provides a rosy overall message that technological advances are a boon to society (and even failure is valuable if it motivates you to continue exploring), through the character of Doris there is at least a cursory acknowledgement of the ongoing debate in philosophical and cultural circles concerning what limits (if any) should be placed on research and to what extent scientists should be held accountable for their creations.

The most innocent of the three protagonists appears to be Captain Neweyes, who is motivated by his desire to fulfill the wishes of 20th century children to see real dinosaurs, the same motive claimed by John Hammond (whom Neweyes physically resembles) in the film *Jurassic Park*, which appeared the same year as *We're Back!* As the dinosaurs run amuck in the park during a power outage, Hammond explains to paleontologist Ellie Sattler that his first attraction designed for public entertainment was a flea circus, which he acknowledges to have been a scam. "I wanted to show them something that wasn't an illusion," he claims in reference to the park of genetically-engineered dinosaurs. "Something that was real.... An idea that is not without merit." Sattler sagely counters that Jurassic Park is as much an illusion as the flea circus (albeit on a much larger, and more sinister, scale).[29] Neweyes and Bleep's plan for having a live dinosaur display in the American Museum of Natural History is likewise an illusion, as they are not dinosaurs in their natural state, but as in the case of Jurassic Park, genetically engineered, in this case made smarter (and far more benevolent than their Mesozoic counterparts!). It is an extreme case of what paleontologist Stephen Jay Gould and others have bemoaned in the museum industry, namely the Disney-fication of the museum experience from education into "edutainment."[30] In addition, the live dinosaur exhibit in *We're Back!* is a secret between the dinosaurs and the children and happens behind a curtain so that the adults cannot take part. The concept of science taking place in secrecy is one of the stereotypes which promulgates public suspicion of the scientific establishment. These films therefore illustrate one of the central lessons of *Jurassic Park*, as painted in the novel version in the words of mathematician Ian Malcolm:

> Science has attained so much power that its practical limits begin to be apparent.... Science cannot help us decide what to do with that world, or how to live. Science can make a nuclear reactor, but it cannot tell us not to build it. Science can make a pesticide, but cannot tell us not to use it.[31]

One of the most misunderstood (and feared) advances in modern science — the concept of genetic engineering — appears in some sense in all three films. *Meet the Robinsons* features at least two examples of artificial life (the malevolent Doris the Bowler Hat and the benevolent Carl the robot) and the Last Mimzy herself is an advanced artificial life form (with an Intel chip) whose nanotechnology astounds the FBI's scientists: "It's almost like it could be alive," one utters in awe.[32] It seems ironic that while the Last Mimzy's mission is to find pure, pristine DNA in our present (her past), in the act of teaching the children how to build the wormhole she alters them and in the process forever alters human evolution. Emma and Noah experience heightened senses and intelligence (for example, Noah can speak to insects and no longer needs his eyeglasses), and Emma levitates and moves objects with her mind on several occasions, much to the terror of the adults around her. When her concerned parents take Emma to a neurologist, his CAT scans find that Emma's brain has been physically altered and continues to be altered at an alarming rate. When Emma's DNA (in the form of a tear which she sheds on the mimzy's stomach) is brought back to the future and used to repair the genetic damage of that time, Emma's new-found psychic powers are somehow transmitted to all future generations, which could only occur if the DNA in all her cells (rather than just her brain) had been altered by the mimzy before the tear was shed. At the end of the film, after the teacher explains to the children (through her telepathic story telling) that Emma was the mother of all humanity now alive, the children fly off through levitation, presumably to their homes, leaving behind a flower petal mandala identical to the one pictured in the story.

We're Back! also contains serious misconceptions about genetics and evolution as part of its plotline, and in doing so reinforces common suspicions and doubts which a not insignificant proportion of the general public have concerning these topics. When the dinosaurs eat the Brain Grain cereal, not only does their intelligence increase exponentially (but without an apparent increase in brain or at least skull size), but in the case of Rex his eyes move from the sides to the top of his head and his teeth decrease in size. If evolution were only that swift or easy, or could take place in a single individual. However, polls conducted by the Gallup Organization and National Science Board have consistently shown that many Americans share this and other misconceptions about evolution.[33] Rex affirms this when he tells Buster the chick that he started life "stupid and violent" but is now "one smart dinosaur."[34] Aboard Neweyes's time travel craft, the four dinosaurs—Rex, Woog the glutinous triceratops, Dweeb the silly "padasaurus" (actually a parasaurolophus) and Elsa the charming and flirtatious female pterodactyl—are as a group appalled at their previous "animal" behavior. Dweeb notes "let's face it—we've evolved."[35] Dweeb may have been artificially mutated, he certainly has not evolved. While it may be argued that the difference is not important for an animated children's film, numerous studies have shown that scientific misconceptions in children are deep-rooted and can hinder the acquisition of new, accurate scientific knowledge.[36] A less obviously modified dinosaur appears in the obligatory chase scene between the MitBH and Lewis in *Meet the Robinsons*, when the MitBH time travels between the far past and the future in order to snare a T Rex to use as his henchman to capture Lewis. But as the dinosaur explains (in dinospeak), he is unable to catch Lewis because his arms are too short.

The general public's lack of scientific knowledge is played upon in two other significant ways in *We're Back!* and *The Last Mimzy*, with only the latter done somewhat tongue in cheek. *The Last Mimzy* humorously uses the widely-cited Clarke's Law—any sufficiently advanced technology is indistinguishable from magic (attributed to science-fiction writer Arthur C. Clarke)—as well as the public's interest in/fear of aliens. When the children find that spinning the black rock shards they call "spinners" will generate a blue sphere of light, they refer to it as a "magic trick" when in actuality it is a part of the Last Mimzy's wormhole technology. Both Noah and the babysitter suspect the technology to be "alien," a thought which evokes interest in the boy and abject fear in the babysitter (who tells the FBI that the entire family is alien). When Louie and Cecilia join the circus of Neweyes's dastardly brother, Professor Screweyes, in *We're Back!*, he uses them as a trap for the dinosaurs by "de-evolving" the children using Brain Drain, in the form of green-glowing pills (their color a stereotype of malevolent scientific potions in science-fiction films). The children turn into monkeys that look suspiciously like chimpanzees, in line with the most common public misconception concerning evolution, namely that humans evolved from present-day monkeys in general, and more specifically from chimpanzees, our nearest living relatives.

Professor Screweyes is himself an obvious stereotype of the mad scientist, described by his brother as being "cruel" and "insane," and who "travels down in this time causing mischief. He was driven mad by the loss of his eye long ago...."[37] As his name implies, Screweyes' left eye is indeed a screw, which he uses to hypnotize the children and the dinosaurs to bend them to his will. The deformed (perhaps even cyborg-like) villain fits in well with many similar villains from the *James Bond* films, including Dr. No (who lost his hands during the course of his atomic experiments), Ernst Blofeld, Jaws, Richard Gettler, and Emilio Largo. He stands in obvious opposition to his kindly elderly brother Captain Neweyes, voiced by Walter Cronkite, himself often termed "the most trusted man in America." In a final affirmation of the Faustian stereotype of the corrupt scientist, Screweyes demands that the children sell their bodies and souls to him, forcing them to sign an invisible contract in blood.

Other serious and deep-rooted stereotypes appear in the films, namely those involving science and gender. All three young male protagonists are portrayed as curious, creative inventors (Lewis and his memory-scanner, Noah and his spider project, and Louie and his Rube Goldberg machine that prepares eggs and toast). All three boys are carefully portrayed as not your stereotypical nerd, for example giving Louie a definitive urban "edge" and having him kiss Cecilia near the end of the film. Lewis walks the geek line very carefully, with his spiky-hair, glasses, and genius-level intelligence. He even jokes about his obsession with inventing: "Nothing says 'adopt me' like a weird invention."[38] When he tries to impress a prospective adoptive family with a notebook full of equations and sketches, and a defective peanut butter and jelly sandwich making hat, he is endeared to the audience rather than made to appear freakish. In the running commentary track to the DVD, the directors acknowledge that their goal was to "make Lewis quirky without making him weird. You always wanted to care about him."[39] The suggestion is, of course, that the audience would not care about a stereotypical nerd.

This stereotype is addressed in *The Last Mimzy*, when Emma is talking to the mimzy during a backyard tea party: "Girls in my class won't talk to me because I like astronomy and I play the violin."[40] Earlier in the film, Noah, her brother, calls her a "mutant" for much the same reason. As a young girl who likes to stargaze with her mother, and ponders deep philosophical issues such as the possibility of life elsewhere in the universe, Emma sets herself apart from "normal" young girls early in the film. She is also obviously different from the rest of her family in her desire to commune with the night sky and music, rather than the household technology which enslaves her parents and brother (including cell phone, video games, and computers). She is thrilled by the prospect of a vacation on a wooded island, while her brother the technocrat complains. It is therefore not surprising when she turns out to be declared "special" in a later scene. Research shows that this peer pressure on girls to feel self-conscious about liking science usually becomes apparent later in childhood — in middle school, near puberty — at the same time that girls are pressured to be more feminine and shun disciplines seen as more masculine (such as mathematics, science, and engineering).[41] The result is that a 2006 study of American girls showed that 75 percent "have no interest in pursuing a career in science, math, or technology."[42] Clearly this has serious implications not only for future opportunities for these girls, but our society at large.

Part of the persistent problem with attracting women into science is the common physical stereotypes of scientists (as seen in Professor Screweyes). Mr. Willerstein, Lewis's science teacher, is a perfect example: short, male, wearing glasses and a bowtie. When asked to picture a scientist, young children will invariably draw someone resembling Mr. Willerstein (often in a lab coat). When asked to draw a female scientist, a female version of Mr. Willerstein often results. For example, a study of third grade students in England found that the most common image was of "thick glasses, flat shoes, big feet, judo types with muscular calves and sensible clothes," often referred to as the "flat chested flat heeled syndrome."[43] This decidedly unflattering and unfeminine stereotype is featured in both *Meet the Robinsons* and *We're Back!* Dr. Lucille Krunklehorn is a visiting judge for Lewis's science fair, a tall, gangly women wearing a lab coat, a tie, and chemistry safety goggles. Her black hair is worn in an exaggerated flip. She babbles incessantly, due to being overly caffeinated thanks to her self-invented caffeine patches (which cover one of her arms). She admits "I just don't get out of that lab much."[44] In opposition to the usual stereotype, Lucille is not an old maid, but is instead married to Bud Robinson, an eccentric man in his own right who likes to wear his clothes backwards. At the end of the film, Lucille and Bud adopt Lewis and foster his metamorphosis into Cornelius, successful inventor.

An even more egregious (and unattractive) stereotype of a woman scientist appears in *We're Back!*, in the character of Dr. Juliet Bleeb, the dinosaur curator at the American Museum of Natural History. Bleep is an older, grey-haired, chubby woman with a mole on her cheek, and she is so absent-minded and oblivious to the world around her that she puts a museum poster *on* one of the dinosaurs at the same time that she is searching for them. She also drives by the dinosaurs on her moped without seeing them (because she neglects to wear her glasses). Her behavior is a repeated sight gag throughout the film, leading one to question whether or not she is grossly incompetent. While Captain Neweyes is voiced by Walter Cronkite, bringing respect to his character, Bleeb is voiced by Julia Child, whose distinctive voice and mannerisms have often been parodied in such venues as *Saturday Night Live*. Clearly Bleeb reinforces negative stereotypes of women in science, and as such the film does a disservice to its young female viewers, especially those who come to the film fascinated by dinosaurs and have the potential to parlay that dino-love into an eventual career in science (as was the case with this author). After all, what young girl would want to grow up to be Juliet Bleeb?

Lest this essay end on too pessimistic and critical a note, there is one persistent stereotype concerning science and scientists which is openly broken by *Mimzy*, namely the perceived war between science and spirituality. Since the time of Galileo, science and religion have frequently come into conflict, due to equal parts misunderstanding and hubris on both sides. From discussion on the origin of the universe to medical advances such as stem cell research, scientists and religious practitioners have more often than not taken a rather intolerant view of each other's perspectives. The film's open breaking with this tradition led at least one reviewer to accuse the film of falling into "New Age nonsense."[45] Science and religion are literally bed partners in this film, in the persons of science teacher Larry White and his fiancée Naomi Schwartz. When we first see Naomi, she is meditating in front of a Tibetan Buddhist altar, repeating "om mani padme hum," the mantra of Chenrezig, the bodhisattva of compassion. They speak wistfully of a recent trip to Nepal, and Larry's recurrent dream of a spinning mandala, a symbolic representation of the universe usually constructed out of sand or painted on cloth (the latter termed a thangka). It is interesting that an Eastern religion is portrayed in this film, most notably Tibetan Buddhism, which has often been called a "science of the mind" by the fourteenth Dalai Lama.[46]

When Larry sees the mandala of his dreams as one of several sketches in Noah's notes, he asks to have the sketches, which he and Naomi match up with centuries-old mandalas in a book. They bring this to the attention of

Jo, Noah and Emma's mother, and ask to conduct a noninvasive body search — a palm reading — to determine if Noah is a tulku, a reincarnation of an important Buddhist teacher. For example, the Dalai Lama is the best known example of a tulku, and the process of looking for reincarnations and other "special" people through marks on the body and other tests has been referenced in *The Matrix* (when the Oracle looks at Neo's hands and face) and the television series *Lost* (in the case of Richard Alpert visiting a childhood version of John Locke). While Noah's hand is disappointingly ordinary, Emma's is extraordinary, and Naomi declares it to be the purest thing she has ever seen. Jo is understandably shaken by this pronouncement, and declaring the method "too strange," asks the pair to leave. When the children manifest further inexplicable powers (such as levitation), Larry gives Jo the name of a neurologist so that they can find a more scientific explanation to what is happening, but all Dr. Rose's fancy technology can do is demonstrate the seemingly inexplicable changes in Emma's brain. Similarly, the FBI agents and scientists fail to comprehend the truth of the situation because they are close-minded in their adherence to the scientific method, rules, and regulations. When Emma tells the FBI and her parents the truth, they are all blind until they see the wormhole open with their own eyes.

In Larry White we see that, despite the common stereotype, a scientist does not have to be an atheist; as in the case of Carl Sagan's book and film *Contact*, there are experiences which fall outside the realm of science, which transcend its explanations and evidence. To admit the existence of such experiences does not make any scientist less so — based on their life experiences and personal philosophies they, like all human beings, can choose to "believe" in something outside of the scientific method, in a spiritual or supernatural power which shapes and guides their life. In this way, Larry White, Captain Neweyes, and the entire Robinson family embody another important lesson for both scientists and society at large — namely the importance of C.P. Snow's warning about the danger of separating human experience and knowledge into disciplinary silos. In doing so, we are often blind to the entire picture in front of us. For example, Jo Wilder sees the symbol-filled green crystal as a featureless black slab, just as she refuses to see the symbolic lines in her daughter's hand.

The word "believe" is a slippery one, as it denotes different meanings to different people, and is used in varying ways depending on the situation. In fact, the word is so fraught with the possibility for misunderstanding that various scientists have called for its ban in scientific conversations.[47] This concern highlights the centuries-old tension between science and religion in Western Culture. Putting aside Biblical literalists and "Young Earth" proponents, authors on both sides of the aisle have increasingly shown that, as Snow argued concerning humanities and science, such dichotomies are artificial and serve no useful purpose in a modern society. Perhaps the most well-known hand of friendship has been extended by the late paleontologist and science writer Stephen Jay Gould, who suggested that both sides agree to what he called the Principle of Non-overlapping Magisteria (NOMA), a "principle of respectful noninterference — accompanied by intense dialogue between the two distinct subjects, each covering a central facet of human existence." In his trademark humor, he succinctly described this as "science gets the age of rocks, and religion the rock of ages; science studies how the heavens go, religion how to go to heaven."[48]

While Gould's respectful division of the disciplines is certainly an improvement over the active hostility seen in previous centuries, others, like the character of Larry White, have taken a more holistic view of the natural world. In this view, the study of science can even deepen one's faith in a spiritual side to reality, and vice versa. For example, Pope Pius XII wrote that "as with art, every science serves God,"[49] and J.R.R. Tolkien offered that while "Those who believe in a personal God, Creator, do not think the Universe is in itself worshipful ... devoted study of it may be one of the ways of honouring Him."[50] While surveys have shown that, as a whole, scientists are less religious than the general public, a study by Elaine Howard Ecklund showed that 48 percent of university science professors identified with a faith tradition and 66 percent consider themselves to be a spiritual person.[51] Given this fact, the fictional character Larry White appears to be far closer to reality than the stereotype of the atheist scientist. If this is the case, then scientists should be encouraged to don their spiritual hats rather than merely their scientist lab coats in debates concerning science and society. As the Dalai Lama notes, "in the first decade of the twenty-first century, science and spirituality have the potential to be closer than ever and to embark upon a collaborative endeavor that has far-reaching potential to help humanity meet the challenges before us. We are all in this together."[52]

As adults we are taught to pigeonhole people and experiences into safe, convenient boxes, but as children we have not yet lost our ability to look at the world in wonder without passing judgment. Neweyes' desire to fulfill the wishes of children by showing them real dinosaurs may be naïve, misdirected, or childish, but at the very least it is honest. The eccentric Robinsons embrace Cornelius's wild inventions, especially the failures, because they provide valuable learning experiences. Larry White is able to help the children by hearing Emma's call in his dreams because he retains that childlike aspect which should be (but unfortunately too often is not) the hallmark of someone who becomes a scientist. It is therefore no accident that the Last Mimzy's creator designed her to attract the interest of a child, someone who is open to new experiences.

But as Emma wisely notes, she will succeed where Alice Liddell (the real-world child-model for *Alice in Wonderland*) failed with her own mimzy, because Alice didn't have a brother like Noah: "you're my engineer."[53] Emma embodies a pure scientific wonder about the world and an appreciation for the arts (and perhaps a spirituality as well). In this way, she typifies a truth espoused by Physics Nobel laureate Sheldon Glashow, who has stated that all children begin with a sense of wonder about the world. Those who retain that wonder become artists, musicians, or scientists. Emma understands that it is in working *with* technology and not being a slave to it (nor shunning it) that humanity can benefit. At the same time, as demonstrated near the end of the film when Emma is temporarily sucked into the wormhole, technology brings with it the possibility of danger and must be used with care and clarity of mind.

In conclusion, it is therefore not a coincidence that time travel forms the backbone of the plot of these three works, for perhaps no other aspect of theoretical science provides such opportunities for wonder, interdisciplinary work, and, yes, even abuse of the laws of physics. But as recent films such as *Star Trek* and *Harry Potter and the Prisoner of Azkaban* have demonstrated, real world science can remain an integral part of the plot without stifling artistry — even in films which can be enjoyed by a younger audience. Perhaps in the future Hollywood will learn this lesson for itself and provide our youngest citizens — our potential future scientists — with both a positive portrayal of realistic science and realistic scientists, all the while continuing to illuminate the controversies surrounding issues of science and its relationship to the greater society in which it is situated and which it serves.

Notes

1. J.R.R. Tolkien, *The Letters of J.R.R. Tolkien,* edited by Humphrey Carpenter (Boston: Houghton Mifflin, 2000), 246.
2. C.P. Snow, *The Two Cultures: and a Second Look* (New York: Cambridge University Press, 1963), 11–12.
3. Snow, *The Two Cultures: and a Second Look*, 17.
4. Brian L. Silver, *The Ascent of Science* (Oxford: Oxford University Press, 2000), 481.
5. Carl Sagan, *The Demon-haunted World* (New York: Ballantine Books, 1997), 11.
6. Sagan, *The Demon-haunted World*, 373.
7. Elaine Howard Ecklund, "Religion and Spirituality Among University Scientists," *Social Science Research Council*, 5 February 2007, http://religion.ssrc.org/reforum/Ecklund.pdf.
8. National Science Board, *Science and Engineering Indicators 2010* (Arlington, VA: National Science Foundation, 2010), Appendix 7–18.
9. Sean Cavanag, "Educators Revisit Girls' Loss of Math, Science Interest," *Education Week* 24, no. 34 (2005): 36.
10. Kip Thorne, *Black Holes and Time Warps* (New York: W.W. Norton and Co., 1994).
11. Michael S. Morris, Kip S. Thorne, and Ulvi Yurtsever, "Wormholes, Time Machines, and the Weak Energy Condition," *Physical Review Letters* 61, no. 13 (1998).
12. S.W. Hawking, "Chronology Protection Conjecture," *Physical Review* D 46 (1992).
13. Ronald L. Mallett, "The Gravitational Field of a Circulating Light Beam," *Foundations of Physics* 33, no. 9 (2003).

14. Readers interested in the details of the ring laser time machine are directed to Mallett and Henderson (2006).
15. Hawking, Stephen W., "Space and Time Warps," http://www.hawking.org.uk/index.php/lectures/63.
16. Ibid.
17. Paul J. Nahin, *Time Machines* (New York: Springer, 1999), 150.
18. Hugh Everett III, "'Relative State' Formulation of Quantum Mechanics," *Reviews of Modern Physics* 29, no. 3 (1957): 454–462.
19. David Deutsch, *The Fabric of Reality* (New York: Penguin Press, 1997).
20. Michael Silberstein, "Space, Time, and Magic," in *Harry Potter and Philosophy: If Aristotle Ran Hogwarts*, edited by David Baggett and Shawn E. Klein (Chicago: Open Court, 2004).
21. *Meet the Robinsons*, DVD, directed by Stephen Anderson (2007; Burbank, CA: Buena Vista Home Entertainment, 2007).
22. *Meet the Robinsons*, DVD.
23. *The Last Mimzy*, DVD, directed by Robert Shaye (2007; Los Angeles: New Line Entertainment, 2007).
24. Snow, *The Two Cultures: and a Second Look*, 64.
25. *The Last Mimzy*, DVD.
26. *Meet the Robinsons*, DVD.
27. *Meet the Robinsons*, DVD.
28. For example, see Baudrillard (2004).
29. *Jurassic Park*, DVD, directed by Steven Spielberg (1993; Universal City, CA: Universal Studios, 2000).
30. Stephen T. Asma, *Stuffed Animals and Pickled Heads: The Culture and Evolution of Natural History Museums* (Oxford: Oxford University Press, 2001), 35.
31. Michael Crichton, *Jurassic Park* (New York: Knopf, 1990), 314.
32. *The Last Mimzy*, DVD.
33. For example, see National Science Board, *Science and Engineering Indicators 2010*.
34. *We're Back! A Dinosaur's Story*, DVD, directed by Dick Zondag, Ralph Zondag, Phil Nibbelink, and Simon Wells (1993; Universal City, CA: Universal Studios, 2009).
35. *We're Back! A Dinosaur's Story*, DVD.
36. For example, see Hammer (1996) and Schoon (1995).
37. *We're Back! A Dinosaur's Story*, DVD.
38. *Meet the Robinsons*, DVD.
39. *Meet the Robinsons*, DVD.
40. *The Last Mimzy*, DVD.
41. Cavanag, "Educators Revisit Girls' Loss of Math, Science Interest," 36.
42. Ronald Roach, "Survey: American Girls Aren't Interested in STEM Careers," *Diverse: Issues in Higher Education* 23, no. 4 (2006): 54.
43. L. Measor and P.J. Sikes, *Gender and Science* (London: Cassell, 1992), 74–75.
44. *Meet the Robinsons*, DVD.
45. Rick Norwood, "The Last Mimzy," 2007, http://www.sfsite.com/04b/lm246.htm.
46. For example, see Dalai Lama, Tenzin Gyatso, *The Universe in a Single Atom* (New York: Morgan Road Books, 2005).
47. For an overview, see Kristine Larsen, "This I ~~Believe~~ Understand: The Importance of Banning the B-word from Science," *Astronomy Education Review* 6 no. 2 (2008): 118–26.
48. Stephen Jay Gould, *Rocks of Ages* (New York: Ballantine, 1999), 6.
49. Michael Chinigo, ed., *The Teachings of Pope Pius XII* (London: Methuen & Co., 1958), 145.
50. Tolkien, *The Letters of J.R.R. Tolkien*, 400.
51. Ecklund, "Religion and Spirituality Among University Scientists," 5.
52. Dalai Lama, Tenzin Gyatso, *The Universe in a Single Atom*, 208–9.
53. *The Last Mimzy*, DVD.

REFERENCES

Asma, Stephen T. *Stuffed Animals and Pickled Heads: The Culture and Evolution of Natural History Museums.* Oxford: Oxford University Press, 2001.

Baudrillard, Jean. *Simulacra and Simulation*. Ann Arbor: Michigan University Press, 2004.
Cavanag, Sean. "Educators Revisit Girls' Loss of Math, Science Interest." *Education Week* 24, no. 34 (2005): 36.
Chinigo, Michael, ed. *The Teachings of Pope Pius XII*. London: Methuen & Co., 1958.
Crichton, Michael. *Jurassic Park*. New York: Knopf, 1990.
Dalai Lama, Tenzin Gyatso. *The Universe in a Single Atom*. New York: Morgan Road Books, 2005.
Deutsch, David. *The Fabric of Reality*. New York: Penguin Press, 1997.
Ecklund, Elaine Howard. "Religion and Spirituality Among University Scientists." http://religion.ssrc.org/reform/Ecklund.pdf.
Everett, Allen. "Time Travel Paradoxes, Path Integrals, and the Many-Worlds Interpretation of Quantum Mechanics." *Physical Review D* 69 (2004): 124023.
Everett III, Hugh. "'Relative State' Formulation of Quantum Mechanics." *Reviews of Modern Physics* 29, no. 3 (1957): 454–462.
Gould, Stephen Jay. *Rocks of Ages*. New York: Ballantine, 1999.
Hammer, David. "More than Misconceptions: Multiple Perspectives on Student Knowledge and Reasoning, and an Appropriate Role for Education Research." *American Journal of Physics* 64, no. 10 (1996): 1316–1325.
Hawking, S.W. "Chronology Protection Conjecture." *Physical Review D* 46 (1992): 603–611.
Hawking, Stephen W. "Space and Time Warps." http://www.hawking.org.uk/lectures/warps.html
Jurassic Park. DVD. Directed by Steven Spielberg. 1993. Universal City, CA: Universal Studios, 2000.
Larsen, Kristine. "This I Believe Understand: The Importance of Banning the B-word From Science." *Astronomy Education Review* 6, no. 2 (2008): 118–26.
The Last Mimzy. DVD. Directed by Robert Shaye. 2007. Los Angeles: New Line Entertainment, 2007.
Mallett, Ronald L. "The Gravitational Field of a Circulating Light Beam." *Foundations of Physics* 33, no. 9 (2003): 1307–1314.
Mallett, Ronald L., with Bruce Henderson. *Time Traveler*. New York: Thunder's Mouth Press, 2006.
Measor, L., and P.J. Sikes. *Gender and Science*. London: Cassell, 1992.
Meet the Robinsons. DVD. Directed by Stephen Anderson. 2007. Burbank, CA: Buena Vista Home Entertainment, 2007.
Morris, Michael S., Kip S. Thorne, and Ulvi Yurtsever. "Wormholes, Time Machines, and the Weak Energy Condition." *Physical Review Letters* 61, no. 13 (1988): 1446–1449.
Nahin, Paul J. *Time Machines*, 2nd ed. New York: Springer, 1999.
National Science Board. *Science and Engineering Indicators 2010*. Arlington, VA: National Science Foundation, 2010.
Norwood, Rick. "The Last Mimzy." http://www.sfsite.com/04b/lm246.htm.
Roach, Ronald. "Survey: American Girls Aren't Interested in STEM Careers." *Diverse: Issues in Higher Education* 23, no. 4 (2006): 54.
Sagan, Carl. *The Demon-haunted World*. New York: Ballantine Books, 1997.
Schoon, Kenneth J. "The Origin and Extent of Alternative Conceptions in the Earth and Space Sciences." *Journal of Elementary Science Education* 7, no. 2 (1995): 27–46.
Silberstein, Michael. "Space, Time, and Magic." In *Harry Potter and Philosophy: If Aristotle Ran Hogwarts*, edited by David Baggett and Shawn E. Klein, 186–199. Chicago: Open Court, 2004.
Silver, Brian L. *The Ascent of Science*. Oxford: Oxford University Press, 1998.
Snow, C.P. *The Two Cultures: and a Second Look*. New York: Cambridge University Press, 1963.
Thorne, Kip. *Black Holes and Time Warps*. New York: W.W. Norton, 1994.
Tolkien, J.R.R. *The Letters of J.R.R. Tolkien*, edited by Humphrey Carpenter. Boston: Houghton Mifflin, 2000.
We're Back! A Dinosaur's Story. DVD. Directed by Dick Zondag, Ralph Zondag, Phil Nibbelink, and Simon Wells. 1993. Universal City, CA: Universal Studios, 2009.

• *Fifteen* •

"Manmade Mess": The Critical Dystopia of *WALL-E*

ALEXANDER CHARLES OLIVER HALL

2008's Pixar film *WALL-E*, directed by Andrew Stanton, is among the best examples of 21st century American films that adhere to the conventions of the critical dystopia. The critique that accompanies *WALL-E*'s dystopian narrative form is of the overconsumption that is increasingly abundant in postmodern society, but the dystopian conditions of the film's world are predicated on a very possible outcome of such overconsumption: the complete destruction of the Earth's environment. Indeed, there is cause for concern in the viewer's empirical world, for as the global hegemony of late capitalism causes levels of consumption to rise, the possibility of environmental sustainability grows weak. *WALL-E* imagines a world in which the collapse of the Earth's environment some seven hundred years before the film takes place (and about one hundred years from the time of its release) forces humanity to flee the planet and live instead on giant spaceships. After hundreds of years aboard the ships, humans have adopted a way of life that robs them of much of their humanity — they have allowed the ships' automated robots to perform all their tasks for them, leading to the deterioration of their bones (a symptom of disuse atrophy that in turn robs them of their ability to walk[1]), they interact with one another only through a computer interface, and they have completely lost any concept of what life would be like otherwise, especially life on Earth. Despite the obviously dystopian conditions of this existence, however, the inhabitants of the ships remain entirely complacent, but actions do transpire in the film to wrest them from their complacency. In this way, the film maintains a utopian impulse in that the dystopian conditions of its fictional world are capable of being transcended in favor of a better life for its inhabitants. Thus, with its dystopian narrative form, inclusion of a figure of hope, and critique of the system under which it is produced, *WALL-E* fits nicely into the category of the critical dystopia.

In a recent essay by utopian studies scholar Kenneth M. Roemer, Utopia in the early 21st century is said "to have retreated to the margins"[2]— this at least insofar as it is viewed as a realistic characterization of America in the wake of the 9/11 attacks, the war in Iraq, and amid the so-called economic "crisis." To be sure, the idea of America as Utopia did find new vitality in the years following what M. Keith Booker has called the "long 1950s [1946–1964]"— "the great period of American Cold War hysteria"[3]— as evidenced by the rise of what Tom Moylan termed the literary "critical utopia," which "was inspired by the movements of the 1960s" and the ensuing "return to the human agenda of the categories of cooperation, equality, mutual aid, liberation, ecological wisdom, and peaceful and creative living."[4] The conservative turn of the 1980s, however, brought about an "era of economic restructuring, political opportunism, and cultural implosion" that resulted in the reappearance of the dystopian narrative in its own new "critical" form.[5] "Critical," as Moylan writes, is meant "in the Enlightenment sense of *critique*— that is expressions of oppositional thought, unveiling, debunking, of both the genre itself and the historical situation. As well as 'critical' in the nuclear sense of the *critical mass* required to make the necessary explosive reaction."[6] Alongside the conservative turn in the 1980s and the critical dystopia's rise, however, utopian rhetoric was taken up by leaders on the right in the United States—Moylan gives the examples of Ronald Reagan's retrieval of "the utopian figure of the 'city on the hill' from colonial history to signify the society of harmony and enterprise that his new administration promised to establish" and George H.W. Bush's deployment of "the utopian figure of the millennium as he called for a new world order of peace and prosperity that would move beyond the era of the Cold War," but points out that "what the Republican presidents celebrated in their 'utopian' tropes was clearly not the betterment of humanity and the earth, but rather the triumph of transnational capital and right-wing ideology."[7] The critical dystopia came as a response to this new anti-utopian vision of America as Utopia instead by engaging in utopian*ism*. Lyman Tower Sargent defines this "broad, general phenomenon" as "social dreaming," suggesting that "if we are frustrated by something in our society, we dream of a society in which it is corrected."[8] The critical dystopia takes a slightly different path, however, upon which frustration with society is expressed, according to Sargent, through "a non-existent society described in considerable detail and normally located in time and space that the author intended a contemporaneous reader to view as worse than contemporary society."[9] The correction of that society is usually implied by the inclusion of "at least one eutopian enclave" in the narrative, or, at the very least, "hope that the dystopia can be overcome and replaced with a eutopia."[10,11] In this way, the critical dystopia, according to Moylan, carries out an "intertextual intervention" that denies the "negation of the critical utopian moment"—a symptom of the conservative turn in America in the 1980s—"and thus make[s] room for another manifestation of the utopian imagination within the dystopias form."[12] Concurrent with the popularity of the critical dystopia in cultural production, utopian rhetoric has continued on the right—Roemer points to the "exceptionalist, go-it-alone, 'City Upon a Hill' concept of America ... re-revived during [Reagan's] funeral services in 2004 and by George W. Bush in campaign speeches."[13] Approaching the end of the first decade of the 21st century, while visions of America as Utopia have been appropriated by the right-wing, the cultural ubiquity that has been achieved by the critical dystopia is a testament to its strength as a narrative framework for the emergence of the utopian imagination.

Concurrent with the rise of the critical dystopia during the conservative turn in the United States during the 1980s, according to ecocritic Cheryll Glotfelty, "the field of environmental literary studies was planted," resulting in a body of ecocriticism that "shares a common motivation: the troubling awareness that we have reached the age of environmental limits, a time when the consequences of human actions are damaging the planet's basic life support systems."[14] Even with the rise of ecocriticism and the awareness that has influenced it, however, the environment continues to suffer, but according to Donald Worster, this "age of environmental limits" has come about "not because of how ecosystems function but rather because of how our ethical systems function."[15] Case in point: the United States government has been reluctant to ratify the Kyoto Protocol (which would set limits on the emission of certain greenhouse gases that contribute to global warming) primarily because of the expenditures that compliance would necessitate—and this despite the environmental benefits of doing so. This failure of the United States to adopt the Kyoto treaty is but one example of how the flawed ethical systems of the hegemonic capitalist system have largely influenced a greater concern in government for the economic cost of trying to achieve environmental sustainability than for the ecological benefit. Still, Worster suggests that "understanding those ethical systems and using that understanding to reform them" is the best prescription for "getting through the [global environmental] crisis."[16] In their work, the ecocritics have sought to further this understanding as a means to inciting the kind of action necessary to get through this crisis. The critical dystopia, on the other hand, uses its cautionary form to envision the outcome of the crisis, and as such warns against the kind of complacency that can suppress this understanding and lead to such an outcome. An ecological dystopia such as *WALL-E*, then, is "a mirror held up by culture to its environment," producing an estrangement that allows its viewers to recognize the flawed ethical systems of their empirical world that might lead to environmental collapse.[17]

WALL-E conjectures a future in which overconsumption — which continues in the viewer's empirical world despite warnings about environmental sustainability and thanks to the flawed ethical systems of late capitalism — has rendered the planet uninhabitable thanks to all the trash it produces. There is, of course, a real need for this kind of ecological concern. Economist Douglas E. Booth, for example, grants that "without growth in consumption, economic stagnation is the result," but is more concerned with the fact that "the pressure of economic expansion within fixed ecological constraints is bound to result in significant environmental harm."[18] Meanwhile, the editors of *Confronting Consumption* wish to challenge what they see as the underlying problem with contemporary attitudes regarding consumption, which is its seeming inviolability: "production reigns supreme because consumption is beyond scrutiny"; in other words, "if ... supplies are tight, one must produce more ... not consume less."[19] The dominant logic regarding consumption follows this model of increased production over decreased consumption, but economic discourses have in the past twenty years begun to reflect the growing concern about the relationship between economic growth and the environment. In addition to these and other academic discourses in which concern for the environment in the age of overconsumption is prevalent, cultural production too reflects these concerns. *WALL-E*'s conjectured future, for instance, is built upon a possible outcome of environmental irresponsibility, a large part of which has to do with consumption.

WALL-E is rife with cautionary energy, which Fredric Jameson associates with dystopia in general, noting that "the dystopia is always and essentially what in the language of science-fiction criticism is called a 'near-future' [narrative]: it tells the story of an imminent disaster — ecology, overpopulation, plague, drought, the stray comet or nuclear accident — waiting to come to pass in our own near future."[20] Although the film takes place in the far future, the catalyst for that future is said to have taken place in the early 22nd century, which is much nearer the film's contemporary moment. In this way, despite Jameson's conception of the postmodern as "an attempt to think the present historically in an age that has forgotten how to think historically in the first place," moving beyond that symptom of the age, *WALL-E* provokes the reader to think historically — to consider the film's dystopian future a direct result of the present.[21] As a critical dystopia, the inclusion of a route out suggests the viability of action in the present to subvert its dystopian conditions for the betterment of the future, which in itself equals a utopian gesture since historicism is fundamentally linked to the utopian impulse in postmodern culture. This is so, following Booker, in that the inverse is true: "a loss of utopian energy is ... part and parcel of ... a loss of the ability to think in terms of coherent historical narratives."[22] A rescue of this ability, however, is attempted in dystopian works such as *WALL-E* via their cautionary energy, which thereby seek — intentionally or otherwise — to transcend what Jameson has argued is perhaps the most important aspect of life under late capitalism and "call our own form of life into question," for "if it is so that the proper articulation of any concrete mode of production structurally implies the projection of all other conceivable modes, then it follows that it implies the future as well and that the hermeneutic contact between present and past" therefore produces "the anticipatory expression of a future society."[23] *WALL-E*'s narrative is consistent with this cautionary, historicist, and therefore utopian function. Still, despite the cautionary measures of the film regarding the environment, Stanton remains steadfast that he did not intend to be ecologically didactic.

WALL-E opens on a "dystopian, post-evacuation" Earth, or so Stanton terms it in his commentary on the DVD release of the film, but the director insists that there is no "message"— that he had no intention of being "preachy or environmental or ecological."[24] Despite his intentions, however, there is an explicitly didactic ecological message inherent in the film's premise, which is that the pattern of humanity's consumption, if taken to its logical conclusion, could result in the kind of future depicted — one in which the Earth has been so contaminated by the waste produced after years of overconsumption that it is no longer inhabitable. Stanton does admit that he was influenced by the reality of the situation in contemporary society regarding consumption:

> you just kind of look at the state of the world as it is, and you just sort of extrapolate a little bit off of the elements that you have, and you go 'well, if we keep buying too much and throwing it all away, sooner or later there won't be enough places to put it all, and once there's no room, what would you have to do?' Well, one of the things might be that you'd have to sort of leave the planet and make room for everything to get cleaned up so you could kind of move back in. So we just went with that simple logic.[25]

Unfortunately, the ecological concerns in American culture that result from overconsumption have only become more widespread, and so, in the years leading up to *WALL-E*'s release, "things just got more timely."[26] This timeliness allows the film to become a more potentially critical cultural product in that it is influenced by the problems of the viewer's empirical world, and participates in the discourses regarding the potential outcome of those problems.

To preserve the human race, the company responsible for the production of the consumables that have led to the Earth's predicament — "Buy N Large" — builds a fleet of automated spaceships — "modern day ark[s]" — upon which the Earth's inhabitants may live until such time as the planet may sustain human life once again.[27] Meanwhile, to try and "clean up the mess," an army of trash compacting robots are deployed to stack the waste for removal and incineration, but the undertaking is soon abandoned because "rising toxicity levels have made life unsustainable on Earth" and so "Operation: Cleanup" is canceled.[28] According to the Global CEO of Buy N Large, Shelby Forthright (Fred Willard), "rather than try and fix this problem, it'll just be easier for everyone to remain in space."[29] Seven hundred years later, one of the trash compacting robots, whose model name — "Waste Allocation Load Lifter Earth-Class" — is shortened to "WALL-E" for the film's title, still remains operational on the Earth's surface, while humanity exists only on the Buy N Large spaceships. It is on the ships that the dystopian theme becomes most apparent in the film.

Due to the destruction of the Earth's environment, as presented in the film, humanity is forced to live in what Stanton refers to as "vacation hell."[30] This "perpetual vacation" atmosphere of the spaceships is achieved thanks to the way in which the automated ships coddle their human inhabitants.[31] One important way they do so is by providing "all-access hoverchairs" for everyone, even though the floating chaise lounges are initially suggested as a convenience for those unable to get around on the ships — a Buy N Large advertisement touts: "with our all-access hoverchairs, even Grandma can join the fun; there's no need to walk."[32] Nonetheless, everyone on the ship is equipped with a hoverchair, which have screens projected directly in front of the faces of their passengers, allowing them access even to people who may be right beside them, and speakers on the left and right "like horse blinders."[33] Reducing human contact to something that occurs only through a machine is a dystopian concept that dates back to the classical dystopia "The Machine Stops," written by E.M. Forster in 1909, demonstrating a dystopian self-awareness in *WALL-E*'s narrative. Despite this parallel, however, Stanton cites a more contemporary influence:

> "it's not that much different than how it feels sometimes when you're on the street of a city ... and everybody's on their cell phone. Or you're in a commuter lane and everybody's in their car, in their own private little universe, even though technically we're all very close to one another."[34]

Stanton recognizes this dystopian aspect of contemporary society, which he exaggerates in the film by "literally cocoon[ing] people in their hoverchairs," but this exaggeration contains a utopian impulse, in that the director sees this isolation as "the thing that should be corrected," which marks another potentially critical angle of *WALL-E*'s dystopian narrative.[35]

The "hell" of life on the Buy N Large starliner is allowed to become perpetual, according to Stanton, because of humanity's "programming," which is used in the film as a metaphor: "that all of us fall into our habits, into our sort of routines; in a way it's a bit of our own self-fulfilling programming, and life just can sometimes pass us by."[36] What Stanton touches upon here is humanity's complacency under dystopian conditions. He continues, "especially with all the distractions that happen in life now, imagine what it will be like in the future, which is what we tried to do."[37] Once again, although the director contends that he has no ulterior motives critically, a utopian impulse can be extracted from the film. In the face of humanity's complacency under these dystopian conditions, Stanton hopes to be able to "force all of humanity ... to wake up," which, he says, was "always the byproduct of what [he] wanted the love story between EVE and WALL-E to do ... to have a positive effect on humanity."[38] That the utopian potential of *WALL-E* comes not from human endeavor but as a result of the love story between EVE and WALL-E, however, reflects the prevalence of fatalism in contemporary culture, which is partially to blame for the cultural loss of utopian figuration. Ruth Levitas writes:

> Where it is no longer assumed that social organization is inherently controllable by human agents, or where it is no longer believed that the agents who are in control can themselves be made accountable to the rest of us, much of the motive for the construction of utopias as goals is lost. They cease to be images of a hoped-for future and become again expressions of desire. The role of fantasy increases and utopia is less and less intended as a literal goal, and less bound by constraints of literal possibility.... Utopia may be critical of present reality, but the transformative element is no longer primary.[39]

In the space left by this abandonment of utopian realization is what Levitas refers to as the "education of desire"—the suggestion of "the desire for a different, better way of being."[40,41] No longer concerned with the establishment of some utopia, "the function of utopia thus reverts from that of goal and catalyst of change to one of criticism, and the education of desire"—enter the dystopia.[42]

The dystopian genre is surely a locus of critique in cultural production, even to the point that Booker characterizes it as "not so much a specific genre as a particular kind of oppositional and critical energy or spirit."[43] In terms of the education of desire, the dystopian genre is consistent with Frederick L. Polak's conception of *u*topia—paraphrased by Sargent as "a constant mirror held up to the present, showing the faults of contemporary society"—which affords dystopia the ability to show readers what is wrong with their world so that they may take action to make it better as time moves forward.[44] *WALL-E* fits in with this logic in that its film world is essentially just an extrapolation of what the world might look like if the ills of contemporary society continue unchecked — a world orbited by a shield of satellites, where the big box chain extends its power and influence to the point of governance, and where concern for the environment has been completely supplanted by the desire to have more stuff. *WALL-E* points out these flaws in the hegemonic order, effectively cautioning against the continuation of the ethical systems of that order and attempting a critique; however, in keeping with the conventions of the critical dystopia, all hope is not lost.

Moylan and Baccolini make it clear in their work on the critical dystopia that the works "not only critique the present triumphal system but also explore ways to transform it."[45] Unlike classical dystopias such as Zamyatin's *We*— wherein the protagonist is resubjugated by the dystopian society he lives in after struggling to subvert it — critical dystopias leave space for "contestation and opposition" in the narrative, suggesting that their imagined dystopian worlds can be overcome, and thereby suggesting that the dystopian nature of the present can be overcome as well.[46] *WALL-E* makes several critical points about contemporary society, but also suggests ways to overcome the ills it identifies.

One of the critical points *WALL-E* (perhaps inadvertently) makes is that the hegemonic system is too readily accepted as final — that somehow there can be no alternative. The basic idea for the film, according to Stanton, was to depict "a robot that was left alone on Earth, and didn't know it could stop doing what it was doing"; he asks, "what if it just kept doing its job for hundreds of years, having no idea it could stop?"[47] There is a kind of parallel here to the widely-accepted view that capitalism is forever, that political struggle cannot displace the capitalist system. Under such an assumption, the system's subjects themselves become metaphorical robots, going about their daily lives without questioning the system in place. One way this robotic existence is maintained is through the production of popular culture — subjects are entertained to the point of passivity. WALL-E himself, for instance, repeatedly watches Gene Kelly's *Hello, Dolly!*, which keeps him happy enough to ignore the futility of the work he is doing from day to day. This aspect of the film suggests a potential critique of the Hollywood system itself, though this is certainly inadvertent. Still, WALL-E is able to "stop," needing only the right stimulus to lead him to do so, and this suggests the possibility of humanity to effect systemic change, which locates a utopian impulse in *WALL-E*'s narrative that might be translated to the viewer's empirical world.

WALL-E's "job" was itself apparently the springboard for Stanton's having come up with the premise of the film: "we always had a character that compacted trash ... so then I had to think backwards, I had to go, 'why would the world be covered in trash?'"[48] The answer Stanton came up with was the ubiquity of the corporation under late capitalism, which, he says, perpetuates "consumerism" to the point of "almost governing how you run your life."[49] The next step was for the filmmakers to pose the question, "what if a company *was* the government?" and to "distort" that concept in a "gross" (read: exaggerated) way, which is consistent with dystopian figuration.[50] The corporation-cum-government in the film, Buy N Large, is to blame for the state of the world, as well as for the displacement of humanity to the starliners, which is a symptom of the condition of the Earth's environment. Once it is assumed that the Earth cannot be salvaged as a home for humans, Buy N Large issues "override directive A113" which allows the automated machinery of the starliners to take control of the human passengers and the starliners.[51] What is more, the autopilots are instructed to "stay the course"—that is, not to return to Earth under any circumstances, dooming the possibility of "Operation: Recolonize" even if conditions on Earth are found to be able to support human life once again.[52]

Clearly, the film is critiquing the corporation in the postmodern age, but there is hope: with the possibility of returning to Earth, the humans on board the Axiom starliner have to pull together to overcome the robots that have been programmed by Buy N Large to maintain the dystopian conditions they live under. Rather than merely accepting the life they have been subjected to, events transpire in the film that allow them to fight for the right to return to the Earth and reclaim their humanity, thereby subverting their "programming" and starting fresh. Viewers can then extend this ability to their own lives and hopefully see the evils of the corporation as it operates in the system they live under. As a result, they might question a system that would allow the corporation to gain the kind of influence that might lead to a dystopian world like the one depicted in *WALL-E*. Still, one of the more powerful critiques that the film makes is of the pollution of the environment.

Although in a broad sense *WALL-E* critiques the system that its viewers live under, the film seems especially interested in the effects of that system on the Earth's environment. The overcoming of these effects, however, does seem a bit too easy, as evidenced by the narrative of the time after the humans' arrival back on Earth that plays during the film's credits, which depicts a suspiciously convenient overturning of the Earth's plight. What began as a single figure of hope, embodied by the plant WALL-E finds early in the film, for instance, becomes an entire hillside of botanical life by the very end. What is more, the people who make it back to the Earth know little about even the most basic things that might help them survive—e.g. the Axiom's captain suggests that they will grow "pizza plants."[53] Even so, it is the condition of the environment by the early 22nd century that forces humanity into space in order to survive, and it is in space that the dystopian conditions are allowed to be fully realized. The "manmade mess" that has been made of the Earth catalyzes those conditions, and it stands to reason that the film implicates environmental awareness as one possible method of circumventing such a dystopian future, even if that solution is in the narrative somewhat unrealistic.[54] And so the situation is not hopeless — even though it has been seven hundred years since humanity has been forced off the planet thanks to environmental destruction, and even though humans have become oblivious to the dystopian nature of their existence, the narrative does allow room for them to "wake up" thanks to an ecological figure of hope. The plant that WALL-E finds among the trash on Earth is the manifestation of that hope. Stanton says:

> "I just kept picturing this dandelion pushing through a cement sidewalk. It's like all this manmade cement — all this manmade stuff — trying to force something organic and natural to just not exist anymore, and it still perseveres.... It took seven hundred years, but it still came up through the cement."[55]

Again, however, Stanton insists that there is not an ecological message here, preferring instead to think of the plant as a metaphor for the perseverance of humanity. To achieve this, the plant is placed in a boot, as a "portentous symbol" of "man walking again," foreshadowing the Axiom captain's having to stand and walk toward the end of the film (despite the symptoms of disuse atrophy), which would suggest that "all of humanity would start to have to get up and walk again."[56] In this way, it is suggested that ecological hope might catalyze human action to subvert the dystopian conditions of its existence. The viewer can then surmise that the preservation of the environment might prevent such conditions in the first place, which locates hope within the narrative that can be transplanted to the viewer's world.

Conclusion

Along with the rise of the critical dystopia, there has been considerable concern for the environment, which has been reflected in the cultural production of the age of environmental limits, not the least of which is the critical dystopia. Nevertheless, the hegemony of late capitalism places economic concern before the environment, which reveals the system's flawed ethics. An ecologically critical dystopia cautions against the continuation of these ethical structures, thereby hoping to incite the kind of awareness that might prevent an ecology-based dystopian future the likes of *WALL-E*. The film points to the prevalence of overconsumption as one symptom of late capitalism that might permanently damage the environment, especially since the system seems all but unconcerned with the growth of consumption, even to the point that it would encourage increased production before decreased consumption, and despite the environmental harm that will surely result from such behavior. *WALL-E* takes this behavior to its logical conclusion, depicting a future world that not only exacts a critique of consumption in contemporary society, but also warns against consumption in the process. In this way, the film, like most dystopias, forces its viewers to think historically, which resists a key symptom of postmodernity — the loss of historicity. There is a utopian impulse inherent in this development because the viewer can then take this new historical awareness and apply it to his or her own life in an attempt to avert the kind of future *WALL-E* depicts.

Interestingly, Stanton does not wish to proffer ecological messages per se, preferring instead to merely look at the world as it is in the early 21st century and imagine what the future may hold if it continues on its current path. Still, the film's concepts are particularly timely for its contemporary audience, who can recognize the environmental irresponsibility of their age as that which might result in environmental destruction. It is the resulting world after environmental destruction, however, that Stanton concentrates on. Humans are displaced from their planet and forced to live in space, where they come to live under considerably dystopian conditions, even if they do not necessarily recognize those conditions as dystopian. As such, the humans become complacent under these conditions, which corresponds with the increase in fatalism in postmodern culture. This fatalism has in many ways superseded utopian figuration in culture, situating the dystopia as a more powerfully estranging narrative form. The critical dystopia is consistent with this power of the genre, except that while it critiques and cautions, it also leaves room for hope that that which it critiques and cautions against can be subverted. It does this by including a figure of hope within the narrative.

WALL-E's critical dystopia contains several critical and cautionary points, including an overall critique of the hegemony of capitalism. The film depicts WALL-E as a character of intense futility — compacting and stacking trash for seven hundred years, with no end in sight — but also depicts humans in this way. Life, it is therefore suggested, cannot be otherwise, and, rather than taking any kind of action to make a change, humanity simply accepts this idea. However, the narrative does see the humans coming together in the end to find their way back to the Earth, which represents a utopian impulse within the narrative, and thus marks one way in which it adheres to the conventions of the critical dystopia.

Similarly, the film critiques the power that the corporation has come to possess in the postmodern world, suggesting it can only lead to a dystopian life as long as it encourages overconsumption. Again, however, the film leaves room for hope in that the people are able to overthrow the corporation-controlled robots that keep them in their state of complacency, equaling a utopian impulse. Finally, the environment has an important role in the setup for *WALL-E*'s narrative — it has reached a point where it can no longer sustain human life, primarily because of the waste humanity has produced over the years. This idea speaks to the wasteful nature of the viewer's empirical world, thereby critiquing and cautioning. Again, however, there is a utopian impulse in the narrative that comes in the form of a lone plant that has managed to brave the conditions on the planet, suggesting that humanity too can persevere. With these hopeful elements despite seemingly hopeless conditions, *WALL-E* becomes a critical dystopia.

And so *WALL-E* fits in rather well with the critical dystopias of the 21st century that are influenced by the conditions of its contemporary moment. Each of these types of works pick their proverbial poison, and while *WALL-E* is critical on several different levels, it is especially interested in the environment — intentionally or not. From this film, the viewer might discover ways he or she might help make the future better instead of worse, and this is consistent with the utopian imagination — the manmade mess of the Earth in the 21st century needs cleaning if the planet is to survive, the hope for which must be retained at all costs.

NOTES

1. Still, Stanton also blames this on the fact that, "in zero gravity, osteoporosis kicks in — you start to have disuse atrophy ... your bones start to sort of deteriorate ... you would lose, eventually, almost all of your bone mass if you were out in zero gravity." This, he suggests, combined with "the lack of ever having to get up for anything," that is, "never needing to do anything for survival," leads to the atrophy of the spaceship passengers' bones.
2. Kenneth M. Roemer, "More Aliens Transforming Utopia: The Futures of Reader Response and Utopian Studies," in *Utopia Method Vision: The Use Value of Social Dreaming*, edited by Tom Moylan and Raffaella Baccolini (Bern, Switzerland: Peter Lang, 2007), 132.
3. M. Keith Booker, *Monsters, Mushroom Clouds, and the Cold War: American Science Fiction and the Roots of Postmodernism, 1946–1964* (Westport, CT: Greenwood Press, 2001), 3.
4. Tom Moylan, *Demand the Impossible: Science Fiction and the Utopian Imagination* (New York: Methuen, 1986), 10.
5. Tom Moylan, *Scraps of the Untainted Sky: Science Fiction, Utopia, Dystopia* (Boulder, CO: Westview Press, 2000), 186.
6. Moylan, *Demand*, 10.
7. Moylan, *Scraps*, 183–184.
8. Lyman Tower Sargent, "The Three Faces of Utopianism Revisited," *Utopian Studies* 5, no. 1 (1994): 3–4.
9. Lyman Tower Sargent, "US Eutopias in the 1980s and 1990s: Self-Fashioning in a World of Multiple Identities," in *Utopianism/Literary Utopias and National Cultural Identities: A Comparative Perspective*, edited by Paola Spinozzi (Bologna: COTEPRA/University of Bologna, 2001), 222.
10. Ibid.
11. The term "eutopia" means simply "good place" — a combination of the Greek words "eu" ("good") and "topos" ("place"). The title of Thomas More's *Utopia*— the work after which the utopian genre is named — is a pun built on the ambiguity achieved by combining "eu" and "ou" ("no" or "not") with "topos."
12. Moylan, *Scraps*, 194–195.

13. Roemer, 133.
14. Cheryll Glotfelty, "Introduction: Literary Studies in an Age of Environmental Crisis," in *The Ecocriticism Reader: Landmarks in Literary Ecology*, edited by Cheryll Glotfelty and Harold Fromm (Athens: University of Georgia Press, 1996), xvii–xx.
15. Donald Worster, *The Wealth of Nature: Environmental History and the Ecological Imagination* (New York: Oxford University Press, 1994), 27.
16. Ibid.
17. Ibid.
18. Douglas E. Booth, *Hooked on Growth: Economic Addictions and the Environment* (Lanham, MD: Rowman & Littlefield, 2004), ix.
19. Thomas Princen, Michael Maniantes, and Ken Conca, "Confronting Consumption," in *Confronting Consumption*, edited by Thomas Princen, Michael Maniates, and Ken Conca (Cambridge: The MIT Press, 2002), 5.
20. Fredric Jameson, *The Seeds of Time* (New York: Columbia University Press, 1994), 56.
21. Fredric Jameson, *Postmodernism, or, The Cultural Logic of Late Capitalism* (Durham, NC: Duke University Press, 1991), ix.
22. M. Keith Booker, *The Post-Utopian Imagination: American Culture in the Long 1950s* (Westport, CT: Greenwood Press, 2002), 5.
23. Fredric Jameson, "Marxism and Historicism," *New Literary History* 11, no. 1 (1979): 71.
24. Andrew Stanton commentary, *WALL-E*, DVD, directed by Andrew Stanton (2008; Burbank, CA: Disney DVD, 2008).
25. Ibid.
26. Ibid.
27. Ibid.
28. *WALL-E*, DVD, directed by Andrew Stanton (2008; Burbank, CA: Disney DVD, 2008).
29. Ibid.
30. Stanton commentary, *WALL-E*, DVD.
31. Ibid.
32. *WALL-E*, DVD.
33. Stanton commentary, *WALL-E*, DVD.
34. Ibid.
35. Ibid.
36. Ibid.
37. Ibid.
38. Ibid.
39. Ruth Levitas, *The Concept of Utopia* (Syracuse: Syracuse University Press, 1990), 195–96.
40. Ibid., 196.
41. Ibid., 181.
42. Ibid., 196.
43. M. Keith Booker, *Dystopian Literature: A Theory and Research Guide* (Westport, CT: Greenwood Press, 1994), 3.
44. Sargent, "Three Faces," 25.
45. Raffaella Baccolini and Tom Moylan, "Introduction: Dystopia and Histories," in *Dark Horizons: Science Fiction and the Dystopian Imagination*, edited by Raffaella Baccolini and Tom Moylan (New York: Routledge, 2003), 8.
46. Ibid., 7.
47. Stanton.
48. Ibid.
49. Ibid.
50. Ibid.
51. *WALL-E*, DVD.
52. Ibid.
53. Ibid.
54. Stanton commentary, *WALL-E*, DVD.
55. Ibid.
56. Ibid.

REFERENCES

Baccolini, Raffaella, and Tom Moylan. "Introduction: Dystopia and Histories." In *Dark Horizons: Science Fiction and the Dystopian Imagination*, edited by Raffaella Baccolini and Tom Moylan, 1–12. New York: Routledge, 2003.
Booker, M. Keith. *Dystopian Literature: A Theory and Research Guide*. Westport, CT: Greenwood Press, 1994.
_____. *Monsters, Mushroom Clouds, and the Cold War: American Science Fiction and the Roots of Postmodernism, 1946–1964*. Westport, CT: Greenwood Press, 2001.
_____. *The Post-Utopian Imagination: American Culture in the Long 1950s*. Westport, CT: Greenwood Press, 2002.
Booth, Douglas E. *Hooked on Growth: Economic Addictions and the Environment*. Lanham, MD: Rowman & Littlefield, 2004.
Glotfelty, Cheryll. "Introduction: Literary Studies in an Age of Environmental Crisis." In *The Ecocriticism Reader: Landmarks in Literary Ecology*. Edited by Cheryll Glotfelty and Harold Fromm, xv–xxxvii. Athens: University of Georgia Press, 1996.
Jameson, Fredric. "Marxism and Historicism." *New Literary History* 11, no. 1 (1979): 41–73.
_____. *Postmodernism, or, The Cultural Logic of Late Capitalism*. Durham, NC: Duke University Press, 1991.
_____. *The Seeds of Time*. New York: Columbia University Press, 1994.
Levitas, Ruth. *The Concept of Utopia*. Syracuse, NY: Syracuse University Press, 1990.
Moylan, Tom. *Demand the Impossible: Science Fiction and the Utopian Imagination*. New York: Methuen, 1986.
_____. *Scraps of the Untainted Sky: Science Fiction, Utopia, Dystopia*. Boulder, CO: Westview Press, 2000.
Princen, Thomas, Michael Maniantes, and Ken Conca. "Confronting Consumption." In *Confronting Consumption*, edited by Thomas Princen, Michael Maniates, and Ken Conca, 1–20. Cambridge: The MIT Press, 2002.
Roemer, Kenneth M. "More Aliens Transforming Utopia: The Futures of Reader Response and Utopian Studies." In *Utopia Method Vision: The Use Value of Social Dreaming*, edited by Tom Moylan and Raffaella Baccolini, 131–158. Bern, Switzerland: Peter Lang, 2007.
Sargent, Lyman Tower. "The Three Faces of Utopianism Revisited." *Utopian Studies* 5, no. 1 (1994): 1–37.
_____. "US Eutopias in the 1980s and 1990s: Self-Fashioning in a World of Multiple Identities." In *Utopianism/Literary Utopias and National Cultural Identities: A Comparative Perspective*, edited by Paola Spinozzi, 221–233. Bologna: COTEPRA/University of Bologna, 2001.
Stanton, Andrew. "Director's Commentary." *WALL-E*. DVD. Directed by Andrew Stanton. 2008. Burbank, CA: Disney DVD, 2008.
WALL-E. DVD. Directed by Andrew Stanton. 2008. Burbank, CA: Disney DVD, 2008.
Worster, Donald. *The Wealth of Nature: Environmental History and the Ecological Imagination*. New York: Oxford University Press, 1994.

• *Sixteen* •

A Bumbling Bag of Ball Bearings: *Lost in Space* and the Space Race

Jonathan Cohn

Beginning in the middle of the Cold War, *Lost in Space* (1965–1968) owed much of its popularity along with its very existence to the Space Race. While filled with a certain degree of patriotic fervor, the series was not simply an hour-long advertisement for this international contest. In fact, it was often critical of the way in which the Space Race melded politics with scientific ventures to a degree that other series in the same vein, like *I Dream of Jeannie* or *Bewitched* did not. At times, the popularity of the series was actually viewed as a hindrance to keeping the American public interested and engaged with the patriotic discourses and daily news concerning actual astronauts and their real space adventures.

Indeed, on March 16, 1966, an episode of *Lost in Space* was pre-empted by coverage of the Gemini 8 space mission, which was rapidly spiraling out of control because of a misfiring thruster. The next day, one CBS station received 160 complaints from viewers who were disappointed because they were not able to see their favorite show.[1] This event was later brought up in July of that year at the 58th National Governors Conference, during which Erwin Canham, the editor of *The Christian Science Monitor*, told the governors that it is the "prime responsibility of the press ... to inform people; not by 'just reporting the bare facts of events' ... but by putting 'the news in some sort of analytical perspective....'" William H. Lawrence, the White House correspondent for the American Broadcasting Company responded by saying that he agreed, "but the problem springs from the human beast,"—in other words, the viewer. He then referenced the Gemini 8 event as proof that the "the human beast" was only interested in the "fictional 'Lost In Space,'" and not the "real people lost in space."[2]

However, *Lost in Space* and other fictional series like it did provide an important though imperfect "sort of analytical perspective" on the Space Race. Throughout its impressive three year run *Lost in Space* helped its largely juvenile audience explore and make sense of the Space Race and its possible effects on their everyday lives. While none of the various plots in *Lost in Space* focused on the Gemini 8 or any other specific NASA missions, the series did continually discuss, celebrate and at times criticize the possible effect that new space-age technologies might have on a wide range of contemporary social issues. In the process, *Lost in Space* showed how the space race and our relationship to technology and exploration could affect our understanding of what it meant to be not just American, but also "human," who and/or what could be referred to as such, and what qualities constitute what it means to be "humane." Indeed, *Lost in Space* critiqued space race rhetoric on a weekly basis in order show how the colonial rhetoric that surrounded it and the technologies that were emerging from it were radically affecting the constitution of American identity as well as the American dream.

The series focused on the Robinson family along with a few other assorted characters, including a comic villain, Dr. Zachary Smith (Jonathan Harris) and the B-9 robot who had aspirations of experiencing emotions and becoming more like his human cohabitants. For the entirety of the series, these voyagers spend their time exploring (and more often than not, crashing into) the planets that they stumble upon while trying unsuccessfully not to annoy the local inhabitants. Fights break out on the show continually between the Robinsons and the aliens, robots and space-vagabonds of unknown origins that they come across, often as a result of either cross-cultural misunderstandings, Dr. Smith's meddling, or of one of the crew members wandering too far away from the ship and into a variety of perilous situations. These confrontations force the Robinsons to question their position as humans within the universe and challenge their perspective and values in light of their meetings with others who are often both smarter and stronger.

Like much of the science-fiction (sf) television of the era, *Lost in Space* has been discussed as a series which arose from, encouraged, and simulated the political rhetoric of the Space Race.[3] However, newspaper articles and advertisements from the period show that it was read in part as political camp in direct opposition to the rhetoric of NASA. By camp, I am referring to both the show's intentionally (and at times seemingly unintentionally) corny plots and style along with the desire this kitsch effect imparts on the viewer to look for and generate alternate readings of the text. Thus, many mutually constitutive discourses exist and are important within the series. These discourses on the related issues of colonialism, new technologies and the American dream served in part to undermine the xenophobic space race rhetoric of the period.

Starting in September of 1965 and running until March of 1968, *Lost in Space* premiered at the height of the Space Race. On May 25, 1961, four years after the Soviets beat the United States to space with Sputnik, John F. Kennedy pledged to have a man on the moon within ten years. This decision was explicitly framed to Congress as an important step in preserving freedom and ridding the world of Soviet tyranny while also cementing the United States' position as not just "a world leader" but "the world leader."[4] After being bested by the Soviets in science, Americans needed a new utopian dream, which they found in Kennedy's New Frontier of space. In his historic 1962 speech at Rice University, Kennedy compared venturing into space to various other world-changing events like the beginning of Christianity, the creation of the printing press and Newton's articulation of gravity. Like these other events, Kennedy felt, the introduction of space travel "cannot help but create new ills as it dispels old, new ignorance, new problems, new dangers. Surely the opening vistas of space promise high costs and hardships as well as high reward."[5] He spoke of America's dual need to be both the first to "conquer space" while also ensuring that it become a sea of peace rather than a "terrifying theater of war."

This contradiction between viewing space as both a place to conquer and colonize while also imagining it as a place of freedom and peace guided much of the overall plot of *Lost in Space*. As Lynn Spigel explains in her essay "From Domestic Space to Outer Space," "the construction of the New Frontier was largely accomplished through media discourses that envisioned new and potent ways to organize past experiences."[6] This new rhetoric was capitalized upon by both the Kennedy administration and television itself, which was suffering from a barrage of critics who believed that its content had decreased in quality. The networks began creating longer news segments and documentaries that focused mainly on creating and sustaining an excitement for the "space-age metaphors, that were based on the tenets of progress, democracy and national freedom" that they helped to generate.[7] These new trends greatly affected those science-fiction and fantasy series that aimed for a mixed audience of adults and children, which critics often felt were too silly for adults, but too scary or serious for children.

With the sudden explosion of "real" nonfiction stories about the space race, it was inevitable that the networks would start creating fictional shows to accompany them.[8] As one *LA Times* reporter pointed out, "With all the hoopla over space men and their achievements, it was only a matter of time before the television programmers would build a series around astronauts."[9] *Lost in Space*, along with *I Dream of Jeannie* followed *Bewitched* as the two newest members of what Spigel has called "the fantastic family sitcom, a hybrid genre that mixed conventions of the suburban sit-com past with the space-age imagery of the New Frontier."[10] While *Lost in Space* is closer in form to a children's action/adventure drama than a sit-com, it does mix the domestic space with that of the New Frontier and encourages an awareness of and interest in the American space program.

The series was created by Irwin Allen, a television and film producer who is known for his disaster and epic films like *Voyage to the Bottom of the Sea* (1964), *The Poseidon Adventure* (1972), and *The Towering Inferno* (1974). Many of his films include struggles between humans and their encounters with an unsustainable world that they had built up around themselves. These struggles were often caused by an often particularly life-threatening desire to colonize and explore their hazardous surroundings. His shows also dealt with this colonialist impulse and other contemporary issues in an entertaining, middle to low-brow, big-budget way.

Lost in Space was Allen's second TV series and ran from 7:30–8:30 P.M. on Wednesday nights during CBS's comedy night schedule, which also included *The Beverly Hillbillies*, *Green Acres*, *The Dick Van Dyke Show*, and *The Danny Kaye Show*. In a *Variety* advertisement for the CBS lineup, *Lost in Space* was billed as a "delightful and exciting spoof on SF involving a modern family marooned on an unknown planet."[11] This classification of it as a "spoof" both groups it with the latest sf shows of the time (which were by and large the fantastic sitcoms), and encourages a campy reading of the show as playing against both this latest genre hybrid and specifically the ways in which they normalized the nuclear family and American dream. While it is true that Allen did not originally envision the show as a spoof, the first screening of the pilot, which featured a serious soundtrack by John (then Johnnie) Williams and a dearth of jokes, was nonetheless greeted with hysterical laughter from CBS executives.[12]

Lost in Space thus began as a deeply polysemic text, with at least two dominant readings: one of the show as a serious sf action adventure, and one of the show as making fun of this genre by seemingly exaggerating the earnestness and sobriety that are often central to sf. After Dr. Smith was added post-pilot, the show became even campier and the serious reading of the show became slowly obscured. Whether intentionally or not, by presenting these multiple meanings and by satirizing the fantastic sitcoms and their goal of bringing together domesticity and space travel, *Lost in Space* also engages in a larger critique of the Space Race, which the popular sf of the time largely supported.

This reading is further influenced by its hour-long, action adventure format. Unlike the shorter sitcoms, which had a closed form that finished a plot in every episode, the structure of *Lost in Space* was based on a long lineage of weekly serials like *Flash Gordon*, which had a much more open form. Although only few of the show's plots continue through more than one episode, the last ten minutes of every episode was devoted to introducing the next episode's plot and whatever terror might befall the poor Robinsons in a week's time. Theoretically, the audience would spend that week agonizing over how Penny (Angela Cartwright), the youngest daughter, would get away from the evil monster or whether Will (Bill Mumy), the adolescent son, would finally die after fiddling with the lightning bolt machine one too many times. Like the many movie and television serials that came before *Lost in Space*, a sense of dread stayed with the Robinsons throughout the entire series and beyond since the last show, having been cancelled, also ended on a cliffhanger. The following episode would always contain the last few minutes of the last show, to catch viewers up on the plot. Then the beginning credits would run, with Johnnie William's exciting score in the background.

By connecting the individual shows together through an endless series of cliffhangers, this dramatic serial style allowed the issues the show addressed to spill over into the rest of the week. These cliffhanger moments turned what might have been isolated death-defying, though campy, incidents into a sustained critique of space as a terrible place where there is always at least one, and usually twenty monsters behind every rock. This challenges television's main discourse of space as an amazing place worth exploring and bringing into your home. Even the title, *Lost in Space*, which was constantly repeated by the announcer, implies that space is not simply a goal, which you win like a race, but rather a huge labyrinth with a three-headed laser-eyed dog at the exit.

While on their search, the Robinsons surrounded themselves with many of the most common trappings of American domesticity, and in the process, this way of life begins to look very strange and inappropriate. This is in contrast to Spigel's "Fantastic Sit-Coms," which brought the fantasy and sf into the house instead of the house into a sf landscape. The 1950's American dream of moving to a suburb and owning a house is made farcical by placing this house on a barren and destitute planet many light-years from Earth. *Lost in Space* becomes a parodic and at times absurdist rendering of suburban sprawl, complete with what the mother, Maureen Robinson (June Lockhart) refers to as her "space washing machine," which conveniently looks the same as one you might have bought at Sears at the time. This machine usually sits in the background as the Robinsons run into any of a number of "space" people, such as "space hillbillies" or "space hippies," while they eat their "space salad" with "space dressing." The "space washing machine" is positioned outside of the spaceship, parked on foreign desert landscapes like a Winnebago which has run out of gas. Even with such appliances, Lockhart, who had previously co-starred on *Lassie* (1954), looks much more foreign against this landscape than the magical women featured in *Bewitched* or *I Dream of Jeannie* ever does. Her character, placed within a world where she looks ridiculous, denaturalizes suburban culture.

This ability to denaturalize those values and ideas which are often taken for granted has long been thought to be a central trait of the science-fiction genre. In the influential book *Metamorphoses of Science Fiction*, Darko Suvin praises this aspect and declares sf to be "the *literature of cognitive estrangement*."[13] Suvin takes the idea of "estrangement" from Bertolt Brecht, who defines it as:

> "a representation which estranges is one which allows us to recognize its subject, but at the same time makes it seem unfamiliar." And further: for somebody to see all normal happenings in a dubious light, "he would need to develop that detached eye with which the great Galileo observed a swinging chandelier. He was amazed by that pendulum motion as if he had not expected it and could not understand its occurring, and this enabled him to come at the rules by which it was governed." Thus, the look of estrangement is both cognitive and creative; and as Brecht goes on to say, "one cannot simply exclaim that such an attitude pertains to science, but not to art. Why should not art, in its own way, try to serve the great social task of mastering Life?"[14]

For Suvin, sf provided a space from which to challenge the most common sense ideas of one's contemporary period. In contrast to the myth, which "claims to explain once and for all the essence of phenomena, SF first posits them as problems and then explores where they lead; it sees the mythical static identity as an illusion, usually as fraud, at best only as a temporary realization of potentially limitless contingencies."[15] By defining sf in this way, Suvin and later Fredric Jameson point to the ways in which sf should "stage an implicit debate with the objections and ideological and political prejudices of its readers."[16] In their view, one of the primary purposes of all sf is to put under an analytical gaze those things which at one point or another were thought of as common sense, as those things which go without saying.[17] For Galileo, this was the swinging of the chandelier. For the Robinsons, it was the American dream.

This cognitively estranging effect, which often manifests itself through a quality of camp, is present from the first pilot episode on and was generally aimed at critiquing the way American lives would change as a result of the space race. The series begins with shots of the Robinson Family, which was chosen above over two million volunteers for their intelligence and strength to lead the first colonial expedition to Alpha Centauri (in the distant, distant future of 1997), which is believed to be the closest habitable planet. This episode starts in a NASA control center, with an announcer's voice (Richard

Tufeld) proclaiming that "This is the beginning, this is the day. You are watching the unfolding of one of history's greatest adventures: man's colonization of space, beyond the stars!" Quickly the announcer makes it clear that Earth has become desperately overpopulated and colonization is humanity's only hope.

Susan Sontag sees this tactic in other sf films and refers to it as giving the mission and space technology "the certificate of utility," which is needed for a "scientific enterprise to be treated entirely sympathetically" by the audience.[18] This is in opposition to space race rhetoric, which as an enterprise did not have an obvious tangible utility, except to beat the Soviets and perhaps also explore. In comparison to the more tangible, though often racist and egotistical goal of colonization, which has a utility of sorts, the U.S. Space mission seems more like a "disinterested intellectual curiosity" which "rarely appears in any form other than caricature, as a maniacal dementia...."[19] Even though *Lost in Space* was certainly part of the rhetoric that brought space into focus for Americans, by showing a utilitarian image of space travel that did not match the messages from the Johnson White House, this series encouraged a discussion about exactly what the purpose of the space program (with its large costs) was and should be.

However, the way the program presents this discussion is problematic, as it poses colonialism as the logical reason for space travel. The voyagers of *Lost in Space* certainly mean well and are at least in the beginning fighting for the survival of humanity, but they still spend each episode killing those monsters and animals which they stumble upon, while also disrupting the day-to-day lives of those they encounter. In sf generally, when the colonists are aliens, the colonial impulse is virtually always presented as a terrifying threat to Earth and/or humanity and while the Robinson's colonialism is treated with a sense of understanding of the series, when aliens try to colonize planets, they are treated as a savage threat. In a first season episode titled "The Sky Is Falling," the Robinson's confront a family of aliens who appear to be only the first of many of their species to begin the process of colonizing the planet the Robinson's have crashed onto. The Robinson's cannot understand the aliens, and when Will disappears and the aliens start shooting at them, they fear for the worst. In the end, they realize that Will and the aliens' son have run off together and they both eventually return to their parents, but not before they realize that if they cannot create a sense of what they refer to as "universal brotherhood" very quickly, "before long there will be thousands of them down here. This is our only chance of survival!" Luckily, the crisis is suddenly averted in a nonsensically campy way when the aliens mysteriously teleport off the planet and off the series, never to be seen again.

While the series originally presented colonialism from the colonizer's perspective, as a necessity for the growth and survival of the species, this episode suddenly displays it from the viewpoint of the colonized. The aliens do not mean any harm, but just by arriving, they become a threat to the Robinsons' existence. This threat as colonists is compounded by their superior technology and firepower, makes the humans suddenly realize that they are no longer the highest step on the evolutionary ladder or even the masters of their domain. In the process, the aliens' arrival and their new technologies begins to shift the very definition of what it means to be human as we cease to be the privileged species. The Robinsons' only recourse is to appeal to a notion of "universal brotherhood," presumably the idea that everyone is equal and worthy of compassion, regardless of their differences. At points like this, the estrangement of space is doubled as the alien encounter denaturalizes not just the common logics that people on Earth use to justify their position within the world, but also the logics that the Robinson's use within the series.

This logic of estrangement can be seen throughout the series and even into the design of the ship that the Robinsons flew, to the disappointment of NASA. Unlike the NASA Gemini and Apollo spaceships, which tended to look like missiles, the Robinson's ship was shaped like a Roswellian UFO. This type of spacecraft appears in countless films, not as a spaceship used by humans, but is instead iconic of the colonizing alien invader. While Allen and NASA originally intended to work together to promote both the space program and "TV's first prime time space opera," NASA quickly realized that Allen was not interested in "science and logic." In other words, Allen was not interested in using *Lost in Space* simply as an advertisement for NASA's brand of "logic" that supported the space race. The partnership did not continue past the first episodes of the series. Chris Craft, the architect of NASA's Mission Control Station and its first flight director, looked at the plans for the Robinson's ship and said it "would never fly." Allen responded by saying: "One hundred years ago, they were saying the same things about your rockets."[20] By not using a design more similar to the NASA spacecrafts, like other shows and films were using at the time, there is an implicit challenge being made to NASA's brand of spaceflight through even the imagery of the series.

This desire to challenge the reasoning behind the space race can be clearly seen even in the pilot episode of *Lost in Space*, "The Reluctant Stowaway," which presents a conflicting discourse concerning the effect of space missions on the world community. First, a long table is shown in the mission control headquarters with a large multicultural cast sitting behind it, reporting on the mission. This opening scene is an attempt to show that the world is "watching" what is happening, and therefore has a stake in it and is part of the community that the space mission is symbolically representing. This sequence was also used in the promotional tape that CBS sent to its affiliates, re-edited to make it seem that the world was waiting and watching for the show, *Lost in Space*, and this representation of a collegial world that it was symbolically creating.[21] This image places the United States as the super power whom all other nations should follow, but the series also attempts to display a world based on principles of collaboration rather than antagonism.

However, this desire to display a united world is countered throughout the rest of the series by the inclusion of an almost entirely homogenous white American cast. The aliens, creatures, and even robots that they come across are virtually always played by noticeably white Americans who only wear a scant amount of makeup and costume to signal their difference from the Robinsons. While such casting choices are inarguably racist and have historically lead to a dearth of roles for people of color on television, they at the same time create a great degree of cognitive estrangement and campy flavor concerning the characters from week to week. While these characters that the Robinsons meet often look and behave like the Robinsons, as white middle class American nuclear families, the series continually asks its audience to think of them as similar to their American counterparts, though they obey a slightly different set of rules and ethics. This is most evident in their often decidedly anti–Robinson (and anti–American) objectives. As a result, these alien characters often personify America's enemy, the Soviets of the era, even as they appear and sound like Americans. As Brecht and later Suvin have argued, this technique of placing the normal in a strange background is often useful for bringing to light the rules and ideologies that govern what we take as being normal. While perhaps not intentional, by having white Americans play every character regardless of what background (whether actual or metaphoric) they are supposed to have, the supposed differences between the Americans and Soviets, as well as the basis for the Cold War are questioned as both sides are made to look the same.

Even with this sense of homogeneity, the character of Dr. Smith seems to clearly be a caricature of a Soviet spy. Strangely, Dr. Smith is identified not as a Soviet, but as a spy from an "unidentified competing country" in the first aired episode in which he manages to thwart the Robinson's mission. There is nothing particularly Soviet about him except his vague European accent, which is enough to tie him to the long lineage of Soviet spy caricatures most commonly seen in James Bond films. This image of Dr. Smith trying to destroy the Robinson's ship is in direct competition with that of the table of world correspondents and expresses the world as not a community, but as a group excluded from the American New Frontier. This is the image that is most clearly created via NASA's politicized space race that created opposition between nations that could have and should have been helping each other.

Although he starts out the series as a somewhat menacing villain that is a genuine threat to America's supremacy, he quickly becomes more comical and silly. However, this change does not stop his greed and idiocy from continually putting the Robinsons and himself in mortal peril. His character became continually campier and was featured in the *LA Times* next to the Penguin (Bergess Meredith) from *Batman* and The Commandant (Werner Klemperor) from *Hogan's Heroes* as one of the three "nicest villains you'll ever meet."[22] Even though CBS specifically requested that Smith be made into a "citizen of the world working for the highest bidder" whose "villainy does not express a personal viewpoint but is done rather for money," any spy or saboteur in this period would have likely been from Americas sworn enemy, the USSR.[23] This character, along with the Robot B-9,[24] was added after the first pilot was shot by the express orders of the CBS network.[25] This is an important change, as in the pilot episode, the space crash is caused by a natural meteor shower, which the Robinson's were unable to avoid. In the first aired episode, this cause is changed to Dr. Smith, who creates the space crash himself. This change makes the Soviet's and other unfriendly earthly foreigners seem more dangerous while simultaneously making space seem much safer.

However, the choice to add Dr. Smith points to ways in which the politics of the space race made the science and exploratory process much more dangerous. The hurry to launch a ship to the moon before the Soviets do created anxiety in the American public, especially after the Vanguard I crash in 1957, just three months after the successful launching of Sputnik. While this competition made the exploration of space possible, it also created an environment in which this exploration was much more dangerous than it needed to be, and did nothing to relieve anyone of their fears of this new and explosive technology. The politics of the Space Race made the use of such technology even more dangerous than it already was. Even as Dr. Smith's character changes to a bumbling idiot, he is still able to turn machines into deadly weapons simply by pushing all the buttons he can find regardless of whether he knows what they do or not.

Dr. Smith's constant fumblings with B-9, the Environmental Control Robot, show the extreme extent to which technology in this series was not just central to the Robinsons' well-being but was also what led to many of the near-fatal confrontations. B-9 was designed by Robert Kinoshita, who also made Robby, the robot from *Forbidden Planet* (1956). Like Robby, B-9 is an extremely wry, intelligent robot, who constantly bickers and jokes with Dr. Smith. Its somewhat ambiguous status as the Environmental Control Robot signifies both that it holds a great deal of power over the rest of the crew and that its existence is central to their well-being. By using the unseen announcer's voice of Richard Tufeld for the Robot's voice, the series reinforces the idea that B-9 is central to and in control of the show's narrative.

This central position of technology is common to many sf films from the 1950's and early 1960's (as well as today), as Sontag points out:

A greater range of ethical values is embodied in the décor of these films than in the people. Things [technology], rather than the helpless humans are the locus of values because we experience them, rather than people, as the sources of power. According to science fiction films, man is naked without his artifacts. They stand for different values, they are potent, they are what get destroyed, and they are the indispensable tools for the repulse of the alien invaders or the repair of the damaged environment.[26]

While *Lost in Space* certainly invests the "artifact" of B-9 as a foci of power and control within the series, B-9 is not simply a static object that stands for a particular value. Instead, it is a robot with a certain degree of intelligence, though one that is easily and constantly manipulated and reprogrammed.

With each reprogramming, B-9's status as a tool suitable for the space race and the American values it stands for completely change, and instead the robot becomes an illustration of how easily values can shift and discourses evolve within a highly politicized society. In the third episode of the series, "There Were Giants in the Earth,"[27] Will tries to repair the robot late at night and it runs off soon after. His father, John Robinson (Guy Williams), scolds Will and tells him that "with a little patience and a little time we could have reprogrammed the robot to do its job, but because you acted without thought or permission we lost a valuable piece of equipment that we need very greatly." B-9 is made to embody the "ethical values" of those who control it. It takes the side and does the job of whoever has programmed it last. If Dr. Smith programmed B-9, it will do evil, and if the Robinsons have, it does good. This thought is echoed in Vivian Sobchack's essay, "Images of Wonder," wherein she references how unlike the visual icons of Westerns and other genres, robots "do not communicate by [their] standard physical presence a constant and specific cluster of meanings throughout" the sf genre.[28] This fluidity of meaning is even apparent from week to week on *Lost In Space*, as the Robot repeatedly changes his allegiances and feelings, depending on whether Dr. Smith has "reprogrammed" him lately.

While the gigantic computers with glowing buttons and teletype printouts created during the space race were portrayed as cold and logical, B-9 is often shown to be extremely emotional. His values may shift and mirror those of whom he is with, his blank robotic, tool-like demeanor is often complicated and contradicted by other aspects of the series that explore B-9's humanity. While the Robinsons often discuss humanity as being privileged over robotic creations because it possesses free will, emotions and the ability to differentiate good from evil, B-9 still often seems to possess an underlying ethical personality of its own. It does not want to perform the evil acts but has to, and its repulsion is expressed only in its witty wordplay. For instance, in "Return from Outer Space,"[29] a first season episode, Dr. Smith says to the Robot, "I should like to hear a brief but compelling statement on the starry character of Dr Smith." The Robot responds with its overly repeated catch phrase: "Does not compute." It is within this witty banter that the morality of the series is located. B-9 intrinsically seems to know the difference between right and wrong and desires to act positively, but because it must always follow commands, this is not always possible.

Throughout *Lost in Space,* the role of technology constantly shifts. Sometimes its purpose is to protect the nuclear family and stand for the ideals of the American dream. Other times its only desire to kill this family with a laser beam. While Michael Ryan and Douglas Kellner believe that in sf, "technology must seem to be intrinsically evil, and this is so if the natural alternatives to technological society — the family and the individual especially — are to seem inherently good,"[30] there is nothing "intrinsic" about the technology in *Lost in Space*. The appearance of an opposition between family and technology in a film for them is a sign of an inherently conservative ideology. Unlike *Lost in Space* and other elements of sf that try to challenge dominant ideology and those things that are taken for granted, these elements of conservative sf serve to uphold common American ideals like the nuclear family by proposing that they are "natural." Thus, they are presented as being ahistorical values that everyone at all times have shared and are thereby beyond critique and are not to be challenged.

While *Lost in Space* certainly celebrates many American values through the example of the Robinsons, the presence of B-9 as a piece of technology that always seems to be more ethical and humane than those humans who surround it undermines the notion that any human value is "natural." The continual reprogramming of B-9 from episode to episode has the effect of making the estranging and deconstructive aspects of the series especially obvious. This is not to say that B-9 is perfect, but rather that it always attempts to be ethically "good," though it does not always reach this goal. It makes mistakes and learns, like many of the human characters, and its humanness is often referred to, challenged, and praised.

Furthermore, the status of B-9 changes throughout the series, and by the third season, it is no longer continually reprogrammed but instead is allowed to choose whom it will obey. This presents a fundamental shift in how the series presents the concept of what it means to be a robot and therefore also what it means to be human. In effect, B-9 has successfully gained intelligence and free will, and those distinctions that exist between humans and robots begin to fall apart. Instead of being simply terrified by this prospect, the series presents both the utopian and dystopian elements of such a change. B-9, on its own, always uses his new free will to help (and often save) the Robinsons from themselves as they are often getting themselves into trouble through their misguided explorations and colonial instincts. In effect, B-9 becomes a technology that is better at the human goal of self-preservation and at being generally humane than any of the humans on the series, who are more often worried about upholding specifically American values and space race goals.

In "War of the Robots,"[31] an episode from the first season before B-9 obtained the ability to resist direct commands and reprogramming from those around him, this question of free will in the face of competing ideologies and in respect to robots is examined. Will stumbles upon a deserted robot and decides to try to repair it. B-9 gets very upset at this and tries to explain that the robot (Robbie, from *Forbidden Planet*) is actually a robotoid: "A robot is a machine which performs as programmed. A Robotoid is a machine which goes beyond programming. It has a free choice." By "free choice," B-9 is clearly referring to only the negative and destructive connotations of this term. Will does not share in B-9's terror of a robot with free choice, and retorts with, "No, I know what's wrong with you, you're jealous." B-9 replies, "I am not jealous, it is a human emotion," and then repeats louder, "I AM NOT jealous, it is a HUMAN EMOTION!" This change of tone implies that B-9 does in fact have emotions and perhaps is jealous of the robotoid. However, unlike a human, while he can voice these emotions, he cannot directly act on them.

His fears of the robotoid are well-founded, as the first thing it does after being turned on, is shoot a laser out of its chest to blow up a tree. The robotoid then spends the rest of the episode trying to trick the Robinsons into being captured by its real masters, an evil group of alien travelers that want to "collect" them. While it appears to have the capacity for free choice and therefore be closer to human, the Robotoid stays extremely loyal to its master in the same way that B-9 stays loyal to the Robinsons. The Robotoid is repeatedly referenced throughout the show as being more advanced than B-9 both because of its free choice and its fancy weaponry. The free choice, however, is definitely the more dangerous of the two upgrades, as it allows the robot to be deceitful and trick the Robinsons.

However, this fear of advanced technology is challenged by the end of the episode, as the roles of the robots are reversed. While the Robotoid seems to be following its free choice, it is actually still following its true master's directives. In the process, the question arises as to what free choice actually consists of and whether there is any difference between the free choice that humans are thought to have and the free choice that cyborgs and this Robotoid could possess. The audience is asked to judge whether B-9 should blame the Robotoid for its evil qualities, or its alien masters who programmed and to some extent control it.

At the end of the episode, B-9 shows that it, too, is capable of the same level of free choice, as it repeatedly does not listen to the Robotoid's voice to "move back," which allows it to get close enough to destroy the evil bot. The quality of free choice, which both makes them more human, and potentially more dangerous, also allows for B-9 to help what the series repeatedly refers to as its "fellow crewmembers." When B-9 gets upset after being referred to as not a human by Dr. Smith and Will tries to cheer him up, he replies coldly by saying, "You forget that a robot has no heart. I am only wires and cold metal parts," and thus does not need to be reassured. Then Will says, "You are more than a machine, you are our friend," to which B-9 quietly, as if it might cry, says, "My computers are deeply affected." While this is a very silly moment, it does show how even if B-9 is not human, it is in many ways depicted as being equivalent to one.

Thus the breakdown of the distinction between humans and machines is shown to be inevitable and within this human-robot dialectic, a liminal space is formed. Donna Haraway, in her essay "A Manifesto for Cyborgs," argues that the continuing and inevitable connection between the human, animal, and machine is a liberalizing force because it implies "transgressed boundaries, potent fusions and dangerous possibilities, which progressive people might explore as one part of needed political work."[32] This "political work" is first and foremost concerned with reshaping American identity away from the idea that there is one singular unifying American dream and towards one where there are many American dreams, each valid and in dialog with each other. For her, and I would argue *Lost in Space*, by becoming comfortable with our cybernetic future of liminality, we are also becoming "not afraid of permanently partial identities and contradictory standpoints,"[33] which, to her, is essential to the breaking down of currently cemented conservative binaries. These binaries serve only to separate humans from both robotic technologies as well as other species, and in the process they enforce a distinction between what can be considered natural and what is artificial. The cyborg's existence avoids established oppositions, such as the human and the machine, emotion and rationality, free will and programmable control. By challenging these distinctions between B-9 and the rest of the crew,[34] *Lost in Space* is engaging in a dialogue "resolutely committed to partiality, irony, intimacy and perversity," which to Haraway, is what the cyborg stands for.[35] Importantly, similar to the goals of cognitive estrangement, "perversity" here refers to the desire to deliberately depict something in a way that is deemed socially unacceptable in order to question and undermine the standards by which something is able to become acceptable. Through such perversions of the American dream and space race rhetoric, B-9 and *Lost in Space* open up the possibilities of what it means to be American and what the American dream can consist of.

In July of 1969, "millions of Americans [sat] before their television sets, with a gleam of hope and a beer can in hand, awaiting ... the realization of a decade-long dream, the biggest crowd pleaser in television memory."[36] However, this dream did not continue past the first trip to the moon. Whether this was due to a national feeling that they had accomplished what they set out to do in space by beating the Soviets to the moon, or rather to a growing pessimism concerning the difficulty and benefits of space travel in general, the funding quickly began to dissipate for NASA, and its far-flung dreams of exploring the universe have not yet come to pass. *Lost in Space* showed that while the Space Race was fueled and caused by a political rivalry that has on many occasions threatened to blow up the world, it also generated a profound desire to look beyond such feuding toward the positive benefits that space age technologies could foster. Such changes importantly include the decline of the American dream as a static and monolithic entity and the creation of B-9's dream of liminality and respect.

NOTES

1. See "Space Fiction Tops the Real Thing," *Los Angeles Times,* March 17, 1966, 9.
2. David S. Broder, "Governors Support Vietnam Policy," *New York Times,* July 8, 1966, 1.
3. For one instance of this rhetoric, see "Television's Race for Space — and Ratings," *Los Angeles Times,* August 15, 1965, L3. Also, while Lynn Spigel does not extensively write about *Lost in Space* in her article, "From Domestic Space to Outer Space: The 1960's Fantastic Family Sit-Com," in *Close Encounters: Film, Feminism, and Science Fiction,* edited by Constance Penley, Elisabeth Lyon, Lynn Spigel, and Janet Bergstrom (Minneapolis: University of Minnesota Press, 1991), included is a picture of the Robinson's and the suggestion that it was part of television's move to discuss and promote the space race.
4. John F. Kennedy, "'Man on the Moon' Speech to Congress," http://www.presentation-magazine.com/kennedy_man_on_the_moon_speech.htm.
5. John F. Kennedy, "We Choose to Go to the Moon...," http://www.historyplace.com/speeches/jfk-space.htm.
6. Lynn Spigel, "From Domestic Space to Outer Space: The 1960's Fantastic Family Sit-Com," 210.
7. Ibid., 211–12.
8. While there were many "fantastic sit-coms" throughout the early 1960s, they rarely dealt so specifically with the space race and the lives of astronauts, but instead focused on the invasion of the fantastic into the household.
9. "Television's Race for Space — and Ratings," L3.
10. Spigel, "From Domestic Space to Outer Space: The 1960's Fantastic Family Sit-Com," 205.
11. "Hey Look, CBS Advertisement," *Variety Weekly,* Sept. 15, 1965, 50.
12. Mark Phillips and Frank Garcia, "Lost in Space," in *Science Fiction Television Series: Episode Guides, Histories, and Casts and Credits for 62 Primetime Shows, 1959 through 1989* (Jefferson, NC: McFarland, 1996), 185.
13. Darko Suvin, *Metamorphoses of Science Fiction: Studies in the Poetics and History of Cognitive Estrangement in Fiction* (New Haven, CT: Yale University Press, 1978).
14. Ibid.
15. Ibid., 7.
16. Ibid., 410.
17. See Fredric Jameson, *Archaeologies of the Future: The Desire Called Utopia and Other Science Fictions* (New York: Verso, 2005), 270: "One of the most significant potentialities of SF

as a form is precisely this capacity to provide something like an experimental variation on our own empirical universe...."

18. Susan Sontag, "The Imagination of Disaster," in *Liquid Metal: The Science Fiction Film Reader*, edited by Sean Redmond (New York: Wallflower Press, 2004), 43.

19. Ibid.

20. Mark Phillips, "The History of 'Lost in Space,' (Part 1)," http://www.lostinspacetv.com/news/history1.html.

21. *CBS Network Presentation* (1965; 20th Century–Fox, 2004).

22. "Nicest Villain You'll Ever Meet," *Los Angeles Times*, December 24, 1967, B17.

23. See "CBS Requested Script Revisions: Episode 1: 'the Reluctant Stowaway,'" in *Box 54, Irwin Allen Papers, 1964–1975 (Collection 18)* (Los Angeles: Arts Library Special Collections, Young Research Library, University of California, Los Angeles).

24. Although no one is credited as playing the Robot, Bob May was the technician inside the suit.

25. *The Fantasy Worlds of Irwin Allen*, SciFi Channel (FoxStar Productions, 1995).

26. Sontag, "The Imagination of Disaster," 43.

27. "Island in the Sky," *Lost in Space*, DVD, directed by Anton Leader (September 29, 1965; Los Angeles: 20th Century–Fox).

28. Vivian Sobchack, "Images of Wonder: The Look of Science Fiction," in *Liquid Metal: The Science Fiction Film Reader*, edited Sean Redmond (New York: Wallflower Press, 2004), 7.

29. "Return from Outer Space," *Lost in Space*, DVD, directed by Nathan Juran (December 29, 1965; Los Angeles: 20th Century–Fox).

30. Michael Ryan and Douglas Kellner, "Technophobia/Dystopia," in *Liquid Metal: The Science Fiction Film Reader*, edited by Sean Redmond (New York: Wallflower Press, 2004), 51.

31. "War of the Robots," *Lost in Space*, DVD, directed by Sobey Martin (February 9, 1966; Los Angeles: 20th Century–Fox).

32. Donna J. Haraway, "A Manifesto for Cyborgs: Science, Technology and Socialist Feminism," in *Liquid Metal: The Science Fiction Film Reader*, edited by Sean Redmond (New York: Wallflower Press, 2004), 161.

33. Ibid.

34. Although out of the scope of this paper, this trope of liminality is also used throughout the series when discussing the human qualities of the aliens the Robinsons meet on their travels.

35. Haraway, "A Manifesto for Cyborgs," 159.

36. Spigel, "From Domestic Space to Outer Space," 205.

REFERENCES

Broder, David S. "Governors Support Vietnam Policy." *New York Times* July 8, 1966, 1.
CBS Network Presentation. 1965. 20th Century–Fox, 2004.
"CBS Requested Script Revisions: Episode 1: 'The Reluctant Stowaway.'" In *Box 54, Irwin Allen Papers, 1964–1975 (Collection 18)*. Los Angeles: Arts Library Special Collections, Young Research Library, University of California, Los Angeles.
The Fantasy Worlds of Irwin Allen, Sci Fi Channel. FoxStar Productions, 1995.
Haraway, Donna J. "A Manifesto for Cyborgs: Science, Technology and Socialist Feminism." In *Liquid Metal: The Science Fiction Film Reader*, edited by Sean Redmond, 158–81. New York: Wallflower Press, 2004.
"Hey Look, CBS Advertisement." *Variety Weekly*, September 15, 1965, 50.
Jameson, Fredric. *Archaeologies of the Future: The Desire Called Utopia and Other Science Fictions*. New York: Verso, 2005.
Kennedy, John F. "'Man on the Moon' Speech to Congress." http://www.presentationmagazine.com/kennedy_man_on_the_moon_speech.htm.
_____. "We Choose to Go to the Moon..." http://www.historyplace.com/speeches/jfk-space.htm.
"Nicest Villain You'll Ever Meet." *Los Angeles Times*, December 24, 1967, B17.
Phillips, Mark. "The History of 'Lost in Space,' (Part 1)." http://www.lostinspacetv.com/news/history1.html.
Phillips, Mark, and Frank Garcia. "Lost in Space." In *Science Fiction Television Series: Episode*

Guides, Histories, and Casts and Credits for 62 Primetime Shows, 1959 through 1989, 185. Jefferson, NC: McFarland, 1996.

Ryan, Michael, and Douglas Kellner. "Technophobia/Dystopia." In *Liquid Metal: The Science Fiction Film Reader,* edited by Sean Redmond, 48–56. New York: Wallflower Press, 2004.

Sobchack, Vivian. "Images of Wonder: The Look of Science Fiction." In *Liquid Metal: The Science Fiction Film Reader,* edited by Sean Redmond, 4–10. New York: Wallflower Press, 2004.

Sontag, Susan. "The Imagination of Disaster." In *Liquid Metal: The Science Fiction Film Reader,* edited by Sean Redmond, 40–47. New York: Wallflower Press, 2004.

"Space Fiction Tops the Real Thing." *Los Angeles Times,* March 17, 1966, 9.

Spigel, Lynn. "From Domestic Space to Outer Space: The 1960's Fantastic Family Sit-Com." In *Close Encounters: Film, Feminism, and Science Fiction,* edited by Constance Penley, Elisabeth Lyon, Lynn Spigel, and Janet Bergstrom, 205–36. Minneapolis: University of Minnesota Press, 1991.

Suvin, Darko. *Metamorphoses of Science Fiction: Studies in the Poetics and History of Cognitive Estrangement in Fiction.* New Haven: Yale University Press, 1978.

"Television's Race for Space — and Ratings." *Los Angeles Times,* August 15, 1965, L3.

About the Contributors

Carol A. Bernard is an assistant professor of English at Northeast Lakeview College, one of the Alamo Colleges. Her research interests include popular culture, science fiction/fantasy, and queer theory. She has sponsored undergraduate presenters at the last two national conferences of the Popular Culture Association in the area of science fiction and fantasy and is currently working to engage more undergraduates in the study of popular culture.

J. P. C. Brown started watching *Doctor Who* at the age of two in 1966, having been set in front of the television so his mother could do the ironing. He now teaches English literature and film at Middlesex University and social and political theory at Birkbeck College in the University of London.

Jonathan Cohn is a Ph.D. candidate in the Cinema and Media Studies Program at the University of California, Los Angeles. He is currently writing his dissertation on the relationship between digital technologies, surveillance, and self-representation.

Brian Cowlishaw is an associate professor in the Department of Languages and Literature at Northeastern State University in Tahlequah, Oklahoma. He has many academic interests, including science fiction and fantasy literature, literature and culture of India, and nineteenth-century British literature.

Patrick D. Enright holds a doctorate from the University of Kansas and teaches English at Northeastern State University in Tahlequah, Oklahoma. Besides Renaissance literature, his interests include science fiction, the Nibelung legends, and little-known composers of the Romantic era. He resides in Tahlequah with his two cats and is a devoted motorcyclist.

Alexander Charles Oliver Hall is institutionally affiliated with Kent State University in Kent, Ohio, where he teaches mostly composition courses. His published work deals primarily with dystopian literature and culture, and he is also the editor of the Society for Utopian Studies newsletter, *Utopus Discovered*.

Holly Hassel is an associate professor of English at the University of Wisconsin–Marathon County and director of the Women's Studies program. She teaches composition, literature, and women's studies courses. Her scholarly work has appeared in *Pedagogy: Critical Approaches to Teaching Literature, Language, Composition, and Culture*; *Feminist Teacher*, and *Teaching English in the Two-Year College*, and she is the coauthor of *Critical Companion to J.K. Rowling*.

Daniel Kennefick is an assistant professor of physics at the University of Arkansas and the author of *Traveling at the Speed of Thought*, a history of the theoretical debates over the existence of gravitational waves. He is also an editor of the *Collected Papers of Albert Einstein*. His physics research focuses on gravitational waves from supermassive black holes and investigating the mass function of supermassive black holes in galaxies throughout the universe.

Kristine Larsen is professor of physics and astronomy at Central Connecticut State University, where she teaches a variety of interdisciplinary courses, such as Science and Society and Women's Contributions to Science. She is the author of two books, *Stephen Hawking: A Biography* and *Cosmology 101*, and coeditor of *The Mythological Dimensions of Doctor Who*.

R. C. Neighbors has degrees in psychology, English, and film from the University of Arkansas, Northeastern State University, and Hollins University. He is currently a Ph.D. student in English at Texas A&M University where he serves as a reviewer for the journal *Callaloo*. He has many scholarly interests, including 20th century literature and culture, the short story, film, theories of narrative, and creative writing.

Daniel O'Brien is a freelance writer and occasional teacher specializing in film and television. Since the late 1980s, he has contributed to encyclopedias, dictionaries, and other reference works, and written books on such subjects as Clint Eastwood, Frank Sinatra, British science fiction, Hong Kong horror movies, the Hannibal Lecter books and films, Paul Newman, and Daniel Craig. He is completing a Ph.D. on sword and sandal films.

Debbie C. Olson is a Ph.D. candidate at Oklahoma State University. Her research interests include West African film, images of African/African American children in film and popular media, transnationalism, and Hollywood film.

Sandy Rankin is a visiting assistant professor of writing at the University of Central Arkansas. She earned her Ph.D. in English at the University of Arkansas, where her dissertation was "China Miéville and the Misbegot: Monsters, Magic, and Marxism." She previously earned an M.F.A. in creative writing-poetry. Her publications include poetry and fiction, and essays in *Extrapolation*, *New Boundaries in Political Science Fiction*, and *Journal of Popular Culture*.

Elizabeth Leigh Scherman is a doctoral candidate in the Department of Communication at the University of Washington. Her research focuses on representations of disability in cinema marketed to children. She is particularly interested in the intersections between cinematic portrayal of disabled people and that of other populations who have been and continue to be underrepresented or simplistically represented in literature, television, film and other media.

Lynn Whitaker was a high school teacher of English and drama for many years before returning to academia to pursue film and television studies at the University of Glasgow. She is interested in all aspects of children's media, and her doctoral research, funded by the AHRC, examines the current production culture of children's public service broadcasting in the UK.

Jacqueline Wiegard is a lecturer in English at Monash University. Her research interests include science fiction and fantasy, children's literature, medieval literature (Chaucer), nineteenth-century and contemporary literature. She has forthcoming publications on Chaucer, alchemy and animal/human boundaries, and also Tarzan, paternal authority, language acquisition, and colonial discourse.

Index

Adorno, Theodor 151
The Adventures of Peter Pan 83, 84, 93–94
AI: Artificial Intelligence 85, 86
Alloway, Lawrence 4
Andrews, Dudley 152
Applebaum, Noga 126–127

Back to the Future (films) 229, 231–232, 234
Banks, Adam 79
Baudillard, Jean 68
Berlant, Lauren 197
Bloch, Ernst 112–113, 157
Booker, M. Keith 9, 113–114, 158, 249, 252, 254
Booth, Douglas E. 251
Bould, Mark 111
Brecht, Bertolt 267, 270
Broderick, Damien 123
Brooks, Peter 7
Buckingham, David 196
Burton, Gabrielle 37–38
Butler, Judith 54–56, 58, 60–61

Calder, Angus 102–103, 107
camp 150–152, 156, 266–268
Clarke, Arthur C. 239–240
Clover, Joseph 123, 126, 133
cognitive estrangement 6, 44, 50, 97, 112–113, 140, 148, 155, 267, 270
the Cold War 114, 249, 262, 270
colonial/imperialism 65–66, 68–69, 72, 74, 77, 111–122, 125, 133, 164–179, 249, 263–265, 268, 274
Cornea, Christine 67
Csicsery-Ronay, Istvan, Jr. 5, 6, 112–113, 140–141, 148

Dalek's Invasion Earth 2150 A.D. 11, 97–109
Darke, Paul 16
D.A.R.Y.L. 70–72

Deutsch, David 232
didacticism 90, 195–196, 199–200, 212,
disability 15–27
Docter, Pete 19
Doctor Who (franchise) 11, 97–109, 161, 180
dystopia 156, 203, 213, 248–259; *see also* utopia

Ecklund, Elaine Howard 244
Edelman, Lee 78–79, 197
Einstein, Albert 88–89, 230–231
environmental concerns 236, 248–259
E.T. 22, 69–70
Explorers 72–74

fairy tales 15, 33, 35, 91, 119, 133, 140
fantasy 2–4, 10–11, 49–50, 85–86, 90
Flash Gordon (serials) 217–226
Flight of the Navigator 73–74, 76
Freedman, Carl 5, 44–45, 112–113, 115, 120, 141
Fritz, Leah 42

Garland-Thomson, Rosemary 17
gender 31–50, 53–62, 118, 121, 191–192, 223
Gilliam, Ken 58–59
Glashow, Sheldon 245
Glotfelty, Cheryll 250
Gould, Stephen Jay 238, 244
grandfather paradox 231–232

Hall, Stuart 116
Haraway, Donna 140, 157, 275
Harry Potter (franchise) 3, 48, 233, 245
Hawking, Stephen 231–232
The Hope Principle 113
Howard the Duck 68–69
Hutcheon, Linda 49, 138

The Iron Giant 11, 139–158

283

James, Edward 97
Jameson, Fredric 5–7, 112–113, 119, 138, 140, 142, 146–147, 151, 158, 188, 191, 251, 267, 276–277
The Jetsons (TV series) 183–193, 234
Johnson, Allan 32–33, 48
Jones, Gerard 211
Jurassic Park 228, 238

Kincaid, James 205–206
Kinnard, Roy 218–219
Kitses, Jim 207
Knight, Damon 2–3
Kohl, Leonard J. 223
Krips, Valerie 159
Kristeva, Julia 127, 134–135
Kuhn, Annette 34
Kurzweil, Ray 193
Kuznets, Luis R. 126

The Last Mimzy 229, 235–236, 238–245
LazyTown 195–215
Le Guin, Ursula 112
Levine, Bruce E. 154
Levitas, Ruth 254
Lilo & Stitch 10, 15–16, 22–29
Lost in Space (film) 76–77
Lost in Space (TV series) 76, 262–277
Lurie, Alison 35

Mackay, Robert 103
Mallett, Ronald 228, 231
Mandler, Peter 163
Marxism 5, 50, 92, 113, 120, 147, 170
McKnight, Utz 23, 25
Meet the Robinsons 229, 233–235, 237–244
Mendlesohn, Farah 206, 215
Michaud, Nicolas 133
Miéville, China 50
Milner, Andrew 132
Monsters, Inc. 10, 16, 18–22, 27
Monsters v. Aliens 32–50
Motion Picture Association of America (MPAA) 8–9
Moylan, Tom 249–250, 255

Nama, Adilifu 66–67, 111, 117
Neale, Steven 16
Nodelman, Perry 9, 144
nostalgia 114–115, 138, 140, 151, 155, 157, 188
novum 113, 139–142, 147–148, 152–154, 157

Orwell, George 170
the Other 18, 23, 66, 68, 74, 79, 123, 135

Papert, Seymour 127
Paris, Michael 165
parody 34, 44, 150, 152, 154, 158, 177
Parsons, Linda 32, 35, 39
patriarchy 32–33, 44, 47, 49, 191–192
Postman, Neil 203

Rabkin, Eric 31, 48
race 64–80, 116–118, 121, 155
ratings system 8
Roberts, Adam 115, 119
robots 10, 53–62, 123–136, 189–190, 248–249, 251–259, 263, 271–275
Roemer, Kenneth M. 249–250
romance 53–62
Routledge, Paul 108

Sagan, Carl 229–231, 243
Sanders, Scott 31
Sargent, Lyman Tower 249–250, 254
Sawyer, Robert 3–4
Seed, David 4
Shavit, Zohar 144
Shrek (franchise) 33, 39
Smit, Christopher 18
Snow, C.P. 229, 236, 243
Sobchack, Vivian 4, 77, 272
Sontag, Susan 149–150, 268, 271–272
Space Camp 74–75
Spigel, Lynn 264, 266
SpongeBob Squarepants 9
Star Wars (franchise) 10, 86, 111–122, 219
Stephens, John 123
Suvin, Darko 3, 6–7, 44, 97, 112–113, 139–142, 148, 157, 267, 270

Thomas, Donald 104
Thorne, Kip 231
Tibbetts, John C. 219
time travel 228–245
Toffler, Alvin 187
Tøssebro, Jan 20
Toy Story 10, 84, 90–91
Transformers 10, 123–136
Trites, Roberta 36, 124

utopia 5, 92, 112, 115, 119, 122, 151, 157, 188, 249–250, 254, 259, 273; *see also* dystopia

The Velveteen Rabbit 84, 87
Verne, Jules 6, 188

Wall-E 53–62, 248–249, 251–259
Wells, H.G. 169, 171, 188, 228–229
We're Back! A Dinosaur's Story 229, 233, 237–244
Westfahl, Gary 111
Wetmore, Kevin J., Jr. 115
Wilde, Oscar 88–90, 139, 142, 145, 147
Winn, Marie 199
Wojcik-Andrews, Ian 8
World War II 66, 99–102, 104, 107, 163–164, 176, 187, 219

Yolen, Jane 27

Zipes, Jack 46, 65
Zola, Irving Kenneth 24

www.ingramcontent.com/pod-product-compliance
Ingram Content Group UK Ltd.
Pitfield, Milton Keynes, MK11 3LW, UK
UKHW041928140426
5217IPUK00014B/371